I0813770

Techniques of Graeco-Egyptian Magic

Techniques of Graeco-Egyptian Magic

Books on the Western Esoteric Tradition by Stephen Skinner

Agrippa's Fourth Book of Occult Philosophy (edited) – Askin, Ibis
Aleister Crowley's Astrology (edited) – Spearman, Ibis
Aleister Crowley's Four Books of Magick - Watkins
Ars Notoria (with Daniel Clark) – Golden Hoard, Llewellyn
Complete Magician's Tables – Golden Hoard, Llewellyn
Cunning Man's Grimoire (with David Rankine) – Golden Hoard, Llewellyn
Dr John Dee's Spiritual Diaries: fully revised edition of *'A True & Faithful Relation'* with all Latin passages translated – Golden Hoard, Llewellyn
Geomancy in Theory & Practice – Golden Hoard, Llewellyn
Goetia of Dr Rudd: Liber Malorum Spirituum (with David Rankine) – Golden Hoard
Grimoire of Saint Cyprian: Clavis Inferni (with David Rankine) – Golden Hoard
Keys to the Gateway of Magic (with David Rankine) – Golden Hoard
Magical Diaries of Aleister Crowley (edited) – Spearman, RedWheel Weiser
Michael Psellus 'On the Operation of Daimones' - Golden Hoard
Millennium Prophecies: Apocalypse 2000 - Carlton
Nostradamus (with Francis King) – Carlton
Oracle of Geomancy – Warner Destiny, Prism
Practical Angel Magic of Dr. Dee (with David Rankine) – Golden Hoard
Sacred Geometry – Gaia, Hamlyn
Search for Abraxas (with Nevill Drury) – Spearman, Salamander
Sepher Raziel: Liber Salomonis (with Don Karr) – Golden Hoard
Sibley's Clavis to the Mysteries of Magic (with Daniel Clark) -
Steganographia (with Daniel Clark) – Golden Hoard, Llewellyn
Techniques of Graeco-Egyptian Magic – Golden Hoard, Llewellyn
Techniques of High Magic (with Francis King) – Daniels, Inner Traditions, Golden Hoard
Techniques of Solomonic Magic – Golden Hoard, Llewellyn
Terrestrial Astrology: Divination by Geomancy – Routledge
Veritable Key of Solomon (with David Rankine) – Golden Hoard, Llewellyn

Books on Feng Shui by Stephen Skinner

Advanced Flying Star Feng Shui – Golden Hoard
Feng Shui Before & After - Haldane Mason, Tuttle
Feng Shui for Everyday Living aka *Feng Shui for Modern Living* - Cico
Feng Shui History: the Story of Classical Feng Shui in China & the West – Golden Hoard
Feng Shui the Traditional Oriental Way - Haldane Mason
Feng Shui: the Living Earth Manual - Tuttle
Flying Star Feng Shui - Tuttle
Guide to the Feng Shui Compass – Golden Hoard
K.I.S.S. Guide to Feng Shui (Keep it Simple Series) – Penguin, DK
Key San He Feng Shui Formulae – Golden Hoard
Living Earth Manual of Feng Shui – RKP, Penguin, Arkana
Mountain Dragon – Golden Hoard
Original Eight Mansion Formula – Golden Hoard
Practical Makeovers Using Feng Shui – Haldane Mason, Tuttle
Water Dragon – Golden Hoard

Techniques of
Graeco-Egyptian Magic

Dr. Stephen Skinner

Golden Hoard Press

2024

Published by Golden Hoard Press Pte Ltd
PO Box 1073 Robinson Road
Singapore, 902123.

www.GoldenHoard.com

First Edition

ISBN: 978-0-9568285-6-9

Printed in Malaysia

Acknowledgements

With gratitude and respect for Hans Dieter Betz who made all this possible by editing, translating and compiling the Graeco-Egyptian magic corpus for the English speaking world.

This book is an amplification of one third of my University of Newcastle Classics Ph.D. entitled *Magical Techniques and Implements present in Graeco-Egyptian Magical Papyri, Byzantine Greek Solomonic Manuscripts and European Grimoires (The Technology of Solomonic Magic)*. I wish to record my thanks to my supervisor Dr. Marguerite Johnson who allowed me the latitude I needed to complete it, and who was enthusiastic about my first tabular analysis of the magical techniques of the *PGM*.

My thanks also to the anonymous thesis examiner who complained that I had arbitrarily and unjustifiably subdivided the *PGM* into different ritual types, thereby spurring me on to extract, and document, the specific Greek headwords occurring in the first line of almost every rite or spell, in order to completely justify my analysis.

Also my thanks to my long time co-author, David Rankine, whose excellent book on *Heka* re-stimulated my interest in Egyptian magic.

The endpapers are a photo of the Metternich Stēlē, copyright the author. The cover illustration is a modified version of a painting by Austrian artist Kurt Regschek. The two yin-yang symbols were removed as they were of Chinese cultural origin and totally out of place in an Egyptian image.

I acknowledge my debt to the sources of several other illustrations whose owners I have not been able to track down. I am happy to acknowledge them in a future edition if made aware of the sources.

Lastly, I admit that there are many details in this huge and fascinating field which I would have liked to expand upon, but have been prevented from so doing by constraints of space and time.

"Magic is not, as the followers of Epicurus and Aristotle think, utterly incoherent, but, as the experts in these things prove, is a consistent system, which has principles known to very few."

- Origen, *Contra Celsus* 1.24.
- (translated by Henry Chadwick, 1953)

Contents

List of Figures

List of Tables

1.0 Introduction

1.1 What is Magic

This book looks at very specific identifiable techniques, consumables, *nomina magica* and implements found in the Greek Magical Papyri, and how they were used, and not just at generalized themes.

These papyri are the source of many of the magical techniques and equipment found in later European magic. The mediaeval Solomonic grimoires, and indeed most of the Solomonic magical tradition in both the Latin and Greek worlds, owe their earliest origins to the Graeco-Egyptian papyri (the *PGM*), not to some unknown Hebrew antecedents, not just in a general or thematic sense, but in the transmission of specific techniques, words and implements from one culture to another.

This book utilises the handbooks written by or used practically by the magicians themselves and approaches this magic as another form of technology. The sources are therefore primarily the ancient papyri written by the practitioners of magic themselves rather than those written by their later (predominantly Christian) adversaries. My approach is very similar to Ritner's when he wrote of Egyptian magic:

> To date, no treatment of Egyptian magic has concentrated upon the actual practice of the magician. Both general studies and textual publications have emphasized instead the religious elements in the contents of recited spell, while the accompanying instructions with their vignettes and lists of materials, instruments, and ritual actions remained uninvestigated. This study represents the first critical examination of such "magical techniques," revealing their widespread appearance and pivotal significance for all Egyptian "religious" practices from the earliest periods through the Coptic era, influencing as well the Greco-Egyptian magical papyri.[1]

While Ritner's book was amongst the first to investigate the actual practices of Dynastic Egyptian magic,[2] this book is the first to examine in detail the practices used in the first five centuries of the common era with its mixture of Greek and Egyptian magic.

By using the term 'magician' there is no implied or overt claim for special powers on the part of the practitioner, simply an assertion that the people so designated were practitioners of magical techniques. Just as the terms 'carpenter' or 'priest' define a trade or a profession, rather than a claim to special skill or special sanctity.

The fact that such techniques have been utilized consistently over long periods

---

[1] Ritner (2008), p.2.

[2] See also Budge (1971), Pinch (2006) and Rankine (2006).

of time often by learned people suggests that some apparent consistency of results was obtained. Otherwise if no such consistency of results had been obtained, then one might expect to find a wide and random diversity of fantasy techniques being independently invented and speculatively tried out at different times and in different cultures: but this is not the case. There is instead a systematic development of techniques with a few being dropped (such as *defixiones*) and some being added (such as the circle of protection) to the repertoire, but with the core techniques remaining the same. As William Brashear once remarked:

> These two papyri, the Philinna papyrus and the Oxyrhynchus parallel, written as they were five to six centuries apart from each other, provide remarkable testimony to the conservatism of magic and magicians in antiquity.[1]

Mankind has a long history of discarding machines and methods that do not work, yet many detailed magical techniques survived literally for thousands of years. As Betz puts it:

> It is one of the puzzles of all magic that from time immemorial it has survived throughout history, through the coming and going of entire religions, the scientific and technological revolutions, and the triumphs of modern medicine. Despite all these changes, there has always been an unbroken tradition of magic. Why is magic so irrepressible and ineradicable, if it is also true that its claims and promises never come true? Or *do* they?[2]

A Working Definition of Magic

Before proceeding, it is necessary to define the term 'magic' as it is the subject of this book. The most fundamental problem for modern academics in defining 'magic' is that any accurate definition of magic *must* involved the concepts of another world of spirits, daimones and gods, because this was the premise from which most magicians worked. For an atheist, for whom these entities simply do not exist, the problem of defining the art or science that deals with them is insoluble. This is not meant as a condescending statement, just one which suggests that analysis of any subject cannot be satisfactorily begun if the basic premises of that subject (be they true or false) are overlooked or completely omitted. This situation is what lies at the root of modern academic difficulties with the definition of magic. Such attempts at defining magic are on a par with the scientist who does not believe in the existence of radio waves, yet tries to explain the functioning of a radio: it cannot be done without making a complete nonsense of the definition.

Maybe the procedure of physicists is an appropriate way of proceeding. They define a theoretical particle which nobody has seen (such as a *quark, lepton or*

---

[1] Brashear (1998), p. 374.

[2] Betz (1996), p. xlvii-xlviii.

boson), and then proceed to see if its behaviour fits their mathematical models. In the present context, the equivalent of this procedure is to accept the theoretical existence of gods, angels, daimones and spirits, and then to move on from there to define magic in terms of their manipulation. In the ancient world the existence of daimones, spirits and gods was a given. Any definition recognizable by, and welcomed by, its ancient practitioners would have to include mention of daimones, gods, spirits, etc. And, more importantly, it would then be a definition which allows for reasonable discourse about the subject.

As so many scholars have laboured unsuccessfully to create a 'modern' definition of the term magic, I intend to cut the Gordian knot by utilising a definition which is much closer to the sense the ancients gave it, by returning to the original meaning of *magia*, with a meaning that would have been understood by its practitioners in Late Antiquity.

If this involves a nod in the direction of the existence of gods, daimones and spirits, then so be it. Without such a nod, the effort resembles that of the man who would describe chess without acknowledging the existence of the invisible rules which govern the movement of the individual pieces. Such rules have no real existence, but without them the game of chess is impossible to play, or even to write sensible commentary upon. Likewise it is very difficult to examine or comment upon magic without acknowledging the 'spiritual creatures' which are part of its basic premises, as understood by its practitioners.

I would therefore like to offer a working definition of magic that is based on how it was practised in the Greek speaking Mediterranean, and which avoids modernisation, social theory, or the moral challenges of theological definition:

> Magic is the art of causing change through the agency of spiritual creatures rather than via directly observable physical means: such spiritual creatures being compelled or persuaded to assist, by the use of sacred words or names, talismans, symbols, incense, sacrifices and *materia magica*.

Here 'spiritual' is defined to mean non-physical, with no ethical connotation, and 'spiritual creature' to mean a non-physical entity, ranging in definition or substance from elementals, spirits, demons, daimones, angels, archangels, gods and goddesses, to discarnate humans (both saintly and prematurely dead).[1] The use of this terminology which was in widespread use in Europe up to the mid-17th century[2] might be hard for modern readers to digest,

---

[1] The term 'spiritual creature' also saves the tiresome need to write out "gods, goddesses, spirits, demons, daimones, angels, archangels and elementals" every time they all need to be mentioned.

[2] This definition obviously does not cover 'natural magic' which was a category mentioned by Agrippa, and in current use by the Renaissance, probably devised

particularly those who come from a Judaeo-Christian background where the notion of 'spirituality' is totally opposed to the very existence of spirits. In modern times the word 'spiritual' does surface in the practices of 'spiritualism' or 'spiritism' where the medium deals with the dead, but the term is still not understood in its wider meaning.

So for the purposes of this book 'spiritual creature,'[1] will be understood in exactly the same way that Dr John Dee understood it in the late 16th century when he wrote:[2]

> Suddenly, there seemed to come out of my Oratory a Spirituall creature, like a pretty girle of 7 or 9 yeares of age…[3]

Dee then began to converse with this girl via his skryer Edward Kelley, certain that she was an angel, a real spiritual creature. Such behaviour was not unique to Dr Dee. Other precedents for this usage exist, and at least one manuscript of the *Key of Solomon* refers in a similar fashion to angels as 'Créatures célestes.'[4] According to Zambelli:

> Ficino and his followers admitted the existence of spiritual beings (demons, angels and devils, anthropomorphic movers of astral bodies etc.) to whom it was possible to address prayers, hymns or innocent spells.[5]

There was no doubt in the minds of most magicians of Late Antiquity, that the effects of magic were attributable to external 'spiritual creatures' be they gods, angels, daimones, or spirits, rather than to either the innate powers of the magician himself, or to some nebulous undefined pseudo-scientific 'force' or 'vibration.' In the Jewish world angels and demons were clearly seen as the driving forces behind the operation of magic, as confirmed by Trachtenberg:

> Demons and angels, to be counted only in myriads, populated that world; through their intermediacy the powers of magic were brought into operation. The most frequently employed [Hebrew] terms for magic were *hashba'at malachim* and *hashba'at shedim*, invocation and conjuration of angels and demons [respectively].[6]

---

specifically to avoid opposition from the Church, by eliminating mention of spirits and demons from its definition.

[1] A better term might have been *creaturum incorporalis.*

[2] Dr. John Dee was an Elizabethan polymath (1527-1608) who wrote books on geometry, navigation, alchemy, rectification of the calendar, and who promoted the idea of the British Empire. His interest in angelic invocation lead him to employ a succession of skryers, such as Edward Kelley, who provided Dee with a large amount of dictated messages and instruction from entities claiming to be angels or spirits. See Casaubon & Skinner (2011) for transcripts of these sessions which ran to many hundreds of manuscript pages.

[3] This description refers to the angel Madimi as described in BL Cotton Appendix MS XLVI, f. 1. See also BL Sloane MS 3188, fol. 8, and Clulee (1988), p. 179.

[4] BL Lansdowne MS 1203, ff. 7-8.

[5] Zambelli (2007), p. 3.

[6] Trachtenberg (2004), p. 25.

It was considered, in the ancient world, that the main skill of a magician was to constrain these entities using the spoken and written word, sigils, talismans, suffumigations and sacrifices. The centrality of spiritual creatures to the operation of Mediterranean magic is again confirmed by Johnston:

> In short, it seems that many Mediterranean magicians considered the control of ghostly or demonic entities to be *essential* to the completion of their work: the better one was at controlling demons, the greater a magician one was.[1]

This definition therefore, leads naturally to the subject of this book: the examination of the technology of these words, sigils, talismans, suffumigations and sacrifices that the magicians used.

Magic divides this universe into a specific hierarchy of spiritual creatures in order to deal with it more effectively. Like any science, one of the first steps is analysis, where the constituent parts of the method need to be identified and labelled.[2] If magic is looked at in historical terms, as a practice, something people actually did, then magic can be examined and documented in the same way that one could research and document the production of parchment for writing, without condemning the process as primitive, or judging the morals or efficacy of the method. Nobody who owns a computer would now ever go to the trouble of pulling the skin off a sheep, soaking, stretching, scraping, liming and processing it for several weeks, before writing on it with ink made of soot and oak galls, but nobody can deny that this procedure produced a very durable writing surface that can last more than a thousand years.[3]

My point is that it is not necessary to take a psychological or even a social anthropological approach to magic. It is sufficient to examine what was done by magicians, on their own terms, and for their own reasons, as documented by its practitioners, in their own handbooks.

Delimiting the Definition

Before proceeding I would like to clarify the scope of this book by eliminating from it a number of subjects and techniques often associated with magic in popular literature, but which are not in fact parts of Graeco-Egyptian magic.

Although divination is often seen as part of magic, divination is essentially a

---

[1] Johnston (2002), pp. 42-43, my italics.

[2] These labels are particularly important in magic, because of one of the primary axioms of magic is that all spiritual creatures can only be addressed and controlled when their true name is known.

[3] I am still surprised that I can easily read the contents of a manuscript from the Middle Ages, but can no longer access digital work written by myself on an obsolete computer just thirty years ago. Parchment may well prove more durable in the long run than easily deleted digital documents.

passive method, whereas magic is nothing if not proactive. Divination seeks to foretell the future, while magic seeks to change the future. Three exceptions to this generalisation will be made, the first in the case of electional astrology. Electional and katarchic astrology have been used from time immemorial by magicians to determine the best time to conduct a rite. A second exception will be made in the case of techniques like *lychnomanteia, lekanomanteia* and *hygromanteia,* where skrying is supplemented by the active ritual evocation of daimones or spirits. The third exception is a divinatory method based on random lines from the works of Homer (*PGM* VII. 1-148). This will be explored in chapter 6.3 because it was used by the magician who owned that papyrus.

Oracles, although a few are present in the *PGM,* are not part of magic. In most cases these 'oracles' are not oracles in the same sense as the oracle at Delphi, but invocations of a god in order to receive answers or advice. The later procedure is part of magic. Emilie Savage-Smith makes the distinction:

> That magic seeks to alter the course of events, usually by calling upon a superhuman force...while divination attempts to predict future events (or gain information about things unseen) but not necessarily to alter them.[1]

As Fritz Graf rightly concludes, the confusion between magic and divination only dates from the early Christian era:

> Only when divination is read in terms of demonology, as in mainstream Christian discourse, do [the definitions of] divination and magic converge.[2]

Otherwise these two fields of endeavour are not really connected. Instead of referring to one of the practices of Graeco-Egyptian magicians as 'bowl divination,' I will instead refer to it rather more aptly as 'evocationary bowl skrying.' The same applies to 'lamp divination' which I will in future refer to as 'evocationary lamp skrying.'

In the ancient world magic was considered to be very real, and not a random assemblage of nonsense actions and words, and the insiders who practised it:

> ...were far from illiterate, and some of these magical texts even display the scribal hands, writing styles, and modes of textual production which come only with many years of scribal learning and practice. Moreover, when we do find evidence outside the actual magical texts as to who practiced such magical rituals, that evidence repeatedly demonstrates the acceptance, and even practice, of magic by members of the Jewish elite, including the religious establishment itself... Most of these sources were not the product of Jewish "folk magic," but of "intellectual magic," produced by learned experts who mastered a specialized body of knowledge and consulted many different sources, sometimes in more than one language.[3]

---

[1] Savage-Smith (2004), p. xiii.
[2] Graf (2011), p. 133.
[3] Bohak (2008), p. 36.

Although these comments were applied to Jewish magic, they are equally applicable to other forms of European or Mediterranean littoral learned magic. Egyptian magicians, especially, were mostly of the priestly class.

Greek Categorisation of Magic

The Greeks made a clear distinction between *goetia* (γοητεία) the magic of the *goes* (γόης), and that of *theurgia* (θεουργία). It is difficult to be sure of what was exactly meant by the ancient Greeks when they used the term γοητεία, as it was associated with rites for the dead. *Goetia* (γοητεία) and *goes* (γόης) were later used in the sense they acquired in the Latin grimoires of 'dealing with spirits,' rather than in the sense outlined in Johnston of 'dealing with the dead.'[1] Chapter 6.7 deals with the interface between Graeco-Egyptian magic and the dead.

Theurgia is a quite separate category, and is a descendant, via Porphyry and Iamblichus of Chalcis,[2] of the ancient Mysteries.[3] This usage has persisted through to 13th century (and later) grimoires.[4] It has been suggested that *theurgia,* meaning "divine work," was a term that might even have been invented by the group of Neoplatonically inclined magicians, including luminaries like Iamblichus, probably based in Alexandria around the 2nd – 3rd century CE.[5] The theurgists were concerned with purifying and raising the consciousness of individual practitioners to the point where they could have direct communion with the gods. The theurgists were in a sense the inheritors of the ancient Greek Mysteries which aimed to introduce the candidate directly to the gods. There are four sections in the *PGM* which give instructions in these procedures, and these are categorised as rite type 'M,' and examined in chapter 7.0.

The *goes* (γόης), the practitioner of *goetia* (γοητεία), on the other hand, attempts to bring daimones/demons onto the physical plane and to manifest them, or their effects. The relationship of the practitioners of *theurgia* to practitioners of the *goetia* is that both attempt to invoke/evoke a spiritual creature (be it god, daimon, angel or demon). The *teletai* (τελεταί) priest does it for the benefit of the client's immortal soul while the *goes* does it to benefit the client's material desires. Dickie is of the opinion that:

> ...although there are indications that *goetes, epodoi, magoi* and *pharmakeis* originally pursued quite different callings, there is no indication when the terms are first

---

[1] Johnston (1999), pp. 102-103.

[2] Apart from Iamblichus, the other main source for theurgy is Proclus, a 5th century Neoplatonist. See also Johnston (2008) and Struck (2004), chapters 6-7 on Proclus.

[3] See chapter 1.2 for a fuller explanation of the relationship between the Mysteries and magic.

[4] The author of the *Juratus* defines 'theurgy' as a "sacramental rite, [or] 'mystery.'"

[5] Johnston (2008), p. 150.

encountered in the fifth century that they refer to specialised forms of magic.[1]

Although it may well be true that there is too little evidence available from their earliest mentions to separate their specialised forms of magic, but these terms definitely identified different practices, and later usage of the terms *goetes* and *magoi* confirms this by being quite distinct. Rather than wrestling with the theoretical identification of these terms, for which there is on the whole too little evidence, I have instead divided these methods according to the type of spiritual creature being used.

Accordingly chapter 6 on Magical Techniques has been divided up according to the type of spiritual creature the magician wished to deal with, ranging from the gods (chapter 6.5) through daimones (chapter 6.6) to the dead (chapter 6.7). Chapter 6.4 deals with visions, dreams and skrying, while chapter 6.1 deals with techniques relying on magical statues, rings and gemstones. Chapter 6.2 deals with inscribed magical devices ranging from simple amulets made for paying clients, through talismans designed to achieve a particular magical end, to phylacteries which were for the personal protection of the magician from the spiritual creatures he called (but only during the rite). Having made this division it became very obvious that the methods used divided along exactly the same lines.

[1] Dickie (2001), pp. 14-15.

1.2 The Relationship between Magic, the Mysteries and Religion

It is useful to first enter into a brief discussion of the relationships between magic, the Mysteries and religion for three very specific reasons:

i) to further refine the definition of magic, in order to successfully avoid any confusion with religion;

ii) to isolate the four passages in the *PGM*, which are in fact Mystery and initiation rites, and not either magic or religion; and

iii) to further appreciate the distinction between the various types of magic.

The dichotomy between magic and religion has caused so much scholarly controversy over the last century or so, that it has even been categorised as an unsolvable dilemma by some scholars.[1] I would like to make some observations which may lead to such a solution, or at least to a very different viewpoint from which to perceive such a solution.

It is still often argued that religion deals with God or the gods, angels and saints, but only to implore their help, not to constrain it. This view, which is now somewhat superseded, dates back to the work of James Frazer in 1890.[2] There is some truth in this contention, but some techniques of magic overlap with the techniques of religion. Techniques such as prayer or consecration span both practices. On the other hand, religion also sometimes uses compulsion, when, for example, it indulges in exorcism. Even techniques such as animal sacrifice, as distasteful to the modern reader as it may be, were originally used by both magicians and priests in the service of their art or religion. One only has to look at the huge quantities of animals sacrificed by King Solomon at the inauguration of his temple in Jerusalem in order to appease Yahweh/El, to see that sacrifice is not the exclusive province of the magician or polytheist. Christ's New Testament miracles have much more in common with magic than they do with religion as currently conceived of by any mainstream church.[3]

Often the same act will produce different responses according to which side of the religion/magic divide the commentator sits upon. Brashear,[4] commenting on Kazhdan,[5] writes:

---

[1] Betz (1991), pp. 244-247.

[2] For Frazer, and many other scholars since, religion was equated with Christianity.

[3] See Conner (2006) and Conner (2010).

[4] Brashear (1998), p. 253.

[5] Kazhdan (1995), pp. 73-82.

> The difference between holy and unholy miracles, he suggests, is in the miracle's aim and result: the saint rescues, feeds and comforts, creating good and exemplifying the Christian ideal. Unholy magic causes death, confusion, sexual misbehaviour and the like. Yet, in the final analysis, ambivalence is the order of the day, and the Byzantines seem to have had no real criterion for distinguishing between a holy and an unholy miracle.

There is in fact no clear distinction because miracles are based on magic. To a large extent, this problem has been created by the Christian doctrinal view of magic. The early Church Fathers were in no doubt that magic was a real and internally consistent body of knowledge. For example, Origen wrote:

> ...magic is not, as the followers of Epicurus and Aristotle think, utterly incoherent, but, as the experts in these things prove, is a consistent system, which has principles known to very few.[1]

The question of the relationship between magic and religion has, I feel, been inappropriately phrased, and the discussion should not centre around *two* opposing terms, but on the consideration of *three* terms. To solve this one needs to look at the whole spectrum of how mankind has attempted to relate to the unseen, to the gods and to other spiritual creatures.

Christian doctrine attempted to suppress magic because it viewed it as a very real force. The basic problem is that the question has been treated as a simple dichotomy of magic versus religion, whereas the missing 'middle term' is the Mystery religions, which is part of a *spectrum* of three modalities: religion - the Mysteries - magic. However, the problem remains a difficult one because the Mystery religions are missing from our 21st century experience, and do not exist any more, in any form, in any Western culture.

In the ancient world these were the three main ways that man sought to approach the unseen. The differences between these three can be defined by a number of criteria, each of which by itself is not sufficient to make the distinction, but taken together clearly demarcate these three modalities:

1. *Audience*. The first category, religion, deals with the gods on behalf of the congregation. The second, the Mysteries, takes a select few[2] of the congregation and exposes them to experiences which (by all accounts) change their view of the world and their life for ever after. The significance of this change can be measured by the very small number of initiates who have ever broken their vows and written down an account of their experiences. The third category will often be performed for just one client, or just for the benefit of the magician himself.

---

[1] Origen, *Contra Celsus* in Chadwick (1965), pp. 23-24.

[2] Of course the numbers applying to Eleusis rose significantly in later years.

2. *Degree of Secrecy*. Religion embraces all-comers and in many cases seeks to convert the non-believer or adherent of a rival religion to join its services. The Mysteries selected or accepted only a few individuals from the congregation who looked for (or paid for) a specific spiritual experience. Magic was even more secretive, and in most cases, actively discouraged new postulants or practitioners.[1] Clients were only included in the practice on a need-to-know or disciple basis.

3. *Degree of Specificity in Objectives*. Religion dealt with the general good, and assisted in various rites of passage such as birth, death and marriage, but the objectives will be general in nature such as blessing (baptism for birth, blessing for marriage, last rites for death). The Mysteries focused on the initiation or introduction to the god(s) of a few candidates, at a personal experiential level, and usually dealt just with one god, such as Dionysus or Demeter, with the single objective of initiation or immortalisation. The prime objective of the immortality offered by the Mysteries should not be confused with "a place in heaven" offered by religion. Magic operates with a very specific end or single objective, but drawn from a very wide field of very concrete possibilities: love, lust, money, power, etc.

4. *Range of Entities encountered*. Religion deals with the gods, angels and saints. The Mysteries dealt with one specific god or goddess. Magic deals with the whole range of spiritual creatures: gods, angels, daimones, demons, elementals, spirits and even the dead.

5. *Privacy*. The nature of these three practices can also be summed up in terms of degree of privacy.

a) Religion is practised in public in temples in front of all adherents by priests.

b) The Mysteries (or holy *teletai*),[2] were celebrated in private by the

---

[1] The degree of privacy was also used as a distinguishing factor between magic and religion by Emile Durkheim. Michael Bailey (2006), p. 3, pointed out that Marcel Mauss (Durkheim's nephew and pupil) defined magic as "private, secret, mysterious, and above all prohibited, while religion consisted of rites publicly acknowledged and approved."

[2] *Teletai*, which is often translated as 'initiation,' derives from the Greek root *tele-* which means 'completion' or 'perfection.' 'Initiation' is a word which has been somewhat devalued in the last century. To the ancient Greeks it meant approaching the perfection of a god, or at the very least receiving a purification which enabled a mortal to meet with and converse with a god, in some form of fellowship, which was indeed the

teletai-priests only for the benefit of one or a very small number of initiates. It is very clearly different from religion which was practised openly in temples.[1]

c) Magic is celebrated in private and/or secretly.[2] It was sometimes practised by the priests of a religion, but also by lay persons with the right training.

6. *Subject and Object.* Another possible way of looking at these three categories is in terms of subject and object.

   a) Religion: the Priest presents the god(s) to the people.

   b) Mysteries: the *teletai* priest presents a specific candidate to a specific god.

   c) Magic: the magician presents himself to, and adjures, the god or other spiritual creature.

If these definitions are applied, it becomes a lot easier to identify when a particular practice pertains to religion, Mystery or magic. To understand the magic of the *PGM,* it is useful to remember that all three modes of communication with the spiritual existed side by side, at that time when magic was considered a worthy and workable practice, and the Mysteries were still highly valued and flourishing.

It is my belief that it is precisely because of the monotheistic Judeo-Christian bias, and because of the missing modern experience of the Mystery religions, that the discussion of the relationship between magic and religion has not, in modern times, ever reached a satisfactory conclusion. By cutting out the middle term, the Mysteries, Christianity forever polarised magic and religion, instead of seeing it as part of a natural continuum in man's efforts to relate to the gods and other spiritual creatures.

Anthropological Interpretations

It is also now popular to embrace the idea that religion and magic can be understood through the work of anthropologists on the customs of primitive tribes in Africa or Australia, and from that to fallaciously deduce that religion and magic cannot be separated. MacMullen puts it:

> Now, the lessons of anthropology grown familiar, it is common to accept the

---

objective of the Mysteries. *PGM* IV contains several such Mystery rituals, for example lines 26-51 or 475-820.

[1] In the Dervani papyrus the practitioners were referred to as *mystai.*

[2] In the Dervani papyrus these practitioners were referred to as *magoi.* See Edmonds (2008), p.17.

> impossibility of separating magic from religion...[1]

This idea may be common, but that does not ensure its truth. The anthropological analysis of the customs of primitive peoples is a world away from the discourse and understanding of pagan and Christian intellectuals living under the Roman or Byzantine Empires. Attempting to draw parallels between these two cultural groups is like suggesting that the architecture of an Azande village can in some way explain the glories of the Hagia Sophia. Reliance upon the conclusions of anthropologists based on completely different cultures to declare religion and magic inseparable is likewise a complete *non sequitur*.[2] It certainly would not have been difficult for the highly cultured occupants of the ancient world to draw this distinction.

Application of the Categorisation of Magic, Mysteries and Religion

One simple example, taken from the *PGM* helps to illustrate the usefulness of this three-fold categorization. One section of the papyri was designated by its early German translator, Albrecht Dieterich, as *Eine Mithrasliturgie*.[3] Dieterich, working in the Frazerian atmosphere of 1903, wanted to see this ritual as a part of religion, allowing him to characterise it as worthy, so seizing upon one of the few god names present, he called it the *Mithras Liturgy*.[4] Despite Dieterich's undoubted fame as a scholar, the text was neither Mithraic nor was it a liturgy.[5] Franz Cumont was quick to point this out,[6] but Dieterich was not to be moved, and the argument continued for the next quarter century. An appreciation that the text was not either religion or magic, but a Mystery rite, might have solved this confrontation.[7]

Even a cursory reading will confirm that 'Mithra' appears once, but only as part of a clear backward reference to a previous event, rather than as the addressee of the current rite.[8] In addition, not one of the known theological or symbolic themes of Mithraic 'ascent of the soul via the seven planetary

---

[1] MacMullen (1997), pp. 143-144. Much of the main thrust of MacMullen's book is concerned with the identity or similarity of pagan religious and Christian religious practice, which while it may well be true, has little direct bearing on the relationship between religion (pagan or Christian) and magic.

[2] The fact that religion sometimes used magic, or that priests were often magicians also does not invalidate the basic distinction.

[3] Dieterich (1966). *PGM* IV, 475-829.

[4] A title which does not appear in the text itself in any form.

[5] Liturgy refers to religious services, more specifically where the worshippers' responses are complementary to the priest's work. This text contains neither priests nor worshippers.

[6] Cumont (1904), pp. 1-10.

[7] See chapter 7.2 for confirmation of this.

[8] *PGM* VI, 482.

spheres' appears in this text. Therefore, it is clearly not a Mithraic religious text. But Dieterich refused to be convinced, thinking that its complex and elegant structure must be part of some formal religion, not a piece of *volkskunde.* German scholars of that period, like Wilamowitz-Moellendorff, felt that classical scholars should only translate poetry, literature, hymns and religious rites, and not sully their hands with what he called *botokudenphilologie,* hence Dieterich's desire to see this text as a mainstream religious text.

In fact this particular passage, despite appearing in the *PGM* collection, is not in the strict sense magic either.

Applying the definition of the three modalities proposed above in terms of audience, degree of secrecy, specificity of objectives, range of entities addressed and privacy, we can clearly see the true nature of this passage:

1. *Audience.* The '*Mithras Liturgy*' is not a religious rite as it is not one designed to be performed in public.
2. *Secrecy.* The degree of secrecy is clear. The ritual is either a solitary one, or one "for an only child," and therefore it is not a religious ritual.
3. *Objectives.* The objective specified in the first line clearly marks it out as a Mystery rite, it being for the benefit of the writer's daughter, that she may become immortal (the most common objective of the Mysteries) and/or for the benefit of the writer.

   > I write these mysteries handed down… for an only child I request immortality, O initiates of this our power… so that I alone may ascend into heaven as an enquirer and behold the universe.[1]

   As Betz writes, "immortality is of course the primary benefit derived from the Mysteries (μυστήρια)."[2] The objectives are not love, wealth, power, sex, and so it is not a magic ritual, even though it is embedded in a papyrus amongst magic rituals. The objective is the immortalization of the initiate rather than the worship of a divinity (religion) or the constraining of other spiritual creatures for material benefits (magic).[3]
4. *Range of Entities.* The number of spiritual entities invoked is very limited, but it mentions Helios, Aiōn and Mithras (as a backward looking reference) and some other lesser daimones, but does not constrain them or threaten them, as would be typical of a magical text.
5. *Privacy.* In fact it is the procedure for a solitary Mystery rite, addressed

---

[1] *PGM* IV, 475-485.

[2] Betz (2005), p. 94.

[3] Also the Mystery rites are more than four times longer than the longest magical rite in the *PGM,* marking it out as quite different from the other sections.

directly to the greatest god, designed to confer immortality upon just one initiate. It is obviously practiced alone or simply between father and his only daughter.

Unsurprisingly, the Mystery rites are not found in later European forms of magic such as the *Hygromanteia* or the *Clavicula Salomonis,* precisely because they are not magic

The obvious conclusion is that it is a Mystery ritual imbedded in a magical papyrus, but not itself either magic, or religion. The point of this excursus is simply to show an example usage of the criterion set out above to practically distinguish between religion, the Mysteries and magic, and to demonstrate the importance and usefulness of these differences.

1.3 Historical Background

Magic was susceptible to changes in the dominant religion, which in Egypt for example, changed from a tolerant polytheistic pagan environment to a far more restrictive Christian monotheistic environment, followed much later by an even more monotheistic Islamic environment. Therefore it is worthwhile flagging some of the major political changes in the eastern Mediterranean over the course of the period being analysed, as they throw some light on the patterns of the diffusion of this magic.[1]

In Ancient Egypt magic existed over several millennia prior to the Christian era. Greek colonists and settlers moved to Egypt in search of work or a better place to live from the 7th century BCE onwards. From the time of Pythagoras and Herodotus, Egypt was seen both as a land of mystery, and of commercial opportunity. The melting pot where ancient Egyptian and Greek magic initially blended was the city of Alexandria, in Egypt, and it is the history of that city which is central to the history of Graeco-Egyptian magic. The main subsequent changes in the political, cultural and religious environment are mapped out below. The dates are merely a guideline, as the process of cultural transmission is of course more gradual.

Alexandria under the Greeks 332 - 30 BCE

Graeco-Egyptian magic was a direct result of the mixing of Egyptian and Greek cultures which began in earnest with the invasion of Egypt by Alexander in 332 BCE. Betz defines the date range of the relevant extant Graeco-Egyptian magical papyri as from 2nd century BCE to 5th century CE.[2] It is probable that the materials incorporated in these papyri date back a further century or so, but few of the extant magical papyri date before the 1st century CE.[3]

Alexandria under the Romans 30 BCE – 395 CE

Although the Romans conquered Egypt in 30 BCE, Greek remained in use as the *lingua franca*. The Romans seemed content not to interfere with local religious and magical customs, hence their culture added very little to the prevailing system of magic. Roman attempts to suppress local oracles and magical practices long associated with the indigenous Egyptian religion were largely unsuccessful.

---

[1] See my Ph.D thesis (University of Newcastle, 2014) for a full account of how magic was transmitted from Egypt to Greek Byzantium, and thence to the grimoires of Latin Europe.

[2] Betz (1996), p. xli.

[3] On dating see Brashear (1995), pp. 3491-3493.

Although Alexandria had a Jewish community from early times,[1] the Romans' crushing of the Jewish revolt in Jerusalem in 70 CE, and the destruction of the Second Temple in Jerusalem, created a surge in the migration of many Palestinian Jews to Alexandria, which for a while became a world centre for Jewry. In fact the Jews in Alexandria in the 1st century CE are said to have made up 40% of the total population.[2] Around this time Jewish magical formulae, holy names, and figures like Solomon and Moses most strongly entered the texts and practice of Graeco-Egyptian magic.[3] The few papyri that can be definitely dated as prior to that date (70 CE) have very few or no occurrences of demonstrably Jewish formulae.

The next most significant change in the region was the replacement of paganism with Christianity. The main events which saw the overthrow of paganism happened in just the space of 30 years. These events included the death of the Roman Emperor Julian, called the Apostate in 363 CE, an event which effectively finally withdrew official backing for the pagan world in the Roman Empire. In Egypt it was also the decrees of the Coptic patriarch Theophilus which resulted in the looting and burning of the Alexandrian Serapeum in 391 CE (which contained the last remaining scrolls and papyri saved from the great Library of Alexandria).

This saw Christianity rapidly rise to become the dominant religion in the region. Christianity then began a steady persecution of pagans and magicians (often one and the same) resulting in the destruction of a vast corpus of magical manuscripts.[4] On 8 November 392 CE, the ancient gods were officially reclassified as "evil spirits."[5] Although the Romans had legislated against the practice of magic on a number of occasions, the impact of Christian persecution was much greater.

---

[1] When Alexander founded the city he looked favourably on Jewish colonists: "Having found among them brave and loyal allies he granted that they might settle in a quarter of the new city with legal rights equal to those of the Greeks." - Josephus, *Wars of the Jews*, II, 18, 7.

[2] Philo Judaeus in *Flaccum*, 6, 8. Even allowing for exaggeration, it was probably only rigid Jewish monotheism that prevented them contributing more than *nomina magica* to the development of magic.

[3] Moses and Solomon are simply used here as the names of famous magicians, whose names can be called upon in any adjuration, and do not specifically indicate a Jewish provenance for the invocation.

[4] The bulk of the surviving Graeco-Egyptian magical papyri are reputed to have come from just one tomb in Thebes. These were bought by Giovanni Anastasi who subsequently sold them to European museums and libraries. See Dieleman (2005), pp. 12-16.

[5] *Codex Theodosii*, 16.10.12. Godefroy *et al* (2012).

Alexandria under the Byzantines 395-641

Rome lost Egypt back to the Greeks four years after the destruction of the Serapeum, but this time to Christian Greeks, not pagan ones. The grisly murder of Hypatia, the last head of the Platonic Academy in Alexandria, at the hands of the Christians in 415 CE, sealed the fate of paganism in Alexandria.

Finally, the loss of Egypt to Islam in 641 CE resulted in the migration (which had begun some years earlier) of Greeks (with their culture, magical practices and manuscripts) northwards to Constantinople, the capital of the Byzantine Empire which had been designated as their capital three centuries before. The ruling Byzantine Emperor at that time was Heraclius (r. 610-641) who looked favourably upon magic and astrology.

Constantinople and the Evolution of Magic after 641

Heraclius was eager to promote classical Greek learning, and rather like Rudolph II of Bohemia, acted as a patron for magicians, astrologers and alchemists. Heraclius' patronage of such subjects was confirmed by his invitation in 617 CE to Stephanos of Alexandria to come to Constantinople and teach the subjects comprising the *quadrivium.* Stephanos (c. 581 - c. 641 CE) was a Neoplatonist philosopher and scientist, probably born in Athens, but residing in Alexandria. He became Heraclius' astrologer and advisor in magical matters.

Abu Ma'shar and the Byzantine historian Georgios Kedrenos both reported that Stephanos wrote an *Apotelesmatikē Pragmateia.*[1] The *Apotelesmatikē Pragmateia* that he wrote has been tentatively identified by modern scholars as an astrological text relating to Islam. However, *Apotelesmatikē Pragmateia* is the original title of the *Hygromanteia,* a handbook of Solomonic magic with parallels in the *PGM.* The specific *Apotelesmatikē Pragmateia* authored by Stephanos might just as likely have been the *Hygromanteia* under its original title.[2]

The electional astrology chapters 7 and 30 in the *Hygromanteia* clearly derive from Hēliodōros. Olympiodorus is recorded as having specifically lectured on Hēliodōros, and Olympiodorus was known to have been Stephanos' teacher in Alexandria. Stephanos was very familiar with katarchic astrology, and lectured on it. This agrees with the great stress laid upon the importance of selecting the correct hour and day for specific magical operations in both the *PGM* and the *Hygromanteia.* This links the magic of the *PGM* with that of the *Hygromanteia.*

In turn it is now certain that the *Hygromanteia* was the ancestor of the *Clavicula Salomonis,* and hence of most of the grimoires in Europe, thereby linking their magical techniques back to the *PGM.*

[1] See Usener (1914), pp. 266–289.

[2] Skinner (2014), pp. 97-99 for a detailed support of this hypothesis. Also Marathakis (2011).

2.0 Sources of the Graeco-Egyptian Magical Tradition

2.1 Ancient Egyptian Dynastic Magic

Hieroglyphic and Hieratic Texts

Although discussion of purely Egyptian texts is not part of the aims of this book, it is necessary to consider them briefly to 'set the scene,' in order to see what Egyptian influences passed into the Graeco-Egyptian papyri.

The oldest hieroglyphic Egyptian texts are the so-called 'Pyramid Texts' (2500-2200 BCE), which are found on the walls of pyramids such as those of the Pharaohs Pepi and Unas. These texts are almost solely concerned with the happiness and safety of the royal dead in the next world, and not at all with the usual magical objectives of this world. So although they are 'magical,' the limitation of their aims to the resurrection and the reunification of the dead with their *ba* makes them less relevant to Graeco-Egyptian magic. These are primarily for the use of the dead rather than for any living person or magician. These texts which are carved in vertical columns of the chambers of these pyramids, total approximately 800 different passages, varying from 228 in the pyramid of Unas to 675 in that of Pepi II. Most are concerned with post-mortem protection, plus words to be spoken by the deceased, to pass through pylons (gates) in the Duat, and to speed resurrection.

The 'Coffin Texts' (2250-1784 BCE) are the lineal successor to the Pyramid Texts, being inscribed on the inside of the coffin rather than the wall of the sarcophagus chamber.[1] These are found in the coffins of less exalted but still powerful members of Egyptian society, and perform the same tasks, but more economically.

The successor to both of these groups of texts is the many copies of the Egyptian *Book of the Dead*.[2] This book contains about 200 passages, sixty percent of which are drawn from the above two classes of text. As such these rites still have the limited objectives of releasing the dead, guiding him through the Judgement Hall of Double Order, and reuniting him with his *ba* so that he can take his place amongst the gods.

Amongst the additional rites in the *Book of the Dead* however are procedures for animating the *shabti*, the small statuettes of servants found in many tombs and designed to serve their masters (or mistresses) in the afterlife. These are relevant as they bear upon later magical practices of statue ensoulment, and

---

[1] Faulkner (1973-1978).

[2] Budge (1961).

the creation of *stoicheia* (στοιχεῖα) or magical statues.[1]

Although the majority of purely Egyptian texts that have come down to us from the above collections are designed to help the dead, there are *formats* that may also have been used in magicians' rites designed to assist the living. One example of these techniques is the identification of the priest or magician with a specific god, for example, the repeated identification of the magician with Osiris in order to secure power over a lesser spiritual creature. This theme will be expanded in chapter 4.5. In the Babylonian context, the identification was usually either with Eridu or with his son:

> I am the magician born of Eridu, begotten in Eridu and Šubari.[2]

One of the few exceptions to the preoccupation with the needs of the dead is exemplified by the *Rhind Mathematical Papyrus*[3] which was found, not surprisingly, in the tomb of a magician and which includes rites relevant to all the usual magical objectives. A handful of passages in the *Book of the Dead* also concern us.[4] Presumably many other magicians' books either perished with their owners or may still be buried in their owners' tombs.

One part of the magic of the *PGM* which is undoubtedly dynastic Egyptian in origin is the part concerned with threats made to the gods. The Egyptians, in common with the Jews, used and valued the knowledge of the 'true name of the god' or spirit in order to do this:

> ...threats to the gods and knowledge of the true name are commonly agreed to be original Egyptian contributions to magic.[5]

In connection with the 'spirit assistant' or *paredros*,[6] Ciraolo says:

> These individualized names would have been of the utmost value and importance to the practitioner. They are valuable because they provide the practitioner with direct access to the [spirit] assistant. Knowledge of the name of the πάρεδρος [*paredros*] enables the practitioner to summon and control him. The practitioner need only utter the assistant's name and he appears, ready to obey.[7]

Both these techniques, threats to the gods/spirits and the utilisation of the knowledge of their true name, endured from dynastic Egypt right through Graeco-Egyptian and Byzantine Solomonic magical texts to 20th century Latin and English grimoires.

---

[1] See rite type 'J' in chapter 6.1.

[2] Thompson (1908), p. xxiii.

[3] British Museum papyrus 10057.

[4] Relevant chapters in the *Book of the Dead* include 17, 20, 122, 77, 119, 167 and Supp. 99.

[5] Brashear (1995), p. 3391.

[6] See chapter 6.6.

[7] Ciraolo (2001), p. 281.

A third technique, which had it roots in early Egyptian magic, was the threat made by the magician to interrupt natural processes such as the rising of the sun each day, or other cosmological processes such as the ceremonies which supposedly revivified the Egyptian gods each day. These were utilised in the *PGM* but not passed on to later Greek or Latin grimoires.

Other Egyptian magical techniques included:

> Execrations, whose goal was total destruction of the enemy, identified by name, whether alive or dead, human or divine, as well as *damnationes memoriae* conducted on inscriptions, individual hieroglyphs and statues deposited in cemeteries are all commonly attested.[1]

Figure 01: The Egyptian god Heka whose name means 'magic' and whose symbol is the pair of raised arms, palms forward.

Heka

In strictly dynastic Egyptian texts, magic is often personified as the god Heka, whose image is two extended forearms pointing skywards.[2] This god does not appear at all in the Graeco-Egyptian papyri, but the Greek goddess Hekate

[1] Brashear (1995), p. 3392.
[2] Ritner (2008), pp. 14-28.

frequently does.[1] It is strange that the most prominent Egyptian god of magic is not found in the *PGM* whilst many lesser Greek gods are.[2]

Most spells of the pharaonic period were apotropaic, that is designed to ward off evil influences. The uniquely Greek contribution to magic seems to be the generation of spells designed to achieve more personal ends, such as the acquisition of a lover, the winning of a court case or the binding of an enemy, rather than the warding-off of snakes or ensuring that the bark of Ra passed safely through the Duat or Underworld.

Demotic Texts

Demotic is a form of script Egyptians adapted for writing on papyrus with a cut reed pen, rather than chiselling onto the walls of a tomb. Demotic texts concentrate upon the pantheon of ancient Egypt, especially Osiris and Anubis. The time span of Demotic texts has been calculated to be about 1100 years (from 643 BCE to 452 CE).[3] The magic that is found in these texts is more adapted to everyday needs and desires (love spells, money, destruction of scorpions, etc) rather than the more cosmic objectives such as ensuring the rising of the sun. As such they form a bridge between the hieroglyphic or hieratic texts and the Graeco-Egyptian papyri, and they are written on the same medium as the latter.[4] In fact the Demotic papyri often combine Greek and demotic in the same passage, and are much closer in method to the *PGM* than to their ancestor texts from dynastic Egypt.

The best known and longest of the *PDM* (Magical Demotic Papyri) is the London-Leyden papyrus.[5] To quote just one example of continuity from ancient Egypt to the *PDM* papyri, the *Ouphōr* invocation,[6] designed to make carved statues come alive, is clearly an adapted version of the ancient 'Opening of the Mouth' procedure which was an essential part of any embalming process.[7] Here it is adapted to a more personal magical objective:

> ...that you may give divine and supreme strength to this image and may make it effective and powerful against all [opponents] and to be able to call back souls, move spirits, subject legal opponents [to your will], strengthen friendships, produce all [sorts of] profits, bring dreams, give prophecies, cause psychological

---

[1] It is conceivable that there is some link between Hekate and Heka, but to date one has not been found, apart from a superficial lexical similarity.

[2] One possibility is that many occurrences of this god's name have simply been translated by the common noun 'magic.'

[3] Brashear (1995), p. 3396.

[4] Translations of the extant *PDM* magical texts are included with the *PGM* in Betz (1996).

[5] *PDM* xii and *PDM* xiv.

[6] *PGM* XII. 270-350, especially 316-350.

[7] Dieleman (2005), p.290. The procedure of 'washing the mouth' of the god to vivify it also occurs in other oriental religions.

> passions and bodily sufferings and incapacitating illness, and perfect erotic philtres.[1]

This is truly a wide ranging list of magical effectiveness. The crux is the phrase:

> Here is truly written out, with all brevity, [the rite] by which all modelled images and engravings and carved stones are made alive.

The Mesopotamian origins of this practice are confirmed by Reiner:

> The most elaborate ritual performed at night with appeal to the stars is the "washing of the mouth" (*mīs pî*). It deals with the all-important ceremony of breathing life into the statues of the gods, a process called empsychosis[2] in Greek. In Babylonia, the ceremony is called the "opening of the mouth" (*pīt pî*), which is preceded by the "washing of the mouth" (*mīs pî*) of the divine statue. Divine statues, we know, were made of wood, and overlaid with precious materials, usually gold; incrustations of precious stones adorned them.[3] Their fabrication was, therefore, placed under the tutelage of the patron gods of carpenters, goldsmiths, and jewellers. Only after the inert materials were infused with breath through the mouth-opening ceremony could the statue eat and drink the offerings, and smell the incense.[4]

The typical Demotic rites are much longer and more detailed than the earlier hieroglyphic or hieratic rites, and are much closer in structure, objectives, and method to the *PGM* rites. They are therefore likely to have been written by magicians who were more comfortable in the Egyptian language rather than Greek, but who were working with the same materials, methods and assumptions as their fellow Greek magicians. Invocations were preserved in Demotic as well as Greek to specifically preserve the correct pronunciations of the *nomina magica* used in these invocations. Another feature of the *PDM* is that they have a preponderance of Egyptian deities, whilst the *PGM* have fewer Egyptian deities but many more Greek and lesser known gods and daimones.

Most of the extant *PDM* rites date from the time of the Roman occupation of Egypt, especially the early 3rd century CE. Hieratic appears occasionally in these Demotic texts, but never hieroglyphic, which was not adapted to writing on papyrus.

Harpocrates, Bes and Khnum are the minor but the most important Egyptian gods of magic who will later be found in the *PGM,* alongside the major Egyptian gods which were strictly limited to: Anubis, Isis, Osiris, Thoth, Horus, Hathor, Apophis, Ra, Phre, Ptah, Amoun, Khepera, Nephthys, Set, Sekhmet, Apis and Geb.

---

[1] *PGM* XII. 301-306.

[2] This word is not italicised in the original text, which is why it is not italicised here.

[3] Oppenheim (1949), pp. 172-93.

[4] Reiner (1995), pp. 139-140.

2.2 The Input of Jewish Magic to Graeco-Egyptian Magic

"Ten measures of magic came into the world. Egypt received nine of these, the rest of the world one measure."

- *Talmud, b. Qiddushin* 49b.

As confirmed by the above quotation, even the *Talmud* acknowledged that magic came primarily from Egypt, rather than from Jewish sources. There are no clear traces of the *methods* of for example Solomonic magic in pre-Christian Jewish sources. Bohak is of the opinion that there was no tradition at all (and therefore no surviving documents) of Jewish scribal magic, apart from general exorcistic hymns, before the 3rd century CE:

> In the Second Temple period, we already have much evidence for the writing down of exorcistic hymns (Nitzan 1994: 227-72; Eshel 2003), but no real evidence for the use of magical recipe books or even of written amulets (cf. Swartz 2001, Bohak 2008: 70-142, and Cohn 2008). But from the 3rd or 4th century CE, and *probably under the influence of Graeco-Egyptian magic*, of the kind reflected in the Greek magical papyri, we witness the rise of a fully scribal Jewish magical tradition, in which writing is used both in the transmission of magical knowhow and in the magical praxis itself (Bohak 2008: 281-85).[1]

The corollary of this statement is that as it appeared first, Graeco-Egyptian magic contributed to the establishment of a Jewish magical tradition, rather than the other way around. Although god and angel names were liberally borrowed from the Jewish tradition, it appears that method was not. Although magical practice may have been frowned upon by the Jewish community, it is however probable that many of the senior Rabbis were well acquainted with its principles by the time of the *Talmud* (after 200 CE):

> Rabbi Yohanan[2] said (b. *Sanhedrin* 17a and b. *Menahot* 65a) that knowledge of magic was one of the prerequisites for sitting in the Sanhedrin, the supreme Jewish court of law — not only in order to detect and deter magicians, but also in order to beat them at their own game, and to gain the upper hand against other offenders as well.[3]

There are a number of very specific and well-documented contributions made from Jewish magic to the *PGM*, and also to later Byzantine and Latin Solomonic grimoire magic. These contributions apparently did not include the Solomonic or grimoire *method*. The main elements that were passed on from the Jewish tradition are clearly defined as follows:

---

[1] Bohak (1999), p. 125. My italics.

[2] Probably Rabbi Yohanan ben Zakai (30-90 CE).

[3] Bohak (1999), p. 120.

a) The god names in the *PGM* derive from a number of sources, including Egyptian and Greek, but characteristic god names like Iao, IHVH, Yah or Sabaōth without doubt come from the Jewish tradition. In the context of the *PGM* they are just other *nomina magica,* and carry no specific hint of monotheistic Jewish religion with them.

b) The vast bulk of angel (and some demon) names are derived from Jewish sources. The biblical archangels Michael, Gabriel, Raphael and Uriel are well documented. They in turn probably derive from Babylonia.[1] In the first centuries of the Christian era, books like the three different *Books of Enoch* generated a range of angel names, especially those of the angels of the seven Heavens, and of the 12 zodiacal signs. No trace of the 168 names of the hours of the week (found in later grimoires) is however to be found in the *PGM.*

c) Just as the concept of angels was probably derived from Babylon, so the practice of oil magic probably entered Jewish practice from the same source. The practices of oil, water and lamp flame skrying accompanied by evocation are commonly attested in the *PDM* (see chapter 6.4).

Bohak is certainly of the opinion that it was the Graeco-Egyptian technology of magic that informed the Jewish magical tradition. His example focuses on the *charaktēres,* but his contention applies to the whole 'massive' entry of the *PGM* magical technology into Jewish magic:

> For the time being, let us return to late antiquity, and note how the *charactêres* exemplify the massive entry of technological innovations from the Greco-Egyptian magic of late antiquity into the Jewish magical tradition, and their absorption there... we see a set of foreign elements which was so fully naturalized in the Jewish magical tradition - and in some medieval cases also fully Judaized - as to assure its survival within that tradition to our very days.[2]

It is probable that both the Jewish and the Egyptian practices came separately from Babylon. Daiches supports the view that Babylon was the source of both Jewish and Egyptian practices on the grounds of "striking parallels to Babylonian magical texts as well as to the Jewish."[3] Their origins can be seen in the parallels between the *PDM* practice (specifically *qmȝ tȝ*, Evocationary Lamp Skrying) and the Jewish tradition ("princes of the thumb"), which are attested in Jewish records in the 11th century commentaries of Rashi.[4]

---

[1] The concept of an angelic hierarchy reputedly came to the fore during the time of the Babylonian captivity from 597-538 BCE.

[2] Bohak (2008), p. 274.

[3] Published in Daiches (1913), pp. 5-6. The Babylonian Maklū text published by Tallqvist to which he refers is also quoted in Daiches (1913), p. 4.

[4] *Sanhedrin* 67b. Other references to this procedure occur in *Chochmat ha-Nefesh,* 16d, 18a, 20c, 28d, 29a; *Ziyuni,* 10c; *Redak* on *Ezekiel,* 21:26; and *Nishmat Chayim,* III, 19.

The largest collection of Hebrew magical documents so far found was retrieved from the *genizah* of the Fustat synagogue in old Cairo. The bulk of this documentation of Jewish magic in Alexandria is still kept in Cambridge and several other repositories. Unfortunately Schechter, who was responsible for retrieving much of it, and his successors, were much more interested in the religious content of the Genizah, and so it is only in the last 25 years that the magical content has begun to receive significant attention. With that limitation, it still seems most likely that Graeco-Egyptian magic influenced Jewish magic rather than the other way around.

The Hekhalot literature

It is relevant to briefly examine the Hekhalot literature, as Morton Smith claimed a great deal of identity between it and the *PGM*.[1]

The gods of Greece such as Helios and Aphrodite may be glimpsed in *Sepher ha-Razim,* but are definitely not to be found in the *hekhalot*.[2] This literature, extant from the 3rd to the 8th centuries CE, is concerned with "rising on the planes" (to use modern terminology) or journeying from one of the seven heavens to another (to use a more traditional image), with the eventual hope of meeting god face-to-face. This literature is also referred to as *merkavah/merkabah* literature because the journey was often visualized as travelling 'downwards' in an astral chariot (the literal meaning of the word).[3] This material is to a large extent a mystical and rabbinic practice, but the use of secret passwords at the various doorways or portals to the Halls or *hekhalot,* to get past their angelic guardians, gives it a superficial magical colouring.

Morton Smith wrote that:

> Much of the celestial personnel of the *hekhalot* is found also in the magical papyri and in Gnosticism. Not only have the papyri and the Gnostics taken over Hebrew names, but the *hekhalot* have taken over Greek names and sometimes have even taken back Greek corruptions of names which were originally Hebrew.[4]

This appears to be a rather sweeping and not altogether accurate statement. The traffic in names was not nearly as reciprocal as Morton Smith implies. The vast majority of the angelic and god names used in the *hekhalot* literature are obviously of Jewish extraction. Some of these god and angelic names have

---

[1] Smith (1963), p. 150.

[2] Lesses (1996), p.46.

[3] It is strange that this procedure is often described as 'descending,' which is suggestive of an Underworld rather than a heavenly setting. See Davila (2001), *Descenders to the Chariot.*

[4] Smith (1963), p. 150.

been taken over into the *PGM*,[1] rather than the other way around. But these names in the *PGM* could easily have come from Jewish sources other than the *hekhalot*. These names could for example have been derived from the *Septuagint* which had been available in Alexandria from the late 3rd century BCE.[2]

The concept of the chariot very clearly comes from Jewish sources, specifically *Ezekiel*, whose vision was of a very detailed and many wheeled and winged chariot.[3] The concept of doorways guarded by angels who required very specific passwords may have passed in the opposite direction, from Egyptian conceptions of the Duat, with its many guarded portals, to the *hekhalot*.

The predominant direction of traffic is however from the Hebrew sources into the Gnostic texts (which were in the early years Hebrew heresies anyway) and the *PGM* where they enjoyed the reputation of being powerful words of coercion, especially Sabaōth[4] and IAŌ (derived from the Hebrew צבאות and יהוה respectively). Lesses confirms that:

> The Graeco-Egyptian ritual texts draw names of divinities from Jewish, Greek, Egyptian, Roman, or Mesopotamian traditions, while the *hekhalot* adjurations [only] use Hebrew names of God and the angels. They do not incorporate the names of the Greek, Egyptian, or Roman deities.[5]

This is a much more accurate statement of the situation than Morton Smith's rather wide ranging remarks.[6] From the point of view of tracing the evolvement of magical methods, it can be seen that although the *hekhalot* literature may have passed some god and angel names to the *PGM*, it did not pass *any* actual magical techniques. Furthermore the procedure used by the *hekhalot* devotees (and still in use today) was one of piety, intense prayer and meditation, with the minimal use of invocation, and absolutely no use of evocation, or any of the other main Graeco-Egyptian magical techniques.

The *hekhalot* literature is basically mysticism, albeit very vivid mysticism, and not part of the magical tradition. Scholem perceptively characterised the *hekhalot* material as 'ecstaticism' as opposed to magic.[7] It is clear that in the context of magic there is always a hierarchy of spiritual creatures,[8] in which any sense of a strictly monotheistic system is lost. If there is only a meditative appeal to the one god, as in Judaism, then this is meditation/prayer, not magic.

---

[1] Such as IAΩ, Elohim, Sabaōth/Tzabaoth, etc.

[2] Its translation was not fully completed till 132 BCE.

[3] *Ezekiel* 1: 15-21; 10: 9-17.

[4] Literally 'of the hosts.' I believe that 'Sabaōth,' used in a magical context should be interpreted as the lord of the angelic hosts, rather than as lord of armies.

[5] Lesses (1996), p. 52-53.

[6] See Lewy (1969) for a discussion of the Greek phrases in *Hekhalot Rabbati*.

[7] Scholem (1955), pp. 50-60, 78.

[8] See chapter 5.1.

2.3 The Relationship of Gnosticism to Magic

Gnosticism is not a single religion but a term used to embrace a collection of Jewish heresies which also intermixed with Christianity (another Jewish heresy) and which flourished in Asia Minor and Egypt (both areas of flight for Jews post the destruction of the Second Temple in 70 CE) from the 1st to the 5th century CE. Common elements across the many Gnostic sects, include the rejection of the Creator god (Yahweh or Ialdabaoth), and often the worship of the serpent who offered knowledge, or *gnosis,* in the Garden of Eden. This serpent appears in a Greek (Abraxas), Egyptian (Chnoubis) or Persian (Aiōn) guise.

Although Gnosticism has been characterised by heresiologists as full of magic, it was essentially a revolt against Yahweh, a Jewish heresy, rather than a part of the development of magic. Where it entwined with Christianity it was simply one Jewish heresy interacting with another, in an era when even the great Fathers of the Church flirted with heresies or converted from one religion to another.[1]

Gnosticism was founded in its early years predominantly by Samaritans.[2] The first eight Gnostic teachers were either Samaritans or lived and taught in Samaria, the most notable of which was Simon Magus. Even Jesus Christ was pro-Samarian.[3]

Most of these teachers were also magicians, including Jesus, who used magic/miracles to impress their converts and draw disciples. However although these teachers used magic, its principles were not taught to the mass of their disciples, nor is there any mention of Gnostic laity using magic or performing miracles, so Gnosticism did not in itself become part of the chain of transmission of magical methods in the Eastern Mediterranean.

Gnosticism's main relevance to magic was that many of its founders (especially Simon Magus) were able to demonstrate miracles using magical techniques, and a lot of the iconography and theological terms (Ialdabaoth, etc) were drawn from magical texts such as the *PGM.* Apart from that Gnosticism is effectively a cul-de-sac from the point of view of the study of the transmission of magical techniques and formulae.

It was a hallmark of almost all of the Gnostic sects that their prophets were expected to do miracles. Nascent Christianity was no exception, as Jesus

---

[1] For example Tertullian and Origen. At the end of the day, a heresy is only that belief among many that did not finally triumph and become accepted.

[2] Confirmation of this statement can be observed in Table 16 in Appendix 1.

[3] Witness the parable of the Good Samaritan, which would presumably have been enormously unpopular amongst his Jewish listeners.

performed many miracles, and was in his day regularly acclaimed as a magician or wonder-worker.[1] This provided later Christians with an ongoing theological dilemma as to how to distinguish magic from miracle.

If we examine the religious competition in Jesus' day we find that Simon Magus, Apollonius of Tyana, Alexander of Abonoteichos, Basilides and many of the Gnostic founders are all reputed magicians. It would seem that in those days, just as in our own days of tele-evangelists, that the fastest growing religions needed miracles or magic to convince the crowd.

Gnosticism was not initially nor essentially Christian, because the basic premises (such as the evil demiurge, the snake and the rebellion against an evil Creator god) were all very clearly Jewish concerns not Christian ones (except in the sense that Christianity also drew on those same Jewish roots). Nascent Christianity reacted by systematically cataloguing the beliefs of competing Gnostic movements, which were (like it) Jewish heresies. It was the job of the early heresiologists to lay out the beliefs of the competing movements in detail so that they could criticize, compete and defeat them. It is highly significant that the heresiologists did not initially attack other mainstream religions such as Judaism itself, merely their fellow competing Jewish heresies.

Gnosticism is therefore not a source of magical techniques, but a utiliser. Gnostic texts cannot be seen as a major contributory source for Graeco-Egyptian magic, but utilised techniques and names drawn from magic. Magic was utilised by Jesus and other Gnostic founders to attract disciples, but in no real sense did those religions enhance the art of magic. Magic was also both older and more established in the 1st century of the current era, than any of the breakaway Gnostic sects.

Gnosticism drew some of its founders' practice from Graeco-Egyptian magic, and some of its theology from Neoplatonic ideas, rather than the other way around. As Betz writes:

> It is known that philosophers of the Neo-Pythagorean and Neoplatonic schools, as well as Gnostic and hermetic groups, used magical books and hence must have possessed copies. But most of their material vanished and what we have left are their quotations [in the works of the early Church Fathers].[2]

Of course this is overstating the case, as a number of Gnostic texts, such as those found by Bruce (*Pistis Sophia*), or discovered at Chenoboskion in Nag Hammadi have survived.[3] However in terms of the understanding of the

---

[1] See Morton Smith (1978).

[2] Betz (1996), p. xlii.

[3] See Mead (1963), Robinson (1977) and Doresse (1986). Chenoboskion was a monastery near to the Nag Hammadi finds, and so these papyri used to be referred to as the Chenoboskion papyri.

evolution of magic they are less useful, as Gnosticism drew material from the magical texts, rather than the other way around. Additionally Gnosticism is an intellectual a cul-de-sac, having no extant lineal descendants.[1]

See Appendix 1 for a tabulation of the main Gnostic teachers demonstrating the frequent occurrence of magicians and Samaritans amongst their early founders.

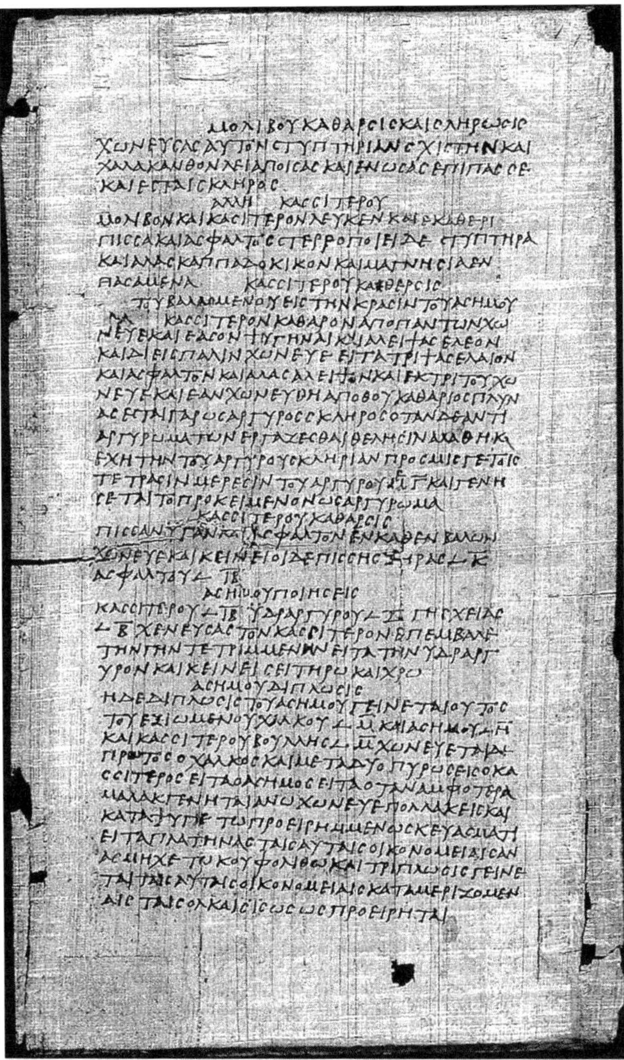

Figure 02: A page from *PGM* XII c. 300 C.E.[2] Note the clear paragraph breaks between sections, which are mirrored in Preisendanz's transcription and Betz's translation.

[1] Efforts by writers such as Thomas Churton, to label certain modern movements as 'gnosticism,' is really just playing with the term, or extending its scope well beyond its original meaning, rather than identifying genuine Gnostic movements.

[2] Rijksmuseum van Oudheden, Leiden.

3.0 The Graeco-Egyptian Magical Papyri

3.1 The Discovery of the Papyri

Translations of most of these papyri into a European language were first made available in German by Preisendanz in 1928/1931.[1] His work on the Greek texts has been supplemented by Betz, who collected and edited English translations, adding in more recently translated Graeco-Egyptian papyri, increasing their number from 81 to 120 papyri. Betz also included translations for the Demotic and Coptic contents of these papyri, which were originally completely ignored by Preisendanz. He followed and expanded Preisendanz's numbering system beyond *PGM* LXXXI, which was the last numbered papyrus in Preisendanz's collection.[2]

The oldest Graeco-Egyptian text (*PGM* XL, the "curse of Artemisia") dates from shortly after Alexander the Great's death,[3] and the most recent from the 5th century CE. The second oldest papyrus (*PGM* XX) was written by, or was in the collection of, two magicians Philinna of Thessaly,[4] and an unnamed magician from Syria, despite the fact that it was found in Egypt. This suggests that this style of magic was already well spread over an area which included at the very least Thessaly, Syria, Palestine and Egypt.[5] It is therefore probably representative of magic in the whole eastern Mediterranean littoral in that period.

There are just four Demotic papyri included in the collection (the *PDM*), all found by Anastasi[6] around Thebes, all dating from the early 3rd century CE, and all written by the same scribe, so they form a consistent whole. This shows that the methods outlined were used by Egyptian and Greek speakers alike. As well as Demotic (and some hieratic) Egyptian, there are passages in Greek and, fortunately, glosses in Coptic which clearly indicate the correct pronunciation for the words so glossed. Although Egyptian hieroglyphs had some phonetic indications, it was not an alphabetic language, so most indications of

---

[1] As we will see in a later chapter, some of these rites made their way into European languages some three centuries before then.

[2] The first edition only covered papyri I-LX, but the Preisendanz reprint of 2001 included I-LXXXI.

[3] Brashear (1995), p. 3413.

[4] Thessaly has always traditionally been the home of 'witches' as far as the Greeks were concerned. See Luck (1987), p. 31.

[5] Of course this is only an indication of the origins of the practitioners, rather than a certain mapping of the actual areas of practice. This is suggestive nonetheless.

[6] Jean d'Anastasi (1780 - 1857) purportedly obtained it from a tomb in Luxor (Thebes) in 1827. Anastasi was an Armenian who worked as a Swedish/Norwegian diplomat at the court of the Khedive of Egypt, based in Alexandria.

pronunciation would have been lost without the Coptic glosses, especially of *nomina magica* and the names of gods, where correct pronunciation was crucial for the magician. The existence of these ancient Coptic glosses show the importance placed upon the correct pronunciation of the Egyptian words of power, *nomina magica,* and god names. Pronunciation, rather than exact palaeographic form, is the best tool for tracking the migration of these names over a range of successor cultures.

The first of the Demotic papyri to be translated into English was published as the *Demotic Papyrus of London and Leiden*.[1] The magical methods outlined in the four Demotic papyri were overwhelmingly Egyptian, suggesting that they had survived in this form for at least seven centuries without significant Hellenic reworking. Methods included the typically Egyptian compulsive formulae, where the magician threatens the god or daimon that he will disrupt the smooth working of the universe if the god does not carry out his commands, formulae that are also found in the earliest Egyptian Pyramid Texts. This threat (to disturb the smooth workings of the universe) is not typical of Greek magic, or Greek religion.

The gods were usually Egyptian, or Egyptian disguised under the name of their Greek counterparts. Often, as in the case of *PGM* XII, both Greek and Demotic rites would occupy the same papyrus, written in the same hand.

Finally the publication of the *Supplementum Magicum* covering a number of small recently discovered papyri (mostly amulets) make up the entire available corpus of Graeco-Egyptian papyri.[2] The *Supplementum Magicum* also partly overlaps with Betz. In the Rite Tables these are listed as '*SM*' followed by their number. A selection of lamellae have been extracted from Kotansky, where they have special interest (such as being a phylactery rather than an ordinary amulet), and have been included in the tables.[3] There are very few discovered magical papyri that remain outside of this corpus, untranslated in any European language. Therefore an analysis of the above resources almost totally covers the whole range of the Graeco-Egyptian magical papyri. A few fragmentary amulets may not have been included in the scholarly corpus.

---

[1] The title refers to the present geographical location of its two halves. See Griffith and Thompson (1904). Betz's numbering is *PDM* xii (and *PGM* XII). The same scribe also wrote *PDM* xiv, lxi, and *PDM* Supp. An exorcism drawn from the original publication of this papyrus, variously entitled 'The Bornless One' or the 'Headless One' was adapted in the late 19th century for use in the ritual of the Hermetic Order of the Golden Dawn.

[2] Daniel & Maltomini (1990, 1992).

[3] Kotansky (1994) followed by the amulet number.

3.2 Analysis of the *PGM* by Source and Type

The material in the *PGM* comes from a range of sources and languages. The contents are a mixture of Egyptian, Greek, Coptic, Gnostic, Jewish, and Christian magic.[1] These strands can be most easily recognized by the type of spiritual creatures or gods called upon:

a. *Egyptian magic.* Egyptian magic calls upon traditional indigenous Egyptian gods such as Harpocrates, Horus, Anubis, Thoth, Isis, Osiris, Set and Bes, and preserves elements of dynastic Egyptian magic. Magical names like Bainchōōōch are also of Egyptian derivation.[2]

b. *Greek magic.* Greek classical magic calls upon a very specific subset of the Classical Greek gods including Selene, Cybele, Zeus, Hermes, Apollo, Helios, Artemis, and specially Aphrodite (for love rites); and then upon the gods of the Underworld, like chthonic Hermes, Hekate, and Persephone; plus gods which personify abstract qualities, such as Aiōn (the All), the Moirai (Fate), Kronos (Time), Physis (Nature) and Tyche (Providence). None of these gods are portrayed or used in the Classical manner, but rather delegated to the same level of functionality as their daimones.[3] For some reason Dionysos, Hephaistos, Hera and other prominent occupants of Olympus never appear. The gods in the papyri were treated in much the same was as they were in later Greek folk religion, as useful, but almost daimonic, tricksy and dangerous. As Betz puts it:

> In the older material, the Greek gods are alive and well. But Zeus, Hermes, Apollo, Artemis, Aphrodite, and others are portrayed not as Hellenic and

[1] Some Babylonian input may have come via Jewish practices adopted in Babylon during the captivity (597-538 BCE). Brashear (1995), p. 3429 also tentatively suggests the possibility of some Buddhist influence, but this seems very unlikely, and is not supported by examples of imported practices. Christian magic is also very much in the minority. Interestingly, there are no obvious traces of Roman magic, despite the fact that Egypt was under Roman domination from 30 BCE - 395 CE, during which time most of the papyri were written.

[2] Possibly derived from the Egyptian *ba* = one of the parts of the soul; and *cho(oo)ch* = darkness, or 'soul of darkness.' See *Pistis Sophia,* IV, 137.

[3] Betz (1996), p. xlii, quotes Ulrich von Wilamowitz-Moellendorff's well known disparaging comment: "I once heard a well-known scholar complain that [it was unfortunate that] these papyri were found, because they deprived antiquity of the noble splendor of classicism." Splendour or not, this is how the Greek and Egyptian gods were treated by magicians in the first five centuries of the Christian era. Occasionally the gods were asked to send their daimones to perform a specific task, but more often they were commanded to do it themselves. The gods were effectively treated as daimones, and feared, as the magicians wore phylacteries for the express purpose of protecting themselves from the malice of these same gods.

> aristocratic, as in literature, but as capricious, demonic, and even dangerous.[1]

Egyptian religion in turn influenced the imported Greek religion, so that the importance of the Egyptian Underworld (the Duat), helped to emphasise the Greek divinities of the underworld like Hekate,[2] Persephone and Korē,[3] and otherwise gods like Hermes and Aphrodite became associated with the Underworld in their magical and chthonic forms.[4]

c. *Jewish magic.* Some Graeco-Egyptian texts call upon the archangels: Michael, Raphael, Gabriel and Uriel/Ouriel plus recognizable Hebrew god names like אדני Adonai (and its Greek variants like Adonias),[5] יהוה IHVH or Yahweh (frequently appearing in the guise of יה Yah or the Greek version ιαω/ΙΑΩ, or the Samaritan version Ipos/Ibas),[6] Elohim (often misspelled), and Sabaōth.[7] Of course, since the translation of the Hebrew scriptures into Greek in the form of the *Septuagint*, in Alexandria, dating from the 3rd century BCE, some Jewish material entered directly and more easily into the predominantly Greek culture of the eastern Mediterranean, but the main period of importation was immediately after 70 CE. The use of Hebrew god names in all these texts is simply a by-product of their having filtered into Graeco-Egyptian magic practice from Jews living in Alexandria rather than an indication of the origin of the techniques. Jewish material brought with it some Babylonian elements (such as the angels), and an elaborately stratified cosmology of the heavens. Although Hebrew names entered the mix, specifically Jewish magical techniques do not appear to have had much impact on Graeco-Egyptian magic.

---

[1] Betz (1996), p. xlv.

[2] Hekate becomes important and is sometimes associated with one of the few Babylonian goddesses in the *PGM*, Ereshkigal.

[3] Kore later becomes a demon in the works of the German Jewish grimoire, *The Sacred Book of Abramelin, the Mage.* See Mathers (1900), Book II, pp. 81, 83.

[4] Hermes is described on a 4th century BCE binding talisman (or *defixio*) as "the underworldly, the treacherous, the restrainer, the luckbringer [not 'roguish' as translated by Jordan]." See Gager (1992), No. 102, p. 201; Jordan (1985), No. 18.

[5] In fact the Hebrew אדני simply means 'Lord' and is often used in Hebrew texts to replace the actual names of god. Despite Judaism being nominally a monotheistic religion, a number of names of god appear in Jewish scripture, which may be traces of separate gods that were later merged. The two classical Hebrew groups of god names were the Elohistic (אל El, Elohim) and the Yahwistic (יה, יהוה IHVH, Yah, Yahweh).

[6] The transformation from יהוה or IHVH to IAŌ is easier to understand if you take into account that ו can be transliterated as V or O, depending on its use as a consonant or a vowel, just as י can equally be transliterated as J, I or Y. IHVH then becomes YHOH, which might then be speculatively pronounced as YaH-OH or ιαο.

[7] Sabaōth retained its use to constrain spirits right up to the later European grimoires, even to the 19th century.

d. *Gnostic magic.* Gnostic elements, and other words derived from creative combinations (or scribal degeneration) of the other traditions listed above.[1] For the purposes of this book, Gnostic material will be treated as a phenomenon separate from Christianity, as even those Gnostic movements which may have started out as an offshoot of Christianity, were later rejected and discarded by the religion which is now accepted as Christianity.

Although scholars have argued over the origins of Gnosticism, it seems clear from the work of Quispel, Stroumsa, Segal and Fossum that the main elements of Gnosticism were derived from Jewish heresies rather than from Christian heresies.[2] Furthermore, the Jewish heresies identified by the above scholars sprang up immediately after the destruction of the Second Temple in Jerusalem, with the tide of dispirited Jewish immigrants who arrived in Egypt (and to a lesser extent Asia Minor) just after 70 CE. The idea of an evil creator god obviously found fertile ground in the disillusioned post-exilic Jewish community in Alexandria, whose temples in both Jerusalem and Egypt had been destroyed by the Romans without any trace of divine intervention.

This disillusioned Jewish Diaspora were the seedbed of Gnosticism therefore giving us an approximate *terminus a quo* of 70 CE for the introduction of Gnostic names and gods into Egypt. Very soon after, in 74 CE, the Romans destroyed the second most important Jewish temple which was Onias' temple located in Leontopolis near Heliopolis, Egypt which must have completed the Jews' sense of total abandonment by their god.[3] Finally after bar-Khokba's revolt failed in 135 CE, Jews were totally banned from living in Jerusalem by the Romans. This must have stimulated a second wave of Jewish migration to Alexandria (as well as to other destinations). This apparent abandonment also helped to launch a number of Jewish heresies. If this date is accepted as the *terminus a quo* for the generation of Gnosticism, we can fairly safely assume that any interaction between Gnosticism and Graeco-Egyptian magic only began in the early 2nd century CE.

e. *Christianity.* Christianity was, in reality, just another Jewish heresy, that managed to survive rather better than its competitors. The fact that the Christian church attacked these other heresies so vigorously was a function of the competitive fear felt by the early Church Fathers, who were concerned to

---

[1] Of course it could well be that these names, instead of being later corruptions, are in fact earlier strata of genuine Egyptian magical practice. As Barb (1964, p. 4, note 16) suggested: "much that we are accustomed to see classified as late 'syncretism' is rather the ancient and original, deep-seated popular religion, coming to the surface when the whitewash of 'classical' writers and artists began to peel off…"

[2] Mastrocinque (2005), p. 82.

[3] Ornias' temple was said to have stood for 243 (or 343 years according to one source) before its final destruction by the Romans.

preserve the purity of their nascent religion against the other Jewish heresies springing up around them.[1] Christianity, in the sense of that religion preserved under that name today, added very little of significance to these magic texts, except the occasional insertion of the name of 'Jesus.'[2] Besides, Christianity did not reach its status as a Roman state religion till 391 CE, and during most of its subsequent existence, disapproved of and sought to vigorously destroy magic.[3]

f. *Roman.* Strangely, although Rome conquered Egypt in 30 BCE, Roman religion and magic added very little to Graeco-Egyptian magical texts.[4] Romans still revered Greek culture, and well-educated Romans spoke Greek. Presumably the same attitude prevailed with regard to their attitude to magic.

g. *Mithraism.* Mithras appears once in one of the longest complete sections of the *PGM*, but only as a backward reference, in the so-called 'Mithras Liturgy.'[5] As already stated, I do not believe that this was a Mithraic rite, as it has none of the usual Mithraic initiatory steps or iconography, but a Mystery rite that happened to mention the god Mithra in a passing reference to a previous event.

Although this list of sources sounds complex, and many of the papyri have two or more ingredients, it is usually fairly easy to identify the *main* root of any particular rite. For example, rites that make reference to all four archangels may be of Jewish origin, although the universal use of Jewish god names makes this less than certain. Likewise, a rite that primarily calls on Anubis or Osiris, or is written in Demotic, will almost certainly have Egyptian roots. Rites referencing Selene or chthonic Hermes will seldom mention an Egyptian god, and will fairly obviously have sprung from Greek roots.

However it is not the purpose of this book to identify the roots of each Graeco-Egyptian procedure, but rather to demonstrate the techniques they employed. It is sufficient to observe that as the Greeks traditionally deferred to the Egyptians in matters of magic (as did the Jews), and that the rites with the

---

1 Marcion and Valentinus and others came from 'Christian' Gnosticism, which was however formulated on the basis of the Jewish heretical vision of an evil creator god.

2 Where Jesus was used his name was used in the same sense as Solomon, or Eleazar, as a great magician of the recent past, who might strike fear into the hearts of the spirits conjured. Such commemoration of the names of powerful magicians of the past remained a feature of magic right up to modern times. See chapter 4.5.

3 Volumes on early Christian magic, such as Meyer and Smith (1999) predominantly contain material with the marginal addition of 'Jesus' as a word of power, plus spells generated in Egypt in a Coptic environment.

4 To quote Tavenner (1966), p. 19: "The only two works in extant Latin literature which at all resemble a treatise on magic are the *Apologia* of Apuleius of Madaura, his defence against the charge of being a magician; and parts of Pliny's *Natural History,* especially the first thirteen paragraphs of book thirty."

5 *PGM* IV 475-820.

predominantly Egyptian elements are likely, but not always, to be the oldest.

Papyri owing the *bulk* of their content to Jewish elements are very few, but the god names IAŌ and Sabaōth are to be found regularly distributed across many rites. The upshot of this is (as a number of scholars have remarked) that the presence of these god names is not an indication of the origin of the rite, but rather a symptom of the widespread use of such words of power that were considered universally effective, regardless of their origin.

With regard to the provenance of the papyri, there is little to go on apart from the fact that Thebes was the reputed source of the Anastasi hoard of papyri, which make up the bulk of the *PGM*.[1] One of the few clear statements of provenance of one papyrus occurs at the beginning of *PGM* CXXII. 1-55 where it says:

> [This is] an excerpt of enchantments from the holy book called *Hermes*, found in Heliopolis in the innermost shrine of the temple, written in Egyptian [Demotic] letters and translated into Greek.

One may deduce that if the book was casually 'found' in the library of an Egyptian temple, it is likely to have been removed at a rather late date, probably after 400 CE when the temple had fallen into ruin. Alternatively 'found' might really mean stolen, which still argues for a late date, or it might simply be a literary device designed to make the papyrus appear to be more valuable. The naming of the book *Hermes* is intriguing, but does not automatically assert that this book was part of the Hermetic literature, merely that the god was an important part of its contents, as he was in a number of magical papyri.

When you first look through either the Greek or English edition of these magical instructions it looks like an impenetrable mass of heterogeneous material, but when you begin to realise how the original scribes thought about magic, and clearly captioned most of the 'spells' it becomes much clearer. Although the list of techniques and ritual procedures in Table 01 may look like a rather mixed bag, these have been distilled from the sum total of all the procedures found in the *PGM*, the *Supplementum Magicum,* plus many of the most important lamellae produced during the first five centuries of this era.

It is not immediately clear from Betz's English edition that the volume actually contains the text of 131 separate papyri. With the addition of the papyri in the *Supplementum Magicum* the number of papyri rises by another 100 papyri (most of which are amulets). Of these 231 papyri only 15 are substantial. These have been analysed in Appendix 5 showing which rite types and subtypes occur in which papyri.

---

1 Interestingly there is a Thebes in Greece with a similar later reputation for magic. *Juratus,* a much later Latin grimoire (*circa* 1225 CE) was reputedly written by Euclid of (the Greek) Thebes. This Euclid was a magician and not the famous geometer.

PGM/PDM number	Papyrus Number & Collection	Papyrus Title	Number of Lines	Number of Rite Types present
IV	Bibliothèque Nat. Supp. Gr. 574	Great Magical Papyrus of Paris	3274	29
XIV/xiv	Leiden I 383 and BM dem. 10070	London and Leiden Papyrus	1227	21
VII	London 121		1026	33
III	Louvre 2391		731	11
XII/xii	Leiden I 384		495	19
V	London 46		489	11
I	Berlin 5025		347	7
II	Berlin 5026		183	3

Table 01: The main Magical Papyri and their contents.

According to Dieleman, papyri IV, V, XII, XIII and XIV come from the 'Theban Magical Library' discovered in a tomb near Thebes by Giovanni Anastasi in the first half of the 19th century, whilst I, II, III, VII, LXI and *PDM* Supplement are probably also from that collection. It is a great pity that it has taken so long for them to be brought fully to the attention of the world.

From the analysis in Appendix 5 (Table 20) it is clear that the core of the Graeco-Egyptian system of magic is to be found in just the first six magical handbooks listed above. Later we will see (in Table 13) how the scribes divided their work, and what specific headings they used to make it easy to find their way around this mass of material.

The techniques and methods used by Graeco-Egyptian magicians can be initially broken down into the following categories listed in Table 02. These are not arbitrary divisions, or invented categories, but closely follow the headings utilised by the authors of these papyri. Categories such as Invocation of Gods, Love or Talismans will later be broken down into subtypes according to their use of specific Greek headwords. The alphabetic codes are however just for convenience, and ease of reference.

Code	Technique or Rite
A	Amulets
B	Evocationary Bowl Skrying
C	Calendrical Considerations
D	*Defixiones*
E	Evocationary Lamp Skrying
F	Face-to-Face Encounter with a God
G	God's Arrival and Invocation
H	Health
I	Invisibility
J	Hymns
K	Foreknowledge and Memory
L	Love
M	Mysteries and Initiation Rites
N	Necromancy
O	Homeric magic and divination
P	*Paredros* or Assistant Daimon
Q	Daimonic Possession and Exorcism
R	Rings and Gemstones, Magical
S	Statues, Magical
T	Talismans
U	Phylacteries
V	Visions and Dream Revelation
W	Prayers
X	Other Magical Procedures
Y	Herbs and Plants
Z	'Evil Sleep,' Blindness and Death
Ω	Composite Rites
-	Excluded Minor Fragments

Table 02: Outline Summary of Techniques and Rite Types to be found in the *PGM*.

4.0 The Theory behind Graeco-Egyptian Magic

4.1 The Hierarchy of Spiritual Creatures

The importance of hierarchy in magic cannot be overstressed. It is one of the basic principles acknowledged and utilised by magicians in all periods. It is well known that knowing the name of a spirit is reputed to give the magician control over that spirit. In order to coerce that spirit into carrying out the wishes of the magician, there are a number of other threats that the magician typically used.

The first of these is to order the spirit in the name of one of its superiors. This technique is found in ancient Egyptian magic, the *PGM*, and much later in the *Hygromanteia* and the *Clavicula Salomonis*. The theory behind 'hierarchical threatening' is that the spirit is not in a position to check if the magician has the authority to make such an order, it simply reacts to the threat. It works on the same principle as a teacher threatening a student that he will be sent to the headmaster, an outcome that no student relishes. At the point the threat is issued, neither the headmaster, nor the superior spirit, has been consulted.

Therefore, clearly knowing the names of the spirit's superiors, at all the levels of the hierarchy, gives the magician leverage. This technique of utilising the power of the name, not necessarily of the supreme being, but of one further up the 'food chain' is a method used in many forms of magic, not just Graeco-Egyptian. Morton Smith puts it in a more jocular fashion:

> So the first thing to do is line up the god (go directly to the provost). Then after that is settled you go, with authorization from the deity, to the subordinate official, the daimon. And then the daimon will do as you tell him and he must do as he is told because you have the authorization of the great god So-and-so whose name you pronounce, and you may also display his seal and the like.[1]

This approach is very clear in the *PGM*, where the supreme gods like Phre/Ra or Osiris are often invoked as a coercive threat. This extends even to using a name with which to threaten the gods themselves:

> Hear me, because I am going to say the great name, AŌTH,[2] before whom every god prostrates himself and every daimon shudders, for whom every angel completes those things which are assigned. Your divine name according to the seven [vowels] is AEĒIOYŌ IAYŌĒ EAŌOYEĒŌIA. I have spoken the glorious name, the name for all needs.[3]

AŌTH purports to be an excellent all-purpose name, as it applies to the whole range of spiritual creatures: gods, angels and daimones. The threat is also

[1] Smith (1988), p.4.

[2] ΑΩΘ.

[3] *PGM* XII. 117. The 7 Greek vowels were recited in a specific order.

closely tied in to the magician's order to complete the task in hand and/or reveal certain information.

The obverse of this threat is to promise the spiritual creature that the magician will praise it to its superiors. One such Demotic inducement to assist in an Evocationary Lamp Skrying, promises that the daimon with be praised by the magician to Ra, the sun god and also to the moon god:

> I shall praise you in heaven before Pre; I shall praise you before the moon; I shall praise you on earth; I shall praise you before the one who is on the throne...[1]

Daimones are below the gods in the hierarchy. Daimones are defined in some detail by Socrates who quotes Diotima as saying that daimones are:

> Interpreters and ferrymen, carrying divine things to mortals and mortal things to gods; requests and sacrifices from below and commandments and answers from above. Being midway between, [*daimones*] make each half supplement the other, so that the whole becomes unified. Through them are conveyed all divination (*mantikē*) and all priestly crafts concerning sacrifices, initiations, incantations, all prophetic power (*manteia*) and magic. For the divine does not mix with the mortal, and it is only through the mediation of [the *daimones*] that mortals can have any interaction with the gods, either while awake or while asleep.[2]

Daimones are therefore essential to any process dealing with the gods. In the sense of messengers of the gods, daimones seem very close in nature to angels, except that they deliver messages in both directions, not just *from* god. The fact that they are also seen as the conduit for magic and divination reinforces the relationship between the magician and the daimones in their later Mediaeval 'incarnation' as demons. As *daimon* was a Greek concept, and *demon* a Christian adaptation of that concept, it is reasonable to maintain that there are no daimones or demons in dynastic Egyptian magic. Of course there are many Egyptian gods, like Apep or Seth to which 'demonic' behaviour has been attributed.

There are numerous texts showing parts of the hierarchy. One of the lamellae in Kotansky gives a detailed, if slightly mixed up, angelic hierarchy.[3] This formula is written on a silver strip which was found in a bronze tubular container in a tomb in Beirut, and dates from the 4th century CE. The text includes a named person, Alexandra daughter of Zoê, and so is certainly a personalised amulet (see 'A2' in chapter 6.2). However the most interesting part of this amulet is the catalogue of angelic names, shown in Appendix 3.

---

[1] *PDM* xiv. 493.

[2] Plato, *Symposium*, 202e-203a as quoted in Johnston (2008), p.10.

[3] Kotansky (1994), No. 52, pp. 270-300.

4.2 Calendrical Considerations (C)[1]

Timing was considered very important for magical operations, and in later Greek grimoires each hour of every day of the week had an angel (and later a demon) assigned to it. These attributions occur in fragmentary form in the *PGM*, but in much greater detail in Byzantine Solomonic texts, and in the European grimoires, right through to modern times. However it is only in the *PGM* (and the *Hygromanteia*) that it is stressed that it is technically *essential* for the magician to call upon the angel of the hour before launching his ritual in that hour in order to gain credibility and help from those spiritual creatures he is attempting to command.

By the time the material reached Latin Europe these angel names had been reduced to a look up table without any indication as to how they should be used. This is therefore just one of many examples where the techniques outlined in the *PGM* can throw considerable light on the exact function of often unexplained data in the European grimoires. Calendrical calculations make up 1.5% of all *PGM* rites. There is no distinctive headword for these passages except κύκλος, *kyklos* (the circle of the heavens), they are therefore primarily gathered together in Table C on the basis of their common calendrical content.

Not only was the timing of many of the rites carefully calculated, but the names of the gods of the hours, days, and months were delineated in considerable detail. The *Hygromanteia* also follows very closely the attributions of planets to the hours of the days of the week, with the gods of these time units being replaced by demons who were said to rule them. This pattern also appears later in the Latin grimoires, where planetary hours are still specified, but often the details of the demons of each hour have been lost.

Timing has always been a very important element of magical preparation, and a mistake in timing has often been given as the reason for the failure of a particular magical operation. A passage in the letter of Thessalos of Tralles (1st century CE) written to the Emperor (Caesar Augustus or Claudius) explains the essential nature of good timing in a magical operation, and in the collecting of herbs for medico-magical purposes:

> Soon the god appeared in a spectacular vision and spoke to Thessalos, telling him that the book of king Nechepso was of limited use, because it required supplementary knowledge of the correct times at which to harvest the herbs - knowledge that could only be acquired directly from [the god] Asclepios himself.[2]

---

[1] Details of the alphabetic coding of every single passage in the *PGM* can be seen in Table 12 and Table 13. Each code has a dedicated Table showing the location of all procedures relevant to that technique.

[2] See Codex Matritensis Bibliotheque Nationale 4631. Summarised in Dodd and Faraone (2003), p. 226.

One of the three completely self-contained books in the *PGM* which relates to the Mysteries rather than to magic, is the pseudepigraphical *Tenth Hidden Book of Moses.*[1] Even in the context of an initiatory rite, it was also considered important for the initiate to be equipped with the names of the rulers of the time when the rite was being performed, the ruler of the hour, day and month, before beginning the rite:

> You should also take, child, for this personal vision, [a list of] the gods of the days and the hours and the weeks, those given in the book, and the twelve rulers of the months [before commencing]...[2]

Planetary Days

The idea that each of the seven Classical planets has a day dedicated to it, goes back a long way. The Indian tradition of attributing seven gods to the seven days of the week probably dates back to Vedic times. Babylonian practices also enshrine exactly the same days for the same corresponding planets. It is therefore not possible to establish the origin of this practice, but it is extraordinary that the attributions are consistent across a large number of cultures, and even more extraordinary, that each planet falls on exactly the same day, in all cultures. The day of the Moon, for example, falls on Monday in all cultures, and the day sacred to Mars (Roman) or Aries (Greek) is the same day as that attributed to Madim (Hebrew) or Mangal (Hindu).

Planetary Hours

In addition to their attribution to the days, the planets are also attributed to the 24 hours of the day. Proclus, for example, affirmed that "general opinion makes the Hours goddesses and the Month a god, and their worship has been handed on to us."[3]

These attributions as well as having calendrical significance also have great importance for the practice of magic. Precise timing of magical rites was always considered a crucial ingredient. Not only must the right day be chosen, according to its planetary attribution (for example rites of the Moon on Monday, or of Venus on Friday), but also the hour must be chosen with care. As the first hour of every day (that is the hour immediately after sunrise) is attributed to the same planet as the whole day, so sunrise is always a potent time, it being doubly attributed to the planet/god of the day. In many examples in the *PGM*, the sunrise hour was recommended for specific rites.[4]

It seems very clear that the emphasis on the 12 hours of day and 12 hours of

---

[1] *PGM* XIII. 734-1077.

[2] *PGM* XIII. 734-741.

[3] Proclus, *In Timaeum,* 248 D.

[4] Although that could be attributed to the focus on Re/Phre in Egyptian thinking.

the night were originally an Egyptian phenomenon, as the most ancient texts describe the bark of Ra ascending through the sky, and then descending under the Earth through the Duat, with the activities, gates and spell of each hour separately described.[1] Each hour that Ra spent in the Duat was described in considerable detail as a separate department. Each of these hours is illustrated in a separate illustrative register in the *Book of the Dead*.

Unequal Hours

The technique was refined even further so that each day was divided into 24 hours, not equal clock hours as we understand them, but unequal 'planetary hours.' No matter where you are in the world, the timing of dawn and dusk change from day-to-day (extremely at the poles and very little at the Equator). The basic principle was that the 24 hours of the day were divided into 12 daylight hours and 12 night hours. The starting point is respectively sunrise and sunset. After the first hour of every day which is attributed to the same planet that rules the day, the following hours rotate in the same sequence. For example, on Sunday (after the first hour attributed to the Sun) come the hours of Venus, Mercury, Moon, Saturn, Jupiter and Mars, starting the cycle again with the Sun (in the 8th hour of the day). So the timing of the evocation of the spirit of Mars would be preferably performed on a day of Mars in an hour of Mars (for example Tuesday on the 1st, 8th, 15th or 22nd hour, counting from sunrise).

The number of minutes from sunrise to sunset is divided by 12, giving the number of minutes in each 'planetary hour.' This will be longer than 60 minutes in summer, but shorter in winter. This number of minutes is then used to count off the hours. These unequal 'hours' came to be known, in later grimoires, as 'planetary hours.'

The planetary hours were also used for civil purposes in Europe until cheap clocks were generally available, but retained in Europe for magic long after the common usage reverted to clock time with an exact 60 minutes. The logic of using unequal hours is that without mechanical clocks, the hour can only be estimated by looking at the angle of elevation of the sun above the horizon. Regardless of the length of the day, the angle of the sun above the horizon, for a specific hour, will always be the same. On short days the sun will appear to travel faster but, for example, it will always be 30° above the eastern horizon at the end of the 2nd planetary hour, or 30° above the western horizon at the end of the 10th planetary hour, whatever the season or latitude. This enabled people to tell the time without clocks, by the simple observation of the elevation of the sun over the horizon. This automatically made for a shorter working day in winter, and a longer working day in summer.

---

[1] See texts like the *Book of Gates* (c. 1300 BCE) for further details.

The Moon's Effect

In addition to the selection of hour and day, it was considered necessary to choose the right Moon phase. For works of construction, the Moon should be waxing (that is increasing in size from New to Full) rather than waning or shrinking (said to be suitable instead for works of destruction). It is also suggested in some later grimoires that the Moon should not be located too close to the Sun, where astrologically it will be rendered 'combust,' which is said to diminish its powers considerably. These rules relate to the belief that the spirits and demons belonged to the 'sublunary regions,' and were therefore affected by the Moon in the same ways that tides are governed by that satellite. These considerations of time are common to the *PGM, Hygromanteia* and *Clavicula Salomonis,* with the names of the respective gods/planets remaining unchanged.

The gods of the day and its hour were very important in Graeco-Egyptian magic in a practical way, for it was said (in the *PGM*) that any magician who does not first call these hour/day gods and propitiate them will have no luck in his operation, because he will be considered by any god to be "uninitiated."

In the *PGM* various natural qualities and rulers were associated with each hour. One papyrus gives a table of the hours with their natural animal, tree, stone and bird correspondences (Table 03). Some of these natural history correspondences appear again later in European grimoires, and in Agrippa's early 16th century *De Occulta Philosophia.*[1]

The God of the Hour

Even the gods have their hourly schedule. It was suggested, for example, that the magician invoke Apollo in the third hour of the day.[2] Several passages in the *PGM* list the all important names of the gods of the hours (see Table 04), although the names differ according to the magician or text.[3]

The appropriate god of the hour which needed to be called before any important rite in any well timed invocation is the god:

> ...in whose hand is the moment, the one who belongs to these hours.[4]

---

1 Agrippa (1530-1533, 1993), pp. 288-289, 294-297.

2 *PGM* III. 335. It later mentions the 10th hour, but the papyrus is much damaged.

3 *PGM* VII. 862-918.

4 *PDM* xiv. 34. Also Griffith and Thompson (1974) p. 53, n. to 1.

Hour	Animal	Tree	Stone	Bird	Alternate animal	Ruler
1st	Young monkey	Silver fir	*Aphanos*[1]			PHROUER
2nd	Unicorn	Persea	Pottery stone	*Halouchakon*	Ichneumon[2]	BAZĒTŌPHŌTH
3rd	Cat	Fig	*Samouchos*	Parrot	Frog	AKRAMMACHAMAREI
4th	Bull		Amethyst	Turtledove	Bull	DAMNAMENEUS[3]
5th	Lion	Prickly shrub	Magnet [lodestone]		Crocodile	PHŌKENGEPSEUARET-ATHOUMISONKTAIKT
6th	Donkey	Thorn tree	Lapis lazuli		[White-faced cow]	EIAU AKRI LYX...[4]
7th	Crayfish		Sun opal [sunstone?]		Cat	
8th					Hippopot-amus	
9th	Ibis			[Ibis]	Chameleon	
10th			Stone[5]			
11th						
12th						ADŌNAI[6]

Table 03: Animal, tree, stone and bird correspondences for each hour of the day.[7]

[1] Maybe clear quartz.
[2] Egyptian mongoose.
[3] One of the constituents of the *Ephesia grammata.* See chapter 4.5 for an explanation of her nature, and a new tentative translation of the *Ephesia grammata.*
[4] And in the sea, the jellyfish [glass fish].
[5] A stone the colour of a falcon's neck.
[6] Notably the only Hebraic godname in this list.
[7] *PGM* III. 494-611. The gaps in the Table are due to damage to the papyrus.

Hour	Animal form[1]	God of the Hour[2]	God[3]
1st	Cat	PHARAKOUNĒTH	Bast
2nd	Dog	SOUPHI	Anubis
3rd	Serpent	AMEKRANEBECHEO THŌYTH	Apophis?
4th	Scarab	SENTHENIPS	Khepera
5th	Donkey/Ass	ENPHANCHOUPH	Typhon
6th	Lion	BAI SOLBAI[4]	Sekhmet
7th	Goat	OUMESTHŌTH	Khnum
8th	Bull	DIATIPHĒ[5]	Apis
9th	Falcon	PHĒOUS PHŌOUTH	Horus
10th	Baboon	BESBYKI	Thoth?
11th	Ibis	MOU RŌPH	Thoth
12th	Crocodile	AERTHOĒ	Sobek

Table 04: The animals and gods of the hours of the day.

During a rite to compel the daimon of the Bear asterism, the time is specified as the 6th hour of the night, i.e. 11pm to midnight, thereby arranging to culminate the operation at midnight, when the direction pointed to by the Bear asterism will accurately indicate the season. For the ancient Egyptians the most appropriate time, in general terms, was at dawn when the Bark of Ra rises over the horizon, and light conquers darkness.[6]

There were also limitations on which days magic could be performed. One passage suggests that the correct hour is sunrise, but only on the third day of

[1] *PGM* IV. 1596-1715.
[2] *PGM* IV. 1596-1715; *PGM* XXXIX. 1-21. The god's secret name.
[3] Inferred from the animal.
[4] Ruler of time.
[5] 'Visible everywhere.'
[6] Brashear (1995), p. 3393.

the (lunar) month.[1] Another instructs that Evocationary Bowl Skrying be done at the seventh hour of the day, which begins seven hours after sunrise, i.e. at midday.[2] Yet another passage lists out the gods of each hour measuring from sunrise to sunset (see Table 04).

Specific times of the day or week were more appropriate for one kind of magic or another. These allocations of appropriate hours also occur later in the *Hygromanteia* and in a number of European grimoires. A different papyrus enumerates the 'angels' of the hours, a system which reappears in the *Hygromanteia,* but with completely different angel names (see Table 05).

Hour	**Angel of the Hour**[3]
1st	MENEBAIN
2nd	NEBOUN
3rd	LĒMNEI
4th	MORMOTH
5th	NOUPHIĒR
6th	CHORBORBATH
7th	ORBEĒTH
8th	PANMŌTH
9th	THYMENPHRI
10th	SARNOCHOIBAL
11th	BATHIABĒL
12th	ARBRATHIABRI

Table 05: The angels for each hour of the day.[4]

[1] *PGM* IV. 169-171.
[2] *PDM* xiv. 73.
[3] *PGM* VII. 900-907.
[4] *PGM* VII. 900-908.

Days

The following is just one illustration of the importance of specific days to the Graeco-Egyptian magician. One very specific day is mentioned in the *PDM* which is used as a threat by the magician to prevent the return of a spirit to its own heaven. These words are addressed by the magician to the spirit, to ensure its obedience:

> "'Do the every command which NN [the magician] will desire!' Is not doing it what you will do, O noble spirit?[1] [If so then] your soul will not be allowed to rise up to heaven on day 25 of the fourth month of Inundation [Khoiak] to dawn of day 26, while the excellent spirits are awake."[2]

Anubis is requested to send the spirit, and the spirit is commanded to go to the target of the rite and tell him, whilst sleeping, that he is to "Do the every command which NN [the magician] will desire!" The punishment for the spirit failing to do this is that the spirit will be prevented from returning to heaven "on day 25 of the fourth month of Inundation" through to the following dawn."[3]

From this passage we may deduce that there was a specific day that was considered to be the time when spirits were allowed (temporarily) to return to their heaven, and that to prevent them from doing so was a form of punishment inflicted (or threatened) by the magician.

Even in a simple Graeco-Egyptian Evocationary Lamp Skrying, the request is to "bring me the god in whose hand the command[4] is today."[5] This is the 'duty' god, of which there are 365 in the course of the year, the names of which were a closely guarded secret, possibly given only to acolytes.

This restriction is particularly prevalent in the Demotic *PDM*. For example, one invocation refers specifically to the god of the day or the hour:

> Send to me the god in whose hand the command is [today] so that he may tell me an answer to everything about which I am asking here today.[6]

Another passage mentions "the god who gives answer today" again confirming that there is also a daily rota of gods, and it befits the magician to know which one is in charge of the day on which he attempts the operation, otherwise the god will purportedly not answer him.

---

[1] In other words "do you intend to disobey me?"

[2] *PDM* Supplement 117-130.

[3] The 26th of Khoiak was the date of the climax of the festival of Sokar (often identified with Osiris). See Smith (2011), p. 25.

[4] Or more correctly, the rulership.

[5] *PDM* xiv. 163.

[6] *PDM* xiv. 227.

'Egyptian Days'

Approx Zodiacal Sign	Months of the Egyptian Calendar[1].	Days Unsuitable for Magical Operations.[2]	Egyptian Mystery Celebrations.	Approximate Month Start Dates.
♈	9. Pachōn	3, 4, 12, 13, 21, 26, 28.	Spring Equinox - Isis	March 17
♉	10. Payni	1, 2, 10, 11, 15, 20.		April 16
♊	11. Epeiph	7, 8, 9, 14, 18, 19, 22.		May 16
♋	12. Mesore	[10, 14,] 20, 23, 24, 25.	Summer Solstice - Seraphis	June 15
	5 epagomenal days		Osiris, Horus, Set, Isis, Nephthys	July 15-19
♌	1. Thōth	1, 4, 12, 13, 22.		July 20
♍	2. Phaōphi	2, 4, 10, 19, 20.		August 19
♎	3. Athyr	7, 8, 9, 17, 18, 23, 27.	Autumn Equinox - Osiris	September 18
♏	4. Choiak	5, 6, 13, 15, 16, 24, 25.		October 18
♐	5. Tybi	3, 4, 12, 24, 26.		November 17
♑	6. Mecheir	1, 2, 10, 14, 19.	Winter Solstice[3]	December 17
♒	7. Phamenōth	7, 8, 9.		January 16
♓	8. Pharmouthi	5, 6, 14, 15, 20.		February 15

Table 06: The Egyptian year, with month names and inauspicious days for performing magical operations.

[1] All months were exactly 30 days long. The month of Thoth was considered the first month. For more detail, see Skinner (2006), Tables W9-W11.

[2] *PGM* VII. 272-83.

[3] The date of the Solstice moves over long periods of time, due to the precession of the Equinoxes, and is closer to 22 December at present.

The Egyptians also set great store on good and bad days for doing various mundane things like starting a business or getting married, but especially for the performance of magic.[1] These days were set out in detailed tables of good and bad days.[2] These remained part of magical practice in Europe through to at least the 17th century, when they were still actually referred to as "Egyptian days." The *Grand Grimoire* for example has tables of lucky and unlucky days, but these days do not correspond with those listed in the *PGM*.[3]

Months

A table of the months occurs as part of "Pythagoras' request for a dream revelation and Demokritos' dream divination:"[4] Interestingly the papyrus gives what might be the sigils of the god for each month.

κριοῦ	ʽΑρ Μονθ ʽΑρ θω χε α'
ταύρου	νεοφοβωθα θοψ
διδύμων	αριcταναβα ζαω
καρκίνου	πχορβαζαναχαυ
λέοντοc	ζαλαμοιρλαλιθ
παρθένου	ειλεcιλαρμου φαι
ζυγοῦ	ταντινουραχθ
cκορπίου	χορχορναθι
τοξότου	φανθενφυφλια
αἰγοκέρωc	αζαζαειcθαιλιχ
ὑδρηχόου	μεννυ Θύθ, Ἰάω
ἰχθῦc	cερυχαρραλμιω

Figure 03: The Zodiac with the god name and sigil of each Sign.[5] See Table 07 for a transliteration. The alignment of the sigils is not always consistent.

[1] This is also a part of Chinese Taoist magic. These days are identified in the Chinese Taoist almanac which is printed every year, with a printrun in the millions. The details of these days and their calculation change each year, and may have also done so in Egypt.

[2] *PGM* VII. 272-83.

[3] Rudy (1996), pp. 13, 105.

[4] *PGM* VII. 795-845. Demokritos of Abdera (c. 460-c. 370 BCE) was a mathematician who was also considered to be a magician, as the Persian *magi* were said to have taught him magic at the specific request of Xerxes. See Diogenes Laërtius, *Lives* 9.34.

[5] Preisendanz (1931), Vol. 2, pp. 35-36.

Zodiacal Sign	Moon in Egyptian Month[1]	Egyptian name/god	Number[2]
Aries	9. Pachōn	HAR-MONTH[3] HAR-THŌCHE	α - 1
Taurus	10. Payni	NEOPHOBŌTHA THOPS	β - 2
Gemini	11. Epeiph	ARISTANABA ZAŌ	Γ - 3
Cancer	12. Mesore	PCHORBAZANACHAU	Δ - 4
Leo	1. Thōth	ZALAMOIR LALITH	ε - 5
Virgo	2. Phaōphi	EILESILARMOU PHAI	6[4]
Libra	3. Athyr	TANTIN OURACHTH	ζ - 7
Scorpio	4. Choiak	CHORCHOR NATHI	[η - 8]
Sagittarius	5. Tybi	PHANTHENPHYPHLIA	θ - 9
Capricorn	6. Mecheir	AZAZA EISTHAILICH	ι - 10
Aquarius	7. Phamenōth	MENNY THYTH IAŌ	ια - 11
Pisces	8. Pharmouthi	SERYCHARRALMIŌ	ιβ - 12

Table 07: The Zodiacal sign with its corresponding Egyptian god and month number.

Moon Phases/Lunarium

The phases of the Moon and the action of the Moon in each Egyptian month were also a key part of the proper practice of magic, and these are set out in detail in several papyri. Table 08 is also effectively a list of some typical Egyptian magical objectives.[5]

---

[1] Not in the papyrus, but inserted here for convenient reference.

[2] The third column which has the corresponding sigil or *charaktēre,* also has a Greek number. Although these are an erratically placed mixture of capitals and lower case, they are simply meant to be numbers 1 to 12. Number 10 - ι has been lost on the facsimile.

[3] Horus-Montu, the Egyptian god of war, and therefore ruler of Aries.

[4] *Digamma.*

[5] Astral magic also considers the Moon in the 28 Lunar Mansions, and even the action of each of the 360 degrees of the heavens.

Approx Zodiacal Sign	Egyptian month	Magic suitable for Moon in specific month[1]	Best for which objective[2]
♈	9. Pachōn		Fire divination or love rite
♉	10. Payni		Incantation using a lamp [for Evocationary Lamp Skrying]
♊	11. Epeiph	Perform spells of binding	Rite for winning favour
♋	12. Mesore	Perform the rite of reconciliation, air [?] divination	Making Phylacteries
♌	1. Thōth	Recommended for making an amulet against gout.[3]	Rings or binding spells
♍	2. Phaōphi	Anything is obtainable, perform bowl divination [skrying], as you wish	Everything is rendered obtainable
♎	3. Athyr	Perform invocation… rite of release…necromancy	Necromancy
♏	4. Choiak		Anything inflicting evil
♐	5. Tybi	Conduct business	Invocation and incantations to the Sun and Moon
♑	6. Mecheir	Do what is appropriate	Say whatever you wish for best results
♒	7. Phamenōth		For a love rite
♓	8. Pharmouthi	…OIŌ [rite] or love rite	For foreknowledge

Table 08: The use of specific Egyptian months for particular magical objectives.

One invocation prescribes "the rising of the moon on the thirtieth day."[4] The 7th hour of the moon is mentioned in a rite to meet with a god:

> Start saying the aforementioned invocation at the 7th hour of the moon, until the god hearkens to you, and you make contact with him.[5]

The implication is that persistence in the correct hour will bring success.

Another Demotic Evocationary Bowl Skrying/Vessel Inquiry states that it

---

[1] *PGM* III. 275-81.
[2] *PGM* VII. 284-99.
[3] *PGM* xiv. 1003-14.
[4] *PGM* III. 335.
[5] *PGM* II. 42-43.

should be performed "from the fourth day of the lunar month until the fifteenth day, which is the half-month when the moon fills the sound-eye."[1] The full moon is the 'sound eye' of Horus. In other words it should be performed during a waxing moon, a specification which is repeated in the *Hygromanteia* and again in almost all Latin grimoires.

Another invocation of Helios suggests the best lunar days to encounter the god:

> ...His encounter with Helios [takes place] on the 2nd [lunar day], but the invocation itself is spoken when [the previous moon] is full. But you will accomplish a better encounter at [sun]rise on the 4th [lunar day], when the god is on the [increase]...[2]

Specific months are also beneficial for specific rites. For example, in one invocation of Imhotep (the deified Pharaoh) it is said that "you will do the 'god's arrival'[3] [best] while the moon is in Leo, Sagittarius, Aquarius, or Virgo."[4] Necromancy and Libra are connected in *PGM* III. 278, as they are also connected in the later grimoire the *Goetia*.

The Moon and its passage through the zodiac have always been important for judging the correct time for a magical operation.[5] In the *PGM* the rules are:

Orbit of the moon:[6]

Moon in Virgo:	anything is rendered obtainable.
In Libra:	necromancy.
In Scorpio:	anything inflicting evil.
In Sagittarius:	an invocation or incantations to the sun and moon.
In Capricorn:	say whatever you wish for best results.
In Aquarius:	for a love charm.
[In] Pisces:	for foreknowledge.
In Aries:	fire divination [Evocationary Lamp Skrying] or love charm.
In Taurus:	incantation using a lamp [Evocationary Lamp Skrying].
[In] Gemini:	spell for winning favour.
In Cancer:	[for making] phylacteries.
[In] Leo:	[for making] rings or binding spells.[7]

---

1 *PDM* xiv. 295.

2 *PGM* VI. 1-47.

3 In Egyptian *peh-netjer*. Operations of the rite type 'G.' See chapter 6.5.

4 *PDM* Supp. 184.

5 This also yields an excellent example of continuity of magical techniques from the *PGM* to the Latin grimoires. A *lunarium* or electional astrology passage is to be found in the *PGM* and later in the *Hygromanteia* and the *Clavicula Salomonis*. See *PGM* VII. 284-99; *Hygromanteia* chapters 7 and 30; and Skinner and Rankine (2008), p. 282.

6 Line breaks have been introduced to help show the structure.

7 *PGM* VII. 284-99. See also *PGM* III. 275-81 which is contradictory, less detailed and fragmentary.

Zodiac

The zodiacal sign in which the Moon currently resides was also often thought by magicians to be of more importance than the presence of the Sun in a particular sign. The Sun remains there for a month rather than the two-and-a-half days of the Moon's transit through a sign. Such electional astrology, dependant on the Moon's position in a particular zodiacal sign, can be directly paralleled with the *PGM* papyrus quoted above.

Another more general specification for Evocationary Lamp Skrying (rite type 'E') is:

> Do this when the Moon is in a settled sign, in conjunction with beneficial planets [i.e. Jupiter, Venus] or is in good houses, not when it is full;[1] for it is better, and in this way the well ordered oracle[2] is completed.[3]

The timing is less restrictive for the making of magical statues such as:

> ...[make] a figure of Hermes wearing a mantle, while the moon is ascending in Aries or Leo or Virgo or Sagittarius.[4]

The nature of the gods utilised in a particular piece of magic was also matched with the zodiacal sign. The Moon waxing in Aries or Taurus[5] was the condition required for making a love charm which utilised an appeal to Typhon.[6]

The specification of the four key quarters of the day (relative to the sun) of sunrise, noon, sunset, and midnight was a specifically Egyptian phenomenon, and related to the passage of Ra/Phre over the heavens and under the Earth. These are sometimes referred to as 'Sun Stations.'

It can be seen that the most popular time was dawn, and that midnight did not feature at all in this table. Dawn is doubly effective as the planetary ruler of the day and the hour coincide during this hour. In addition, dawn was easy to visually identify, but without a clock midnight is not so easy to determine. For example, an invocation of the goddess of the Bear asterism (Ursa Major) should be done facing north, but specifically on the third day of the lunar month. By contrast the 14th day of the lunar month is recommended for the performance of a love rite.[7] A table of all occurrences of calendrical information to be found in *PGM* follows.

---

1 Or "when it is full" in another text.

2 Here μαντεία means 'rite' not 'oracle.'

3 *PGM* V. 49-53.

4 *PGM* V. 379-380.

5 The Moon is exalted in Taurus, but the rationale for Aries is not so obvious.

6 It uses the blood of a black ass, sacred to Typhon. See *PGM* VII. 300a-310.

7 *PDM* xiv. 772-804.

Gods, Angels, Daimones, names of magicians, *nomina magica*	Non-Roman PGM Nos.	Category	No. of lines	Betz Papyrus *PGM/PDM* Reference number	Objective/ Technique	Greek Headwords
	3	C	7	*PGM* III. 275-281	Types of magic relevant to each zodiacal sign. [Hermonthis]	[Κύκλος][1]
	4	C	15	*PGM* IV. 835-849	Astrological text listing the influence of each zodiacal sign in each period of life. Luck cycles	[n/h][2]
Typhon, Helios, Aberamenthōou	7	C O	13	*PGM* VII. 155-167	Days and hours of the Moon – times for Homeric divination	Ἡμερομαντίαι κ[αι] ὧραι[3]
	7	C	12	*PGM* VII. 272-283	Astrological calendar of the days of the 12 Egyptian months unsuitable for magical operations.[4]	[n/h]
	7	C	16	*PGM* VII. 284-299	Type of magic operation relevant for the moon in each zodiacal sign. [Hermonthis archive]	κύκλος [σ]ελήνης[5]
Demokritos of Abdera	12	C	14	*PGM* XII. 351-364	Demokritos' "sphere" – the day of the month used to determine potential mortality	Δημοκρίτου Σφαῖρα[6]
				PGM XXXVIII. 1-26	*See L7* [7]	
Zeus, Hermes	62	C	5	*PGM* LXII. 47-51	Divination using dice, isopsephy and arithmetic to determine if a man is alive	[n/h]
	62	C	24	*PGM* LXII. 52-75	Natal horoscopes for three years[8]	[n/h]
	110	C	12	*PGM* CX. 1-12	Making a horoscope on a board using semi-precious stones as planetary markers	[n/h]
Total C		**9**	**118**			

Table C: Calendrical Considerations.

[1] Circle of heavens, glossed by Betz as 'horoscope,' which it is not. This passage is just a list of various types of magic and their corresponding Zodiac signs: for example λεκανομαντεία line 277 and φίλτρον line 280 just indicate two such types of magic.
[2] [n/h] indicates no headword found.
[3] Calendar of days. The parts of the day and their usability for magic.
[4] Day of the month unsuitable for magic. See Table 06. See also Delatte (1927) I, 631-332 for the Byzantine Greek version.
[5] Circle of the Moon.
[6] Demokritos' Sphere. Name and birthdate numerology. A similar 'sphere' is attributed to the Egyptian Petosiris.
[7] Cross-reference to a rite which is mainly relevant to another category.
[8] Not included in Preisendanz (2001), Vol II, p. 194.

4.3 Preliminary Procedures and Preparation

Spatial Orientation

A number of formulae suggest that the rites take place in sunlight, facing the sun, often at dawn or sunset. In many cases the operation could take place in the enclosed courtyard of the home, or upon its flat roof (both architectural features still to be found extensively in Egypt and the Middle East).

However some Graeco-Egyptian invocations suggest that:

> You [should] do it in a dark place whose door opens to the east or the south, and under which there is no cellar.[1]

One rite confirms that the ground floor of a house is the best place from which to conjure, even for the god of the sun, Helios.[2] Conversely, it is recommended that rites which involve the heavens, or the Moon, or the Bear asterism goddess be conducted "after going up to a roof top."[3]

Many religions orientate their temples to face East, the rising sun, but the orientation of magical operations is more complex. The time and direction faced are of prime importance in magical operations, and this has been the case since antiquity. The following passage from 460 BCE, demonstrates that it was a real concern. Even if the passage appears to give the practitioner free rein in these matters, the point is that they were acknowledged as an important consideration.

> If a person wants to purify himself from attacking ghosts [*elasteroi*], he is to call on the ghost wherever he wants and at whatever point in the year he wants and in whatever month he wants and on whatever day he wants and facing in whatever direction he wants.[4]

For the evocation of other spiritual creatures, especially spirits and daimones, the time of the year, season, day, hour and direction of evocation were more important issues than they apparently were for ghosts, presumably because ghosts were only bound to a specific location, but not to a direction or time.

In Egyptian magic (and religion) facing the rising or setting sun is a very common prerequisite of a rite. At night the ancient Egyptians had other cosmological points of reference, such as the direction of Sirius (Sothis), Orion or of the Pole Star with its attendant circling Bear asterism (Ursa Major).

---

1 *PDM* xiv. 766.

2 *PGM* VI. 4.

3 *PGM* LXXII. 1. Of course that is really only practicable in locations where houses have open flat roofs.

4 Selinus, *Lex sacra* (eds. Jameson, Jordan, and Kotansky, 1993, col. B) as quoted in Ogden (2002), p. 162. See also Clinton (1996), pp. 159-179.

Conjuration made to the four quarters (when direction is critical) is a method utilised in the *PGM* and the later grimoires. In one *PGM* rite, the description of conjuration to the four quarters utilises the vocalisation of the seven sacred Greek vowels:

> ***The instruction***: Speaking to the rising sun [east], stretching out your right hand to the left and your left hand likewise to the left, say "A [α once]."[1] To the north, putting forward only your right fist, say "E [ε twice]." Then to the west, extending both hands in front [of you], say "H [η three times]." To the south, [holding] both [hands] on your stomach, say, "I [ι four times]." To the earth, bending over, touching the ends of your toes, say "O [ο five times]." Looking into the air, having your hand on your heart, say "Y [υ six times]." Looking into the sky, having both hands on your head, say "O [ω seven times]:"[2]

Because of its obvious importance as a ritual action instruction, this description is followed in the papyrus by a diagram relating the vowels to the directions, which makes it clear that the letters were repeated a specific sequentially increasing number of times (see Figure 04).

<u>**A:**</u>

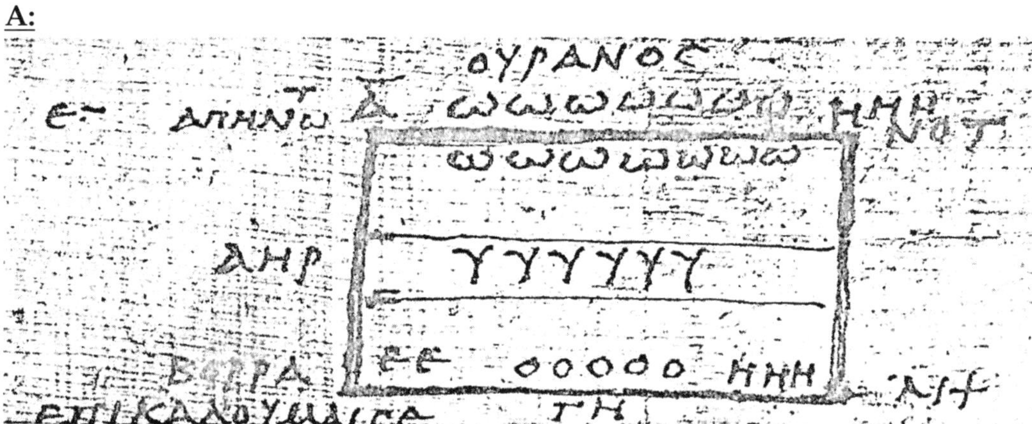

Figure 04: Schematic of an invocation to the four Cardinal directions: [3]

A: the original Greek papyrus.

B: after the translation of Betz/Smith.[4] (See next page.)

C: a re-drawing made in the light of the original Greek and the vowel sequencing of the rite (the association of the seven Greek vowels with the compass points plus the three levels of earth, air and sky).

D: The reconstructed version reflecting the original intention of the scribe, with the 'A' and 'IIII' inside the box, and excess 'ω' above the box removed (next page).

---

[1] The first of the seven Greek vowels.

[2] *PGM* XIII. 821-870 gives the full procedure.

[3] *PGM* XIII. 835-841. Betz's illustration (Figure 04 B) has been corrected (Figure 04 D), in line with the text of the original Greek illustration, and the logic of the associated Greek descriptive text.

[4] Betz (1996), p. 191.

B: Betz's illustration

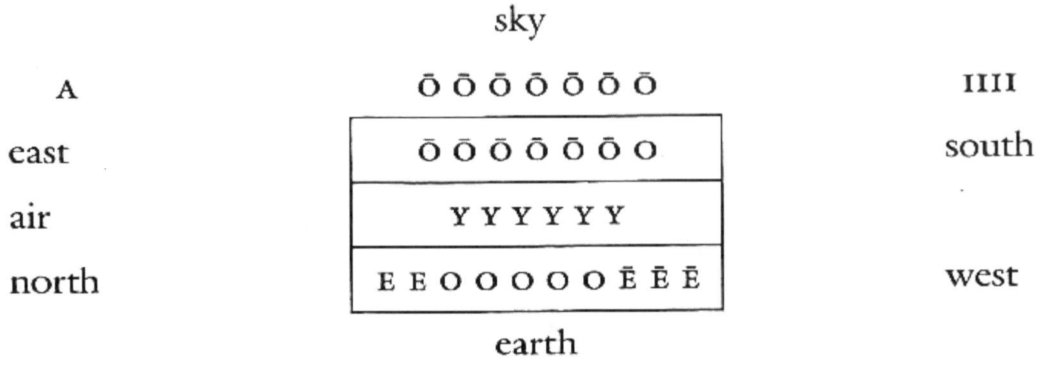

	sky	
A	Ō Ō Ō Ō Ō Ō Ō	IIII
east	Ō Ō Ō Ō Ō Ō O	south
air	Y Y Y Y Y Y	
north	E E O O O O O Ē Ē Ē	west
	earth	

C: Re-drawn to reflect the illustration in the papyrus

ϵ- east	A[1] sky ωωωωωωω	IIII[2]
	ωωωωωωω	south
air[3]	YYYYYY	
north	εε ooooo HHH	west
	earth	

D: Reconstructed to reflect the scribe's original ritual intention

ϵ-	sky	
east	α ωωωωωωω ιιιι	south
	air υυυυυυ	
north	εε ooooo ηηη	west
	earth	

[1] The 'A' and the 'IIII' should be inside the square, but have been left in the same position as in the Greek papyrus original, for purposes of comparison.
[2] The Greek text has HHH, which is obviously an error. It should be IIII, repeated four times not three.
[3] Applies to the centre of the diagram despite the fact that it is written on the left in the Greek original.

The procedure, as shown above is to invoke in a circle moving east, north, west then south. Using the seven vowels the invocation begins with α, then εε, ηηη and ιιι, increasing the number of repetitions each time, after which an invocation to the earth with οοοοο, then air with υυυυυυ followed by ωωωωωωω to heaven.[1]

After a short diversion, which looks like an interpolation, the text resumes with the cardinal directions invocation:

> "I call on you as the south." (Looking to the south say, "ι οο υυυ ωωωω αααααα εεεεεε ηηηηηηη.")[2]
> "I call on you as the west." (Stand [facing] the west, say, "ε ιι οοο υυυυ ωωωωω αααααα εεεεεεε.")
> "I call on you as the north." (Standing looking towards the north say, "ω αα εεε ηηηη ιιιι οοοοοο υυυυυυυ.")
> "I call on you as the earth."(Looking towards the earth say, "ε ηη ιιι οοοο υυυυυ ωωωωωω ααααααα.")
> "I call on you as the sky." (Looking into the sky say, "υ ωω ααα εεεε ηηηηη ιιιιι ωωωωωωω.")
> "I call on you as the cosmos,"ο υυ ωωω αααα εεεεε ηηηηηη ιιιιιι."
> Accomplish for me [the] NN thing quickly.
> I call on your name, the greatest among gods."[3]

Notice that although the vowels are used in different sequences, according to the direction, the pattern of saying each vowel first once, then twice, then thrice, etc., persists.

The four directions of the universe play an important part in magic, both from the point of view of marking out the boundary of a protective circle, and establishing directions for the magician to face for evocation. The equivalent Egyptian 'angels' of the four directions are mentioned in one 3rd century papyrus:[4]

> For I do this on order from PANCHOUCHI THASSOU at whose order you are to act, because I conjure you by the four regions of the universe, APSAGAĒL CHACHOU MERIOUT MERMERIOUT and by the one who is above the four regions of the universe, KICH MERMERIOUTH.[5]

A few lines below this, the names of three of the four angels of the directions are spelled slightly differently:

> ACHACHAĒL CHACHOU … MARMARIOUTI.

---

[1] It can be seen that the scribe accidently wrote HHH twice instead of HHH and IIII.

[2] The vowel strings are here rendered back into lower case Greek for clarity.

[3] *PGM* XIII. 856-871. Line breaks have been inserted to clarify the structure of the invocation.

[4] Dating from Brashear (1995), p. 3492.

[5] *PGM* VII. 478-490.

This rite involves the goddess of the Bear asterism, which symbolically relates to the turning of the Earth on its axis, and therefore also relates to the four cardinal directions.

On the other hand for invocations of the goddess of the Bear asterism,[1] it was customary to turn to the North, which is its position in the sky near the North Pole.[2]

One dream-producing rite specifies specific cardinal directions to face during the course of the ritual:

> After sunset raise the first [reed], look to the east and say three times: "MASKELLI MASKELLŌ...
> Raise the second [reed] to the south and say again the "MASKELLI" formula...; hold the reed and spin around;
> look towards the north and [then] the west and say three times the same names, [as] those of the second reed.
> Raise the third [reed] and say the same names and these things: "IĒ IĒ,[3] I am picking you for such-and-such a rite."[4]

Although the procedure of calling to the four quarters is repeated in later grimoires, the specific names used in the *PGM* are not.

Purity and Sexual Abstinence

Magic would often have been done within the temple precincts where privacy and purity were presumably assured. By the time the main Egyptian temples were closed down (the last one in 550 CE), the priests had left their accustomed quarters and probably operated from their homes. Its later translation to the more prosaic environment of the magician's home or workshop meant there might be an increased need for purification, but no fear of prosecution in either case. Egyptian priests would often freelance as magicians during the time they were not on temple duty:

> The "private" magician is revealed to be none other than the cultic priest, in "private practice" during interims in temple service.[5]

The specification of ritual purity involving chastity was almost universal in ancient magic. The modern Western use of sex in magic (following a supposed Tantric practice) is an exception that does not appear in the *PGM*.[6]

---

[1] Ursa Major.

[2] See *PDM* xiv. 117. Strangely, in the same passage, it is recommended that the magician should retire to a dark room that opens to the south.

[3] IĒ IĒ indicates that the name of the magician is to be inserted here.

[4] *PGM* IV. 3172-3208.

[5] Ritner (2008), p. 2.

[6] Nor in the *Hygromanteia, Clavicula Salomonis* or in any later vernacular grimoire.

As Samson Eitrem wrote:

> Ritual "cleanliness" or "purity" is everywhere [in magic] the overall important prerequisite…[1]

This is not some latterly introduced Calvinist "cleanliness is next to godliness" imposition, but is a condition that goes all the way back to Graeco-Egyptian magic, and before in to dynastic Egypt. It was well established in the *PGM* that the magician needs to have high standards of personal cleanliness, wear clean cotton clothes, preferably new and use only instruments that have been either made new, or bought new.[2] Egyptian priests were even obliged to be circumcised.[3] Apparently "priests were also inspected for suitability and lineage by Roman officials prior to the circumcision required of them."[4]

What was the point of all this purity? Was it to give the magician the purity and holiness to approach the gods and other spiritual creatures? The theory offered in the *PGM* was that the gods would reject an impure man, and not act on his request.[5] This translates into a number of specific requirements.

Sexual abstinence was not only enjoined on the magician, but virginity was imposed upon his skryer. Chastity is of course imposed upon the priests of many religions. For the magician a period of three, seven or nine days before was advised as a period of sexual abstinence. This abstinence is to a large part tied to the idea of purity, and to lie with a woman who was having her period was thus completely forbidden.

Sexual abstinence was specified for Egyptian priests, but only for the relatively short time they were actually serving in the temple. There was a system of rotation of priests, which entailed service for three separate months in every year, and they were not obliged to observe sexual abstinence when living with their families outside the confines of the temple in between these periods. In addition women who were menstruating were forbidden to enter the temple. Similar thinking also goes into current Hindu practice. In this case, menstruation is seen as the other end of the continuum of sexual purity/impurity. As often Egyptian priests were also magicians, the rules applied to the Egyptian magician as well.

---

1 Faraone and Obbink (1991), p. 177.

2 Later grimoires would also insist that such tools that were bought, must be bought without haggling. That is an instruction found in a number of Latin grimoires. It shows the extreme length to which magicians would go, so as to not even slightly besmirch the purity of the instrument they were buying, by arguing over it.

3 It is possible that the Egyptian captivity was the origin of this Jewish practice.

4 Moyer (2003), p. 53.

5 In later Christianised grimoires it gave the magician extra protection against demons, on the basis that if he were not 'corrupted' then they supposedly could not easily overcome him.

Other forms of bodily purity were enforced. One practice which has not carried through into later magic is the Egyptian practice of shaving off *all* the bodily hair.

Purity was also specified in one example of Evocationary Lamp Skrying where the magician should be:

> Robed and refraining from all unclean things and from all eating of fish[1] and from all sexual intercourse, so that you may bring the god into the greatest desire toward you.[2]

This is a very telling passage as it shows that the main objective of purification before a magical ritual was not just to make the human acceptable to the infinitely more refined god, but actually to make the operator desirable to the god.

One Evocationary Bowl Skrying utilises a virgin boy as a skryer, describing him as "a pure youth who has not yet gone with a woman."[3] This is not only the concern of Jewish or Christian magicians, but dates right back to the Demotic papyri of Egyptian magicians. As one Egyptian magician wrote:

> If you do not purify it, it does not come about. Purity is its chief factor.[4]

In fact, this is one of the invariable constants within the magical tradition. Just one example amongst many, taken at random, illustrates this rule as it was applied by Graeco-Egyptian magicians:

> It is necessary to keep yourself pure for three days in advance... [If] you wish [to see], look inside, wearing clean [white] garments [and crowned] with a crown of laurel...[5]

Repeatedly 'clean', 'white' and 'pure' are specified. The use of a tripod by skryers and prophets is another long running feature of magic: from the *PGM* magicians and the pythoness at Delphi to the French seer Nostradamus.[6]

The main theoretical reasons why the magician prepares himself in this manner are:

i) To be in a state of ritual purity so that the spiritual creatures could approach the circle without difficulty or pain.

---

[1] There is an element here of the belief that drowning in the Nile immortalises the creature so drowned. The taboo on eating fish in ancient Egypt is also covered in Darby (1977), pp. 380-404.

[2] *PGM* I. 290-292.

[3] *PDM* xiv. 67-68.

[4] *PDM* xiv. 515.

[5] *PGM* III. 291-306.

[6] Nostradamus mentions his use of the tripod in the first verse of his first *Century* of predictions.

ii) As a protection against the spiritual creatures he evokes.

iii) To provide a certain degree of apparent spiritual superiority, necessary to enable him to command them.

Physical purity is also enjoined, with prohibitions against the presence of dirt, urine, a menstruating woman or any other impurities.

Fasting and Food Prohibitions

Fasting is another very important ingredient in magic in all periods. Typically a three or nine day fast, or bread and water diet,[1] is recommended. This practice has a number of dimensions:

i) Fasting purifies the body by allowing the gross matter to pass leaving the intestine empty.

ii) Fasting promotes a sense of purpose and acts as a reminder of the intention of the operation over the days leading up to the operation.

iii) Fasting is thought to purify spiritually, so that the magician is in a superior spiritual state.

iv) It has sometimes been remarked that the spirits fear the spittle of a fasting man.[2] Trachtenberg mentions that:

> Maimonides wrote, in his capacity of physician, that the spittle of a fasting person is hostile to poisons. In consequence of this belief charms to heal an ailment or to *drive off demons* or to counteract magic were usually prefaced by a threefold expectoration.[3]

v) A fasting man's perceptions may be more refined, and hence his ability to see and converse with spiritual creatures may be heightened by the fasting.[4]

This practice has deep roots in ancient Egyptian magic.[5] Spittle is consistently used in such magic for creation in much the same way as semen.

Food prohibitions for priests (which would have also mapped onto their magical practice) were complicated by the rules of the *nome* in which they lived.[6] Thus in the nome of Oxyrhynchus they would be prohibited from eating the long-nosed fish of the same name. In Cynopolis they would be

---

[1] Four ounces of bread a day is recommended.

[2] Anyone who has lived in a Muslim country during Ramadan will understand what is meant here.

[3] Trachtenberg (1939, 2004), p. 121. My italics. See also Thorndike Vol. I, p. 93.

[4] Or maybe as the psychologists would have it, he is more likely to hallucinate.

[5] Ritner (2008), chapter 3 "Spitting, Licking, and Swallowing," pp. 74-91.

[6] Ancient Egypt was divided into 42 *nomes,* or administrative areas.

forbidden dog meat as food. Fish however seems to have been one of the most consistently forbidden foods, and this may relate to the Egyptian idea of the holiness of the Nile.[1] Despite the fact that fish were normally part of the staple Egyptian diet, there are numerous references to the ritual uncleanliness of fish, and upon entering the temple, a devotee would often announce: "I am clean. I have not eaten fish…"

The prohibition against eating fish is also found in Babylonian texts:

> One of the more common proscriptions, that of eating fish and leeks, is on day 7 of month VII said to be prohibited by "Šulpae, lord of the date grove"…that is, Jupiter…[2]

Garlic was another common banned food, suggesting that part of the reason for the ban might be the smell of the breath after consuming such foods.

One method suggests the fast should run from the 11th day of the Moon, in order to finish on the "14th and a half "day, in time for the Full Moon. Interestingly the fasting is often only specified as daylight fasting, like a Muslim fast, rather a full three day fast.

Fasting was also very much a part of Egyptian spiritual practice so that Lucius Apuleius fasted for ten days before being initiated into the Mysteries of Isis.[3] This event was undoubtedly part of the Mysteries rather than just an ordinary religious ceremony in the temple of Isis. As was the function of the Mysteries, he was introduced to the goddess at first hand:

> I approached the gods from below and from on high, I saw them face to face and I worshipped them near at hand.[4]

It would therefore seem to be obvious that purity and fasting procedures involved in preparing for a magic rite were common to the PGM and the Mysteries.

---

[1] Creatures or humans who drowned in the Nile were often accorded divine status, on the grounds that "Osiris has taken them."

[2] Reiner (1995), p. 114.

[3] Lucius Apuleius, *The Golden Ass,* Book XI: 23. Griffiths (1975), p. 99.

[4] Quoted in Sauneron (1960), p. 50.

4.4 Protection for the Magician

After the magician has selected the right date and time for the operation, and kept himself pure, his next concern is to protect himself during the course of the operation. Protection was achieved in two main ways: by inscribing a floor circle around his area of working to protect him and his assistants, and by wearing a protective phylactery or lamen. Daimones, demons, spirits and even gods, needed to be kept at arms length, and this was achieved in Solomonic magic by drawing such a consecrated circle upon the ground, and keeping within it for the duration of the rite. This protective circle is less obvious in the *PGM* but the phylactery is specified in many operations in the *PGM* (see 'U' in chapter 6.2).

Early Evidence

This idea of a protective floor circle dates back at least two thousand five hundred years. Classical Indian magic in the *Ramayana* (dating from 4th to 5th century BCE) records Lakshman drawing a circle on the ground to protect Sita from a demon, showing that this practice has very deep roots in other cultures as well. In the event Sita was persuaded to cross the circle and so was taken by the demon Ravana.

The circle drawn upon the ground is probably the most ancient form of protection for the magician, and Ronald Hutton mentions an early form of the circle:

> An Assyrian rite has the magician make an *uşurtu,* usually translated as a ring, of sprinkled lime around the images of deities on whom he is going to call.[1]

In the Assyrian texts, protective circles were drawn on the ground with a mixture of water and flour.[2] These two substances were, respectively, sacred to Ea and Nisaba, water being the "shining waters of Ea" and the flour forming circle being the "net of Nisaba, the corn-god." Campbell Thompson remarks that:

> It seems to have been the custom to fence about the patient (or perhaps the magician) with a ring of flour or meal as a magic circle, just in the same way that the mediaeval sorcerers stood within a similar charmed ring when invoking spirits.[3]

The circle was then consecrated with the following invocation:

[1] Hutton (2003), p. 164. It is not clear if the magician remains within that circle.

[2] Modern voodoo *vevas* are also constructed by tracing out lines on the floor with flour.

[3] Thompson (1908), p. 123.

> Ban! Ban! [O] Barrier that none can pass,
> Barrier[1] of the gods, that none may break,
> Barrier of heaven and earth that none can change,
> Which no god may annul,
> Nor god nor man can loose,
> A snare without escape, set for evil,
> A net whence none can issue forth, spread for [against] evil.
> Whether it be evil Spirit, or evil Demon, or evil Ghost,
> Or Evil Devil, or evil God, or evil Fiend,
> Or Hag-demon,[2] or Ghoul, or Robber-sprite,
> Or phantom, or Night-wraith, or Handmaid of the Phantom,
> Or evil Plague, or Fever sickness, or unclean Disease,
> Which hath attacked the shining waters of Ea,
> May the snare of Ea catch it;
> Or which hath assailed the meal[3] of Nisaba,
> May the net of Nisaba entrap it…[4]

For any piece of magical equipment, including the circle, to be effective it must be consecrated. A typical (Mesopotamian) blessing of the circle to be said before an evocation:

> We, therefore, in the names aforesaid, consecrate this piece of ground for our defence, so that no spirit whatsoever shall be able to break the boundaries, neither be able to cause injury nor detriment to any of us here assembled, but that they may be compelled to stand before this circle and answer truly our demands.[5]

According to Thompson, the use of the protective magical circle in Jewish magic dates back to Babylonian practice.[6] There are also explicit references to drawing a protective circle during a 3rd century BCE evocation in Mesopotamia reported by Menippus, an author who lived in Gadara,[7] and later in Thebes.

---

[1] Barrier = *Uşurtu*. Elsewhere Thompson concedes that *uşurtu* might also be translated as 'the magic circle, or perhaps ban' or barrier (cf. Thompson (1908), p. xxiii). This word is translated as *zauberkreis* (or 'magician's circle') by Zimmern.

[2] Labartu, a female demon who attacks children.

[3] Bran.

[4] Thompson (1908), pp.123-124. The introduction of 'snare' seems like the introduction of a Christian concept of setting a snare for the devil, rather than a faithful translation, although I cannot be sure of this.

[5] Thompson (1908). p. lx.

[6] Thompson (1908), p. lviii.

[7] The site of Jesus' exorcism of the demonaic that lived in tombs, on the shore of Galilee, and whose demons Jesus ordered to possess a herd of swine, which promptly killed themselves by charging off a cliff and drowning.

> [6] I resolved to go to Babylon and ask help from one of the Magi, Zoroaster's disciples and successors; I had been told that by incantations and other rites they could open the gates of Hades, take down any one they chose in safety, and bring him up again. I thought the best thing would be to secure the services of one of these, visit Tiresias the Boeotian, and learn from that wise seer what is the best life and the right choice for a man of sense. I got up with all speed and started straight for Babylon. When I arrived, I found a wise and wonderful Chaldean; he was white-haired, with a long imposing beard, and called Mithrobarzanes. My prayers and supplications at last induced him to name a price for conducting me down [to Hades].
>
> [7] Taking me under his charge, he commenced with a new moon, and brought me down for twenty-nine successive mornings to the Euphrates, where he bathed me, apostrophizing the rising sun in a long formula, of which I never caught much; he gabbled indistinctly, like bad heralds at the Games; but he appeared to be invoking spirits. This charm completed, he spat thrice upon my face, and I went home, not letting my eyes meet those of any one we passed.[1] Our food was nuts and acorns, our drink milk and hydromel[2] and water from the Choaspes, and we slept out of doors on the grass. When he thought me sufficiently prepared, he took me at midnight to the Tigris, purified and rubbed me over, sanctified me with torches and squills and other things, muttering the charm aforesaid, then made a magic circle round me to protect me from ghosts, and finally led me home backwards just as I was; it was now time to arrange our voyage.
>
> [8] He himself put on a magic robe, Median in character, and fetched and gave me the cap, lion's skin, and lyre which you see, telling me if I were asked my name not to say Menippus, but Heracles, Odysseus, or Orpheus.[3]

Although Menippus was a Cynic and satirist, and the above account may have been fictional, but it reflects current beliefs. Although his description of the technique of making a magic circle "to protect from ghosts [spirits]" is set by the Tigris in Mesopotamia, he lived in both Coele-Syria and Egypt. Therefore the technique was probably already known in these regions. If not it would have been made known by Menippus through his widely distributed writings.

In the *PGM* many of the rites involve a circular motion, as the magician turns to face first East then North, West, South during the course of the rite (see Figure 04). From this the presence of a protective circle may be inferred. It is highly likely that the Graeco-Egyptian magicians inherited the Mesopotamian and ancient Egyptian practice of encirclement, which was so commonplace that maybe it was not otherwise considered worthy of a more than passing mention in the *PGM*.

---

[1] A common specification found in many European grimoires. See Mark 5:2-13.

[2] A kind of mead or fermented honey.

[3] Menippus (3rd century BCE), *A Necromantic Experiment* as quoted by Lucian of Samosata (c.120-c.180 CE), pp. 159-160.

There is also linguistic support for the use of protective circles in Egyptian magic. For the ancient Egyptians, magic could only take place in an appropriately protected place, in a temple or in an area delineated by the magician. Daimones were seen as dangerous, but not evil in the sense later ascribed to demons.[1] In fact the Egyptian word for conjuring *šnjt* also means 'encircling.'[2]

The Egyptian verb *pẖr* means "to go around or encircle." The concept that enchanting derives from encircling is also common in Egyptian thought.[3] Ritner sees "that which encircles/contains/controls" as a possible root of, or at least intimately connected with, "that which enchants/protects." As Ritner explains:

> The magical ritual of "encircling" (*dbn, pẖr*) for purification is almost coeval with Egyptian civilization itself, being attested from the earliest archaic funerary rituals to the temple ceremonies of the Graeco-Roman periods... Comparable rituals of circumambulation comprise both public, cultic ceremonies and private, 'magical' ones.[4]

The hieroglyphic determinative for "to go around" (the walking legs) is sometimes replaced by scribes with the determinative "to enchant" (man-with-hand-to-mouth).[5] It may be dangerous to extrapolate that this use of encircling by the Egyptians, or its connection with enchantment, implies that the circle was used in Graeco-Egyptian magic, but it is most likely. If not, then it was certainly a parallel concept.[6]

Circle of Protection

One of the most relevant Egyptian magical images is the ouroboros, the snake devouring its tail, forming a natural circle. Although this image has mostly been examined in terms of early Greek alchemy, or Gnosticism, it is in fact of ancient Egyptian origin, where it is alluded to as an "encirclement as protection."

The Circle of protection drawn on the ground before evoking the spirits is a constant feature of later grimoire magic. The earliest form of the circle in ancient Egypt may have been inscribed upon the ground in the form of the ouroboros,

---

[1] For more about the nature of *daimones* see several of the essays in Kousoulis (2011).

[2] Brashear (1995), p. 3393.

[3] Ritner (2008), p. 57.

[4] Ritner (2008), pp. 57-58.

[5] Ostracon Naville 11 in Smith (1977), p. 124.

[6] It is a well known feature of magic that the knowledge of someone's true name gives the magician power over that person. A similar concept of protection from adverse magic may possibly lie behind the Egyptian procedure of encircling the written names of rulers or important people in an oval cartouche.

the snake biting its own tail. It is only specifically mentioned in the PGM on two occasions, but one mention even gives the letters to be drawn inside it. Most Graeco-Egyptian magicians probably took the circle for granted, and so its presence is probably covered by such ritual phrases as "do the usual."

In one image, Harpocrates, one of the gods especially revered by magicians, is depicted seated in an ouroboros which is in turn embraced by the arms of Heka (the prime god of magic) further helping to confirm the importance of such a circle to the magician (Figure 05). A figure of Osiris found in Tutankhamen's tomb shows Osiris standing in a circle made by an ouroboros. He has an ouroboros not only around his feet, but also round his head (Figure 06). In addition there are a number of images of the ouroboros being used as a boundary. Ouroboros ground circles are depicted as being used by Egyptian magicians to restrain poisonous insects/animals usually associated with magic. In these Bes-Pantheos carvings an ouroboros encircles a number of dangerous animals and poisonous reptiles (Figure 10 and Figure 11).

All this suggests that such a protective ground circle was taken for granted by the magicians of the *PGM*. The presence of a circle as part of the magical preliminaries is further reinforced by instructions to circumambulate or face each of the cardinal points in order whilst invoking. It seems therefore a very likely conclusion that Graeco-Egyptian magicians also stood in an inscribed circle when invoking, and that possibly this circle was in the form of an ouroboros, either a drawing or an actual snake skin or body. The use of this is supported by later European grimoires showing the circle in the form of a snake devouring its tail, surely too much of a parallel to be just a coincidence (see Figure 08 and Figure 07).

Ritner sums up the centrality of the circle to Egyptian magic:

> Thus, although ritual encirclement is well documented in many cultures, the centrality of the rite in Egyptian magic is striking, and its uses and terminology uniquely Egyptian… That the rite was of fundamental significance to the success of Egyptian magic is evident not merely by the presence of specified directions in rubrics and depictions in literary, religious, medical, and even historical texts, but also by the very turns of phrase which the Egyptian employed to describe magic.[1]

This is an image which has endured, both in Gnostic gems, and as late as the 18th century grimoire, *Treasure of the Old Man of the Pyramids*, which is notionally set in Egypt.[2] The structuring of the circle as a snake also occurs in later grimoires such as the *Goetia*, although that particular version might simply be attributable to fortuitous artistic licence.

---

[1] Ritner (2008), p. 68.

[2] This grimoire is undoubtedly corrupt, but the image might preserve some distant memory of the practice, and of its Egyptian origins. See Figure 08.

Figure 05: Harpocrates within the ouroboros, with sidelock and characteristic finger to his lips, embraced by the arms of Heka, supported by the two lions of the horizon and flanked by the eye of Horus.[1]

[1] 21st Dynasty.

Figure 06: Figure of Osiris standing in an ouroboros circle and with another around his head.[1] The lower and upper ouroboros have the hieroglyphic determinative for "to go around" (the walking legs). The lower one also includes the hieroglyphs of the sun, the arm and the spitting head (in each case twice).

[1] Found in Tutankhamen's tomb.

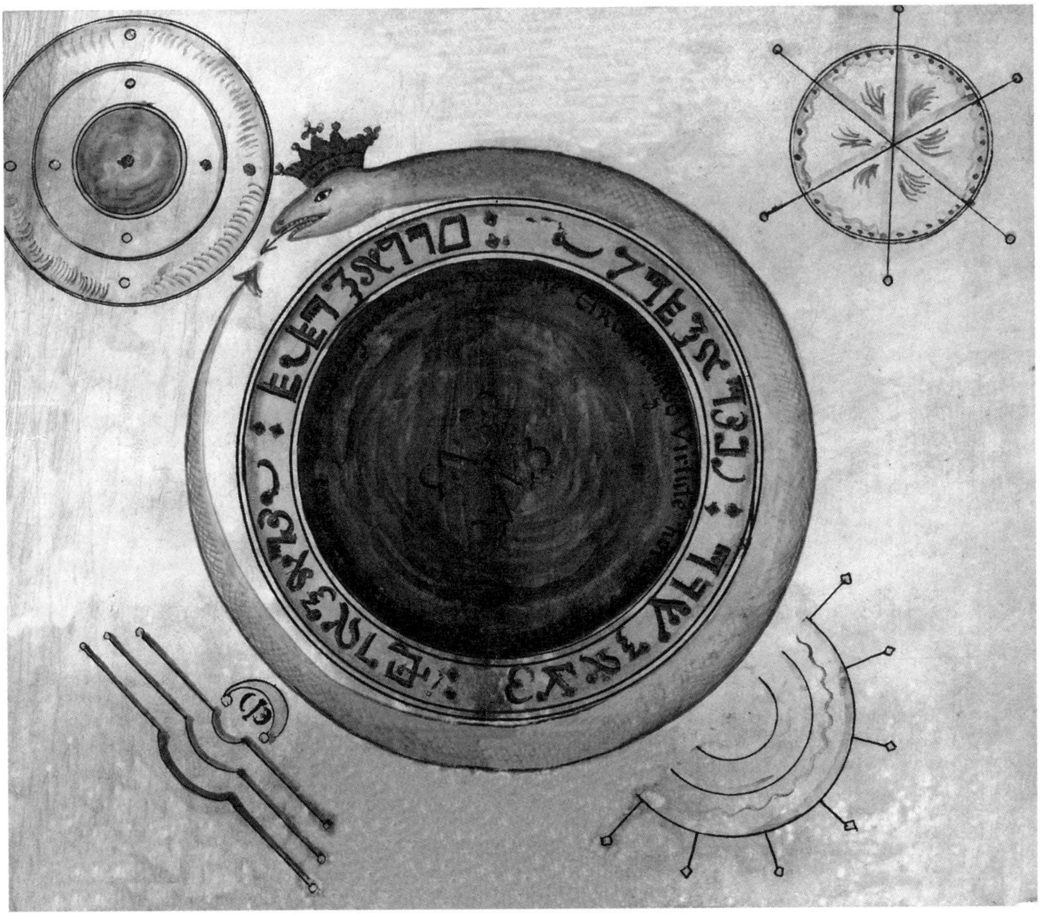

Figure 07: The ouroboros in a 1757 grimoire, *Clavis Inferni*, as the main frontispiece motif of this grimoire.[1]

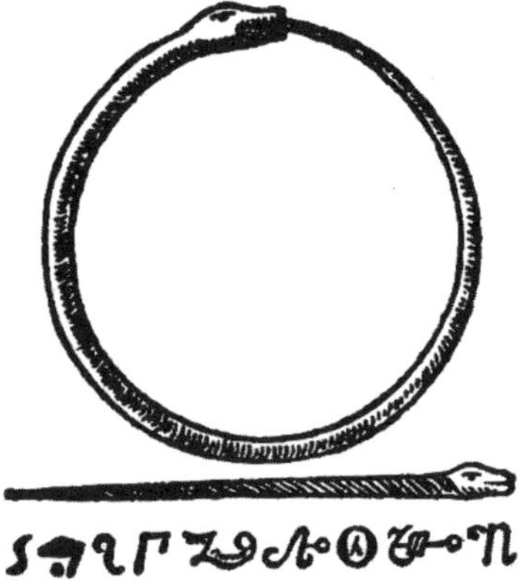

Figure 08: An ouroboros circle in a late 18th century grimoire, the *Treasure of the Old Man of the Pyramids* (also often called the *Black Pullet*).

[1] See a discussion of the dating in Skinner and Rankine (2009), p. 25.

In Figure 08 the snake circle also has a second snake stretched out in an unnaturally straight and rigid pose. This may have been a representation of the snake wands used by both Moses and the Egyptian magicians in their confrontation in front of Pharaoh. A more detailed ouroboros appears in the 18th century grimoire *Clavis Inferni* (see Figure 07).

The four sigils at the corners of Figure 07 are sigils of the four Demon Kings positioned outside the circle in the Cardinal directions. Although this grimoire illustration is of relatively late date, it sums up several of the techniques which Latin grimoires inherited from the Graeco-Egyptian magicians:

1. The use of a protective circle in the form of the ouroboros.
2. The directions as marked by the four corner sigils of the Demon Kings.
3. The opposition of the four thwarting archangels' names (G[a]brial, Urial, Mika[e]l and R[a]pal (*sic*), written in the ring just inside the ouroboros) to those Demon Kings.
4. The sealing or consecration of the circle, as stated in the Latin inscription that explains that the circle is sealed by virtue of the names of the four archangels written around it written in 'Crossing the River' script.[1]

In the *PGM*, the magician needs protection from the gods as well as daimones and spirits. The gods were not seen as universally beneficent, but as dangerous as spirits and daimones, and so the magician needed to be protected from them as well. This was usually achieved by the wearing of a phylactery.[2] Given that the magic in the *PGM* tends to treat the gods like inferior daimones, rather than worshipping them, this need for protection is not surprising.

In a number of passages the phrases "do the usual" or "add the usual," occur, indicating that well-known background procedures were not usually specified in the *PGM*. This may also have applied to prefatory procedures such as drawing the protective circle. The fact that a circle appears to be only mentioned several times in the whole corpus of the *PGM* suggests that the circle was taken for granted. This phenomenon of unwritten instructions was common in the *PGM,* as these papyri were meant to be used as an experienced magician's reference book, not as a primer in magic.

There is however one clear mention of the drawing of a protective circle with chalk on the ground in the *PGM* in a rite which is an invocation of a daimon referred to as a "shadow on the sun," probably a solar daimon. The rubric

[1] *Ego me circumcingo virtute horum nominum alubus hic circulus est consignatus,* "I surround myself with the virtue of these names with which this circle is sealed."
[2] See chapter 6.2, rite types 'U' and 'U2.'

concerning the protection of the magician mentions both a circle and a phylactery:

> ***Phylactery*****:** The tail [of the cat][1] and the characters with the circle (κύκλῳ) [on which] you will stand after you have drawn it with chalk. [2]

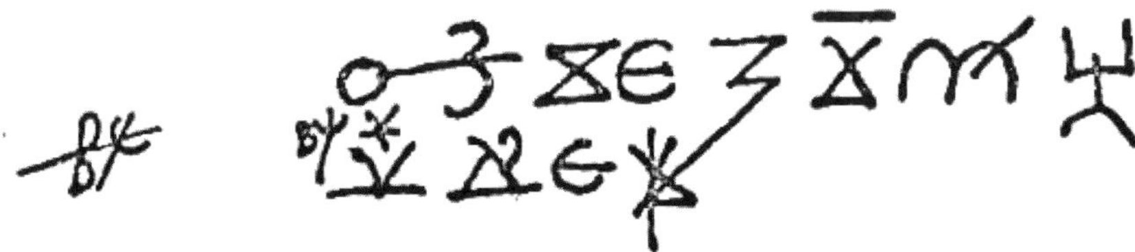

The text concludes with the seven characters shown above, the first of which is definitely Mars, so these are possibly symbols of the seven planets. Another one of the characters echoes a form which occurs later in the 15th century angel seals of de Abano's *Heptameron.* Below them is another sequence of four *charaktēres*, at least two of which look like either astrological aspect signs or elements. These are likely to be the forerunners of the names and symbols later inscribed in more detail in the protective circles of the grimoires.

The point is that the passage clearly gives instruction to stand within a chalk-drawn circle with inscribed astrological figures. This circle is mentioned in the same section as the phylactery and so it is also associated with protection. It is also instructive that this particular invocation has a strong Egyptian flavour with no admixture of Greek words or gods, suggesting an early usage.

In the setup instructions for one experiment of direct vision, a Table of Practice, and floor markings are prescribed:

> ***The preparation for the operation:*** For direct vision, set up a tripod and a table of olive wood or of laurel wood, and on the table carve in a circle these characters:
>
> Cover the tripod with clean linen, and place a censer on the tripod…
>
> In the centre of the shrine, surrounding the tripod, inscribe on the floor with a white stylus the following character…
>
> It is necessary to keep yourself pure for three days in advance. The shrine and the [tripod] must be covered. [If] you wish [to see], look inside, wearing clean [white] garments [and crowned] with a crown of laurel…[3]

The floor inscription, inscribed with a white stylus, is probably a chalk circle as the instruction locates it "surrounding the tripod." This passage is highly significant as it also shows that a circle should also be cut in the surface of the

---

1 The opening line of the rite instructs the magician to be "crowned with a tail of a cat."

2 *PGM* VII. 846-861. The crossed out 'βψ' should be ignored, as these two letters appear again without crossing out. From Preisendanz (1931), Vol. 2, p. 37.

3 *PGM* III. 291-306.

table, which is echoed in the 16th century practice of inscribing characters on the Table of Practice, as was done by Dr. John Dee.

Figure 09: A Greek tripod similar to the one mentioned in the *PGM* passage just quoted. In this example Apollo is attacking the python in order to secure the Pythian tripod for his oracle.[1] It is probable that the Greek tripod was imported into the Graeco-Egyptian milieu. Both Apollo and the serpent are important elements in both prophecy and in the *PGM*. The serpent was an even more important element in many Gnostic sects that saw it as the giver of knowledge or *gnosis* in the Garden of Eden. There are many parallels between the knowledge granted by direct vision or prophecy and the knowledge granted by *gnosis*.

Although references to a protective chalk circle are not very detailed in the *PGM*, detailed diagrams of a protective circle designed to constrain a number of poisonous animals and reptiles often associated with magic are clearly shown in illustrations of Bes-Pantheos (see Figure 10 and Figure 11). The god is Bes, one of the main gods associated with magic, so the illustrations of him standing on an ouroboros circle enclosing such animals and reptiles and helps to confirm that the ouroboros was used as a magical boundary.

---

1 Silver stater coin, Croton, c. 420 BCE. Although this coin was minted more than 500 years before the date of the papyrus, it is likely that the form of the tripod remained very similar in Graeco-Egyptian magic.

Figure 10: Bes-Pantheos and the encircling ouroboros shown with four wings, a three pronged crown and multiple wands.

Figure 11: Bes-Pantheos and the ouroboros circle upon which he stands. The ouroboros circle is being used as a magical boundary to restrain an array of animals and venomous insects and reptiles. The faces on his knees appear again in mediaeval depictions of demons.[1]

[1] Lindsay (1965), p. 24.

4.5 Spoken Words

Conjuration of Angels

The original meaning of ἄγγελος or ἄνγελος, *angelos* (angel) was simply 'messenger' or 'envoy,' with no special religious connotation. Liddell and Scott note in their lexicon that it was an imported Persian word meaning "a mounted courier, such as were kept ready at regular stages throughout Persia for carrying royal despatches." This word could be as easily applied to the messengers of a king as to the messengers of a god. Angels have been an important object of invocation from the *PGM* through the *Hygromanteia* and the European grimoires to the present day, when their popularity with New Age enthusiasts appears to be undiminished.

The Graeco-Egyptian papyri usually only mention the four well-known Biblical angels, Raphael, Michael, Gabriel and Uriel.[1] These have obviously been derived from Jewish sources, and they usually only appear in a line-up of god and angel names, rather than being individually conjured. In the *PGM* the names of angels were just part of the list used to threaten lesser spiritual creatures.

The concept of thwarting angels dates back at least to the *Book of Tobit,* in which the angel Raphael advises Tobias how to repel the demon Asmodeus by burning the liver and heart of the γλάνος or γλιάνος fish.[2] This is followed by the angel binding the demon, demonstrating that certain angels have control over specific demons.[3] The story is set in the 8th century BCE, although most scholars date the appearance of the book to the 2nd century BCE. A number of thwarting angels are also very clearly listed and identified as such in the 1st/2nd century CE text the *Testament of Solomon.*[4] Of the 60 demons listed in that text, as least half are listed with the name of the specific angel that binds or constrains them.[5]

Evocation of Daimones

One surprising example of a straightforward invocation of an infernal daimon occurs as part of an invisibility rite in the *PGM*. One might assume that such a rite would not normally need such a procedure. The magician initially identifies himself with Osiris as part of his magical 'credentials.' The form of

---

1 The first three angels are mentioned in the Bible, the fourth in the *Book of Tobit.*

2 McCown (1922), pp. 55, 125.

3 *Tobit* 8:1-3.

4 McCown (1922); Duling (1983).

5 The rest are controlled by specific words written on papyrus, herbs or pious expletives.

the evocation is very like the form of later grimoire evocations:

> I am Anubis, I am Osir-Phre,[1] I am Osot Soronouier, I am Osiris whom Seth destroyed. Rise up, infernal daimon, Iō Erbēth Iō Phobēth Iō Pakerbēth Iō Apomps;[2] whatever I, NN, order you to do, be obedient to me.[3]

Using his identification with Osiris, the magician conjures the daimon. Its uniqueness lies in the subject of the invocation (Erbēth Phobēth Pakerbēth) which is identified specifically as an infernal daimon (δαῖμον καταχθόνιε, *daimon katachthonie*),[4] rather than some nebulous category of *nomina magica*. Erbēth is Set, as at least one rite clearly refers to him as killing his own brother (Osiris).[5] The evocation of chthonic daimones is definitely a part of *PGM* practice, and may date back to dynastic times.It is therefore likely that the words used in the last two lines of this rite, MARMARIAŌTH MARMARIPHEGGĒ to reverse the rite are also daimon names. The common phrase is MARMARI followed by AŌTH the supreme god, and PHEGGĒ, φέγγη, meaning 'light, splendour or lustre.)

Finally the angels Mikhaēl, Barakhēel, Phamothēel, Ourouēl, Gabriēl and Rhaphaēl are used as 'thwarting angels' to force the appearance of these 13 daimones. Later in the evocation the power of "the God of Abraham, the God of Isaac, the God of Jacob and the God of Israel" is used to compel the spirits' appearance. This particular formula, obviously of partly Jewish origin, also appears in several passages in the *PGM*.

Nomina Magica

The most important of all spoken words used in magic are the names of the spiritual creatures being evoked or invoked. Next in importance are the *nomina magica* that are used to constrain these creatures. The pseudepigraphical *Tenth Hidden Book of Moses* found in the *PGM*, begins by addressing this need:

> You should also take, child, for this personal vision, [a list of] the gods of the days and the hours and the weeks, those given in the book, and the twelve rulers of the months,[6] and the seven-letter name which is in the first book,[7] and which you also have written in the *Key*,[8] which [name] is great and marvellous,

---

[1] Osiris-Ra conjoined.

[2] 'Iō' performs the same function in Graeco-Egyption invocations as 'Om' does in Hindu invocations, the function of calling.

[3] *PGM* I. 247-262.

[4] Literally a chthonic daimon.

[5] *PGM* XXXVI. 5.

[6] As we have seen, the names of the gods of the hours and months is an important adjunct to the practice of evocation.

[7] Not identified.

[8] The text of this Egyptian *Key* has not been identified. It is an interesting thought that this *Key* might in some way be connected with the *Clavicula Salomonis*.

> as it is what brings alive all your books.[1]

The idea of a supreme name which gives life to all the other words, or books of magic, is intriguing indeed. Great secrecy is enjoined:

> ...you are to keep it secret, child, for in it there is the name of the lord, which is Ogdoas,[2] the god who commands and directs all things, since to him angels, archangels, he-daimones, she-daimones, and all things under the creation have been subjected.[3]

This name is being put forward by the scribe as the name that commands all the other spiritual creatures. It is possible that 'Ogdoas'[4] is just a title for the set of the eight primal Egyptian gods, and the name it represents is actually still hidden from the reader.

The same passage continues to enumerate the other names which are needed by the magician to enforce his will, in some cases to be used through the boy medium necessary in evocationary skrying operations:

> There are also prefaced [to that book] four other names, that of nine letters [AEĒ EĒI OYŌ] and that of fourteen letters [YSAU SIAUE IAŌUS] and that of twenty-six letters [ARABBAOUARABA] and that of Zeus [CHONAI IEMOI CHO ENI KA ABIA SKIBA PHOROUOM EPIERTHAT]. You may use these [names] on boy-mediums who do not see the gods, so that one [medium] will see unavoidably, and [also use them] for all spells and needs [such as]: inquiries, prophesies by Helios, prophecies by visions in mirrors. And for the compulsive spell [to call tardy spirits] you should use the great name which is Ogdoas, the god who directs all things throughout the creation. [For] without him simply nothing will be accomplished.[5]

Such names play an important part in the magic of the *PGM* . The name of nine letters (AEĒ EĒI OYŌ) is obviously a version of the Greek seven vowel invocatory combinations. ARABBA_ OUARABA may have later morphed into ABRACADABRA,[6] and IAŌUS is obviously closely related to IAŌ. Although some of the words changed over time, words such as IAŌ and SABAŌTH remained constant across all periods from the *PGM* for the following two millennia.

The *nomina magica* are a particularly important part of magic. The inherent conservatism of ancient magicians about these words comes from their desire to retain the original pronunciation, rather than the original spelling, which

---

[1] *PGM* XIII. 734-741.

[2] This name, being just a Neoplatonic term, is rather a disappointment.

[3] *PGM* XIII. 734-747.

[4] Similar to 'Ennead.'

[5] *PGM* XIII. 747-755.

[6] An alternative derivation from the Hebrew *Ha-Brachah-dabarah* ([in the] Name of the Blessed) is suggested by Skemer (2006), p. 25.

anyway is often from a different and imperfectly understood language. As Johnston concludes:

> They were never supposed to be translated into more familiar languages, lest they lose their particular power to please and attract the god to whom they belong.[1]

A classic case is the well-known translation of יהוה to IAΩ. Transliterated into the Roman alphabet the words IHVH and IAŌ don't appear to have very much in common. However if you know that ו or 'V' can be used as a vowel 'O' and that י or 'I' can equally be pronounced 'Y' then you are half way to seeing how this transliteration occurred, as the two apparently different transliterations can both be pronounced something like 'Yah-ooh.'[2] The point is that determination of the original words of the *nomina magica* relies much more on sound-alike considerations than the checking of exactly the same spelling in lexicons of culturally adjacent foreign languages.

As there are very few gaps and almost no punctuation in many of the *PGM* names, it is assumed that the original reader would have known where the word breaks occurred. Not so easy however for the modern reader without the same cultural background. Some of the word breaks in the *nomina magica* proposed by Betz and his fellow editors do violence to the original *nomina*. Using techniques like isopsephy/gematria it is sometimes possible to break up these words, or at least separate out specific words from the mass of letters. Others can be separated out by comparison with their occurrence elsewhere. A good example of this is SESENGENBARPHARANGĒS which is also found divided up as SESENGEN bar PHARANGĒS, a word which now takes on the structure of a Semitic name, 'Sesengen son of Pharangēs.' [3] Despite considerable controversy about the meaning of this name, it is probably a Semitic rendering of the god Harpocrates, as supported by this passage:

> ...the figure of an infant child seated upon a lotus,[4] O rising one, O you of many names, SESENGENBARPHARANGĒS.[5]

Harpocrates is the "child seated upon a lotus." 'Sesengen bar Pharangēs' also appears in Gnostic texts in the *Nag Hammadi*,[6] which is no surprise because of

---

[1] Johnston (2008), p. 154.

[2] The correct pronunciation of the Hebrew word יהוה was allegedly lost by the Jewish community shortly before the destruction of the Jerusalem Temple in 70 CE, but the Greek IAΩ might in fact offer some help in reconstructing its pronunciation.

[3] 'Bar' is Aramaic for 'son of' as 'ben' is Hebrew for the same designation.

[4] Harpocrates is the rising sun, and the child seated upon the lotus with his finger to his mouth in a gesture of silence. In one specialised sense he is the god of the magicians.

[5] *PGM* II. 107-108.

[6] *Nag Hammadi,* III, 2 and IV, 2.

the close connection between Harpocrates and some Gnostic doctrines.[1]

According to Brashear, the *nomina magica* were absent from the earlier Greek papyri in the centuries BCE, and first started to appear only in the 1st century of the Christian era.[2]

The *nomina magica* resolve into several types:

a. Names of spirits, demons, angels or gods that may be either Greek or Egyptian in origin like the daimon 'Erbēth Pakerbēth.' As Porreca states:

> ...the celestial and infernal hierarchies have been part of the traditional sources of potency for ritual practitioners from the very beginning of the Western magical tradition...the names of angels and/or demons were seen as inherently powerful in themselves.[3]

Fritz Graf stated unequivocally that "the magician thought them all to be names, ὀνόματα [*onomata,* names] or ἐπωνυμίαι [*epōnumiai,* name or title]."[4] Hence the names were not to be changed or translated. This results in a lot of transliteration, which often obscures their original source whilst retaining their sound.

b. Words ending in *-el,-iel, -im* or *-oth,* implying a definite Hebrew origin.[5] These are then often transliterated. For example Sabaōth is the Latin/Greek form of the Hebrew god name **צבאות**.

c. Strings of Greek vowels which rely upon the associations built up between each vowel, its angel, musical note, planet, god/goddess, etc. *PGM* V. 24-30 and VII 766-779 tell exactly how these vowels should be pronounced or sung. The doctrine of the Greek vowels which relies on musical harmonics and other measures familiar to ancient Greek philosophers proves that these particular *nomina magica* are of Greek origin.[6]

d. The instruction to hiss or make popping or barking sounds. These

---

[1] Schwartz (1996), p. 254 suggests that this name relates to *ssn mgw,* 'Sesen the Mage,' on a Sassanian seal-amulet who was associated with date palm fronds, but this sense seems a little distant from the name under consideration.

[2] Brashear (1995), p. 3430.

[3] Porreca (2010), p. 17.

[4] Graff (1997), p. 191.

[5] The *-el* and *-iel* ending is the name of god El added to a stem to form an angelic name. The endings *-im* and *-oth* are respectively the male and female plural endings in Hebrew.

[6] The singing of the seven vowels was an important invocatory skill and very pleasant to listen to, according to Pseudo-Demetrius in *On Style,* 71: "In Egypt the priests, when singing hymns in praise of the gods, employ the seven vowels, which they utter in due succession; and the sound of these letters is so euphonious that men listen to it in preference to flute and lyre."

relate to the traditional animal associations of specific gods, such as the snake (hiss) and crocodile (pop) of Harpocrates, or the dog (bark) of Hekate. These are exactly the sounds the magician was to make, which called to mind, and helped invoke, a specific god.

e. Palindromes such as Ablanathanalba.[1] These words really only have a visual effect. When they are pronounced they are not obviously palindromic. Their ingredients are however often extensions of real Greek or Hebrew words.

f. Letters arranged in geometric shapes like triangles or 'wings.' These are often a single word, repeated on each line, with one letter successively chopped off it, till only one letter remains at the final point. See Figure 32.

g. Words from other languages as yet unrecognisable or unrecognised, sometimes referred to as *voces mysticae* for that reason. I believe that very few of these words are arbitrary inventions, but simply have as yet unrecognisable roots. A fertile source of these words might have been the copying of Demotic words into Greek.

One classic case of three apparently unrecognisable and unattested 'nonsensical' words is "Thoulal, Moulal and Boulal." They were found in a Yale papyrus containing some Coptic Psalms which was published in 1974. The editor assumed they were *nomina magica* and probably the names of spirits. Only later, when correctly transliterated were they recognised as the Coptic version of the names of the three *magi* (or magicians) who visited Jesus soon after his birth. As magi/magicians they were very legitimate additions to an invocation by the Coptic magician who wrote the papyrus.[2] Their names anyway derive from a Greek manuscript written in Alexandria circa 500 CE, at the end of the *PGM* period.[3] I believe there are many more cases like this, where apparent *nomina magica* have real meaning, especially where transliteration from one language to another has been at play.

On the whole Greek, Hebrew and Egyptian words provide the bulk of the derivations of the *nomina magica*. Babylonia appears to only lend a few god/goddess names like Erishkigal, and none of the *nomina magica* except *eulamo* ('eternal') to the *PGM*. It is tempting to ascribe a Gnostic origin to some of the words, but when they are analysed these words are simply either Hebrew, Greek, or a Greek rendering of Hebrew or Demotic. It is most likely that the Gnostics borrowed from the magicians, rather than the reverse, as magicians were often the founders of Gnostic groups. I agree with Jackson who is quite certain that the direction of borrowing was from the magical texts to

[1] This is claimed in the text of *PGM* V. 475 to be Hebrew.

[2] Brashear (1995), p. 3438.

[3] Translated into Latin as *Excerpta Latina Barbari*.

Gnosticism, not the other way round:

> I think that we can indeed be quite sure that the direction of the borrowing runs, as in the Sethian texts…from the magicians to the author of the *Pistis Sophia* and not the reverse, for, as in the three cases above, where any meaning at all has been wrung from them, the words [*aberamenthō, agrammachamarei* and *bainchōōōch*] are quite peculiar and appropriate to a magical context but not to a Gnostic one.
>
> …one or all of the forms attested in the magic papyri are the original(s), of which those that occur in Gnostic literature are derivatives.
>
> …The case for derivation of the Sethian Gnostic names Ialdabaoth and Barbelo from the magic tradition is strengthened by the sheer number of other cases in which names in the Sethian Gnostic system either undeniably or at least quite possibly [are] derived from the incantatory *voces magicae* and *nomina barbara* of the magicians.[1]

Ephesia Grammata

As an example of how apparently meaningless *nomina magica* may actually have a concrete meaning, and how a knowledge of magical methods may help in such an analysis, I would like to address a line that has caused considerable controversy. Perhaps the oldest Greek *nomina magica* are the Ephesian Letters. These are relevant to the current discussion as they also appear in two *PGM* passages:[2]

ΑΣΚΙΟΝ ΚΑΤΑΣΚΙΟΝ ΛΙΞ ΤΕΤΡΑΞ ΔΑΜΝΑΜΕΝΕΥΣ ΑΣΙΟΝ

Many interpretations have been proposed for this sentence. My interpretation is that it is actually a spirit binding (directly related to the statue upon whose pediment the inscription was first seen in Ephesus).[3] It is made up of the following ingredients:

> *Askios* means 'unshaded,' and *Kataskios* means 'in shadow.' These first two words form an attractive contrast of opposites, and this meaning has therefore attracted most scholarly approbation. But I think that the *exact* spelling produces a more cogent result: *Askion* means 'empty threats,' such as you might use to bind a spirit.
>
> *Kata-* means (amongst other possibilities) 'down.' *Katadein* means "to bind up" or "to tie down." In a magical context κατάδεσμος, *katademos* is

[1] Jackson (1989), pp. 70-72, 75.

[2] *PGM* VII. 215-18; LXX. 4-25.

[3] If this interpretation is correct then archaeologists might well find something rather interesting *under* the pediment on which the *Ephesia grammata* were inscribed, if the original pediment can be identified.

literally 'binding down.'[1] So *kataskion* then might conceivably mean 'empty threats used to bind down.'

Lix Tetrax is the name of the fourth demon catalogued in the *Testament of Solomon*.[2]

Damnameneus is clearly identified as a goddess in the *PGM*, specifically the goddess of the fourth hour.[3]

Aisios means auspicious or opportune.[4]

Put this together, and the *Ephesia Grammata* might be translated as:

> "I threaten and bind down Lix Tetrax [by the power of] the auspicious goddess Damnameneus."

Assuming, for the moment, that the *Testament of Solomon* demons (after Ornias) are attributed sequentially to the hours, then the goddess and the demon both relate to the fourth hour. One well known magical formula is the use of a specific angel who thwarts the corresponding demon. This is highly significant as it means that this goddess may have been the thwarting angel/goddess corresponding to Lix Tetrax, whose job it was to bind him. Faraone and Kotansky add support for this role for the goddess by suggesting that Δαμναμενευς "seems to derive from δαμνάω/-άζω (meaning "Tamer")."[5]

If this interpretation proves to be correct, then this most mysterious of magical sentences is finally revealed as a cogent binding formula of the demon Lix Tetrax by the goddess Damnameneus, rather than merely a string of meaningless *nomina magica*. This is just one demonstration of how a knowledge of magical techniques (in this case the use of empty threats, binding and the

---

1 See chapter 6.6 rite type 'D' for examples of *katadesmoi* to be found in the *PGM*.

2 Ornias is not part of the series as he was the assistant demon who introduced Solomon to each of the other demons in turn. Lix Tetrax is described in the *Testament of Solomon* as a dust-devil, said to be the "offspring of the Great One," and to reside in the "horn of the Moon in the South."

3 Damnameneus is referred to as an "avenging goddess, strong goddess [in the] rite of ghosts..." (*PGM* IV. 2780). Damnameneus is also the Egyptian ruler of the 4th hour of the day in a Helios invocation (*PGM* III. 510-511). She is also featured amongst the *nomina magica* on the underside of a throne (*PGM* II. 164) and on a *Stēlē* of Aphrodite (*PGM* VII. 215-18) which confirms her goddess nature. See also Kotansky (1995, 2001), p. 256.

4 The spelling is uncertain, being either *asion* or *aisia*. But related words produce similar meanings such as happiness, luck, good omen, or destined. Therefore, the interpretation "auspicious or opportune" seems to be quite likely. If however the correct spelling is ἄσιος, then 'Asian' in the sense that it was in ancient times applied to Lydia would be correct. In which case "auspicious Damnameneus" should read "Lydian Damnameneus," which is also quite appropriate, as Lydia is just a short distance inland from Ephesus, which is where Pausanias claims these words were first found.

5 Faraone and Kotansky (1988), p. 264.

use of a thwarting angel/goddess of the same hour) can help in the decipherment of *nomina magica*. A number of other examples could easily have been instanced.

The attempt to preserve the original language of the *nomina magica* is rooted in the concept that the gods and other spiritual creatures best understand the sound of their original language. Any changes to this may render the invocation unintelligible to the god or spiritual creature concerned, and therefore be ineffective. This is reinforced by Iamblichus' 3rd century CE comments on the use of such *nomina magica* in Egyptian magic and Mystery Religions:

> But "why, of meaningful names, do we prefer the barbarian [foreign names] to our own?" For this, again, there is a mystical reason. For, since the gods have shown that the entire dialect of the sacred peoples such as the Assyrians and the Egyptians is appropriate for religious ceremonies, for this reason we must understand that our communication with the gods should be in an appropriate tongue. Also, such a mode of speech is the first and the most ancient. But most importantly, since those who learned the very first names of the gods merged them with their own familiar tongue and delivered them to us, as being proper and adapted to these [religious] things, forever we [must] preserve here the unshakeable law of tradition...
>
> It is therefore evident from this that the language of sacred peoples is preferred to that of other men, and with good reason. For the names do not exactly preserve the same meaning when they are translated; rather, there are certain idioms in every nation that are impossible to express in the language of another. Moreover, even if one were to translate them, this would not preserve their same power... For all these reasons, then, they [the barbarian names] are adapted to [communicate with] the superior beings.[1]

Of course the result of conserving the ancient pronunciation is that the spelling gets more and more corrupted as the words are passed from one culture to another and from one alphabet to another, especially in the case of Egyptian to Greek, via the medium of Coptic.[2] It is for that reason that many of the passages in the *PGM* have their *nomina magica* glossed in 'Old Coptic' by the scribe or the original owner of the papyrus, so that Greek readers will know how to pronounce words that were originally Egyptian. The upside of this is that the presence of a Coptic gloss almost guarantees that the original words were Egyptian. Secondly, it leaves the reader with a reasonable chance of getting the pronunciation right. The downside is that the hieratic spelling (and therefore the meaning) of the word may well have been lost.

Although *nomina magica* are names whose uncorrupted derivation is in many cases unknown, I believe they are not deliberately fabricated nonsense

---

[1] Iamblichus, *De Mysteriis* VII. 4-5 in Clarke *et al*, (2003), pp. 296-299.

[2] Coptic is effectively Egyptian words spelled in Greek, with the addition of at least seven further letters designed to convey sounds that don't exist in Greek.

syllables, as their function was to coerce gods, daimones, angels or spirits. To be an effective form of coercion they must have originally had a meaning, rather than just being nonsense. No ancient magician would have thought that some random nursery nonsense syllables would have been effective in ordering around a recalcitrant, and possibly dangerous, spirit or demon. These words will, in many cases, be names, as the theory behind such coercion falls into three name-related methods:

i) The named entity can be used to coerce the lesser entity, as it is of a higher rank, (i.e. the name of an arch-demon may be used to coerce a lesser demon, or the name of a god used to coerce a daimon) or the name of a specific thwarting angel.

ii) The name of a famous magician or exorcist who in the past has effectively commanded the spirits is used, such as Solomon, or even Jesus. In this context the operation is not necessarily of Jewish or Christian derivation, but simply utilising the name of a famous magician to terrify the spirit.

iii) A more Egyptian approach to this appears with the identification of the magician with such an ancient worthy or god, like the claim "I am Paphro Onosophris..."

In all these cases the *nomina magica* will in all likelihood be a name, and not a nonsense word.[1]

The Rationale of Spirit Belief in the Irrational

The technique of dressing up to fool or impress the spirits is one that has been passed down from the *PGM,* via the *Hygromanteia,* to the Latin and vernacular grimoires. This is a real technique and more than just play-acting, as confirmed by Iamblichus when he wrote:

> ...there exists a certain class of powers in the cosmos [spirits] - limited, devoid of judgement and highly irrational...[that is] led by appearances and to be influenced by other things through a foolish and unstable imagination.[2]

This is a rationale for the magician's play-acting when wearing a crown or a lion-skin belt. If we suspend disbelief temporarily, it might seem strange that spirits would fall for such false claims made by a magician acting in the name of a god or a dead magician, who the current performer has never met. The explanation for this is threefold: that the spirit is unwilling to risk it; that the spirit cannot read the magician's mind; or that the power of words is real in these realms. All three explanations have been given at various points in the history of magic. The practical result is that coercion can only be effective if the

[1] All these procedures are later found passed on in the *Hygromanteia* and the *Clavicula.*

[2] *De Mysteriis* VI. 5.246.

names named are correctly pronounced, have some basis in real words, and represent beings of a superior rank to the entity being evoked. It is therefore certain that, with this in mind, no competent magician, believing in their power, would consciously generate nonsense syllables for the purpose of coercion, as that would be completely self-defeating. Therefore, in many cases, the *nomina magica* will be proper nouns like Solomon or 'Sesengen bar Pharanges.'[1] Rebecca Lesses summarises the possible derivations of these *nomina magica* as:

> The names consist of proper names of particular deities and angels, name-formulas (*logia*) such as "Sesengen bar Pharanges," strings of letters of the Hebrew or Greek alphabet (especially vowels), permutations of the Tetragrammaton, and combinations of the names [or titles] of God with other letters.[2]

As already noted the latter is definitely a proper noun, as it has the structure of 'Sesengen *son of* Pharanges.' Pharanges may be related to Phre, and Harpocrates was the son of the sun (Horus or Phre).[3] Daniel and Maltomini admit that:

> It is a well-known fact that editorial division and analysis of magical words is often nothing other than guess work, among other reasons because so many are unparalleled, because the ancient texts for the most part lack word division, and because much is meaningless gibberish that cannot be explained by Egyptian, Hebrew and other languages. A number of the shorter "words" listed below will of necessity be wrong divisions. Also a number of the longer "words" must occasionally contain shorter, meaningful elements that have not been correctly isolated.[4]

One binding talisman has a long catalogue of these names in which each is shown to be the name of a god.[5] I believe that these are not fanciful attributions but the real meaning of these as understood by a 3rd century magician in Carthage. As such this talisman strongly supports the explanation of many *nomina magica* as the actual or secret names of gods. See Appendix 4 for a listing of many of these words.

The reason why many of these words cannot be found in lexicons is that they are mostly transliterated *proper nouns*, and not that they are gibberish. Proper nouns don't normally make it into dictionaries. As such there is much scope for hunting down precursors and incorrupt forms of such names, a process

---

[1] Sesengen bar Pharanges also occurs in *Nag Hammadi* III, 2 and IV, 2 as well as *PGM* IV, 964-67.

[2] Lesses (1996), p. 52.

[3] Scholem suggested that it was an angel's name, implying 'the purifier,' which is inherently unlikely. Mastrocinque (2005), p. 120 suggests 'Sesenggen son of Tartarus' (assuming *Pharanges* = *pharangos* = Tartarus), but this interpretation also seem rather unlikely.

[4] Daniel and Maltomini (1991), p. 325.

[5] Gager (1992), No. 10, pp. 62-64.

that has been begun by Porreca.[1]

The correct pronunciation of the letters making up Greek *nomina magica* is not often specified in the original texts, but just one passage in the *PGM* actually gives what that scribe considered to be the 'correct' pronunciation of the Greek letters:

> the "A" with an open mouth, undulating like a wave;
> the "O" succinctly, as a breathed threat,
> the "IAŌ" [directed] to earth, to air, and to heaven;
> the "Ē" like a baboon [screech?];
> the "O" in the same way as above;
> the "E" with enjoyment, aspirating it,
> the "Y" like a shepherd, drawing out the pronunciation.[2]

When Mesopotamian, Greek and Semitic magic were added to the mix, so the range of words of power increased from just Egyptian ones by the addition of such names as Hekate, Ereshkigal, Neboutosoualēth, Abraham, Adonai, Solomon, Moses, Sabaōth, Anael or Boel.[3] These names, with a few exceptions (for example Neboutosoualēth, the Moon), remain part of the literature of magical handbooks up to the present day.

The scribe of the *Eighth Book of Moses* (part of the *PGM*) is very conscious that it draws its *nomina magica* from different linguistic sources and makes a determined effort to identify them. This is not so obvious in Betz's continuous text translation, but comes to life when the lines are separated out:

I call on you, lord, [whose name is]

> [written] in 'birdglyphic': ARAI;[4]
> [written] in hieroglyphic: LAILAM;
> [written] in Hebraic: ANOCH[5] BIATHI ARBATH[6]
> [written in] Berbir:[7] ECHILATOUR BOUPHROUMTROM;
> [written] in Egyptian: ALDABAEIM;
> [written] in Baboonic:[8] ABRASAX; [85]

---

[1] Porreca (2010), pp. 23-25.

[2] This suggests that O and Ω should be pronounced in the same way. *PGM* V. 24-30.

[3] See Brashear (1995), p. 3396. Bo'el is mentioned more than a dozen times in the Demotic, as well as in the mediaeval parts of the *Sepher ha-Razim*. The name also occurs later in several other Latin grimoires.

[4] Bird form hieroglyphs.

[5] Should be *'anoki'* according to Betz (1996), p. 174.

[6] The last word has been divided, as ARBATH clearly means 'four' in Hebrew. It relates to the Greek Αρβαθιαω, meaning the fourfold god Ιαω.

[7] I suggest that this is yet another linguistic category (Berber) that has been mistakenly worked into the text as if it were part of a long *nomina magica*.

[8] Κυνοκεφαλιστί, "after the manner of [the Gnostics?]." It is not clear to me why this was translated by Morton Smith as 'Baboonic' except for the association of the baboon with Thoth = Hermes = Hermetic or Gnostic.

[written] in Falconic:[1]	CHI CHI CHI CHI CHI CHI CHI TIPH TIPH TIPH CHA CHA CHA CHA CHA CHA CHA;[2]
[written] in Hieratic:	MENE PHŌIPHŌTH.[3]

These seven languages may in fact be seven different scripts, but obviously it is not just a case of straight transliteration. They have here been split into separate lines for ease of comparison. The inclusion of all these forms is an attempt, by the scribe, to preserve all the clues necessary to the correct pronunciation of these *nomina magica.* Hieroglyphic and Hebrew are subject to ordinary linguistic analysis. Egyptian is likely to be a phonetic rendering of the commonly spoken Egyptian of the time (maybe Coptic?). Hieratic is simply a script form of ancient Egyptian. Falconic seems like an onomatopoeic rendering of a bird's cry. The positioning of 'Birdglyphic' at the beginning suggests that it performed a specific function in relation to the other languages rather than being a language on its own. It seems possible that it was prefaced by the glyph of a bird designed to indicate a special function, possibly a method of pronunciation for all the following languages.

Even though the language labels might seem a little strange, like 'Baboonic' for Gnostic Coptic, there is no doubting a scholarly striving by the original scribe to correctly define the *nomina magica,* their pronunciation, and their origins. He is following the warnings in Hermetic and Neoplatonic texts (such as Iamblichus) not to translate or change the spelling of such words of power.[4]

Some gods have their own specific formula, which can then be used to identify the god being invoked, such as the invocation to Typhon/Set which uses "Iō Erbēth Iō Pakerbēth Iō Bolchosēth."[5] Some words are derived from a *description* of the original word, such as Αρβαθιαω, Arbathiaō. This is derived from the Hebrew ארבעת *arboth,* meaning 'four' and Ιαω derived from the Hebrew IHVH or יהוה: in other words this is yet another Greek form of the four-lettered Hebrew name of God, IAŌ or יהוה, IHVH.

---

[1] ἱερακιστί, "in the language of the hawk."

[2] The "CHA CHA CHA CHA CHA CHA CHA" was originally placed after the hieratic by the editor, but is clearly an overflow from the Falconic line, and so has been moved up one line, where it now forms a symmetrical *nomina magica.* This name now repeats its elements in the familiar 7-3-7 format.

[3] The last word has been split. *PGM* XIII, 81-89.

[4] Iamblichus, *De Mysteriis* VII. 4-5.

[5] See *PGM* IV. 3267. As already mentioned 'Pakerbēth' is a daimonic name associated with Set, and Iō performs the function of calling.

Figure 12: Zeus with thunderbolt fighting with Typhon, the deadliest monster in all Greek mythology.[1] Typhon was identified by the Greeks with the Egyptian god Set, and he appears frequently in the *PGM*.

One of the first things that needs to be done in order to map the transmission of *nomina magica* fully is the production of lists or tables of these names, drawn from all available texts and grimoires. One of the first attempts to do this was Crowley's *777* followed more recently by my *Complete Magician's Tables*.[2]

The second necessary step is the matching of these names, including their variants, across different sources. This has been begun with Porreca's excellent study of just three sources.[3] However his study has only listed obviously matching names, rather than exhaustively listing all possible gods, angels, daimones, demons or spirits. Obviously this table could be widened much further. Such a tabulation of the names of spiritual creatures is key for showing the dependency and transmission of texts, as these words are (in theory) the most jealously guarded or carefully preserved parts of any invocation.

In Porreca's study, exactly half of the names identified were of Hebraic origin.[4] Greek was the next most common language,[5] then Egyptian, as might have

[1] Drawing based on a Greek bronze shield band panel from Olympia. From the *Routledge Handbook of Greek Mythology*.

[2] Skinner (2006), Table M.

[3] Porreca (2010), pp. 23-25.

[4] 21-22 out of 43 names. Porreca (2010), p. 25.

[5] With seven to nine names identified by Porreca as Graeco-Roman, which are in all likelihood just Greek.

been expected. Only about three names may have been Persian/Babylonian, and one name of possibly Muslim origin, the latter confirming the very minor *direct* influence that relatively late-occurring Islam had on European grimoires.[1] I have however, listed most of the main god, angel and daimon names to be found in each *PGM* rite, with a selection of the most frequently occurring *nomina magica* in each Rite Type table. Full extraction of the names in the *PGM* would have boosted the Greek numbers.[2]

The *PGM* borrowed many of its god and angel names from Hebraic sources, with others coming from the Greek tradition. From Egypt came some less easily identified Demotic words plus a few of the major gods of Egypt.

These proportions varied over time. In the 13th century grimoire *Juratus,* of the 100 god names analysed, only 17 were of definite Hebraic provenance, and 49 were of definite Greek origin, thus neatly reversing the percentages achieved by Porreca. The remaining 34 names were of doubtful origin, but most likely either Greek or Hebrew.

Historiola and Commemoration

The procedure of reciting an abridged version of the myths associated with the god being invoked, or commemorating their deeds, is a well-established practice in both religion and magic. As Brashear remarks:

> This idea that mythical events...retain their supernatural forces forever and can be reactivated at any given time by the simple act of recounting them is a technique common to all times and places. The precedent having been cited, the god is obliged to act the same way now as then, this time to the benefit of the conjuror/suppliant. Even a simple allusion to deeds done in the past will suffice to incite a god to action. The same thought is implicit in the magician identifying himself with a certain deity. Having once been in the same situation as the person for whom the rite is performed, the god is induced to act in a way favourable to the magician.[3]

The ritual use of *historiola* dates from ancient Egypt, and is also an enduring part of the magical tradition. The thinking behind it includs demonstrating to the god knowledge of its background, thereby making it more compliant to the commands of the magician. Just as the god had triumphed in some previous contest, so now he was expected to aid the magician and triumph again.

Claiming to be that god is a further extension of that idea. In the same vein, claiming to be a famous magician, like Nectanebus, Solomon or Jesus, was designed to impress the spiritual creature that was being invoked, so repeating

---

[1] Some later names such as Maymon may have Arabic roots.

[2] A full index to the names in *PGM* is still a major *desideratum,* but see Appendix 4 for a limited list.

[3] Brashear (1995), p. 3439.

historiola associated with either the god or a famous magician was also a perennial technique. Mentioning the names of previous famous magicians is designed to convince the god/spirit that the present magician has inherited some of their techniques and abilities, and therefore ought to be obeyed.[1]

In this context, it is worth mentioning that in some procedures the name of 'Jesus' is recalled (as he had a considerable reputation as an exorcist and commander of demons). In one episode a magician uses his name as a spirit-cowering credential as well as that of St. Paul, who had reputedly also developed some magical abilities. The spirit states categorically that it recognised the power of the name 'Jesus' and comprehended that of 'Paul,' but refused to cooperate with the exorcist, as it did not recognise *his* power:

> God did extraordinary miracles through Paul, so that when the handkerchiefs or aprons that had touched his skin were brought to the sick, their diseases left them, and the evil spirits came out of them. Then some itinerant Jewish exorcists tried to use the name of the Lord Jesus over those who had [been possessed by] evil spirits, saying, 'I adjure you by the Jesus whom Paul proclaims.' Seven sons of a Jewish high priest named Sceva were doing this. But the evil spirit said to then in reply, 'Jesus I know, and Paul I know; but who are you? Then the man with the evil spirit leapt on them, mastered them all, and so overpowered them that they fled out of the house naked and wounded.[2]

At this point it appears that even the spirit, as well as the sons of the Jewish high priest, acknowledged Jesus' reputation and abilities as a magician, despite being less than competent themselves. Justin Martyr makes it clear that some names work, and some names (predominantly human names such as St. Paul) do not:

> But though you exorcise any demon in the name of any of those who were amongst you -- either kings, or righteous men, or prophets, or patriarchs - it will not be subject to you. But if any of you exorcise it in [the name of] the God of Abraham, and the God of Isaac, and the God of Jacob, it will perhaps be subject to you. Now assuredly your exorcists, I have said, make use of craft when they exorcise, even as the Gentiles do, and employ fumigations and incantations.[3]

The phrase "the God of Abraham, and the God of Isaac, and the God of Jacob" is a rather long winded way of identifying the Jewish god, Yahweh or IHVH.

License to Depart

The licence to depart is a traditional part of any magical rite, and the last of the

---

[1] Preisendanz in his *Überlieferungsgeschichte* 230.29, lists 30 such names of magicians including Pitys (or Bitys), Astrampsychos, Ostanes, and Zoroaster, all of which are found fulfilling this function in *PGM*.

[2] Acts 19: 11-16. *New Revised Standard Version.*

[3] Justin Martyr 85.3.

five stages of any Solomonic rite.[1] The point of it is to dismiss the spirits that have been evoked, and to ensure that they do not harm the magician and his disciples when they leave the circle. There are many tales of what happens if the magician (or his disciples) steps over the boundary of the circle or leaves before the spirits have retired to their own abode. A classical example of this is related in the *Autobiography* of Benvenuto Cellini in which he participates in a Solomonic evocation in the Colosseum in Rome.[2] The priest responsible for the ceremony only orders the burning of asafoetida at the end of the rite (to drive away the spirits) rather than properly licensing their dismissal. The result is that a number of the spirits accompany Cellini and his terrified skryer home.[3]

There are other techniques for banishing demons, some of them more concrete, for example those mentioned in the *Testament of Solomon* and *The Book of Tobit*, like the burning of catfish entrails.[4] One common denominator in all the dismissals is a bad smell, be it asafoetida, ape's dung or burning fish entrails,[5] accompanied with appropriate words. It makes a sort of sense that the gods and spirits rejoice in the burning of sweet smelling incense, and are by these encouraged to arrive, but cannot abide a bad stench.

Such dismissals are present from dynastic Egyptian, through the *PGM*, the *Hygromanteia* and the *Clavicula Salomonis* to the later European grimoires. From the *PDM*, the following method is obviously of ancient Egyptian provenance:

> If you wish to send them all away:[6] You should put ape's dung on the brazier. They all [will] go away to their place. And you should recite the spell for dismissing then also..."Go well, go in joy!"[7]

Another Egyptian dismissal is expressed simply as a farewell:

> ***His dismissal: Formula***: "Farewell, farewell, the good oxherd, Anubis, Anubis, the son of a wolf and a dog, ..." Say [it] ***seven*** times.[8]

The provision to say it seven times indicates the importance attached by the Egyptians to the dismissal. The word most frequently used in the *PGM* for dismissal or banishing of a god or a spirit when its services are no longer required was ἀπόλυσις, *apolysis,* which literally means 'loosing.' Bell, Nock and

[1] The five stages are: *consecratio, invocatio, evocatio, ligatio,* and *licentia.*

[2] It is possible that the Colosseum was chosen as a site to evoke spirits because of the large amount of blood known to have been spilled there in the past. See also Kieckhefer (1997), pp. 186-189 for a more psychological viewpoint.

[3] Symonds (1946), chapter LXIV.

[4] *Tobit* 8: 2-3.

[5] Fish were also thought to be impure in Egypt.

[6] This applies to invoked gods, living men, spirits, drowned men, and dead men, as listed in the previous lines of the procedure.

[7] *PDM* xiv. 85-86.

[8] *PDM* xiv. 422-424.

Thompson suggest that:

> Possibly ἀπολύω here implies that the power [of the god or spirit] addressed is fettered by the magician and released for a particular task as it were on ticket of leave…[1]

The word ἀπολύω is used in a very specific technical sense. It means "to set free or release from the bonds" that were imposed on the spirit by the previous part of the ceremony (the *ligatio)*. The *licentia* follows on immediately after the *ligatio*. Although these Latin terms apply to later grimoires, the method is still the same.

Dismissing a god is more complex, and in the case of Kronos, the following formula is to be recited:

> ANAE OCHETA THALAMNIA KĒRIDU KOIRAPSIA GENECHRONA SANĒLON STGARDĒS CHLEIDŌ PHRAINOLE PAIDOLIS IAEL, go away, master of the world, forefather [of the gods]; go to your own places in order that the universe be maintained. Be gracious to us, lord."[2]

A more polite form is:

> ***Dismissal***: "I give thanks to you because you came in accordance with the command of god. I request that you keep me healthy, free from terror and free from demonic attacks, ATHATHE ATHATH ACHTHE ADONAI. Return to your holy places."[3]

Another dismissal at the end of an Evocationary Lamp Skrying rite begins by changing the hand in which the wand is held by the magician, and concludes with the usual request not to harm the magician or his assistant(s):

> And after the inquiry, if you wish to release the god himself, shift the aforementioned ebony staff [wand], which you are holding in your left hand, to your right hand; and shift the sprig of laurel, which you are holding in your right hand, to your left hand; and extinguish the burning lamp; and use the same burnt offering while saying:
>
> Be gracious unto me, O primal god,
> O elder-born, self-generating god.
> I adjure the fire which first shone in the void;
> I adjure your power which is greatest over all;
> I adjure him who destroys even in Hades,
> That you depart, returning to your ship,[4]
> And harm me not, but be forever kind.[1]

---

[1] Bell, Nock and Thompson (1931), pp. 261.

[2] *PGM* IV. 3120-3124.

[3] *PGM* LXII. 36-41. This is almost exactly the wording of one 17th century European grimoire dismissal.

[4] The ship that ferries Ra (Phre) across the sky and through the Underworld.

A dismissal of Sarapis at the end of one skrying operation also includes protection for the boy skryer:

> Go, lord, to your own world and to your own thrones, to your own vaults, and keep me and this boy from harm, in the name of the highest god, SAMAS PHRĒTH.[2]

After the successful invocation of the daimon the Headless One, the magician is instructed to release this daimon and dismiss him in an honourable fashion:

> After you have learned all you want, you will release him, doing honor to him in a worthy manner. Sprinkle dove's blood round about, make a burnt offering of myrrh, and say, "Depart, lord, CHORMOU CHORMOU OZOAMOROIRŌCH KIMNOIE EPOZOI EPOIMAZOU SARBOENDOBAIACHCHA IZOMNEI PROSPOI EPIOR; go off, lord, to your seats, to your place, leaving me strength and the right of audience with you."

The burning of myrrh at the dismissal seems contrary to the instructions that advise dismissing the demons with a bad smell like asafoetida, but the request for continued "right of audience" is certainly consistent with such texts, and an important addition.

One rite which was erroneously described as a "charm,"[3] is in fact Solomon's invocation to be said into a skryer's ear in order to put him into a trance. It ends with a classic dismissal:

> ***Dismissal of the lord:*** into the ear of NN [the skryer]: "ANANAK ARBEOUĒRI AEĒIOYŌ."
> If he tarries, sacrifice on grapevine charcoal a [portion of] sesame seed [and] black cumin while saying: "ANANAK ŌRBEOUSIRI AEĒIOYŌ, go away, lord, to your own thrones and protect him, NN [the skryer], from all evil."[4]

A simpler dismissal simply orders:

> ***Dismissal.*** Say: "Go away, Anubis, to your own thrones, for my health and well-being."[5]

The Graeco-Egyptian magicians saw their gods as very palpable,[6] and so the Licence to Depart is also done in a very physical manner:

---

[1] *PGM* I. 334-347. Poetic contractions in the English text, like 'e'en' for 'even,' have been silently expanded.

[2] Shamash Phre, the sun god in Hebrew and Egyptian guise. *PGM* V. 41-49.

[3] The Greek Σολομῶντος κατάπτωσις, and the German *Salomon's Niederfallen* both indicate "Solomon's fall" rather than "charm." The precise meaning is "Solomon's [invocation] that [induces the skryer] to fall." This interpretation is confirmed by lines 910-911 where suddenly falling into trance literally floors the skryer.

[4] *PGM* IV. 917-921.

[5] *PGM* VII. 319-334.

[6] Although I have already instanced this passage as an example of the palpability of Egyptian gods, it is here used also as an example of the Licence to Depart.

> ***Dismissal***: close your eyes, release the pebble which you have been holding,[1] lift the crown up from your head and your heel from his [the god's] toe, and, while keeping your eyes closed, say 3 times: "I give thanks to you lord BAINCHŌŌŌCH, who is BALSAMĒS. Go away, go away, lord, into your own heavens, into your own palaces, into your own course. Keep me healthy, unharmed, not plagued by ghosts, free from calamity and without terror. Hear me during my lifetime.
>
> ***Dismissal of the brightness***:[2] "CHŌŌ CHŌŌŌ CHŌŌCH,[3] holy brightness." In order that the brightness [of the god's appearance] also go away: "Go away, holy brightness, go away, beautiful and holy light of the highest god, AIAŌNA." Say it one time with closed eyes, smear yourself with Coptic kohl;[4] smear yourself by means of a golden probe.[5]

In this instance, the magician is instructed in very physical terms specifically to restrain the god by standing on the god's toe, only releasing him by raising his own foot:

> ***Charm to retain the god [Holding fast to the god]***:[6] when he[7] comes in, after greeting him, step with your left heel on the big toe of his right foot, and he will not go away unless you raise your heel from his toe and at the same time say the dismissal.[8]

---

1 The stone is inscribed with the number '3663,' which is Bainchōōch's isopsephic number, derived by adding together the numeric equivalents of all the letters in his name.

2 'Brightness' should be understood as a ray of light from the sun god, rather than just light.

3 Corresponds to "depart, depart, O darkness," in other words 'Bainchōōch depart.'

4 Powdered antimony or stibnite used for eye makeup.

5 *PGM* IV. 1057-1070.

6 This is not a (physical) 'charm.' Κάτοχος τοϋ θεοῦ simply means holding fast to the god, or binding in a very literal sense.

7 Probably Bainchōōch.

8 *PGM* IV. 1052-1057.

4.6 Sacrifice and Spirit Offerings

Sacrifice is part of the compact made between the magician and a spiritual creature. The idea of making a pact which required the magician's soul as part of the bargain is not found anywhere in the *PGM*, but seems to be solely part of the fictional Faust tradition. However reference is often made to offerings made to the spirits, usually in the form of incense, sometimes as food, and less commonly in the form of a sacrificed animal. Sacrifice was also an integral part of Second Temple Jewish religion and a common part of Roman pagan religion as well as Graeco-Egyptian magic. Solomon was famous for the quantity of oxen and other animals he sacrificed for Yahweh at the inauguration of his Temple: 20,000 oxen and 120,000 sheep, prodigious numbers for those days.[1] Although Jewish sacrifice on a large scale ceased with the destruction of Herod's Second Temple in 70 CE, examples of sacrifice (especially of doves) persist in Jewish magical texts at least into the 15th century CE.[2]

In one of King Pitys' necromantic rites,[3] a sacrifice is offered to a spiritual creature (in this case a daimon) as a 'payment' for a successful conclusion of the unnamed objective of the rite:

> Fulfil, daimon, what is written here. And after you have performed it, I will pay you a sacrifice. But if you delay, I will inflict on you chastisements which you cannot endure.

Sacrifice is therefore distinctly a form of spirit bribery. Sacrifice is specifically instructed in a general purpose rite, but the first application for which sacrifice is recommended, is to attract a lover:

> After saying these things, sacrifice. Then raise loud groans and then go backwards as you descend. And she will come at once. But pay attention to the [arrival of the] one being attracted so that you may open the door for her; otherwise the spell will fail.[4]

The Classical Greeks offered sacrifice to the chthonic gods, via a pit in the earth, usually accompanied by libations of wine and blood poured into the pit. Similar procedures are also to be found in the *PGM* for example, in the following case to aid in the consecration of a magic ring:

> Making a pit in a holy place open to the sky, [or] if [you have none] in a clean, sanctified tomb looking towards the east, and making over the pit an altar of wood from fruit trees, sacrifice an unblemished goose, and 3 roosters and 3

---

[1] *1 Kings* 8:62.

[2] For example the *Sepher Raziel ha-Malekh* translated in Savedow (2000).

[3] King Bitys/Pitys was reputed to be a Thessalian magician, Thessaly being famous for its magic practitioners.

[4] *PGM* IV. 2491.

> pigeons. Make these whole burnt offerings and burn, with the birds, all sorts of incense. Then, standing by the pit, look to the east and, pouring on a libation of wine, honey, milk, [and] saffron, and holding over the smoke, while you pray, [the ring or stone] in which are engraved the inscriptions…[1]

Sacrifice also has its place in the consecration of an iron lamella:

> Go, I say, into a clean room. Set up a table, on which you are to place a clean linen cloth and flowers of the season. Then sacrifice a white cock, placing beside it 7 cakes, 7 wafers, 7 lamps; pour a libation of milk, honey, wine, and olive oil.[2]

A more detailed account of a sacrifice is to be found in an auto-initiation rite:

> Keep yourself pure for seven days beforehand. On the third of the month, go to a place from which the Nile has recently receded, before anyone walks on the area that was flooded - or at any rate, to a place that has been inundated by the Nile. On two bricks standing on their sides, build a fire with olive wood…when half the sun is above the horizon; but before the sun [fully] appears, dig a trench around the altar. When the disk of the sun is fully above the horizon, cut off the head of an unblemished, solid white cock… Throw the head into the river and drink up the blood, draining it off into your right hand and putting what's left of the body on the burning altar.[3]

Sacrifice also appears amongst the compulsive formulae designed to force a god or spirit to manifest if they have been dilatory:

> Take a completely white cock and a pinecone; pour wine upon it, anoint yourself and remain praying until the sacrifice is extinguished. Then rub yourself all over with the following mixture: laurel bayberries, Ethiopian cumin, nightshade, and "Hermes' finger."[4]

The white cock (but not the pinecones) survives as a magician's sacrifice through to the late European grimoires.[5]

One 2nd century CE rite gives sacrifice instructions for a sacrifice of a white piglet that is to be cooked and eaten (except for the innards which are to be burned).[6] Sadly the papyrus is damaged along both edges, leaving a lot to be guessed at.

---

1 *PGM* XII. 201-269.

2 *PGM* IV. 2188-2193.

3 *PGM* IV. 26-51.

4 *PGM* II. 74-76.

5 Sacrifice of a white cock also appears in modern occult fiction, for example in novels by Dennis Wheatley.

6 *SM* 75, line 8.

4.7 Herbs and Plants (Y)[1]

Lists of the magical properties of herbs are an important section in the *PGM,* as they provide concrete items whose use in magic can be tracked across various cultures. This is slightly more complicated in the *PGM* by the habit of priests and magicians of listing quite common ingredients such as herbs and other items with flowery and alarming names. These 'code' names are listed in Table 09. The magical use of herbs and plants makes up 0.9% of all the *PGM* rites.

Techniques in the *PGM* extend to meticulous attention to detail when preparing the equipment or *materia* to be used in a rite, and procuring herbs for such use is no exception.

Picking the Plant

Catalogues of herbs and their uses can be traced back to Mesopotamia. Paying careful attention to the procedure for uprooting medical or magical herbs is derived from Mesopotamian magical practice. A typical description of such precautions found in a Mesopotamian herbarium suggests the magician should:

> [Look for] a gourd which grows alone in the plain;
> when the Sun has gone down,
> cover your head with a kerchief,
> cover the gourd too,
> draw a magic circle with flour around it,
> and in the morning,
> before the Sun comes out,
> pull it up from its location,
> take its root ...
>
> These instructions specify the time for picking the plant, and the precautions to be observed in regard to both the plant and the herbalist. The scene is night (between sunset and sun-rise); the plant is isolated by a magic circle and covered; and the herbalist protects himself by covering his head. Night time may be specified in other ways: sometimes it is sufficient to say that the sun must not "see" the herb: for example, a root "which the sun did not see when you pulled the plant and surrounding it with a magic circle are necessary because the plant may not willingly give up the root, leaf, or shoot needed for preparing the medicine; one must buy it from the plant, or at least give some compensation for it."[2]

Theophrastus makes fun of the latter instructions:

> That one should be bidden to pray while cutting is not perhaps unreasonable, but the additions made to this injunction are absurd: for instance, as to cutting

[1] Details of the alphabetic coding of every passage in the *PGM* can be seen in Table 12 and Table 13. Each code has a dedicated chapter rite table showing the location of all procedures relevant to that procedure.
[2] Reiner (1995), pp. 36-37.

> the kind of all-heal (*panakes*) one should put in the ground in its place an offering made of all kind of fruits and a cake; and that, when one is cutting *gladwyn* [Gk., ἰπὶ;[1] = iris?], one should put in its place to pay for it, cakes of meal from spring-sown wheat, and that one should cut it with a two-edged sword, first making a circle round it three times. . .[2]

There is also a common injunction not to use an iron instrument in digging, even though a two-edged sword of a different metal would be acceptable. This is a very old limitation, and reoccurs in a slightly different form in many Latin grimoires where iron instruments, specifically an iron sword are used to threaten the spirits.

In the *PGM* attention was also paid to how medical and magical herbs were uprooted, and this care survived through the *PGM* formulae to Latin and English grimoires right up to the 18th century herbals. The reason for this care is supposedly so the herb's power is retained and no adverse luck is incurred by the magician for uprooting it. The procedure is spelled out in some detail:

> Among the Egyptians herbs are always obtained like this: the herbalist first purifies his own body. First he sprinkles with natron and fumigates the herb with resin from a pine tree after carrying it [the smoking resin] around the place 3 times. Then, after burning *kyphi*[3] and pouring the libation of milk as he prays, he pulls up the plant while invoking by name the daimon to whom the herb is being dedicated and calling upon him to be more effective for the use for which it is being acquired...
>
> After saying this [invocation], he rolls the harvested stalk in a pure linen cloth (but into the place of its roots they (*sic*) threw seven seeds of wheat and an equal number of barley, after mixing them with honey), and after pouring [this mixture] in the ground which has been dug up [to propitiate the plant so harvested], he departs.[4]

This latter procedure is a form of compensation to both the plant and the earth, for what has been taken, so that no resentment by the earth (or its spirits) will hinder the magical operation that the herbs are destined to be part of.

Another example in the *PGM* of the special precautions taken when uprooting herbs includes a spell to be addressed to the plant to ask its forgiveness:

> ***Spell for picking a*** plant: Use it before sunrise. The ***spell to be spoken***: "I am picking you, such and such a plant, with my five-fingered hand, I, NN, and I am bringing you home so that you may work for me for a certain purpose. I adjure you by the undefiled name of the god: if you pay no heed to me, the earth which

---

1 The *gladwyn* is an English herb usually called "stinking iris." The Greek in this quote may not be correct, as ἰπὶ is only listed in Liddell as "a worm that eats horn and wood."

2 Theophrastus, *Historia Plantarum* 9.8.7. See Hort (1916).

3 A standard Egyptian temple incense.

4 *PGM* IV. 2967-3006.

> produced you will no longer be watered as far as you are concerned - ever in [your] life again...[1]

One of the most significant sections in the *PGM* gives a key to the description of herbs and other items with flowery and alarming names. This key may be of use in interpreting some of the items that have made their way into the grimoires.

Codename in the papyri	Actual ingredient
blood [of a Titan]	wild lettuce
blood from a head	lupine
blood from a shoulder	bear's breach [a herb][2]
[blood] from the loins	camomile
blood of a goose	mulberry tree's milk [sap]
blood of a hamadryas baboon	blood of a spotted gecko
blood of a hyrax	truly [blood] of a hyrax[3]
blood of a snake	hematite
blood of an eye	tamarisk gall
blood of Ares	purslane
blood of Hephaistos	wormwood[4]
blood of Hestia	camomile
blood of Kronos	[sap?] of cedar
bone of an ibis	buckthorn
crocodile dung	Ethiopian soil
eagle	wild garlic[5]
fat from a head	spurge

[1] *PGM* IV. 286-95.
[2] Scarborough (1991) suggests *Acanthus mollis L.* or *Helleborus foetidus L.*
[3] Scarborough (1991) suggests the rock hyrax, *Procavia capensis.*
[4] Supposedly attractive to the gods.
[5] Scarborough (1991) tentatively suggests *Trigonella foenumgraecum* or *hellebore.*

Codename in the papyri	Actual ingredient
[fat] from the belly	earth-apple
[fat] from the foot	house leek
hair of a lion	'tongue' of a turnip[1]
hairs of a hamadryas baboon	dill seed
heart of a hawk	heart of wormwood
Kronos' spice	piglet's milk
man's bile	turnip sap[2]
physician's bone	sandstone
pig's tail	leopard's bane [a herb][3]
semen of a bull	egg of a blister beetle
semen of a lion	human semen
semen of Ammon	house leek
semen of Ares	clover
semen of Helios	white hellebore
semen of Hephaistos	fleabane
semen of Herakles	mustard-rocket[4]
semen of Hermes	dill
snake's 'ball of thread'	soapstone
snake's head	leech
tears of a hamadryas baboon	dill juice

Table 09: Egyptian code names for common ingredients used in magic in the *PGM*.

[1] Scarborough (1991) suggests the taproot of a turnip.

[2] Scarborough (1991) suggests *Brassica napus l.*

[3] Scarborough (1991) suggests 'scorpion tail,' a variety of leopard's bane (genus *boronicum*), or heliotrope.

[4] Scarborough (1991) suggests *Eruca sativa.*

Codename	Actual ingredient
blood of Isis = *asphos*	black horehound = *ballota nigra*
Fox testicles = *testiculus vulpis*	*Orchis*
Dog testicles = *testiculus canis*	*Orchis militaris.*[1]
Ram's horn	a herb like wild fennel
Wild onion	Asphodel or wild garlic[2]

Table 10: Egyptian code from other sources in the *PGM*.

After translation some of these ingredients may have still been taken literally.[3] This passage from the *PGM*, which has been tabulated in Table 09, is described as "interpretations which the temple scribes employed, from the holy writings, in translation," explaining that they have encoded the names of herbs and other materials, to protect the masses from practicing magic without a full understanding.[4]

These codenames for plants appear to have come originally from a Sumerian source.[5] In each case there seems to be very little intuitive connection between the code word and the actual item.

[1] Hermann Fischer, *Mittelalterliche Pflanzenkunde,* Hildesheim: Olms, 1976, p. 276.

[2] *PGM* xiv. 966-69.

[3] Betz and John Scarborough (1988) indicate that similar key lists can be found in *De succedaneis* which was included among the works of Galen; in C G Kuehn [ed.], *Claudii Galeni Opera Omnia*, vol. 19, 1830, pp. 721-47; and in the adapted version of this in Paulus Aegineta, *Corpus Medicorum Graecorum*, IX/2, I. L Heiberg, [ed.], vol. II, pp. 401-8; and also in Dioscorides' *Materia Medica*. Therefore these substitutions were more widespread in use than just in a magical context.

[4] The order has been changed to facilitate comparison of similar code-words.

[5] Reiner (1995), pp. 27-28.

Gods, Angels, Daimones, names of magicians, *nomina magica*	**Non-Roman *PGM* Nos.**	**Category**	**No. of lines**	**Betz Papyrus *PGM/PDM* Reference number**	**Objective/ Technique**	**Greek Headwords**
	4	Y	10	*PGM* IV. 286-295	Procedure for picking a plant	βοτανήαρσις[1] ἐπαοιδήν[2] - line 295
Kronos, Hera, Zeus, Helios, Hermes, Selene, Osiris, Ares Ouranos, Ammon, Mnevis, Pan, Athena, Good Daimon	4	Y	40	*PGM* IV. 2967-3006	Rite associated with picking a plant	βοτάναι λαμβάνονται[3]
Kronos, Hermes, Ares, Hestia, Helios, Herakles, Hephaistos, Ammon,	12	Y	44	*PGM* XII. 401-444	Glossary of terms used by the temple scribes, such as plant secret name, e.g. "blood of goose."	μεθηρμηνευμένα[4] βοτάνας –line 403
	14	Y	11	*PDM* xiv. 886-896	Herbs, for Sun and Moon	[Demotic] [n/h]
	14	Y	14	*PDM* xiv. 897-910	List of herbs and minerals	[Demotic] [n/h]
Total Y		**5**	**119**			

Table Y: Herbs and Plants.

1 Picking plants. Βοτάνη = plants or herbs.

2 Incantation, not 'charm.'

3 Picking plants/herbs.

4 Interpretations [of secret plant names].

Incenses

One of the oldest indications of the systematic use of incense to help in the invocation of planetary entities is a set of seven precious oils which was found on an Egyptian calcite oil tablet, with seven oil depressions and corresponding hieroglyphic labels, dating from the Old Kingdom.[1] The names of the oils inscribed on the tablet were: *seti-heb, heknu, sefeti, ni-chenem, tewat,* best *ash,* and best *tiehenu.* These oil names occur first on jar labels from the royal tombs of the first dynasty (3100-2857 BCE). Although the museum which displayed this object suggested they may have been connected with the process of embalming, the fact that they are a set of seven, with depressions holding quantities too small to be of any use in embalming a corpse, militates against this. It is more likely that they actually contained the incense oils of the seven planets.

One papyrus romanticises the generation of the key incenses by associating them with particular Egyptian gods:

> Horus cried. The water fell from his eye to earth and it grew. That is how dry myrrh came to be. Geb was sad on account of it. Blood fell from his nose to the ground and it grew. That is how pines came to be and resins came to be from their fluid. Then Shu and Tefnut cried exceedingly. The water from their eyes fell to the ground and it grew. That is how incense came to be.[2]

In the *PGM,* myrrh is particularly significant, as talismanic writing of any sort is almost always recommended to be written with perfumed myrrh ink. Apart from the Horus connection, myrrh was also intimately connected with Anubis, god of the Underworld:

> Open to me, O you of the underworld, O box of myrrh that is in my hand!... O box of myrrh which has four corners. O dog who is called Anubis by name, who rests on the box of myrrh, whose feet are set on the box of myrrh…[3]

Other incenses used include:

> …a wolf's eye, storax gum, cassia, balsam gum and whatever is valued among the spices...[4]

The invocation of Selene mandates the burning of an offering of Cretan storax on pieces of juniper wood.[5] It makes a clear distinction between the use of the rite for beneficent operations (using only incense) and for coercive operations

---

[1] Calcite oil tablet from Giza tomb item 4733 E, 19.5 cm x 9.2 cm x 2.2 cm found by the Harvard University Museum of Fine Arts in 1914. See D'Auria (1992), pp. 81-82.

[2] Papyrus Salt 825, translated in Derchain (1965), p. 137; Ritner (2008), p. 39.

[3] *PGM* xiv. 188.

[4] *PGM* I. 285-286.

[5] *PGM* IV. 2622-2707.

(using the same incense on the first and second day, but with less appealing *materia magica* on the third day):

> ***The beneficent offering, then, is:*** Uncut frankincense, bay, myrtle,[1] fruit pit,[2] stavesacre, cinnamon leaf, kostos. Pound all these together and blend with Mendesian[3] wine and honey, and make pills the size of beans.

Another passage suggests the following oil for a face anointment which will win favour and respect:

> …in first-quality lotus oil (or *tšps* oil) or moringa oil…;[4] add styrax to it together with first quality myrrh and seeds of "great-of-love" plant in a faience vessel... anoint your face with it; place the wreath in your hand; go to any place; [and be] among any people. It creates for you very great praise among them indeed.[5]

To consecrate a lead lamella, it was recommended that the magician cense the lamella with a mixture of myrrh, bdellium, styrax, aloes, thyme and [Nile] river mud.[6]

Roses and sumac are also mentioned as an offering.[7] One passage in the *PGM* lists incenses for doing virtuous things, such as:

> …storax, myrrh, sage, frankincense, and a fruit pit.[8]

Sulphur and the seeds of Nile rushes were used as incense to the Moon and Isis.[9] Key planetary incenses from the *PGM* are shown in Table 11.

As a general rule frankincense belongs to the solar gods, while myrrh belongs to the Moon (Selene).[10] Confirming this, frankincense was used at dawn and myrrh in the evening.[11] Plutarch claimed that in the temples myrrh was burned at midday, and *kyphi* at sunset.[12]

---

1 *Myrtus communis.*
2 The fruit pit represents nascent life, as it is the seed of a whole fruit tree.
3 From the city of Mendes in the Nile delta.
4 Βάλανος μυρεψική, *Moringa pterygosperma* or *Moringa aptera.* Moringa was used in cosmetics, cooking and pharaonic medicine. It is still popular in Africa and India as a food, and has a growing reputation worldwide as a supplement and alternative medicine.
5 *PDM* xiv. 330-333.
6 *PGM* VII. 429-458.
7 *PGM* IV. 2232.
8 *PGM* IV. 2870-2879.
9 *PGM* VII. 490-504.
10 LiDonnici (2001), p. 76.
11 *PGM* I. 42-195.
12 Plutarch, *Isis and Osiris,* 372d, 383c, 384c.

Greek god/ Planet	Incense	Botanical Source of the Resin	*Book of Jubilees* 160 BCE[1]	*PGM* c. 100 CE[2]
Kronos	Storax Styrax	*Styrax officinalis* (Liquid *amber orientalis* tree)	Stacte[3]	Styrax
Zeus	Tejpatra Tamaalpatra Indian Bay leaves	*Cinnamomum tamala* or *albiflorum*	Mixed spices[4]	Malabathron[5]
Ares	Costus Kostos	Root of *Costus Arabicus*, *Costus Speciosus, Saussurea lappa, Saussurea costus*	Costum	Kostos[6]
Helios	Frankincense Olibanum (oil of Frankincense)	*Boswellia cartierii* & *Boswellia thurifera*	Frankincense	Frankincense
Aphrodite	Spikenard	*Nardostachys grandiflora* or *Nardostachys jatamansi*	Nard	Indian nard
Hermes	Cassia Kasia	*Cinnamomum Cassia*	Galbanum	Cassia Galbanum
Selene	Myrrh	*Balsamodendron myrrha, Commiphora myrrha*	Myrrh	Myrrh

Table 11: The planetary incenses in the *PGM* and the *Book of Jubilees* showing continuity between Jewish and Egyptian sources.

---

1 Some scholars have dated this to 100 CE, thereby making it contemporary with the *PGM* passage.

2 *PGM* XIII. 16-22. These are the "secret incenses" of the planets. It adds "prepare sun vetch [Egyptian bean] on every occasion." They are listed in a different order, but without planetary correspondences in *PGM* XIII. 353-354.

3 Stacte or στακτή is defined as 'oil of myrrh' by Dioscorides.

4 Probably so specified because the translator did not know how to handle Malabathron.

5 Or Malabatrum. Leaves of *Cinnamomum tamala* or *C. albiflorum.* Liddell-Scott gives "the aromatic leaf of an Indian plant, the *betel* or *areca.*" See also Dioscorides 1.12; Galen 12.66; Pliny HN12.129; Horace *Odes* 2.7.8. The word is probably derived originally from the Sanskrit *tamāla-pattra.*

6 *Saussurea lappa* root.

5.0 The Equipment used in Graeco-Egyptian magic

Mention of specific items of magical equipment is dispersed throughout the *PGM,* mostly located in a separate section at the end of each rite, along with instructions for making phylacteries, inks, and incenses applicable to that particular operation. To get a better perspective on the equipment of Graeco-Egyptian magicians, it is useful to first examine the equipment preserved by a dynastic Egyptian magician.

The Equipment of an Egyptian Magician

In 1896 a Twelfth Dynasty[1] tomb near the Ramesseum at Thebes, excavated by Quibell, was identified as the tomb of a magician-priest by the nature of the papyri found therein,[2] all of which related to magic or magico-medicine.[3] Buried in the tomb were the usual types of tomb furnishings including two sorts of *ushabtis,* the magical servants often buried with the dead in Egypt. One sort was made of green faience and the other of unbaked clay painted yellow. There were also figures of the four sons of Horus, Mesti, Duamutef, Hapi and Qebesenef, who usually stood guard over the internal organs of the deceased, but also had a part to play in the restraining of spirits. However, in this tomb, these were different inasmuch as they were made of wax, not stone or pottery. Wax figures feature in magic from ancient through to modern times.

Inside the tomb was a wooden box measuring about 18″ x 12″ x 12″ covered with white plaster slip upon which was painted a black ink image of Anubis (who features in many spells in the *PGM,* and who might be considered as one of the magician's special gods). The contents of the magician's box were as follows:

1. Fragments of 23 papyri which included magical spells, magico-medical treatises, and the *Discourses of Sisobek.*
2. Four broken throwing- stick shaped ivory wands on which were carved a series of real and mythical animals. Wands have always been associated with magic, but only Egyptian wands were of this shape. See Figure 17.
3. Four deformed female dolls, two made from wood, and one from limestone, two missing their lower legs.[4] These would have been used in the same way that wax or clay dolls have been used by magicians ever since, to damage an enemy.

---

[1] Roughly 2000-1800 BCE.

[2] Most of the magical papyri of the *PGM* also came from tombs in the Thebes area.

[3] Quibell (1898).

[4] All probably used as fith-faths, or magical dolls.

4. A bronze uraeus crown tangled with a ball of hair, probably belonging to the magician. This crown was probably worn by the magician when identifying himself with a god, famous ruler or magician of the past, in order to impress the daimones, in the same way that later European grimoire magicians wore parchment crowns for the same purpose.[1] See Figure 13.

5. Seeds from the *dom* or *doum* palm.[2] These seeds may have been used for divination, just as they are in Ifa divination in sub-Saharan Africa, and in North African geomancy.[3]

6. A statue of Bestet, a goddess of magicians (or possibly a female magician), holding a snake wand in each hand. See Figure 14.

7. An ivory herdsman carrying a calf, an Hermaic image.[4]

8. A bundle of reed pens, for writing phylacteries and amulets.

9. Sundry amulets, beads and other minor utensils.[5]

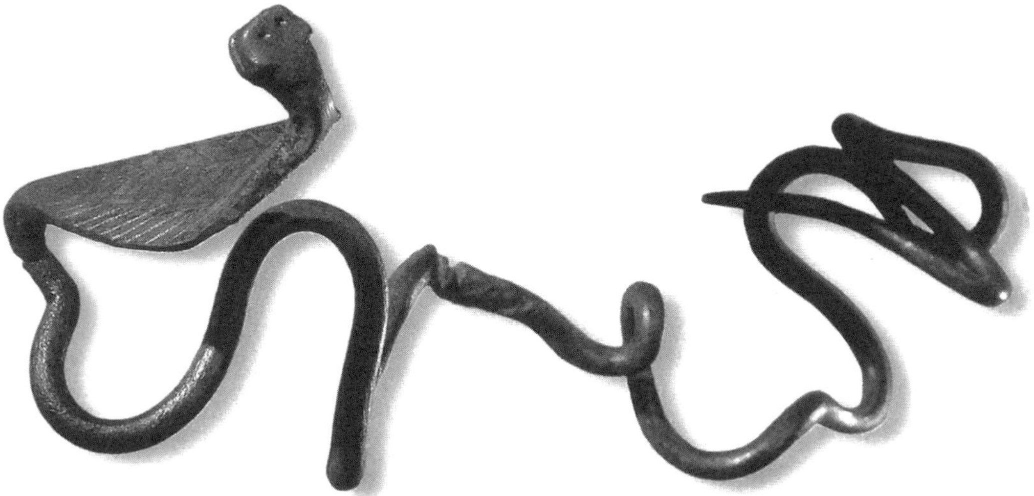

Figure 13: The serpent crown tangled with a ball of hair, part of the equipment of a magician, found in a tomb beneath the Ramesseum in western Thebes. This is sometimes mistakenly said to be a wand because Egyptian magicians did use serpent wands, but straighter ones.[6]

---

[1] The hair tangled in it suggests that it may have been removed from the magician's head post mortem, taking some of his hair with it.

[2] A tree that grew in Nubia and Egypt since ancient times.

[3] For details of seed use in Ifa divination see Skinner (1980, expanded in 2011), chapter 3. The Latin name of this plant is suggestive of the area around Thebes: *hyphaene thebaica*.

[4] See Ritner (2008), pp. 223-227 for more on such images.

[5] See Brier (1980), pp. 46-50 for the full description. See also Ritner (2008), p. 223.

[6] Copper alloy, Middle Kingdom, Fitzwilliam Museum, Cambridge.

Figure 14: Statue of Bestet with two metal snake wands.[1] Bestet is one of the few Egyptian goddesses ever portrayed naked.

The figure of Bestet, found in the same tomb, clearly illustrates the use of snake like metal wands by Egyptian magicians as well as by the goddess Bestet, who was intimately connected with magic.

Table of Evocation

The ancestor of the grimoire Table of Evocation can be seen in a passage from the *PGM*:

> ***The preparation for the operation:*** For a direct vision , set up a tripod and a table of olive wood or of laurel wood, and on the table carve in a circle these characters: [characters]. Cover the tripod with clean linen, and place a censer on the tripod. It is advantageous to place on the table a [hollow figurine] of Apollo [made] out of laurel wood. Engrave [on a lamella] of gold, of silver, or of tin these characters: [characters]. Place the lamella under the censer, near the wooden image, which was set up [at the same time as the] censer, and place [next to] the tripod a beaker or a shell containing [pure] water. In the

[1] Wood and copper alloy, Ramesseum tomb, Middle Kingdom. Manchester Museum.

> centre of the shrine, surrounding the tripod, inscribe on the floor with a white stylus the following character...[1] It is necessary to keep yourself pure for three days in advance. The shrine and the [tripod] must be covered. [If] you wish [to see], look inside, wearing clean [white] garments [and crowned] with a crown of laurel, which [is] on the head... [before the] invocation, sacrifice laurel to him [Apollo]...[2]

Note that olive or laurel wood is used, just as it is in late 18th century French grimoires. These tables of laurel or olive wood are often inscribed with specific characters, foreshadowing the elaborate Tables of Evocation found in the *Sepher Maphteah Shelomoh,*[3] the *Summa Sacre Magice,* and Dee's 16th century 'Table of Practice.'

The small table upon which offerings were made to the gods, the τραπέζιον, *trapezion* is sometimes mentioned alongside the *iynx* in the context of Classical Greek magic, and this may have been another ancestor of the Table of Evocation. Another example of a 3rd century Greek magician's kit found in Pergamon also included a bronze table and base.[4] Conjecturally this may have had the same use as the Graeco-Egyptian Table of Evocation.[5]

Figure 15: A third century Greek magician's equipment found in Pergamon in 1897, possibly a Table of Evocation with three Hekate figures, vowels and 'Celestial script.'[6]

---

[1] Missing in Preisendanz (1928), p. 44.

[2] *PGM* III. 282-409. The characters are a mixture of 'Celestial script' and Egyptian symbols.

[3] Gollancz & Skinner (2008), p. 42.

[4] Luck (1987), p. 19, from the detailed report in Wünsch, *Antikes Zaubergerät,* 1905, no. 2, p. 8.

[5] Not a talisman as suggested, as it has a base or ritual support attached to its centre. In addition the kit contained a large bronze nail with Greek letters on its flat sides, two bronze rings and three polished black stones inscribed with *nomina magica.*

[6] Berlin, Staatliche Museen zu Berlin, Antikensammlung. Misc. 8612, 6. 12cm width.

Wand

In ancient Egypt, according to Geraldine Pinch:

> Staffs of various kinds were standard symbols of office in Ancient Egypt, so magicians who wished to command demons and spirits naturally used them too. In the *Book of Exodus,* Pharaoh's magicians and the Hebrew leader Aaron are all able to turn their staffs into live snakes but Aaron's snake is said to have overcome and swallowed the others.[1]

When exiting Egypt, Moses used a rod or wand (מטך) to part the Red Sea. The magician's wand in the form of an elongated bronze cobra[2] survived in the 16th century BCE tomb in Thebes. This is almost certainly the type of wand used by Aaron and Pharaoh's magicians. The use of magician's snake wands therefore has a very long history. The use of a snake as a wand also correlates with the use of the snake as an ouroboros to form the protective floor circle.

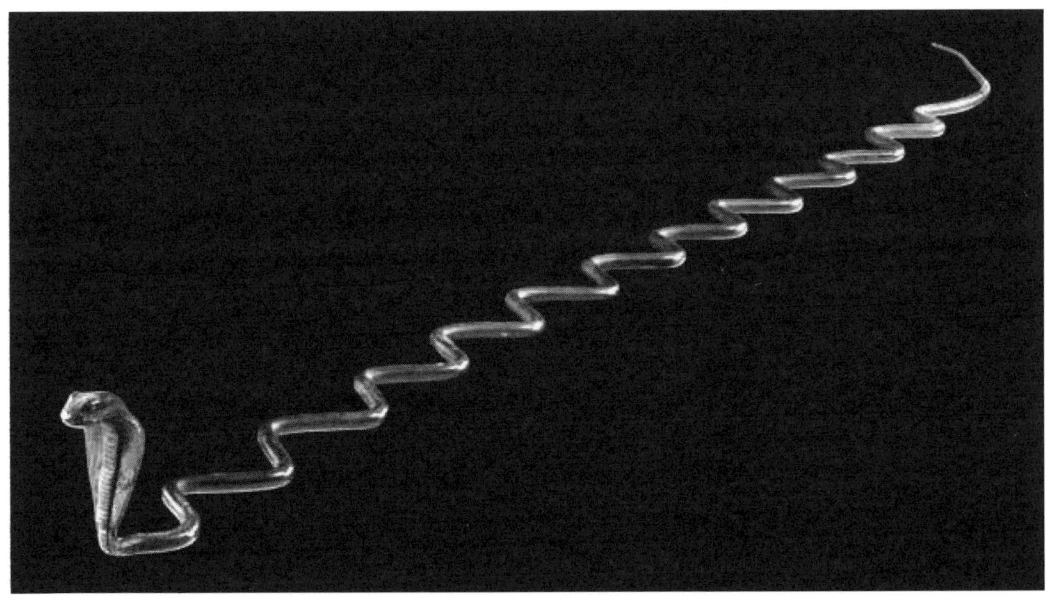

Figure 16: An Egyptian magician's bronze snake wand, from just prior to the Hellenisation of Egypt in 332 BCE. The 12 folds probably correspond to the 12 hours of the night.[3]

A different variety of ancient Egyptian ivory wands was shaped like the curved throwing sticks used by the ancient Egyptians to bring down birds. They are often found broken and carefully mended, and may therefore have been actually thrown as part of a rite. Other rods, which may have been used

---

[1] Pinch (2006), p. 78.

[2] Probably representing Weret Hekau, literally 'Great of Magic' who was the cobra goddess on whose form the wands have been modeled.

[3] Louvre.

as wands were made of glazed steatite or soapstone, heavily decorated with attached images of crocodiles, lions, turtles, frogs, etc. These wands were almost always made from the incisor of a hippopotamus, one of the most feared, unpredictable and deadly animals in Egypt. This animal is the form taken by Taweret (Thoeris), and the sacred animal of Seth, one of the magician's gods often invoked in the *PGM*. As the points of these wands are often worn, it seems possible that they were either thrown or maybe used for inscribing the protective circle on the ground.

Figure 17: Typical Egyptian 'throwing stick' wand, like the one found in the magician's tomb below the Ramesseum.[1] Note the figure of Bestet holding two snake wands.

The earliest Greek references to the wand probably occur in connection with Hermes who was characterised as the "god with the golden wand."[2] It may be a coincidence that the addition of a pair of intertwined serpents reflects the Egyptian use of the serpent wand.

There are references in the *PDM Supplement* to the use of an iron staff by Anubis, which may have also have been some kind of wand. In later grimoires, iron has always been something that spirits feared, which is part of the rationale behind the magician threatening the spirit with an iron sword.[3] An iron spear was used by Seth against the serpent Apep, and perhaps iron's rarity in ancient times contributed to its reputed ability to defeat evil.[4] The *PDM* passage instructs Anubis to "Give your iron staff which is in your hand

---

[1] British Museum 18175.

[2] *Odyssey*, X. 27. Circe's wand, or ῥάβδος, *rhabdos,* is also mentioned in *Odyssey*, X. 20. The same word is applied to Hermes' wand. Rhabdos was later personified as the 14th demon in the *Testament of Solomon.*

[3] Aleister Crowley owned an iron Janus-headed wand.

[4] Iron was rare in ancient Egypt and apparently until the first millennium BCE only imported or meteoric iron was available.

to the spirit!"[1] The passage continues with Anubis being instructed to send the spirit to the person the magician is trying to influence:

> Let him go to NN, whom NN bore. Let him stand before the image of the god who is great in his heart until he brings him to the road which NN is in, he [the spirit] seeking after him [NN]. And may you send a breathing spirit to NN so that he may stand before [him] in the image of the god who is great in his heart.[2]

This is a classic piece of magic, a theme repeated in many guises in later grimoires. Here the magician sends a "breathing spirit," in other words a living spirit, to enter NN's dreams and thereby influence his actions. The point of sending the spirit disguised as the god that NN most venerates ("the god who is great in his heart"), is to get NN to believe whatever it is the spirit says to him, which will of course have been of the magician's devising.

The Graeco-Egyptian wand was however more often made of ebony. In one Evocationary Lamp Skrying rite which incorporates an invocation of Apollo, the magician is instructed to:

> Hold an ebony staff in your left hand...[3]

There seems to have been a considerable significance attached to the hand in which the wand was held. In another invocation designed to obtain answers and revelations either during the epiphany of a god, or afterwards in lucid dreams, the ebony wand was held in the left hand whilst the right hand held a sprig of laurel (sacred to Apollo).[4]

In one Classical invocation of Apollo, the wand to be held in the right hand was the seven-leafed sprig of laurel.[5] This was used to summon both heavenly and chthonic deities. The seven characters to be written on the wand were the "seven characters for deliverance."

Another rite praises the qualities of this wand which also acts as a phylactery in this particular case:

> For this is the body's greatest protective charm [phylactery],[6] by which all [daimones] are made subject, and seas and rocks tremble, and daimones [avoid] the characters' magical powers which you are about to have. For it is the greatest protective charm [phylactery] for the rite, so that you fear nothing.[7]

---

[1] *PDM* Supplement 105.

[2] *PDM* Supplement 101-116.

[3] *PGM* I. 279.

[4] *PGM* I. 334-341.

[5] *PGM* I. 262. The laurel was used to make the crown that was placed on the head of the victor in the Apollonian/Olympic games, and so by implication, conferred high status upon the magician.

[6] φυλακτήριον.

[7] *PGM* I. 274-276.

Although the magician's wand is mentioned in the *PGM*, it is not illustrated. A possible exception occurs in an illustration which shows a drawing of a man wearing an Egyptian loin cloth (but described as naked in the rite) holding a knife or sword. The figure also wears a crown (with three poppy heads) and in his left hand he carries a wand or plant stalk. This is probably a laurel, a single stemmed wormwood, or a bulrush stem with a single leaf.

Figure 18: Graeco-Egyptian magician with sword wearing a crown surmounted by three poppies, holding a plant stem wand.

Sword

The iron sword has been used from time immemorial to threaten spirits. The oldest reference to using a sword to exorcise or threaten spirits comes from a Babylonian tablet which reads:

> When I perform [the Incantation][1] of Eridu,
> When I perform the Incantation…
> May a kindly Guardian stand at my side.
> By Ningirsu, master of the sword, mayest thou be exorcised!
> Evil Spirit, evil Demon, evil ghost, mayest thou be exorcised.[2]

Theophrastus wrote in *Inquiry into Plants*[3] in the 4th century BCE that before picking a mandrake it was usual to draw three circles around it with an iron sword. It is not clear at what point the practice of using an iron sword to draw

---

[1] Thompson's interpolation.
[2] Thompson (1903), p. 3, Third tablet.
[3] Hort (1916).

three circles round the magician before evoking was introduced, but it was probably related. There is no direct evidence in *PGM* of magicians using a sword to draw the circle of protection, but absence of such a description does not necessarily mean absence of the practice.

The theory behind the use of the sword is that spirits do not like iron, and an iron sword brandished in their direction is something to be feared, as it can reputedly damage them.[1] One of the three 'helpers' who rout demons in an early Aramaic formula is called σίδηρος, *sidēros* (Greek for 'iron').[2] Many more Latin grimoires mention a sword than those that mention a wand.

There are no explicit mentions of the use of a sword to constrain the spirits in the *PGM,* although one rite to secure love is entitled the 'Sword of Dardanos.' Dardanos was the founder of the Mysteries of Samothrace, and so may have been accounted a magician. One 'sword' is later revealed to be simply a list of angel names to invoke, rather than a physical sword:

> Monas[3] THOURIĒL MICHAĒL GABRIĒL OURIĒL MISAĒL IRRAĒL ISTRAĒL.[4]

The usage echoes that of the Jewish grimoire, the *Sword of Moses,* where the sword is also a list of angel and god names. Speculatively, this list of names may have been those originally engraved on an actual physical sword. If so then it seems more likely that the use of a physical sword sprang from a different tradition, perhaps as old as Mesopotamia, that valued sharp iron as a direct threat to the spirits.

Papyrus Reed Pen and Ink

Because the written word is such an important part of magic, so the surface it is written on must also be pure and consecrated. Obviously papyrus was the writing surface par excellence in dynastic Egypt. Papyrus came in different grades of quality, and hieratic papyrus,[5] the best quality, was recommended in the *PGM* for the written works of magic. Parchment (later discovered in Pergamon) was not as yet used.

Reed pens were used for writing on papyrus not only in a dynastic Egypt, but also in a Graeco-Egyptian context, and later in a Muslim context. Quill pens only came into use later, with the replacement of papyrus by parchment. For

---

1 Early Byzantine amulets (circa 5th century) featuring Solomon as the master of demons, on the same pattern as the rider-saint, were often made of haematite, a form of iron oxide, and therefore inimical to spirits.

2 See Spier (1993), pp. 35-36.

3 O'Neil in Betz translates this as 'One,' when it obviously has the technical meaning of the Unity as the prime mover of creation rather than a simple ordinal number.

4 *PGM* IV. 1815.

5 Χάρτης ἱερατικός.

magical use, just like the hazel wand, the reed pen must be cut with a single stroke. The consecrated knife is used for this purpose, and the operation was to be accompanied by an invocation or short prayer.

It is interesting that even though quills would have become the norm in Byzantium after the 7th century, five exemplars of chapter 20 of the Greek magical text, the *Hygromanteia,* still preserve the techniques for cutting and consecrating a reed pen in the 15th century, showing the antiquity of this line of transmission. However, the reed pen did not survive the later cultural transmission from Byzantium to the Latin grimoires of Western Europe.[1]

Smell was very important to the ancient Egyptians, so much so that they are depicted in wall paintings as wearing cones of fragrant material melting on top of their heads, to ensure they smelled attractive throughout the day.

Smell was an important issue in magic, with sweet incenses being used to attract spirits and sour ones like asafoetida used to drive them away. It is therefore not surprising that the other medium of communication with spirits, the written word, be it phylactery, talisman, pentacle, or lamen, had to be written with sweet smelling inks. The most common recommendation found in the papyri is to use 'myrrh ink' so that the gods or other spiritual creatures would take sufficient notice of the words so written.

The ink is sometimes made of cinnabar:[2]

> ...write on strips of papyrus made from a priestly scroll, with ink of cinnabar, juice of wormwood, and myrrh.[3]

This method of using incensed ink on consecrated papyrus or parchment endured for at least another 1500 years. Myrtle leaves are also mentioned as a writing surface, and single stemmed wormwood is often specified as an additive to the myrrh ink.[4]

To give the ink its necessary staining quality soot was often added. Apart from myrrh, soot and herbal matter, the other key ingredient in inks used in magic was blood. Sometimes just blood alone would be used as a writing material although it is ill adapted for such use. In King Pitys' first necromantic rite, the

---

[1] As the use of the reed pen petered out in Byzantium around the 7th century, this is circumstantial evidence for both an early date of composition of the *Hygromanteia,* and is also an example of the very conservative nature of magical handbooks.

[2] Mercuric sulphide. This is vermillion and it was used for the rubrification of text. As a compound of mercury, cinnabar is particularly appropriately as an ink, an instrument of communication. This material was also used in China for the same purpose, the creation of very important scrolls, and for magic talismans

[3] *PGM* IV. 2394.

[4] *PGM* IV. 2233-9. Single stemmed wormwood is ἀρτεμισίᾳ μονόκλωνος, *artemisia monoklōnos.*

writing is to be done with ink made from serpent's blood mixed with the soot from a goldsmith's workshop.[1] Soot was a standard ingredient of black inks since antiquity right up to the 19th century, for everyday as well as magical use. The soot from a goldsmith's workshop would presumably also have some traces of sublimed gold in it, and this echoes the usages of inks containing metals.

In King Pitys' second necromancy rite,[2] the writing is done with black ink on a leaf of flax or on a roll of hieratic papyrus. The ink is made from the blood of an ass[3] mixed with coppersmiths' soot. The leaf of flax is inscribed with a falcon's blood, mixed with goldsmiths' soot. The hieratic papyrus is to be inscribed with eel's blood mixed with acacia.[4] Another rite adds blood to the usual myrrh ink, but also specifies the spell must be written on leaves of flax.[5] A short necromantic rite for questioning corpses also attributed to King Pitys requires the *nomina magica* to be written on a flax leaf,[6] with a special ink made from:

> ...red ochre, burnt myrrh, juice of fresh wormwood, evergreen and flax.[7]

One rite for business success requires the words to be written on a male egg,[8] with the following ink:

> ***Drawing made with Typhonian ink***: A fiery red poppy, juice from an artichoke, seed of the Egyptian acacia, red Typhon's ochre,[9] unslaked quicklime, wormwood with a single stem, gum, rainwater.[10]

The egg is to then be buried "near the threshold where you live" or "in the house [where] I do my business."

Another use of ink consisted of writing a spell with "Hermaic myrrh ink," then washing the ink off the papyrus in order to drink it and thereby absorb the qualities of the spell. One example of this practice designed to strengthen the memory enjoins the practitioner to make the ink with spring water from seven springs, and drink the resulting ink wash on an empty stomach for seven days. The ingredients of this ink are:

> Myrrh troglitis,[11] 4 drams; 3 karian figs, 7 pits of Nikolaus dates, 7 dried pinecones,

1 *PGM* IV. 2006-2125.
2 *PGM* IV. 2006-2125.
3 An indication of Seth/Typhon.
4 Presumably acacia ash.
5 *PGM* XIXb. 1-3.
6 Flax, which was extensively cultivated in ancient Egypt, was associated with the dead and necromancy. Pictures of flowering flax have been found on the walls of tombs in Thebes.
7 *PGM* IV. 2140-44.
8 Presumably a fertilised egg, or maybe a code word for some other item.
9 Possibly the blood of an ass.
10 *PGM* XII. 96-106.
11 Possibly fossilised myrrh. See Betz (1996), p. 5.

> 7 piths of the single-stemmed wormwood,[1] 7 wings of the Hermaic ibis,[2] spring water. When you have burned the ingredients, prepare them and write.[3]

Another typical aromatic ink recipe involved similar food items:

> Preparation of the ink: 3 dried figs, 3 stones of Nicolaus date,[4] 3 fragments of wormwood, and 3 lumps of myrrh; [mix together, then] after pulverizing them, [write] the following formula.[5]

The practice of washing the ink off the writing surface and drinking the resultant solution occurs as far afield as in Taoist magic, as well as in the Bible. In the latter case the solution is drunk as a way of determining the truth, and enforcing a curse as a penalty, if the subject has sworn falsely. Here it is referred to as the 'water of bitterness':

> Then the priest shall put these curses in writing, and wash them off into the water of bitterness. He shall make the woman drink the water of bitterness that brings the curse, and the water that brings the curse shall enter her and cause bitter pain... when he has made her drink the water, then, if she has defiled herself and has been unfaithful to her husband, the water that brings the curse shall enter into her and cause bitter pain, and her womb shall discharge, her uterus drop, and the woman shall become an excration among her people.[6]

The Maskelli formula for revealing answers in a dream, uses a similar ink for writing upon both papyrus and cloth:

> ...single-stemmed wormwood, vetch, 3 pits of Nicholaus date palms, 3 Karian dried figs, soot from a goldsmith,[7] 3 branches of a male date palm, sea foam.[8]

For invocations of specific gods, specific inks were used, just as specific incenses were burned. For example, drawing an image of Anubis on a papyrus for magical purposes requires the correct ink, in this case mixed with "the blood of a black dog."[9]

Another ink also using myrrh and wormwood is made as follows:

> In a purified container burn myrrh and cinquefoil and wormwood; grind them to a paste, and use them [as an ink].[10]

Cinquefoil has an enduring place amongst the herbs used in European grimoires.

---

[1] Sweet wormwood.

[2] The association of Hermes and Thoth (the ibis) with the art of memory is obvious.

[3] *PGM* I. 232-247.

[4] Niclaus/Nikolaus/Nicholas is spelled inconsistently in Betz.

[5] *PGM* VII. 993-1009.

[6] Numbers 5:23-27. *New Revised Standard Version.*

[7] Presumably containing tiny flecks of gold.

[8] *PGM* IV. 3172-3208.

[9] *PDM* Supplement 113.

[10] *PGM* II. 35-37.

Another ink formula, for an operation involving the god Besas:

> Take red ochre [and blood] of a white dove, likewise of a crow, also sap of the mulberry, juice of single-stemmed wormwood,[1] cinnabar, and rainwater; blend all together, put aside and write with it and with black writing ink…[2]

A very similar ink formula is also associated with the god Besa,[3] which confirms that the ink ingredients are conditioned by the nature of the god associated with the rite:

> ***This is the ink with which you* draw** [the figure]: Blood of a crow, blood of a white dove, lumps of incense, myrrh, black writing ink, cinnabar, sap of mulberry tree, rain-water, juice of single-stemmed wormwood and vetch.[4]

Garments

The act of claiming to be some famous personage, god or magician (part of the standard armoury of magicians in all ages) was assisted by the wearing of appropriate garments. It follows the tradition, which recurs again in the *Key of Solomon,* of dressing up as someone imposing, such as a prophet, or Solomon, in order to awe the spiritual creatures invoked.

Egyptian priests and magicians wore linen, and no clothing made of animal products such as wool. Strangely the High Priest or *sem*-priest wore a leopard skin. It is also likely that the *sem*-priest was amongst the most learned in the temple (and therefore more likely to practise magic). He inhabited the *per-ankh* or House of Life, a combined library, scriptorium and college, in which priests would perform magic, interpret dreams and make amulets, for clients who paid for them. It will be seen later in the section on amulets ('A' and 'A2') that the production of these items for clients makes up numerically (if not volumetrically) a large part of the *PGM.*

The skin of any big cat, especially a lion, was held in awe, as it related to the fierce goddess Sekhmet. Sekhmet also had associations with magic.[5] High Priests of Sekhmet were often associated with magic, such as Heryshefnakht, who was both Chief of Magicians and High Priest of Sekhmet. On the reverse of the Edwin Smith Surgical Papyrus (which dates from 1700 BCE) the title of one rite refers to "the demons of disease, the malignant spirits, messengers of Sekhmet,"[6] which identifies this goddess also as a ruler over evil spirits. If that

---

[1] ἀψίνθιον, ἀρτεμισίᾳ, *absinthium.*

[2] *PGM* VII. 222-249.

[3] Another spelling of the same god.

[4] *PGM* VIII. 70-72.

[5] The House of Life at Edfu, which was occupied by priests and scribes dealing with magic, had a library list of papyri on an interior wall. One of the papyri on this list, probably dealing with magic, was entitled the *Book of Appeasing Sekhmet.*

[6] Breasted (1930), p. 477.

is so, then wearing a belt made of her animal's skin conferred a certain authority on the magician when dealing with such spirits. The leopard skin of the Egyptian priest and the lion nemyss[1] is met with within the Latin grimoire tradition in the form of a belt made of lion skin. This practice lasted through to the 17th century, and a belt of lion skin is recommended in the 1641 *Goetia*: a girdle of "Lyons skin 3 Inches broad."[2] Even today such belts are sold online to aspiring magicians. I think it is quite clear that this is a continuation of the same ancient Egyptian tradition, echoing the practice of Egyptian priests. In modern times MacGregor Mathers, in imitation of the Egyptian magicians, wore a leopard skin when conducting Golden Dawn 'Rosicrucian' rituals in Paris in the early 20th century.[3]

I suggest that this practice originally related to Sekhmet, but later it may simply have become part of the dress of the magician designed to cower the spirits. The thinking being that any man who had mastered a lion, Sekhmet's animal (as he was wearing its skin) must truly be powerful, and so the belt of lion skin would be like wearing a magical 'badge of courage' and authority.

This perhaps explains why mere paper crowns, or flimsy lamens in later grimoires, were able to do the job imputed to them. An ivy wreath likewise gave the magician a semblance of status as a hero or a senator:

> Crown yourself with dark ivy while the sun is in mid-heaven, at the fifth hour [after sunrise], and while looking upward, lie down naked on the linen, and order your eyes to be completely covered with a black band…[4]

One description of an Evocationary Lamp Skrying rite gives details of the prescribed clothing:

> Whenever you seek [to do ritual] divinations, be dressed in the garb of a prophet, shod with fibres of the *doum* palm[5] and your head crowned with a spray from an olive tree – but the spray should have a single-shooted garlic tied around the middle. Clasp a pebble numbered 3663[6] to your breasts,[7] and in this way make your invocation.[8]

It is interesting that Bainchōōch should be chosen, and that garlic should be used.

---

[1] A typical Egyptian cloth headdress.
[2] Peterson (2001), p. 47.
[3] A photo of him so dressed exists and has been reproduced in a number of books.
[4] *PGM* IV. 171-174.
[5] This palm was also listed as one of the items in the Egyptian magician's box mentioned in chapter 5.0.
[6] The isopsephic numeration of the letters of Bainchōōch.
[7] As a phylactery.
[8] *PGM* IV. 930-938.

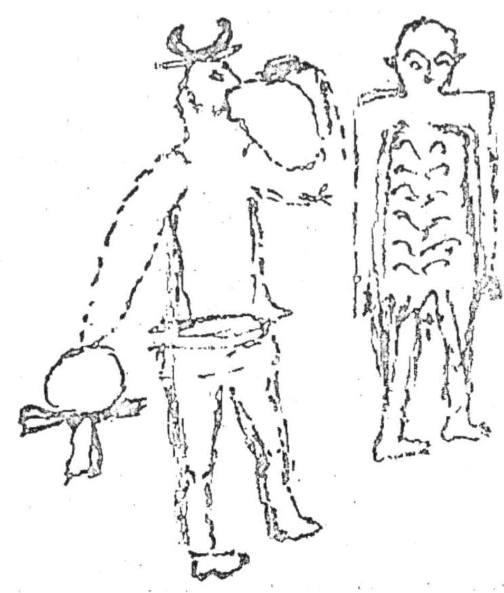

Figure 19: A horned Bainchōōch daimon holding an ankh.[1] He is clearly horned and accompanied by a figure that is probably wearing an animal skin.

The Symbola of the Gods

Egyptian gods are often portrayed with the symbols of their power (like the Pharaoh). Typical *symbola* (σύμβολα) are the throne of Isis, the feather of Maat, the eye of Horus, the crook and flail of Osiris or the cow horns of Hathor. Greek gods also carry indications of their power, like the playthings of Dionysus (e.g. the *iynx* or spinning top), the caduceus wand of Hermes or the laurel of Apollo. The use of laurel wreaths in magic as well as in religious usage occurs in the *PGM*:

> While praying, wear a garland of laurel of the following description: Take 12 laurel twigs; make a garland of 7 sprigs, and bind the remaining five together and hold them in your right hand while you pray, and lie down to sleep holding this…[2]

The purpose of that particular rite was to secure a dream revelation from the god, and the purpose of the laurel wreath was to identify the magician with the god.

In one ritual designed to invoke the 'Egyptian Selene,' the instruction is to "Heed your sacred symbols, and give a whirring sound…"[3] This is likely to refer to one specific concrete tool of magic (especially in the context of the rest of the sentence) rather than to abstract symbols. As Betz writes: "the 'symbols' of the gods were thought not to be mere signs representing them but objects

---

[1] *PGM* IX *verso*. Illustration from Preisendanz (1931), Vol. 2, plate 7.

[2] *PGM* II. 27-33.

[3] *PGM* VII. 884.

and formulae by which they could be controlled." Betz suggests that this is the sound of the sistrum of Hathor.[1] The hiss and clatter of the sistrum does not seem to me to match the sound of 'whirring.' The *iynx* spinning top, which reputedly made a whirring sound, is a much more likely fit.

A passage in the *PGM* lists out some of the *symbola* of Korē's power:[2]

> ...do this task for me,
> Mare, Korē, dragoness, lamp, lightning flash,
> Star, lion, she-wolf, AĒŌ ĒĒ.
> A sieve, an old utensil, is your[3] symbol,
> And one morsel of flesh, a piece of coral,
> Blood of a turtledove,[4] hoof of a camel,
> Hair of a virgin cow, the seed of Pan,
> Fire from a sunbeam, colt's foot, spindel tree,
> Boy love, bow drill, a gray-eyed woman's body
> With legs outspread, a black sphinx's pierced vagina:
> All of these are the symbol[a] of my power.[5]

Some of these may also be code words for some other, often more innocuous but less poetic ingredient (see chapter 4.7).

During the invocation of the Moon goddess (Nephthys/Selene) the magician is told to show:

> ...in your right hand a [single-stemmed] wormwood and in your left a snakeskin, and recite the [specified] formulas [and ask] what you wish [for], and it will happen.[6]

All the inscribed clothing of the magician (including the crown) might be construed as a form of protection, but it is more likely that these inscriptions and symbology (such as the lion skin belt) were meant to impress the spirit with the power or royalty (symbolised by the crown) of the magician, so that the spirit might more readily take orders from that magician.

---

[1] Betz (1996), p. 79.

[2] This goddess morphed into a demon in the grimoire *The Book of the Sacred Magic of Abramelin the Mage*. See Mathers (1900).

[3] Corrected.

[4] Particularly popular with Jewish magicians, a "symbolic" ingredient that lasted well into the 17th century.

[5] *PGM* IV. 2303-2310.

[6] *PGM* III. 702-705.

6.0 Graeco-Egyptian Magical Techniques

In order to understand Graeco-Egyptian magic it is necessary to analyse and categorise the rites. What initially looks like a confusing mass of heterogeneous material in the English translation is considerably clearer in the original Greek, where specific headwords are often used by the scribe in the first line of each rite to identify its type and purpose. For example Evocationary Bowl Skrying or Vessel Inquiry operations will almost always be identified as *šn-hne* in Demotic, whilst operations designed to cause love or lust will be identified in Greek with up to seven possible headwords, according to the exact technique used to influence the behaviour of the subject or person desired. These headwords range from ἀγωγή (*agōgē*) which is designed to draw the subject to the magician, ἀγώγιμον (*agōgimon*) which is designed to bind the subject's will, φίλτρον (*philtron*) which uses potions and salves, to ἀγρυπνητικόν (*agrupnētikon*) which proceeds by torturing the subject with hunger or insomnia till they give in. To translate all of these terms simply as "spell" or even "love spell" does not do justice to the fine precision of Graeco-Egyptian magical terminology.

The almost 40 key headwords defining these practices are listed in Table 13, demonstrating how this wide range of techniques has been identified.[1] In the Demotic texts these headwords are often rubricated, or written in red, showing the importance attached to them by the scribe. Some of these appear in bold face in Betz but where they have been simply translated as "spell" are useless for the purpose of identifying the actual technique used. Essentially the ancient Greek language of the *PGM* was much richer in esoteric terms than any modern European language.

Following this categorisation to its logical conclusion reveals that the original scribes have been quite systematic in their categorisation, using either the method or the objective as their criterion.[2] Although upon first sight the following may appear to be an overly ridged and contrived division of the rites, an examination of the original Greek/Demotic text fully justifies this approach.

It was the habit of the original scribes to clearly designate the type of magical operation at the beginning of each rite, as magic for them was a system of techniques, not just an amorphous mass of "spells." I have therefore added each of the relevant Greek/Demotic headwords to the last column of each of the 41 Rite Tables, to clearly demonstrate that these divisions are not arbitrary or imposed, but part of the system used by the original scribes/magicians.

---

1 These headwords are spelled exacly as they appear in the Greek text, rather than being presented in their lexical form, so that the exact usage can be seen.

2 Where a particular rite has both an identifiable method and a categorised objective, then it is classified under the method, rather than the objective.

Each of these categories has then been assigned an arbitrary alphabetic code for convenience of analysis. A full list of the codes together with a count of the number of instances (and the number of lines) will be found in Table 12. Table 13 gives the percentage breakdown of each type (in terms of both line count and number of instances) with the Greek headwords and their basic meaning.

Greek Headwords

The alphabetically coded Rite Tables list out every single passage in the *PGM, PDM and Supplementum Magicum*[1] and allocates them to one category or another. This taxonomy relies in the first instance upon the original scribe's Greek or Demotic categorisation. Where this is missing (mostly due to damage to the papyrus rather than scribal carelessness) a repeat of the headword in the body of the rite, or the precise content of each rite is used to ascertain the category. The specific Greek headwords which exactly identify the type of rite are given in Table 13. This headword is frequently obscured by the English translation, which will commonly use an imprecise equivalent like 'charm' or 'spell' rather than attempting an exact translation of the Greek name for the technique. These headwords are listed in the last column of each Rite Table. If a significant word appears further down in the body of the rite, then this occurrence is also mentioned with its line number.

In the course of this analysis, three large sections of the papyri were seen to be complete books within themselves, as indeed has been identified by other scholars.[2] These relate to the Mysteries and initiation rather than magic and have been categorised as 'M.' Rites categorised as 'Z' are technically φαρμακεῖα, (*pharmakeia*) practices concerned with drugs, ointments and poisoning, also not strictly magic.

A few rites are listed by objective rather than technique, such as Health 'H.' Where one of these operations utilises a specific technique (e.g. amulets or *defixiones*) the rite has been allocated to that technique category rather than to the objective (e.g. 'A' – Amulets or 'D' – *Defixiones* rather than 'H' - Health), as technique rather than outcome is more germane to the objectives of this book. If a rite uses an amulet but has health as its objective, it will be categorised as an Amulet ('A' or 'A2') rather than under Health ('H'). In these cases the rite will not be duplicated in the objective section. In practice few conflicts of identification arise.

In the case of amulets ('A' and 'A2') the Greek title will often begin with the preposition πρὸς , *pros* (for) followed by the objective or name of the disease.[3]

---

[1] Plus a selection of significant amulets from Kotansky (1994).

[2] For example the *Monas* in *PGM* XIII, lines 1-733, the *Tenth Hidden Book of Moses* in *PGM* XIII. 734-1077, and the so-called *Mithras Liturgy* in *PGM* IV lines 475-829.

[3] See Kotansky (1988), p.65.

Fortuitously Amulets 'A', 'A2' and 'H' Health are the only cases where this preposition is used at the very beginning of the first line, and so acts as a special form of headword.

Where there are (in a few cases) clearly two techniques used in a particular rite, the rite will be listed under the main technique, but a second code will appear in the Code column, and a cross-reference will appear in the minor table. Where more than three techniques are identified as used in one procedure (this occurs in only five cases) the rite is listed at the end under Composite Rites ('Ω').

Very fragmentary or very short formulae with no identifiable method or objective have been passed over without comment, but are listed in Appendix 2, for the sake of completeness. For all of these the amount of material available for analysis of objective, method or implement is minimal or non-existent. The point of listing these in Appendix 2 is to show that every single scrap of Graeco-Egyptian magic has been examined, categorised and tabulated.

Other techniques which are universal (like the ritual use of incense or invocation, neither of which appears as a headword at the beginning of any rite) will not be used as a category identifying criteria, but have been considered in some detail in chapter 4 and chapter 5.

Aside from the rite specific headwords in the *PGM* the general Greek terms for a magical operation or rite were all very practical and include πρᾶξις (*praxis*), literally 'action, transaction or exercise'; πραγματεία (*pragmateia*) literally 'operation'; and οἰκονομία (*oikonomia*) literally 'management' or 'a magical plan.'[1]

The word '*logos*' has many meanings in Greek, and the identification by St John with the creative word or Jesus Christ is more of a literary flourish rather than a core meaning of that word. In the *PGM, logos* usually indicates an invocation. In fact tracking the occurrence of this word in the so-called *Mithras Liturgy* has thrown new light on the way this rite is sequenced (see chapter 7.2).

Λαβών (*labōn*) which means 'to take,' as in taking ingredients, is often encountered at the beginning of a magical or medical recipe which requires a list of ingredients, but is not a headword *per se*. Likewise ἐπικαλοῦμαι, (*epikaloumai*), 'to summon' or invoke will sometimes be found at the beginning of a rite, but in itself does not constitute a headword.

Table 12 gives an overview of the analysis, dividing it by broad themes. This Table also acts as a more detailed contents list for the following chapters. Table 13 is an alphabetical listing of each of the rite types with the precise identifying headword (and its translation) and the percentages of each category.

---

1 Pachoumi (2007), pp. 15-16. Pachoumi adds μυστήριον (*mystērion*), but that term relates to the Mysteries rather than to magic.

Chapter & Code	Category of Rite	Number of rites	Total Number of lines	Average Number of lines per rite
4	***Preparation***			
C	Calendrical Considerations (see chapter 4.2)	9	118	13
Y	Herbs and Plants (see chapter 4.7)	5	119	24
6.1	***Magical Equipment***			
S	Statues, Magical	10	368	37
R	Rings and Gemstones, Magical	8	295	37
6.2	***Words Written & Worn***			
A	Amulets for general protection	60	427	8
A2	Amulets Personalised for named Clients	32	591	19
T	Talismans, general	19	338	18
T2	Victory Talismans	11	137	13
T3	Restraining Anger Talismans	11	160	15
T4	Binding or Coercion Talismans	6	85	14
U	Phylacteries	7	171	25
U2	Phylacteries (integral parts of another rite)	*28*	*210*	*8*
6.3	***Specific Magical Methods & Objectives***			
H	Health	44	327	8
I	Invisibility	4	35	9
L-L7	Love Rites of Attraction	93	1697	19
O	Homeric magic and divination	10	286	29
K	Foreknowledge and Memory	9	244	27
X	Other Magical Procedures	35	423	12
Z	'Evil Sleep,' Blindness and Death	13	74	6
6.4	***Skrying and Dreams***			
B	Evocationary Bowl Skrying/Vessel Inquiry	18	430	24
E	Evocationary Lamp Skrying	15	483	32

Chapter & Code	Category of Rite	Number of rites	Total Number of lines	Average Number of lines per rite
V	Visions and Dream Revelation	27	577	21
V2	Sending Dreams	11	209	19
6.5	***Dealing with Divinity***			
F	Face-to-Face Encounter with a God	5	232	46
G	God's Arrival	14	589	42
G2	Invocation of a god	17	580	34
G3	Invocation of the Bear asterism goddess	5	265	53
W	Prayers	5	216	43
J	Hymns (as integral parts of other rites)	*33*	*846*	*26*
6.6	***Dealing with Daimones***			
P	*Paredros* or Assistant Daimon	5	349	70
Q	Daimonic Possession and Exorcism	4	200	50
6.7	***Dealing with the Dead***			
N	Necromancy	5	130	26
D	*Defixiones*	26	1300	50
6.8	***Composite Rites***	7	672	96
7.0	***The Mysteries***			
M	Mysteries and Initiation Rites	6	1451	242
App. 2	Excluded Fragments	29	269	10
	Total	585	13,847	24

Table 12: Analysis and statistics for Graeco-Egyptian magic in chapter and thematic order. The occurrence tallies measure numbers of rites, quantity of lines, and average line length.[1]

[1] Figures in *italics* are not added into the total, as they are already parts of other rites already totalled. Totals differ from the same Table in my thesis because of the addition of data from the *Supplementum Magicum*.

Code	Category of Rites Procedure/Objective	Percent of *PGM* rites	Percent of *PGM* lines	Rubricated Greek Headwords or key word	Literal Translation of Greek Headwords
A	Amulets	15.7	7.4	πρὸς (*pros*)	for…
A2	Amulets personalised for named client				
B	Evocationary Bowl Skrying/ Vessel Inquiry	3.1	3.2	λεκανομαντεία (*lekanomanteia*), *šn-hne (shen ben)*	bowl skrying vessel inquiry
C	Calendrical Considerations	1.5	0.9	κύκλος (*kuklos*)	circle/cycle [of the heavens]
D	*Defixiones*	4.5	9.4	κατάδεσμος (*katadesmos*), νεκυδαίμων	*defixio,* ghost of a dead man
E	Evocationary Lamp Skrying	2.6	3.5	λύχνου (*lychnou*), *wᶜ šn* [Demotic] λυχνομαντείον (*lychnomanteia*),	lamp lamp skrying
F	Face-to-Face Encounter with a God	0.9	1.7	αὔτοπτος (*autoptos*)	self-revealed (by the god)
G	God's Arrival	6.2	10.4	συστάσις (*systasis*), *pḥ-nṯr* [Demotic]	god's arrival
G2	Invocation of a god			-	-
G3	Invocation of the Bear goddess			Ἀρκτικὴ (*Arktikē*)	Bear goddess/ asterism
H	Health	7.6	2.4	*pẖre.t, mt.t a* [Demotic]	prescription, magical formula
I	Invisibility	0.7	0.3	ἀμαύρωσις (*amaurōsis*)	darkening/ making invisible
J	Hymns (as integral parts of another rite)	*5.7*	*6.2*	ὕμνος	hymn or ode in praise of god
K	Foreknowledge and Memory	1.5	1.8	μνημονική (*mnēmonikē*) πρόγνωσις (*prognōsis*)	memory foreknowledge
L	Love Rites of Attraction or 'Love's Leash'	15.9	12.3	ἀγωγή (*agōgē*)	leading or drawing (love)
L2	Love Fetching			ἀγώγιμον (*agōgimon*)	Fetching the lover, or love tie
L3	Love Potions, worked at close quarters			φίλτρον (*philtron*)	love potions and salves
L4	Love Binding			φιλτροκατάδεσμος (*philtrokatadesmos*)	love binding
L5	Love Enforced by hunger or insomnia			ἀγρυπνητικόν (*agrupnētikon*)	love enforced by insomnia/hunger
L6	Love Separation			διάκοπος (*diakopos*)	separation of lovers/friends
L7	Other Love Rites			-	-

Code	Category of Rites Procedure/Objective	Percent of *PGM* rites	Percent of *PGM* lines	Rubricated Greek Headwords or key word	Literal Translation of Greek Headwords
M	Mysteries and Initiation Rites	1.0	10.5	μυστήρια (*mystēria*), τελετή (*teletē*)	the Mysteries, initiation into the Mysteries
N	Necromancy	0.9	1.0	νεκυδαίμων (*nekudaimōn*)	ghost of a dead man
O	Homeric magic and divination	1.7	2.1	ὁμηρομαντεῖον (*homēromanteion*)	Homeric verses rite/oracle
P	*Paredros* or Assistant Daimon	0.9	2.6	πάρεδρος (*paredros*)	assistant daimon/ familiar spirit
Q	Daimonic Possession and Exorcism	0.7	1.5	δαίμονε (*daimone*)	daimon
R	Rings & Gemstones, Magical	1.4	2.2	δακτύλιον (*daktulion*), *w'gswr*	[seal] ring
S	Statues, Magical	1.7	2.7	[στοιχεῖα (*stoicheia*)]	magical statue, shadow
T	Talismans, general	8.1	5.2	στήλη (*stēlē*), τέλεσμα (*telesma*)	lamella (or its text), talisman
T2	Victory Talismans			νικητικὸν (*nikētikon*)	[talisman for] victory
T3	Restraining Anger Talismans			θυμοκάτοχον (*thymokatochon*)	binding anger
T4	Binding or Coercion Talismans			κάτοχος (*katochos*)	restraining, holding down
U	Phylacteries	1.2	1.3	φυλακτήριον (*phylaktērion*)	[magician's] phylactery
U2	Phylacteries (integral parts of another rite)	*4.8*	*1.5*		
V	Visions and Dream Revelation	6.5	5.7	ὀνειραιτητόν (*oneiraitēton*)	dream revelation
V2	Sending Dreams			ὀνειροπομπὸς (*oneiropompos*)	sending dreams
W	Prayers	0.9	1.6	εὐχή (*euchē*)	prayer
X	Other Magical Procedures	6.0	3.1	-	-
Y	Herbs and Plants	0.9	0.9	[βοτάνη (*botanē*)]	herbs/plants
Z	'Evil Sleep,' Blindness and Death	2.2	0.5	*nktk bin* [Demotic only]	catalepsy and death
Ω	Composite Rites	1.2	4.9	-	-
-	Excluded Fragments	5.0	1.9	-	-
	Total	100.5%	101.1%		

Table 13: Rite Types with identifying headwords and their percentages by line and rite.

6.1 Magical Equipment Carved and Cast

Statues, Magical - στοιχεῖα (*stoicheia*) (S)[1]

Magical statues have been known in many cultures, from the tomb servant *ushabtis* to the giant statues of ancient Egypt, or the στοιχεῖα of Greek magic. According to Gager the earliest mention of making a wax image of a personal enemy designed "to be buried in a grave for harsh treatment by Osiris" dates from the Middle Kingdom (c. 2133-1786 BCE).[2]

The point of any magical statue was to enliven them or ensoul them with a resident spiritual creature, be it a god, daimon or a minor spirit. One of the standard magical procedures related to magical statues was the opening of their mouth, or the introduction of breath, to enliven them, a procedure derived from the ancient Egyptian practice of ensouling statues. The Opening of the Mouth also relates to the last step in the embalming process, opening the mouth of the deceased so he could 'breathe' in the afterlife. The magical statues or *stoicheia* may originally have developed from temple statues, or possibly from the speaking statues of the Egyptian temples.

One very clear example of the creation of a magical statue in the *PGM* was designed for a very modern purpose, bringing customers into a business premise.[3] This particular Graeco-Egyptian type of statue had obviously been often produced, as it even had a pet name, "the little beggar." Its function is translated by R. F. Hock simply as a 'charm,' but the original Greek is a very specific word: κατακλητικόν (*kataklētikon*). The suffix '-ῖκον' indicates an ikon, image or statue. The rest of the word is derived from κατακαλέω, to summon, to call upon, to appeal to. A more precise translation would therefore have been "a statue that summons [customers]" rather than just a 'charm.'

This statue, according to the instructions, is to be made of a single block of hollowed juniper made in the likeness of a man:

> ...having his right hand in the position of begging and having in his left a bag and staff. Let there be around the staff a coiled snake, and let him be dressed in a girdle and standing on a sphere that has a coiled snake, like Isis...and have an asp covering the top as a capital.[4]

---

[1] Details of the alphabetic coding of every passage in the *PGM* can be seen in Table 12. Each code has a dedicated Rite Table showing the location of all rites relevant to that code.

[2] Gager (1992), p. 15.

[3] Such animated statues, particularly those of a golden cat with a mechanical paw beckoning potential customers are a common feature of business premises throughout S. E. Asia. Although there is no suggestion of cultural transmission, it is sometimes enlightening to find instructive parallel magical usages that have survived longer in Asia than in Europe.

[4] *PGM* IV. 2380-2389.

The snake is of course the Agathos Daimon, the good daimon, as is clearly confirmed by the inscriptions which the practitioner is enjoined to write on various parts of the statue.

In relation to the Agathos Daimon, the author makes reference to Epaphroditos who suggests various alternative names for the inscription. However, I believe the image is "Harpon Knouphi,"[1] a form of Harpocrates Chnoubis, which also explains the presence of the snakes. Despite the fact that Betz remarks that "nothing is known about him," this remark probably refers to Epaphroditos (20/25-95 CE), Nero's secretary. As unlikely as this may seem, Epaphroditos was the owner of a slave who was Epictetus of Hierapolis, a well-known Stoic philosopher. He in turn had been taught by Musonius Rufus, who was reputed to have written letters to Apollonius of Tyana. Whether he did or not is not important. What is important is the reputed indirect connection between Epaphroditos and the most famous magician of the age, which considerably increases the likelihood that it was this Epaphroditos who was most able to comment cogently on that particular magical procedure.[2]

The consecration of this statue is complex, and includes the sacrifice of a whole animal, which has been variously suggested to be a wild ass or a wild ram.[3] But both those interpretations are based on adding modifiers to the existing word ἄγριον, *agrion,* which is clearly written by itself both in line 2399 and line 3148. The animals suggested are those of Typhon (ass) or Khnum (ram), neither of which gods coincide in any way with the modelled image. As ἄγριον simply means 'wild,' there is no implication of a specific animal, except that we know it should have a white forehead. I suggest that the animal may have been a wild cow, as the invocation continues: "I receive you as the cowherd who has his camp toward the south."[4] After consecration, the statue is set up in a shop or business to "bring to me silver, gold, clothing, much wealth."

Another example of a magical statue, this time made of clay is used in the process of invocation of the goddess Selene (with a nod toward Aphrodite-Urania):

> ***The preparation for Mistress Selene is made like this:*** Take clay from a potter's wheel and mix a mixture with sulfur, and add blood of a dappled goat and mold an image of Mistress Selene the Egyptian,[5] as shown below,[1] making her in the

---

[1] See Harpon-Knouphi in *PGM* III. 435-6, 560-63; IV. 2433; VII. 1023-25; XXXVI. 219-20. Harpon-Knouphi is not derived from the Egyptian phrase "Horus the pillar of Kenmet" as suggested by several scholars.

[2] Further evidence of Epaphroditus's involvement in magic may be seen in Gager (1992), No 75, pp. 165-166, provided that the Epaphroditus mentioned there is the same man.

[3] Jacoby (in Preisendanz Vol. I, p. 147) suggests 'ass' whilst Eitrem (*ibid*) suggests 'ram.'

[4] Line 2435. In other words Hermes.

[5] This suggests that the image would actually have been of the Egyptian sky goddess Nut (or Tefnut) rather than the Greek Selene. That means the image might well have

> form of the Universe.[2] And make a shrine of olive wood and do not let it face the sun at all. And after dedicating it with the ritual that works for everything, [put it away] and thus it will be dedicated in advance. And anoint it also with lunar ointment and wreathe it. And late at night, at the 5th hour [midnight], put it away, facing Selene in a [pure] room. And also offer the lunar offering and repeat the following in succession and you will send dreams, and you will bind spells [with its aid], for the invocation to Selene is very effective. And after anointing yourself in advance [with] the ointment, appeal to her.[3]

Following the same principle of using the image of an animal sacred to the god, another rite suggests using the figure of an ape and a fish made of wax, for an invocation of Thoth, thus utilising animals sacred to that god.[4]

Statues of the gods, especially Anubis, were often utilised by magicians. The dog Kerberos, being a guardian of the entrance to hell, is sometimes invoked so that the dead may be allowed to carry out the magician's wishes (in the same way they do with a *defixio*) and bind a woman. The rite requires a statue of a dog (symbolic of Anubis), made of wax, pitch, virgin fruit, and manna. The dog is to be eight fingers long, and have its mouth wide open as if barking. It is activated by placing a suitably inscribed bone (from a man who died violently) in its mouth; or by sitting it on a papyrus strip inscribed with the words "IAŌ ASTŌ IŌPHĒ." An invocation is then made, and the statue of the dog will bark if it succeeds.[5]

In two consecutive rites the magician asks Anubis to send a spirit to influence someone else's dreams. In each case an image of Anubis is used. In the first example:

> On a new papyrus: you should draw an image of Anubis with blood of a black dog on it; you should write these writings under it; you should put it [in] to the mouth of [the statue of the] black dog of the embalming house; you should make great offerings before it; you should put frankincense on the brazier before him; you should do it as a libation of milk of a black cow...and you should put its recitation [invocation] in its mouth.[6]

In the second passage:

> On an [image of a] jackal of clean clay which is lying down,[7] its body moistened with milk and fluid of a jackal of the embalming house... You should write your

---

been that of a dark blue cow with many stars painted on her hide. Plutarch equates Nut with Rhea rather than Selene.

1 The figure is missing.

2 With the five-pointed stars of the heavens printed on her hide.

3 i.e. invoke her. *PGM* VII. 866-879.

4 *PDM* xiv. 330.

5 *PGM* IV. 1872-1927.

6 *PDM* Supplement 112-116.

7 The usual couchant form of Anubis.

> words on a new papyrus; you should put it in the jackal's mouth; and you should leave the jackal on a copper lamp which a brazier is heating.[1]

In each case the papyrus on which the spell is written is put into the mouth of the Anubis statue, which is then heated, censed, and in one case libated. The ritual is not religious, but aimed at forcing the god to enforce the spirit to influence the intended 'victim.'

In a Byzantine context, the word *telesma* was often applied to these statues as well as to metal (or parchment) talismans. According to Magdalino, the first Byzantine use of *stoicheia* as a technical term to describe these statues was in the *Parastaseis,*[2] in the early 8th century.[3]

As the process of making a talisman consists of fixing a particular power or specific spiritual creature to an inscribed parchment or metal disk at the correct time, so the Byzantine στοιχεῖα, *stoicheia* probably were originally statues which the magician wished to ensoul, by fixing to them a particular god or spirit. It appears that the word *stoicheion* can also apply to the spirit so fixed. As such it is sometimes defined as "an elementary spirit." Some scholars have suggested the definition "personally active spiritual being," which is only marginally correct, only in the sense that some magician has personally fixed the spirit to a statue or talisman.[4]

Wax and Clay Images

Wax and clay were the ingredients most easily to hand for the creating of figurines to represent the person who was the object of a rite, or to make an (ensouled) spirit statue. Wax was also valued for its ability to absorb a 'spiritual impression,' because of its semi-organic beehive origin.

In ancient Egypt, creator gods like Khnum were reputed to form gods and people from clay, on the potter's wheel, before breathing life into them. It is therefore logical for Egyptian magicians to use clay to make images into which life could be breathed. Dough and wax were also used for this purpose. Wax images of Apep were made before being deliberately destroyed as a counter-measure to his malevolence.

As well as the making of images, clay is also used for making the 'brick,' an item mentioned in both Babylonian magic and the *PGM* where it acts as both a seat and an altar. I suspect that this item was not simply a house brick, which would not be appropriate in such a magical context, where purity was so important, but was in fact a clay tablet. If this were so then it makes a lot more

---

1 *PDM* Supplement 125-130.

2 Παραστάσεις σύντομοι χρονικαί. See Cameron and Herrin (1984).

3 Magdalino (2006), p. 134. However I surmise the term was used much earlier than that.

4 See Blum (1946) for various other opinions about the meaning of *stoicheia*.

sense, because the placing of ritual impedimenta on it would then see it acting as an altar.

One rite of attraction, for binding a lover, uses two clay figures, with the male figure like Ares plunging his sword aggressively into the female.[1] This aggressive pose is surprisingly designed to cause longing in the female rather than pain. Although it is tempting to see a Freudian interpretation, the imagery reflects the idea of compulsion through pain, rather than sexual pleasure. The formula also mandates the use of 13 copper needles to be inserted into parts of her anatomy.[2] The rite is to ensure "she may remember no one but me, NN, alone." Such figures in clay and wax are fairly universal to magic, but images pierced with needles, nails or pins are now usually assumed to be examples of hate magic rather than love magic.

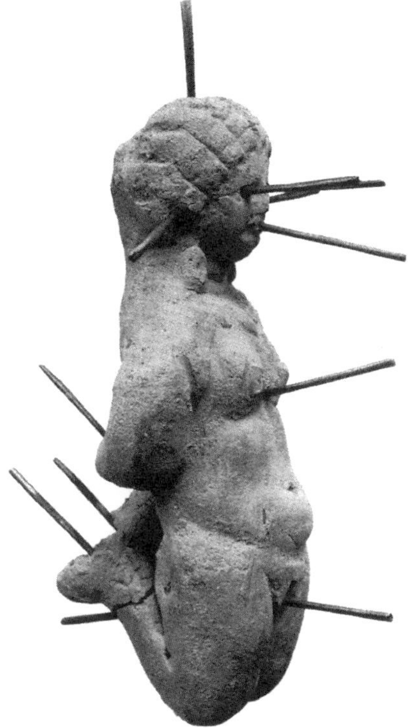

Figure 20: The figure of a woman, the object of a love or lust ritual, bound like a prisoner. The 13 needles thrust into all her orifices were so that she would not love, or even remember anyone but the magician, or his client. The full instruction mandates the writing of *nomina magica* on the figure, which has not been carried out in this case.[3]

[1] *PGM* IV. 296-466.

[2] The image's brain (1), ears (2), eyes (2), mouth (1), midriff (2), hands (1 each), pudenda (2), soles of the feet (2).

[3] Louvre inventory item E.27145.

The rite continues by tying a lead tablet to the figure with 365 knots whilst saying "Abrasax, hold her fast!" The 365 refers both to all the days of the year and to the isopsephy of the name Abraxas. The lead tablet indicates that it is to be used as a *defixio* and buried by or in the grave of someone unrelated (and preferably untimely dead). Although this sounds a rather macabre place for a love image, the theory is that the soul of the newly dead person can pass the message on to one of the chthonic gods: Korē, Persephone, Erishkigal, or Anubis,[1] or a daimon which is then able to carry out the magician's wishes.[2] The predominant use of lead shows that *defixiones* were under the rulership of Saturn, which is most appropriate considering that the grave was the site of most of these. Perhaps the most complete formula for making a magical statue in the *PGM*, this time of Hermes, for the purpose of dream sending, uses a special clay mix:

> Take 28 leaves from a pithy laurel tree[3] and some virgin earth[4] and seed of wormwood, wheat meal and the herb [called] calf's snout (but I have heard from a certain man of Herakleopolis that he takes 28 new sprouts from an olive tree, which is cultivated, the famous one).[5] Those are carried by an uncorrupted boy.[6] Also pounded together with the foregoing ingredients is the liquid of an ibis egg[7] and made into a uniform dough and [then] into a figure of Hermes wearing a mantle, while the moon is ascending in Aries or Leo or Virgo or Sagittarius. Let Hermes be holding a herald's staff. And write the spell[8] on hieratic papyrus or on a goose's windpipe... and insert it into the figure for the purpose of inspiration;[9] and when you want to use it, take some papyrus and write the spell and the matter [being enquired about]; and shave your head[10] and roll a hair into the papyrus, binding it with a piece of purple cord, and put on the outside of it an olive branch, and place it at the feet of the [clay statue of] Hermes (but others say: place it upon him). And let the figure lie in a shrine of lime wood. But when you want to use it, place the shrine beside your head along with the [image of the] god and recite [the spell] as on the altar you burn incense, earth from a grain-bearing field and one lump of rock salt. Let it rest beside your head, and go to sleep after saying the spell[11] without giving an answer to anyone... Recite this both at sunrise and moonrise.[12]

---

1 Anubis Psirinth is specially characterised as "holding the keys to Hades."

2 *PGM* IV. 296-466.

3 The laurel is sacred to Apollo.

4 Probably clay.

5 An interpolation by the scribe, or an early redactor.

6 Such as might have been used by the magician as a skryer.

7 Symbolic of Thoth.

8 The invocation (λόγον), not 'spell,' appears at *PGM* V. 424-435.

9 To enable the statue to breathe.

10 In the manner of a priest.

11 *PGM* V. 400-421.

12 *PGM* V. 370-446.

Another love spell utilises a wax image of Osiris embedded with the hair of the woman desired by the magician, together with the hair of "a donkey[1] together with a bone of a lizard" all of which should be buried under the doorsill of her house.[2] The use of a lizard is a recurrent theme, possibly because it was an easily obtainable animal. In one example a spotted lizard[3] is cooked in an iron vessel, to encourage hatred, as "Helios and all the gods have hated you." This utilises the 'slander spell' technique, implicating the object of desire, and suggesting she has been lying about the lizard, in order to infuriate and hence activate the god.[4] A large number of figurines in beeswax and clay (but also in lead, bronze, magnetite, etc.) are listed by Versnel in the course of his commentary on one particular text.[5] He highlights the deformities of these figures, such as twisted heads and broken necks.[6] Sometimes, a rite in the *PGM* will specify a drawing of a figure rather than a wax or clay three-dimensional execution. One such example gives the following detailed description of Bes-Pantheos:

> Take a clean linen cloth, and (according to Ostanes) with myrrh ink draw a figure on it which is humanlike in appearance but has four wings, having the left arm outstretched along with the two left wings, and having the other arm bent with the fist clenched. Then upon the head [draw] a royal headdress and a cloak over its arm, with two spirals on the cloak. Atop the head [draw] bull horns and to the buttocks a bird's tail. Have his right hand near his stomach and clinched (*sic*), and on either ankle [thigh?] have a sword extended.[7]

Bes has long been known as a helpful god assisting in both childbirth and magic, but Bes-Pantheos (literally "Bes all gods") is more cast in the mould of a magician or master of spirits (see Figure 11). One rite explains in some detail how a statue is to be deified, so that it acts as a guardian of a shop or a temple. After it has been set up and fixed in its place:

> ...sacrifice to it a wild white-faced [falcon], and burn [this offering] entire; also pour to it, as a libation, the milk of a black cow, the firstborn [of its mother] and the first she suckled... And [now] feast with [the god], singing to him all night long the names written on the strip [of papyrus] put in the hollow [inside it]. Wreathe the little temple with olive and thus [you will prosper] throughout life.[8]

---

[1] For lust, or symbolic of Typhon like the ass.

[2] *PDM* lxi. 112-27 and *PDM* xii. 50-61 has the same instruction, to bury it "under the doorsill of the house." This procedure was a common usage in Mediaeval magic in Europe, where the magical image was buried in a place often crossed by the intended victim of the rite.

[3] Which must be "taken from the place where bodies are mummified."

[4] *PDM* lxi. 197-216 [*PGM* LXI. 39-71].

[5] Versnel (1988), pp. 287-292.

[6] Such deformities are apparent in the 'poppets' used in magic later in northern European witchcraft.

[7] *PGM* XII. 121-143.

[8] *PGM* IV. 3125-3171. The libation of milk is not unlike Hindu practice.

Gods, Angels, Daimones, names of magicians, *nomina magica*	Non-Roman *PGM* Nos.	Category	No. of lines	Betz Papyrus *PGM/PDM* Reference number	Objective/ Technique	Greek Headwords
Iaō, Kerberos	4	S L	56	*PGM* IV. 1872-1927	Magical statue in the form of the dog Kerberos, to attract a specific woman.	[n/h]
Hermes, Psentebeth	4	S	14	*PGM* IV. 2359-2372	Magical statue for business	Πρακτικόν[1]
Hermes	4	S	69	*PGM* IV. 2373-2440	Talismanic statue, for acquiring business customers. The 'Little Beggar.'	Καταπρακτικὸν καὶ κατακλητικόν ἐργαστηρίου [2]
Tyche, Aiōn, Agathos Daimon	4	S	47	*PGM* IV. 3125-3171	A magical statue to gain favour for a shop or temple	[n/h] φυλακτήριον[3] - line 3126
Iaō Iō Sabaōth Abrasax Typhon Iō Erbēth Pakerbēth Bolchosēth Apomps Iaōth Iabaōth Aberamenthōou	4	S	20	*PGM* IV. 3255-3274	Talismanic inscription on a clay tablet ('brick') invoking Seth/Typhon.	[n/h]
Hermes, Selene, Helios, Ereschigal, Iaō	5	S E	77	*PGM* V. 370-446	Making a magical statue of Hermes to send dreams and prophesy. It uses a goose windpipe to allow the statue to "breathe."[4]	[n/h] [name facility] στηλη[5] - line 424 λύχνον[6] - line 440
				PGM VII. 862-918 [7]	*See Ω*	
				PGM VIII. 64-110	*See V*	
				PGM XII. 14-95	*See P*	

1 Effective business [rite].
2 For workshop business and customers.
3 Phylactery, but in this context it means a guardian, not a phylactery as worn by the magician. The procedure deifies the statue.
4 See *PGM* VII. 664-685 for an identical invocation.
5 *Stēlē* is the talisman to be placed inside the statue, as part of its consecration.
6 A lamp is mentioned in an alternative procedure (rite type 'E') set out in lines 440-446.
7 This rite, and the next two, just use statues as ancilliary equipment or focus.

Gods, Angels, Daimones, names of magicians, *nomina magica*	**Non-Roman *PGM* Nos.**	**Category**	**No. of lines**	**Betz Papyrus *PGM/PDM* Reference number**	**Objective/ Technique**	**Greek Headwords**
Osiris, Isis	61	S L7	16	*PDM* lxi. 112-127	Making a woman love using a wax image of Osiris	[Demotic] [n/h]
Knēph	111	S	15	*PGM* CXI. 1-15 *SM* 70	Instruction for making magical figures	[n/h]
Thathē, Barouch,[1] Olamptēr[2]	124	S	43	*PGM* CXXIV. 1-43 *SM* 97	Summoning statue and procedure to inflict illness,[3] using a potsherd and a wax manikin.	[n/h]
[Harpocrates], Sabatiaō, Sabaōth		S	11	*SM* 6	Haematite magical falcon statue[4]	[n/h] [named person]
Total S		**10**	**368**			

Table S: Statues, Magical.[5]

[1] The principal angel of "those below the earth."

[2] The angel of many forms.

[3] Not a "charm" as per the translation.

[4] Symbolic of Harpocrates, as its text says "I am he upon the lotus…"

[5] See also *PGM* VII. 862-918 in Composite Rites 'Ω.'

Magical Rings and Gemstones - δακτύλιον (*daktulion*) (R)

Magical rings are most commonly associated with Gnosticism, especially those including carved gemstones, but they have been used for much longer periods and in many cultures, such as the Babylonian seal stones. Magical rings were very much a part of Gnostic practice, many of which now lie in museums around the world. Solomon's ring was a very specific magical ring, reference to which occurs in the *PGM*, the *Testament of Solomon*, the Bible, *The Arabian Nights*, the *Hygromanteia*, the *Clavicula Salomonis*, the *Goetia* and in many other derived Latin and vernacular grimoires. The *Testament of Solomon* describes the Ring (δακτυλίδιον, *daktulidion*) as having been given to Solomon by God, via the hand of the archangel Michael. This magician's ring was reputed to be an integral part of Solomon's ability to command the spirits. The Ring was not usually made of the obvious choices like gold or silver, but was made of iron (for the same reason as an iron sword was used), and of brass (as brass was the metal of the spirit-confining Brass Vessel).

The *Jewish Encyclopaedia* explains that Solomon's Ring:

> ...was partly brass and partly iron. With the brass part of the ring Solomon signed his written commands to the good genii, and with the iron part he signed his commands to the evil genii, or devils. The Arabic writers declare also that Solomon received four jewels from four different angels, and that he set them in one ring, so that he could control the four elements. The legend that Asmodeus once obtained possession of the ring and threw it into the sea, and that Solomon was thus deprived of his power until he discovered the ring inside a fish, also has an Arabic source.[1]

Such stories would have been in circulation in Egypt in the first few centuries CE. The supreme ritual for the consecration of rings and their gemstones is given in *PGM* XII, with another similar consecration in an earlier section.[2] The invocation calls on a wide range of gods,[3] but finishes by revealing that the procedure primarily called upon is the OUPHŌR.[4] The rubric explains that towards the end of the consecration, the ring and gemstone should be inserted into the body cavity of a live rooster and left there for a whole day, rather than simply being anointed with blood.

The attributions of semi-precious stones are mentioned in one passage, in connection with the representation of the planets on an astrological board,

---

[1] 'Solomon, Seal of' in *Jewish Encyclopedia*, 1906.

[2] *PGM* XII. 270-350, 201-269.

[3] Including Helios, Ouroboros, Kheperi, Iao Sabaōth, Abraham, Isaac, Jacob, Astaphaios, Bainchōōch, Amoun and Osiris.

[4] OUPHŌR refers to the the ancient Egyptian procedure of Opening the Mouth (*wp.t-r3*), rather than the name of a god. This is confirmed by Dieleman (2005), p. 173; Thissen (1991), pp. 299-230; and Vergote (1961), pp. 213-214.

however the list equally also serves for the construction of magical rings:

Planet	*Metal/Stone*
Sun	gold
Moon	silver
Kronos (Saturn)	obsidian
Ares (Mars)	yellow-green onyx
Aphrodite (Venus)	lapis-lazuli streaked with gold
Hermes (Mercury)	turquoise
Zeus (Jupiter)[1]	[dark blue] stone, but underneath of crystal.

In the following Rite Table relating to magical rings and gemstones 'R' you can see that the headword δακτύλιον occurs in all the Greek passages, with the equivalent word occurring in one of the two Demotic passages.[2]

The manufacture of magical rings and the use of gemstones in magic detailed in the following table constitute 1.4% of the *PGM* rites, but 2.2% of its lines. One of the most popular motifs was that of the solar god Abraxas.

Figure 21: Abraxas seal with an ouroboros shield inscribed with IAΩ/ιαω (*left*)

Figure 22: Abraxas seal right facing (*right*), both with shield, whip and snake legs.

[1] The planets are indicated by the name of the corresponding Greek god.

[2] *PGM* CX. 1-12.

Figure 23: Abraxas with Chnoubis, the lion headed serpent with solar rays, surrounded by three of the same animals that Harpocrates holds in his hand on the Metternich *Stēlē*: crocodile, snake, oryx, etc.

Figure 24: Christian seal with Jesus (enthroned within a *vesica piscis* with four apocalyptic animals) plus the lion-snake, a crab and *charaktēres* (*left*). [1]

Figure 25: Abraxas seal enclosed within the protective ouroboros (*right*).

[1] Bonner (1950), Plate XVII, No. 324. Kelsey Museum 26119.

Gods, Angels, Daimones, names of magicians, *nomina magica*	Non-Roman PGM Nos.	Category	No. of lines	Betz Papyrus *PGM/PDM* Reference number	Objective/ Technique	Greek Headwords
				PGM IV. 1596-1715	*See U* [1]	
Hermes, Helios, Thouth, Heron, Phoenix, Em, K[n]eph, Anoixis	5	R	91	*PGM* V. 213-303	Hermes' ring: carving and consecration	Ἑρμοῦ δακτύλιος[2] δακτύλιον - lines 224, 233 τελετή[3] - line 229
Sarapis	5	R V	12	*PGM* V. 447-458	Magical ring	[n/h] δακτύλιον - line 451
Asklepios of Memphis [Imhotep], Menōphri	7	R	15	*PGM* VII. 628-642	Magical ring of iron of Asklepios, involving the Pole Star	δακτύλιον - lines 632, 638, 641
Abraxam	12	R	15	*PDM* xii. 6-20	Iron ring to cause praise	[Demotic] A ring to cause praise
Abraxas, Ouroboros, Helios, Selene, IAŌ Sabaōth, Abrasax, Chrates [Sokrates], Nemesis, Phoinix, Aphrodite, Typhi, Kronos, Osiris, Isis, Ēsenephys, Souchos, Agathos Daimon, Aion, Adōnaie, Sabaōth, Ouertō	12	R	69	*PGM* XII. 201-269	A ring for favour and victory, "useful for every magical operation." Engraved on a jasper. See also *PGM* XII. 270-350 for an older version.	Δακτυλίδιον[4] *w'gswr*[5] στοιχεῖα - line 250[6]

[1] The ring is merely one of the objects designed to be consecrated by this rite. It is also used to consecrate stones and phylacteries.

[2] Hermes' ring.

[3] Mystery.

[4] Ring.

[5] Ring (Demotic).

[6] *Stoicheia,* in the sense of an image rather than a magical statue.

Gods, Angels, Daimones, names of magicians, *nomina magica*	**Non-Roman *PGM* Nos**	**Category**	**No. of lines**	**Betz Papyrus *PGM/PDM* Reference number**	**Objective/ Technique**	**Greek Headwords**
Ouphōr, Helios, Ouroboros, Khepera, Iaō Sabaōth, Adōnai, Thoth, Maskelli, Seiseng[en] Pharangēs, Bainchōōch, Abraham, Isaac, Jacob, Astaphaios, Marmariōth, Bainchōōch, Akrammachamarei, Amoun, Osiris,	12	R	81	*PGM* XII. 270-350	The Rite of Ouphōr to make carved stones come alive. A ring for success and favour and victory. Uses Heliotrope, herb of the Sun. includes a rite usable for consecrating all stones or rings.[1]	Δακτυλίδιον[2] *wp.t-rȝ*[3]
				PDM xiv. 376-394	*See Ω* [4]	
	94	R H	5	*PGM* XCIV. 22-26 *SM* 94 e	"Gothic" ring to protect the eyes	ποίησ[ον δακτυλίδιον][5]
	14	R L2	7	*PDM* xiv. 1090-1096	A ring to fetch a woman	[Demotic] [n/h]
Total R		**8**	**295**			

Table R: Magical Rings and Gemstones.

[1] The ring also claims the power to make daimons flee, to call back souls, move spirits, restrain legal opponents, strengthen friendships, produce profits, bring dreams, give prophecies, cause illness, and make love potions.
[2] Ring.
[3] Ring (Demotic).
[4] This is a Complex Rite involving a number of objectives and animal parts. The ring is only a minor element.
[5] Gothic ring.

6.2 Words Written & Worn

Many Graeco-Egyptian magical procedures depended upon the written word. Ritner demonstrates the importance of written magical material by showing that a scribal term was often used to define the magician himself in ancient Egypt:

> In literature from the Old Kingdom through Greco-Roman periods, the priestly qualifications of the magician protagonist are almost invariably specified, being indicated as either "chief lector priest" [*hry-tp*] or "scribe of the House of Life."... From the later designation derive also the simple references to magicians as "good scribes" (*sh̠ nfr*) and magical acts as "deeds of a (good) scribe" (*wp.t n sh̠ nfr, sp n sh̠*).[1]

This chapter will examine the various forms of magic which involve the written word, as distinct from verbal invocation or ritual actions.

Definitions

It is not my intention to be unnecessarily pedantic, but simply to clear the way to effectively separate out and explain the reasons for the different uses, materials and methods, for example the separation of those items made for clients for everyday wear (amulets) from those items specifically used by the magician in a ritual context for protection (phylacteries), or made to simply effect one specific change (talismans).

A number of words related to magic have changed meaning over the centuries, and so it is useful to revisit these definitions so that we can relate to the distinctions that were important to the Graeco-Egyptian magician. It is therefore necessary to define more closely the terms Charm, Amulet, Phylactery, Tefillin, Lamen, Talisman, *defixio* and Pentacle, as the popular perception (and even sometimes the academic one), is that the above terms are roughly equivalent.

Betz, for example, categorises one item (in his Table of Spells) as a "phylactery for earache."[2] The fact that it is designed to cure earache, for a specific patient, definitely marks it out as an amulet, not a phylactery. Furthermore the word φυλακτήριον 'phylactery' does not appear anywhere in the Greek text of that particular passage. This is not meant as a criticism of Hans Betz's scholarship, but merely as an illustration of the generally loose modern application of these terms, and the difficulty of translating technical terms in one language into another language which no longer has the same range of terminology.

These words are often used interchangeably, even by professionals.[3] These

[1] Ritner (2008), pp. 221-222.

[2] Betz (1996), p. 281. *PGM* XLIV. 1-18.

[3] A recent exhibit in the newly refurbished Ashmolean Museum in Oxford showed a photograph of a Rabbi who clearly had a *tefillin* bound to his forehead, captioned by professional museum staff as a "Rabbi with an amulet."

distinctions are further blurred by some translators who translate, for example, φυλακτήριον as "charm" or "amulet." Preisendanz more specifically translates that term as "Amulet des Zaubers"[1] which at least suggests its use by magicians, rather than as an everyday amulet for his clients.

Important technical words like the Greek word συστάσις, *systasis* need to be correctly translated if the exact procedure is to be identified, but Betz points out for example that "*systasis* and cognate words are translated in a variety of ways throughout this volume."[2] This makes the identification of specific methods impossible if based solely on the English text. The worst offenders however are the words 'charm' and 'spell' which are applied randomly to as many as 20 different Greek words. I have tried to keep the translation of Greek technical words relating to magic as consistent as possible, instead of just reaching for a blanket term like 'spell,' as it is crucial to understand which kind of 'spell' is being dealt with in each passage. The undeniable fact is that Greek vocabulary of magic is much more detailed and extensive than the English vocabulary for the same subject.[3]

Skemer, in his note on terminology, makes some very useful and necessary distinctions, affirming that:

> Imprecise terminology has been an impediment to the serious study of textual amulets... Modern scholarship has used different terms to signify textual amulets and has applied them inconsistently.[4]

It is important to make these distinctions before proceeding in order to make sense of the different written magical procedures present in the *PGM*. The definitions are listed below in order of specificity, ranging from the very general and all-embracing word 'charm' to the very specific and technical term 'lamen.' These detailed definitions are necessary to enable the identification of the function of each passage in the *PGM*, regardless of the sometimes very generalised translation of their descriptors in English. As the translations of these papyri have been undertaken by a range of different scholars, it is inevitable that a specific Greek word will sometimes be translated in a number of quite different ways. Categorisation has therefore been done on the basis of either the original Greek headword, rather than the English translation or even

---

1 'Magician's amulet.' Preisendanz (1928), p. 17.

2 Betz (1996), p. 339.

3 The same is true for the Greek vocabulary of geometry, which meant that the early translations of Euclid into English in the 16th century (by Billingsley and Dee) had to rely upon transliterated Greek terms because there were no English equivalents for most of the technical terms (like *rhombus* or *isosceles* for example). In both cases, magic and geometry, the Greeks had developed the technology, and hence the terminology, very much further than the equivalent thinking in English.

4 Skemer (2006), pp. 6, 10. With this view I totally concur.

the translator's suggested title. Table 13 lists the main Greek headwords that have been used for this categorization.

The definitions set out below are formulated solely on the basis of their use in the *PGM*, and will therefore often expand, or sometimes even contradict, the definition to be found in a typical non-specialist English dictionary.[1] Even the *OED* is fairly vague about these distinctions, often simply defining one term in terms of another, which is not very helpful.

Rite

The term 'rite' covers any ritual or magical procedure. I have therefore often preferred 'rite' to 'spell' although both terms are very general.

Spell

The term 'spell' is the least precise term and will seldom be used, but where it is used it simply refers to any technique practised by a magician involving verbal invocation. Often the word λόγος, *logos* is translated as 'spell' or 'prayer.' Although *logos* has many different meanings (which extend over a number of pages in standard Greek lexicons), its meaning which comes closest to the sense it is used in the *PGM* is 'an invocation.'

Charm

The word 'charm' is also a very non-specific term, and therefore not a very useful term when considering detailed magical techniques. 'Charm' may be used as a verb. As it is derived from the Latin *carmen,* meaning 'song' or 'invocation' it can also have a vocal dimension as well as indicating the written form of such a song. It is sometimes applied to a small item designed to be worn and bring good luck, where 'amulet' might have been more appropriate. Charm is therefore too general and imprecise a word for the present purposes. Unfortunately some *PGM* translators have used this blanket term quite often where a much more specific or technical term, like φυλακτήριον 'phylactery,' or κατακλητικόν 'summoning statue,' occurs in the Greek. This term will therefore be used as little as possible in this book.

Amulet

This simply means a thing worn on the person to attract luck or protect the wearer from evil influences, danger or illness generally.[2] Seligman, quoted by

[1] For example, *phylactery,* although a Greek term, is often incorrectly defined in English dictionaries as a solely Jewish religious item (which is really a *tefillin*), whereas in the papyri it is *only* used to describe an Egyptian magicians' ritual item, and has no religious or Jewish connotation at all.

[2] A common mediaeval synonym for amulet was ligature, something bound to the body.

Budge,[1] was of the opinion that 'amulet' was derived from the Old Latin *amoletum*, meaning "a means of defence."[2] Skemer may be closer to the truth when he states that *amulet* is derived from the Latin *amuletum* which he traces back to the Arabic *hamalet*, meaning an object "worn on the body, especially around the neck, as a "preservative" against a host of afflictions.[3]

An amulet may be made in the form of a gem (especially an engraved gem), a coin, pendant, ring, or plant or animal part (like a rabbit's foot), or it may be a textual amulet.[4] A typical Mediterranean example of a mass produced amulet, which is still current, is the blue circular eye-shaped amulet designed to protect the wearer from the evil eye. Ancient Egyptian amulets were also mass-produced using certain standard formats such as the scarab (perhaps the most popular form), *ankh*, *tyet*, *djed* pillar, *ab* heart or the *wedjat* Eye of Horus.[5]

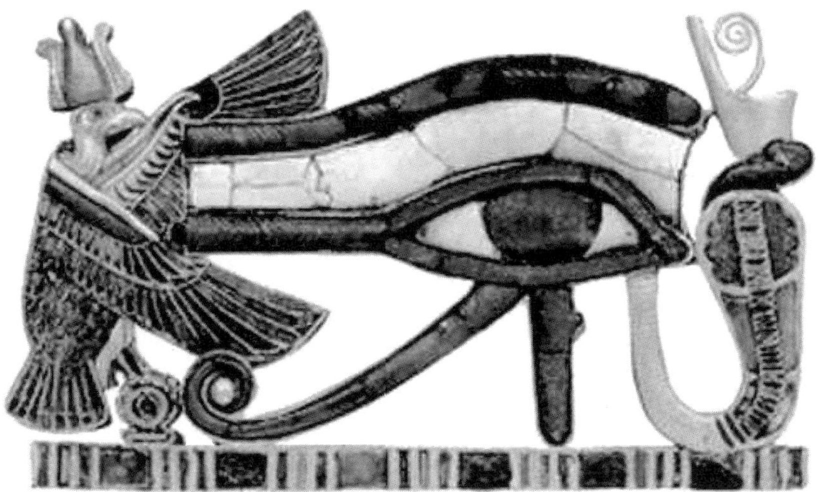

Figure 26: A standard Egyptian amulet: the Eye of Horus.

One key distinguishing feature of an amulet is that it is made for a client, either mass-produced (with maybe the later insertion of the client's name), or specifically made for a very specific client. In the context of the *PGM* amulets

[1] *Heil und Schutzmittel*, Stuttgart, 1920, p. 26.

[2] Budge (1961), p. 13.

[3] Skemer (2006), p. 6. In this sense an amulet may be referred to in Latin as an *alligatura*, *ligature*, *gestamen*, *suspensio* or *filacterium*. See Lecouteaux (2014), pp. 32-33.

[4] Mediaeval textual amulets are well covered in Skemer (2006).

[5] Examples of Egyptian amulets can be seen in Budge (1970), p. 133-176; Andrews (1994), p. 6; and Pinch (2006), pp. 104-119. Examples of Hebrew, Palestinian and Syrian amulets can be found in Budge (1970), p. 212-238, 250-282 and Naveh and Shaked (1985), pp. 40-122. In each of those 15 Palestinian/Syrian examples (except number 6 which is missing at least four lines), the name of the specific person for whom it was made is inscribed on it, thus guaranteeing that it is an amulet.

are primarily made by the magician for his clients, as witness the large number of examples which incorporate specific names.[1]

One example of a 4th century amulet found in Beirut which has been labelled as a 'phylactery' occurs in an article by Jordan. In his translation the repeated order to protect a specific woman from sundry possible ills confirms, without any doubt, that this particular lamella is an amulet for general protection, not a phylactery for the magician's use during a rite:

> Protect Alexandra, whom Zoë bore, from every demon and every compulsion of demons and from demonic (forces?) and magical drugs and binding-spells...free Alexandra, whom Zoë bore - quickly, quickly, at once, at once![2]

Skemer usefully further narrows the definition of amulet by referring to 'textual amulets' as:

> Textual amulets...were generally brief apotropaic texts, handwritten or mechanically printed on separate sheets, rolls, and scraps of parchment, paper, or other flexible writing supports of varying dimensions. When worn around the neck or placed elsewhere on the body, they were thought to protect the bearer against known and unknown enemies...[3]

Taweez

In modern India and the Middle East the wearing of a small metal (often gold) cylinder with an enclosed religious text for protection is quite widespread. These also occurred in ancient Egypt.[4] Although these items are sometimes referred to as phylacteries, they function like amulets, and do not occur in the *PGM*. The usual word for these in Urdu and Arabic is *taweez* or *tabeez*. The *taweez* will be worn every day, and it must contain a religious not a magical text.

Phylactery

The phylactery (as the term is used in the *PGM*) is *always* for the use of the magician, and only then during a rite, not worn on a day-to-day basis. It will also definitely *not* incorporate his name.[5] A phylactery is also worn, but it *must*

---

[1] These specific personalized client amulets have been listed separately in Table 12 and Table 13 as 'A2.'

[2] Jordan (1991), pp. 66-70. Also Kotansky (1994), No. 52, pp. 270-300. We will examine this lamella in a later chapter in relation to the angelic hierarchy to be found thereon.

[3] Skemer (2006), p. ix.

[4] Illustrated in Pinch (2006), p. 115.

[5] Heintz (1996), pp. 295-300, analyses a mass-produced amulet, which interestingly uses just lines 6-9 cut from a much longer inscription recorded in *PGM* XIXa. 1-54. Heintz correctly identifies it as a mass-produced amulet (p. 296) but nevertheless still entitles her article "A Greek Silver Phylactery..."

only used by him during a rite.[1] This term will only be used in this book in the same way as it is used in the *PGM*. The difference between an amulet and a phylactery thus is highlighted by both its usage and user. The amulet is made for a client, but the phylactery is made by the magician for the magician. Phylacteries, almost without exception form part of a larger rite, and are always detailed in a sub-section at the end of the rite. Phylacteries ('U' and 'U2') are always described as φυλακτήριον (*phylaktērion*). Another reason why these distinctions need to be clearly made is that amulets made for a client later merge with folk magic, whilst phylacteries, talismans and lamens always remain part of learned magic, for use solely by the magician himself.

In the *PGM* amulets usually occur in short free-standing passages with no elaborate ritual preparations ('A'). Where a specific client is named in the text, conclusively indicating that it is an amulet, it has been coded as an amulet 'A2.'

Although there is often a confusion (in English), there is no such confusion in the original Greek.

One of the clear indications that a lamella is a mass produced amulet is where the name of the person appears to have been added afterwards, sometimes by a different scribe, in a different hand, or squeezed into a previously blank space.[2] An excellent example of this is the lamella now preserved by the Xerox Corporation in Connecticut, where the phrase "cure and preserve Eugenia whom Galenia bore" is squeezed into lines 14-16. The mass-produced nature of this amulet is confirmed by Faraone and Kotansky, yet their article's title is still 'An Inscribed Gold Phylactery...' a phrase which is then immediately contradicted in the first sentence which correctly states that it is "an excellent example of a common type of amulet."[3]

Tefillin

Phylacteries are defined in most modern dictionaries as associated with Jewish religious practice. Kotansky points out the less than precise use of 'phylactery' in scholarly literature, and pinpoints the difference between it and the *tefillin*. He also traces the probable origin of this confusion to the gospel of *Matthew*:

> These inscribed magical amulets, or *lamellae*, are regularly referred to as "phylacteries" in the scholarly literature. The main drawback in using this term is that 'phylactery' is easily confused in modern parlance with the traditional Jewish *tefillin*...carrying Bible verses worn as frontlets by pious Jews since

[1] Phylactery (φυλακτήριον) is a Greek word and *may* have been derived from the Greek *phylaktikos*, which means 'fit for preserving, or a preservative.'

[2] In Jewish amulets the give-away phrase is *Peloni bar Peloni*, or simply פ ב פ. This is not a *nomina magica*, but an indication that this is the point where the client's name should be inserted, when the amulet is sold.

[3] Faraone and Kotansky (1988), p. 257.

> ancient times. Our modern usage derives wholly from the vituperative use found in Matt[hew] 23:5.[1]

Kotansky's definition needs further refining: when applied to the phylacteries in the *PGM,* the meaning is specifically for the protection of the magician during the rite to which each of the phylactery descriptions are appended.

Although *tefillin* were called by Hellenised Jews *phylaktēria,* the more correct use in Hebrew is the word *tefillin* (תפלין). A *tefillin* is structurally quite different from any other magico-religious pendant, and consists of a small leather case (originally cylindrical but now usually cubical) made either of parchment or of black calfskin, containing slips of parchment or vellum on which are written specific scriptural passages: *Exodus* 13: 1-10 and 11-16; *Deuteronomy* 6: 4-9, 11: 13-21.[2] They are traditionally bound tightly on the forehead and the left arm by orthodox Jewish men, but only during Morning Prayer. *Tefillin* as such do not occur in the *PGM,* or in any of the later magical texts, as their use is and was solely for Jewish religious purposes.

Jewish Tradition

A more massive version of the phylactery was used by the high priests in the Temple of Jerusalem, before its destruction in 70 CE. This is documented in the Bible.[3] In the light of the later use of the phylactery, it seems that the High Priest wore the breastplate (חשׁן) primarily for protection when he entered the 'holy of holies', given the fearsome reputation that the Ark of the Covenant contained there had for killing large numbers of people.[4] Protection is the basic function of any breastplate. The idea of a spiritual breastplate worn on the High Priest's chest is clearly similar in function to the magician's phylactery but dealing with a god (Yahweh) not just a daimon or spirit (see Figure 38).

Lamen

The lamen or 'magician's phylactery' is the most specific term. It is possible than 'lamen' derives from λαμνη, *lamnē* which is usually translated as 'lamella' in scholarly works, but the two should not be confused.[5] In mediaeval and later magical texts, *phylacterium* was often rendered as *lamen.* Lamen always has the technical sense of something worn solely by a magician for protection from the entities he evoked/invoked, specifically at the time of the ritual. The

---

[1] Kotansky (1994), p. xv, fn. 3.

[2] The *tefillin* found at Qumran also had extracts from *Deuteronomy* 10:12 - 11:12 and 32:1-33.

[3] *Exodus* 28:17-20.

[4] See *1 Samuel* 6: 1; *2 Samuel* 6: 2-7. The idea that the Ark was capable of killing people was not confined to Indiana Jones films.

[5] See *PGM* IV. 2146; *PGM* IX. 8.

lamen of the mediaeval magician is a direct descendant of the *PGM* phylactery. At no point was the word 'lamen' used in the sense of a general amulet, or used in a context outside of ritual magic. Interestingly the lamen often became a double (or double-sided) piece of parchment bearing the sigil of the spirit being invoked (on the *recto*) and that of the thwarting angel understood to control that spirit on the *verso*.[1]

The consecration of such a lamen or breastplate was of considerable importance for both priest and magician. One such Jewish rite of consecration of a golden plate (which was obviously a phylactery/lamen) is documented in a Genizah fragment:

> You shall perform all of these (procedures) in the fear of God. Protect yourself well from any bad thing. And when you perform all of these (procedures) you should go out to the [water] trough,[2] and say many prayers and supplications, and ask that you not fail again. Then speak this glorious name in fear and trembling. If you see the image of a lion of fire in the trough, know that you have succeeded in wearing this holy name. Then you shall take the golden plate (*ṣiṣ*) on which this holy name is engraved and tie it around your neck and on your heart. Take care not to become impure again when it is on you, lest you be punished. Then you may do any [magical][3] thing and you will succeed.[4]

There is no doubt that the golden plate engraved with a holy name worn over the heart was a magician's phylactery or lamen. The water trough acted as a variety of skrying bowl to check the success or otherwise of the rite. It would seem in this context that its function was more than protective, in as much as it also granted success in all (magical) operations. This secondary function also appears to have carried over into later grimoires.

Talisman

Although this word is commonly used interchangeably with 'amulet' it will here be used in its more restricted (grimoire) sense, which implies something created with a magical rite for a specific intention. A talisman is not personalised, and not often worn. A talisman is something written or drawn, with a specific magical objective in mind, often planetary. Unlike an amulet or a phylactery it is not designed for personal or general protection, but to do something positive. In the context of the *PGM, stēlē* probably comes closest to the meaning of talisman. Stroud makes the distinction very clearly:

---

[1] See Skinner & Rankine (2010), p. 103.

[2] Instead of a river which would be more usual.

[3] The insertion of 'magical' into this text at this point is justified as no ordinary tasks (except religious or magical) were envisaged whilst wearing the phylactery, in case such actions caused the impurity warned against.

[4] Genizah fragment MS JTSA ENA 6643.4, lines 4–13. See Swartz (2000), pp. 67-69.

> Amulets are protective charms; they fend off evil. They are passive objects and although they can absorb or deflect all manner of dangerous magic, they cannot be actively controlled by their owner. They are thus the opposite of *talismans*, which have active magical powers that can be used at their owner's discretion.[1]

The talisman is *always* made for a definite reason whilst an amulet can be used for generic purposes such as averting evil or attracting good luck.

The title of one *PGM* passage is translated as a "*Stēlē* of Aphrodite,"[2] but its true nature is revealed in the next line, which confirms that it is to be engraved on "a strip of tin...with a bronze stylus" and carried by the client. Therefore it is a talisman designed "to gain friendship, favour, success, and friends." This passage also throws an interesting light on the Egyptian understanding of '*stēlē*.'

'*Stēlē*' in Egyptological literature is usually understood to mean "an upright stone slab or column typically bearing a commemorative inscription or relief design."[3] In other procedures in the *PGM*, '*stēlē*' can equally refer to a simple square of natron to be written on.[4] Here it refers to a strip of tin to be engraved. The actual text or formula of the inscription can also be referred to as a '*stēlē*.'[5] The meaning of *stēlē* is therefore much wider than that usually used by archaeologists, to refer to any rectangular surface engraved or written on with a (commemorative, magical or religious) text. Betz defines it:

> The term *stēlē* occurs in the *PGM* with several meanings. Originally it refers to a plate of stone or metal on which texts could be inscribed (e.g. VIII. 42), but most of the time the term is a literary device suggesting the text was copied from a stone slab. It can also refer to an amulet in the shape of a *stēlē* (as in *PGM* VII. 215).[6]

I certainly agree with this, but would modify the word 'amulet' to 'talisman' in the last sentence.

Pentacle

This term is almost synonymous with talisman, but carries the additional suggestion that the figure inscribed may be in the shape of a pentagram, and will relate to a specific planet. This term is not used in the *PGM*.

These defining characteristics, which are based on their actual usage and

---

[1] Stroud, *Bartimaeus: the Amulet of Samarkand*, New York: Hyperion, 2003, p. 88.
[2] *PGM* VII. 215-18.
[3] *Concise Oxford Dictionary*, 1999. Greek lexicons such as *LSJ*, *Autenrieth* and *Middle Liddell* all define *stēlē* (στήλη) as no more than a gravestone, block of stone, slab, monument or boundary post, without taking into account the more extended meaning implicit in *PGM* passages.
[4] *PGM* VII. 215-218.
[5] See also Ritner (2009), p. 68ff. on a magical healing *stēlē*.
[6] Betz (1996), p. 60.

specifically on the Greek text of the *PGM*, rather than just on the limited dictionary definition of the English words, will be used in this book to distinguish between the different items of magical equipment that were written and worn.

Figure 27: A gold lamella from the early 2nd century bearing a number of well known *nomina magica*: Iaō, Adōnaei, Akramachamari, Ablanathanalba, Simelsam, and Pip.[1] The god entwined by a serpent might be Aiōn, who holds three poppies and a key (or wand?). This was probably a talisman, but as there are only *nomina magica* and no specific objective, this may possibly have been used as a phylactery.[2]

---

[1] The word 'Pip[i]' derives from ΠΙΠΙ which was sometimes written in Greek to visually replicate the original יהוה in Hebrew.

[2] Kotansky (1994), No. 29, p. 118-120.

Amulets

Amulets are περιάμματα, *periammata,* but they are seldom labelled as such in the *PGM.* They are instead identifiable by the presence of personal names identifying the client(s) they were to be made for. Another useful form of identification, equating with a headword, is that they very often begin with the preposition πρὸς, meaning 'for…' followed by their purpose. In the *PGM,* πρὸς is only found in the first line of instructions for making an amulet ('A' and 'A2') or for health ('H'), and not at the beginning of any other passages, and so its presence is a clear indication that the passage is definitely one of these.

The term amulet has come to be used rather loosely in modern literature. Amulets were not designed to be used in the context of a magical rite, but to be worn day-to-day. They will often have been made by the magician for a client who just wanted to be luckier in love or gambling, or protected from disease or accidents in a general way.

Such amulets made for clients are common to all cultures, and have survived thousands of years, from the faience scarabs of dynastic Egyptian times to the "lucky rabbit's foot" of the 21st century. Amongst Jewish amulets manufactured for use by an individual, formulae from ancient Palestinian and Babylonian sources can be found both on amulets from the Cairo Genizah and on amulets currently for sale to the Jewish community in New York and London, attesting a long history of transmission.[1]

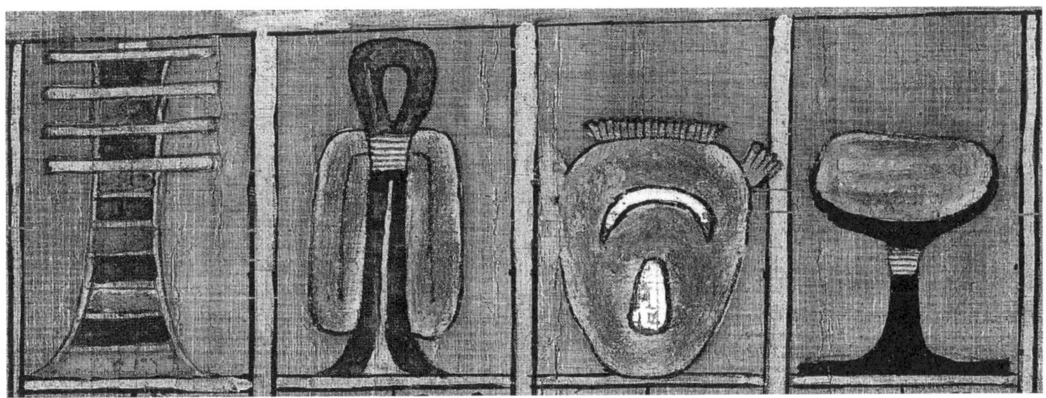

Figure 28: Four ancient Egyptian amulets: the *djed* pillar, knot, heart and headrest from the papyrus of Ani.[2]

[1] Swartz (1990), p. 166.

[2] Papyrus of Ani. British Museum 10470/33.

The ancient Egyptians made a clear distinction between magic (*hekau*) and amulet making (*sau*),[1] a distinction that was carried over into Graeco-Egyptian magic. The Egyptians wore many amulets, of which the most common was probably the pottery, stone or wood scarab which was set into rings, used as pendants or buried with a mummy. A number of standard designs prevailed such as the *tyet* or the Eye of Horus.[2] The fact that *wḏ3w*, the general term for an amulet also means "health" suggests that the bulk of such amulets were meant as general protection especially against disease, but also against injury by snakes, crocodiles, and other unseen menaces that lurked in river junctions, canals, pools and wells.

There are in excess of 65 separate formulae for creating such popular amulets in the *PGM*, many of them for reasons of health or love. These are very simple formulae, with an average length of less than ten lines.[3] These are obviously meant to be manufactured for clients, and so thousands of them have survived as artefacts as well as the details of their preparation in the papyri texts. Most of the more recently recorded papyri in the *Supplementum Magicum* are in fact amulets.

The most common type of Graeco-Egyptian amulet is simply a single narrow column of text often with magical *charaktēres* such as Figure 29 (shown sideways, with top to the right).

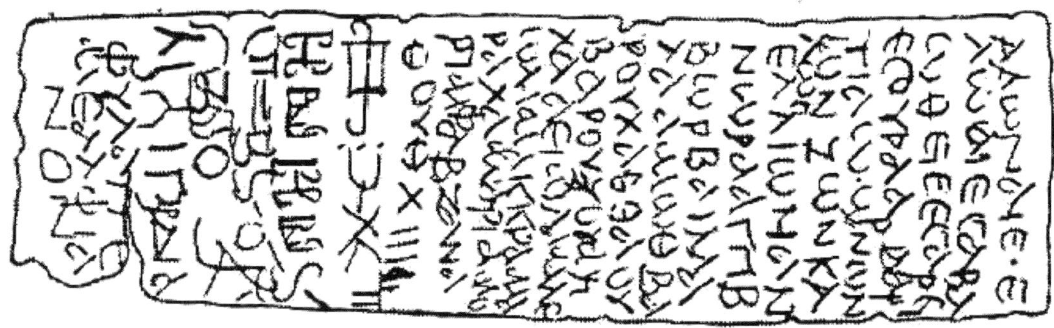

Figure 29: Typical amulet, being a narrow column of text on a gold lamella dating from 1st/2nd century CE and found in Caernarvon Wales, demonstrating the wide geographic and cultural distribution of such items. The text is a Greek translation of a Jewish liturgical text, beginning *Adônai Elôaie Sabaôth*...[4]

---

[1] *Sau* applies to both the practice and the practitioner. See Pinch (2010), p. 56; Rankine (2006), p. 16.

[2] See Budge (1970). Budge's book on amulets is a useful source of examples.

[3] The longest only measures 30 lines because it includes a drawing.

[4] Kotansky (1994), No. 2, pp. 3-12, turned sideways.

Many *PGM* amulets have wing-shaped text with a *nomina magica* being repeated a number of times, each time with the number of letters decremented by one. One such amulet (see Figure 32) was designed to attract Herakles (the small gladiatorial figure at the back) to Allous (daughter of Alexandria) using the good offices of the god Bes (in the foreground).[1] Note the *nomina magica* written down each side of the amulet, decremented by one letter on each line. Such wing formations survived thousands of years into the later vernacular grimoires, for example the wing formation copied by the cunning-man Anders Ulfkjaer from a grimoire by pseudo-Cyprian in 1858 (see Figure 33). Other formats occur but most were closely written in a single narrow column (such as Figure 29).[2]

Although most of the amulets recorded in the *PGM* are very crude in design, there was a parallel Greek and Roman culture of amulets made to a much higher artistic standard, that were inherited by Byzantium. The manufacture of amulets in Byzantium was very sophisticated, with designs engraved upon gems, cameos, enamel pendants, bronze tokens, or disks of gold, silver, bronze and lead, or fashioned in the form of rings. These complex designs nevertheless followed standard patterns, each for a specific purpose. Typically one of the most common amulets was designed to protect the newborn child from the demoness Gyllou (although the name 'Gyllou' does not actually occur on any of them), or counter the imaginary medical phenomena of the so-called 'wandering womb.'[3]

Late Antiquity amulets sometimes dated to the 5th-7th century, which is after the period of the *PGM*, portrayed either Solomon or St. Sisinnios of Antioch mounted on a horse and aiming a lance at a female demon (see Figure 30). I believe that initially these may have been used as phylacteries, because of the connection with Solomon and his reputation for subduing spirits, but later became popularised as amulets. These amulets also had celestial *charaktēres* inscribed upon them similar to some passages in the *PGM*.[4] The earliest example of this style of iconography comes from the 5th century monastery of St. Apollo at Bawit in Egypt. The saint's name hints at a pagan origin. St. Sisinnios (c. 708) hailed from Antioch where the use of the rider saint motif on Syrian amulets was very common.[5]

---

[1] *PGM* XXXIX. 1-21.

[2] Hebrew amulets as recorded in Naveh and Shaked (1985) are often for named clients and arranged in columns. These amulets refer to themselves here and in Genizah fragments as 'proper amulets' or קמיע טב. See Amulet 2:1 and 13:2.

[3] The *hysteria* formula. See *PGM* VIII. 260-271 for an amulet designed for the same purpose.

[4] See Spier (1993), pp. 25-62 for a more extensive discussion.

[5] See British Library Or. MS 6673 for examples. Also Budge (1961), pp. 274-281.

Figure 30: A figure of Solomon mounted with a lance and attacking a recumbent demon is shown on the *recto*. Such a figure is often interpreted as an amulet showing the rider-saint St. Sisinnios,[1] but in this case it is definitely Solomon, as confirmed by the spaced out Greek inscription CoλoMωN (Σoλoμov, *Solomon*). Here Solomon is shown as mastering a demon, and as such it is possible this design was originally designed as a magician's phylactery. The *verso* reads σφραγίς θεον (*sphragis theon*) or 'seal of god,'[2] with a Chnoubis triple-S seal, which also suggests a phylactery rather than an amulet.[3]

Amulet formulae are strongest numerically in the *PGM,* and they were predominantly made for commercial reasons. Note that in Table A, all passages either start with πρὸς (24 examples), or have a distinctly amuletic format (23 examples). Only seven examples of amulets have been identified by their content. In Table A2 *all* examples are identifiable as amulets because of the inclusion of personalisation, and more than 22 also have an amuletic format.

Interestingly, none of the personalised amulets ('A2') appear in the main papyri (see Appendix 5) but only in the smaller papyri, probably because the main papyri are magician's handbooks containing the formulae and general instructions on method rather than actual examples of personalised amulets.

---

[1] Because of the image these figures were later conflated with St. George.

[2] *Sphragis ourania* is the phrase used later in the *Hygromantia* to designate a phylactery.

[3] Bonner (1950), Plate XIV, seal 294. Recently sold by Christies, sale item D4821734r.

The only controversial examples are seven small mostly Christian amulets where the word φυλακτήριον appears.[1] Most of these are late (5th century) and Christian, by which time the functional distinction between amulet and phylactery had become blurred. Given the post 5th century Christian aversion to magic, these items are unlikely to have been phylacteries. This blurring is also very obvious in the two Christian amulets number 65 and 66 (both begin with a cross and containing Christian formulae) analysed by Kotansky,[2] who rightfully calls them amulets despite the presence of the word '*phylacterion*' on the first line of each.

One complex amulet against fever invokes the protection of the five angels Ouriēl, Michaēl, Gabriēl, Souriēl and Raphaēl down the left hand side; the ouroboros (enclosing Semesilam and a vowel string); Ablanathanabla, Achrammachamari, Sesengh[en] B[ar] Pharagēs, Iaō, Sabaōth and Ōripherlou on the right side; and a personalisation for the client Touthous over Adōnias, Adōnaei. The triple crossed 'ZZZ' and 'SSS' also feature in the middle (see Figure 31).

A number of amulets were designed for health reasons and could have been marked both 'A' and 'H' but these have been categorised by method as Amulets 'A,' rather than by outcome, Health 'H.' As a further guide to identification in Table A and A2 those items are marked that have an 'amulet format.' Amulet formats include wing shaped amulets, narrow columns systematically folded, or narrow columns with *charaktēres* written on small scraps of papyrus which contain no ritual instructions.[3]

Αδωναι Ελο[αι Cα]βαωθ Αβλαναθαναβ[λα Ακρ]α̣μμαχαμαρι /
Cεcενγ[ε]ρ Βαρφαρ̣[αν]γηc / αεηιουω / Ιαω Φρη[c.5]ηαω ιαω εαω

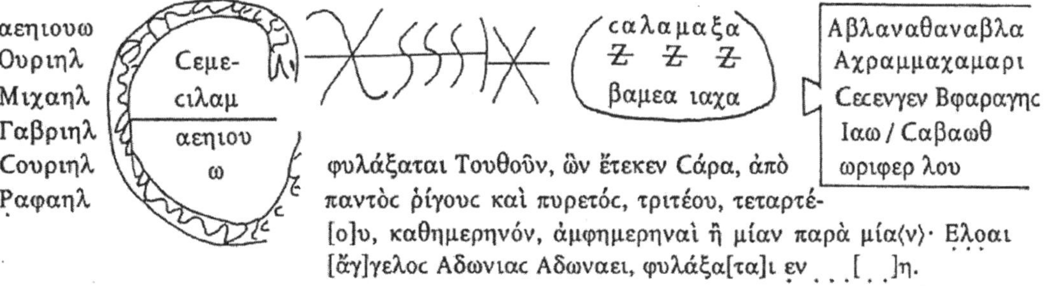

Figure 31: A complex amulet against fever, for a named client, with many typical *nomina magica*.[4]

---

[1] *PGM* VII. 218-221; LXX. 1-4; XCIV. 10-16; CXXVIII. 1-11; XC. 14-18 (*aka SM* 92b); *SM* 34; *SM*.64.
[2] Kotansky (1994), pp. 377-382.
[3] See *PGM* XVIIc. 1-14 and XVIIIB. 1-7 for examples.
[4] SM 10 and *PGM* CVI. See Daniel and Maltomini (1990), Vol 1, p. 27.

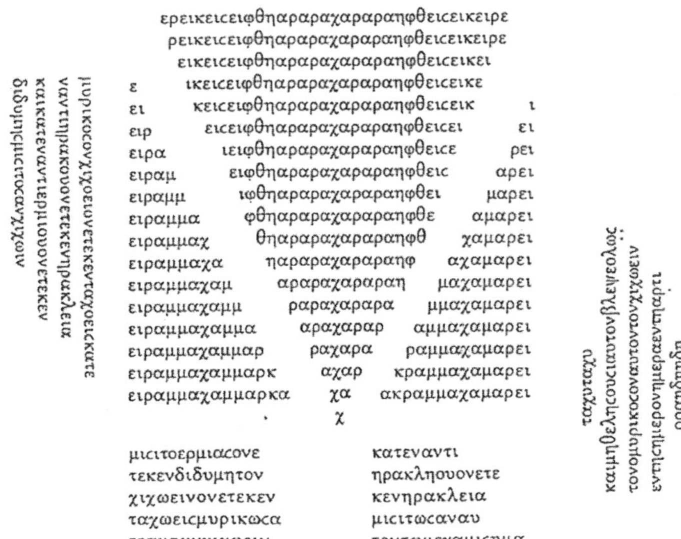

Figure 32: A Graeco-Egyptian wing formation amulet.[1]

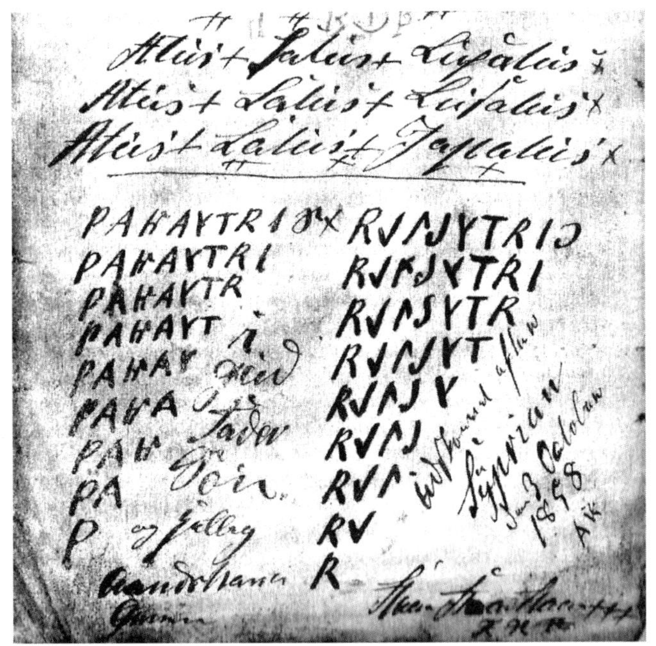

Figure 33: A similar wing formation in a 19th century cunning-man's grimoire.[2]

Amulets, which were the day-to-day 'bread and butter' of client sales for magicians, make up 15.7% of all the *PGM* by rite, or 7.4% in numbers of lines.

[1] *PGM* XXXIX. 1-21 in Preisendanz Vol. 2 (1931), p. 177.

[2] A grimoire written by Anders Ulfkjaer in or before October 1858, copied from 'Sÿpran' i.e. the *Grimoire of St. Cyprian,* reproduced in Davies (2009), p. 130.

Amulets (A) πρὸς (*pros*)

Gods, Angels, Daimones, names of magicians, *nomina magica*	Non-Roman *PGM* Nos.	Category	No. of lines	Betz Papyrus *PGM/PDM/SM* Reference number	Objective/ Technique	Greek Headwords
	7	A	4	*PGM* VII. 193-196	Amulet against scorpion sting	πρὸς[1]
	7	A	2	*PGM* VII. 197-198	Amulet against eye discharge	πρὸς
Zeus	7	A	2	*PGM* VII. 199-201	Amulet against headache, migraine.	πρὸς
Abrasax	7	A	2	*PGM* VII. 201-202	Amulet against headache, migraine.	ἄλλο [πρὸς] [2]
	7	A	3	*PGM* VII. 203-205	Amulet against coughs	πρὸς
	7	A	3	*PGM* VII. 206-207	Health amulet on hyena parchment	ἄλλο [πρὸς]
	7	A	2	*PGM* VII. 208-209	Amulet against hardening of the breasts	πρὸς
	7	A	3	*PGM* VII. 209-210	Amulet against swollen testicles	πρὸς
Sabaōth	7	A	2	*PGM* VII. 211-212	Amulet against fever with shivering fits	πρὸς
	7	A	2	*PGM* VII. 213-214	Amulet against daily and nightly fever	πρὸς
Aiōn	7	A	4	*PGM* VII. 370-373	Amulet against wild animals & robbers	πρὸς [name facility][3]
	12	A	4	*PGM* XII. 397-400	Amulet made of wormwood to attract favour and friendship forever	πρὸς
Ablanathanalba	17	A	14	*PGM* XVIIc. 1-14	Amulet	[n/h] [amulet format]

1 For.

2 Another [for].

3 'Name facility' indicates where "NN" or more often "NN daughter/son of NN" (δεῖνα or δεῖνα τῆς δεῖνα) provides a place to insert the client's name. Where the actual client's name is inserted then the amulet is categorized as 'A2.'

Gods, Angels, Daimones, names of magicians, *nomina magica*	Non-Roman *PGM* Nos.	Category	No. of lines	Betz Papyrus *PGM/PDM/SM* Reference number	Objective/ Technique	Greek Headwords
Sabaōth	18	A	4	*PGM* XVIIIa. 1-4	Amulet against headache	[n/h]
	20	A	4	*PGM* XX. 1-4	Amulet against headache	[πρὸ]ς
Sabaōth, Ouriel	42	A	10	*PGM* XLII. 1-10	Amulet	[n/h] [amulet format]
Michaēl	44	A	18	*PGM* XLIV. 1-18	Amulet against fever and earache.[1]	[n/h] [amulet format]
Satoucheos, Sabaōth	47	A	17	*PGM* XLVII. 1-17	Amulet against fever	[n/h]
Aiōn	49	A	1	*PGM* XLIX	Amulet	[n/h] [amulet format]
	62	A	31	*PGM* LXII. 76-106	Amulet to prevent harm to a woman's womb and genitals. Moon/heart shaped	[n/h] [amulet format]
	63	A	2	*PGM* LXIII. 24-25	Contraceptive amulet	[n/h]
	63	A	3	*PGM* LXIII. 26-28	Contraceptive amulet	[n/h]
Ochthia	65	A	4	*PGM* LXV. 1-4	Amulet for pregnancy prevention	πρὸς
	65	A	4	*PGM* LXV. 4-7	Amulet against headache, migraine cure.	πρὸς
	70	A	26	*PGM* LXX. 26-51	Amulet against fear and to dissolve spells	πρὸς φόβον καὶ ἀναλύων[2]

[1] Not a phylactery as suggested by Kotansky.

[2] For fear, and to dissolve [spells].

Gods, Angels, Daimones, names of magicians, *nomina magica*	Non-Roman PGM Nos.	Category	No. of lines	Betz Papyrus *PGM/PDM/SM* Reference number	Objective/ Technique	Greek Headwords
Iao, Michaēl, Gabriēl, Rhaphaēl, Ouriēl, Ēlēlyth, Iabaōth, Phabriēl, Ebriēl, Soboōs, Abēl, Ariēl, Anaēl, Kemouēl, Abaal, Sabaōth	90	A	13	*PGM* XC. 1-13 *SM* 92 a	Amulet to protect a horse. With signs.	[n/h]
	90	A	5	*PGM* XC. 14-18 *SM* 92 b	Amulet against shivering.	φυλ[ακτήριον][1] - line 14
	94	A	3	*PGM* XCIV 7-9 *SM* 94 b	Amulet for easy childbirth	πρ[ὸς]… περιάπτω[2] - line 7
	94	A	7	*PGM* XCIV. 10-16 *SM* 94 c	Amulet against fever.[3]	[φυλακτή]ριον[4]
	94	A	9	*PGM* XCIV. 27-35 *SM* 94 f	Amulet to protect against tumours	πρ[ὸς]
Bainchōōōch	96	A	8	*PGM* XCVI. 1-8 *SM* 15	Amulet, with the phrase 'protect the wearer'	[n/h] [amulet format]
	97	A	4	*PGM* XCVII. 10-13	Amulet	[n/h]
	99	A	3	*PGM* XCIX. 1-3 *SM* 33	Fragment, maybe an amulet with *crux ansata*	[n/h]
Sebaōn, Sbaōth (*sic*)	112	A	5	*PGM* CXII. 1-5 *SM* 16	Amulet against a scorpion sting	[n/h] [amulet format]
	113	A	4	*PGM* CXIII. 1-4 *SM* 17	Amulet against a scorpion sting, with drawing of a scorpion	[n/h]

[1] Despite the very speculative reconstruction of φυλ[ακτήριον], as this is made to counteract fever it is much more likely to be an amulet. By the 5th century the distinction between amulet and phylactery was fading, particularly in the early Christian millieu.

[2] Amulet.

[3] This is part of a list of other amulets, is against fever, and it is not set out at the end of a rite, therefore it is definitely an amulet.

[4] A very suspect reconstruction based on the last four letters, which Betz translates as 'salve.' Furthermore Betz notes that "the charm apparently served as a fever amulet."

Gods, Angels, Daimones, names of magicians, *nomina magica*	Non-Roman *PGM* Nos.	Category	No. of lines	Betz Papyrus *PGM/PDM/SM* Reference number	Objective/ Technique	Greek Headwords
	120	A	13	*PGM* CXX. 1-13	Amulet in a grape-shaped wing formation against inflammation of the uvula	[n/h] [amulet format]
Marmarithi, Brimō, Christ, Ablanathanapa-mbalanathanath, Raphaēl	123	A	23	*PGM* CXXIIIa. 1-23 *SM* 96A 1-23	Multi-use amulet for love, childbearing, sleep, against shivering, fits and for victory	[n/h] [amulet format]
Christ	123	A	3	*PGM* CXXIIIa. 48-50 *SM* 96A 48-50	Christian Amulet for childbearing	πρ[ὸς]
Thara Tharō	123	A	2	*PGM* CXXIIIa. 51-52 *SM* 96A 51-52	Amulet for sleep	[n/h] [amulet format]
	123	A	3	*PGM* CXXIIIa. 53-55 *SM* 96A 53-55	Amulet for strangury (a urinary condition)	[n/h] [amulet format]
[A]blanathanapa mbalanathanath, Raphaēl, EI	123	A	13	*PGM* CXXIIIa. 56-68 *SM* 96A 56-68	Amulet against fever with shivering fits	[n/h] [amulet format]
	123	A	3	*PGM* CXXIIIa. 69-71 *SM* 96A 69-71	Victory amulet using a hyena tooth	νίκᾶ[ν][1]
	123	A	1	*PGM* CXXIIIb. *SM* 96B	Fragmentary amulet	[n/h] [amulet format]
	123	A	1	*PGM* CXXIIIc. *SM* 96C	Fragmentary amulet	[n/h] [amulet format]
	123	A	1	*PGM* CXXIIId. *SM* 96D	Fragmentary amulet	[n/h] [amulet format]
Adonaei, Eloei, Menouba, Sabaōth	123	A	1	*PGM* CXXIIIf. *SM* 96F	Amulet with a crude necklace drawing	[n/h] [amulet format]
	129	A	7	*PGM* CXXIX. 1-7 *SM* 81	Fragmentary amulet to be written on a lamella	[n/h]
	-	A	13	*SM* 1	Amulet with wing formation	[n/h] [amulet format]
Obach, Bararathan baroch Abraham sabaraam	-	A	20	*SM* 2	Silver fever amulet	[n/h]

1 Victory is an objective, but not 'T2.'

Gods, Angels, Daimones, names of magicians, *nomina magica*	Non-Roman PGM Nos.	Category	No. of lines	Betz Papyrus *PGM/PDM/SM* Reference number	Objective/ Technique	Greek Headwords
	-	A	4	*SM* 5	Note concerning an amulet against tonsillitis	τὸ πρὸς
Solomon, God	-	A	12	*SM* 24	Amulet containing a spirit binding in the name of Solomon.[1]	[n/h]
Ēl, Sabaōth, Emmanuēl	-	A	7	*SM* 27	Christian amulet	[n/h] [amulet format]
Jesus Christ	-	A	9	*SM* 30	Christian amulet	[n/h]
Jesus Christ, Virgin Mary, Father, Son, Holy Ghost	-	A	4	*SM 31*	Christian amulet against fever	[n/h]
Toumēēl Êl, Sabaōth, Adonaei, Aoth, Michaēl, Gabriēl, Ouriēl, Raphaēl	-	A	12	*SM* 32	Christian amulet against migraine and eye discharge	[n/h]
Adōnaie, Sabaōth	-	A	7	*SM* 64	Silver lamella amulet for favour, love, success and charm.	[n/h] φυ[λα]κττήριον[2] – lines 6-7
Ablanathanalba	-	A	10	*SM* 67	Wing format ostracon amulet with fragmentary instructions on the reverse	[n/h] [amulet format]
	-	A	4	*SM* 68	Ostracon amulet	[n/h]
[Seth]	-	A	3	*SM* 69	Drawing of Seth, possibly an amulet or simply a list of his qualities	[n/h]

[1] This has the intriguing possibility of perhaps being a papyrus attached to a seal for a bottle designed for spirit capture, because of the reference to Solomon who "seized all the demons…vessel (?) and having bound [them in a] brazen [bottle]."

[2] It is an amulet despite the use of the word φυλακττήριον (*sic*). According to Kotansky (1994), p. 356 this is anyway a very subjective reading. If it was a phylactery then it would be providing protection from conjured spiritual creatures rather than material benefits like love and success.

Gods, Angels, Daimones, names of magicians, *nomina magica*	Non-Roman *PGM* Nos.	Category	No. of lines	Betz Papyrus *PGM/PDM/SM* Reference number	Objective/ Technique	Greek Headwords
Gē, Abraham	-	A	19	*SM* 88	Medico-magical recipes against erysipelas and the 'red eruption.' Probably two amulets	πρ[ὸς] πρ[ὸς] – line 4
Total A		**60**	**427**			

Table A: Amulets.

Amulets Personalised for Named Clients (A2)

Gods, Angels, Daimones, names of magicians, *nomina magica*	**Non-Roman PGM Nos.**	**Category**	**No. of lines**	**Betz Papyrus *PGM/PDM/SM* Reference number**	**Objective/ Technique**	**Greek Headwords**
Anubis, Ablanathanalba Akrammachamari	17	A2	25	*PGM* XVIIa. 1-25	Amulet for love or attraction, with diamond shaped wing layout	[n/h] [amulet format] [named person]
Gorgōphōnas [Gorgon slayer]	18	A2	7	*PGM* XVIIIb. 1-7	Fever amulet with a wing formation	[n/h] [amulet format] [named person]
Ablanathanablana Mach Aramarach, Kok, Kouk Koul	33	A2	25	*PGM* XXXIII. 1-25	Fever amulet with large V-shaped wing formation	[n/h] [amulet format] [named person]
[Bes]	39	A2	21	*PGM* XXXIX. 1-21	Love amulet. Large double wing format	[n/h] [amulet format] [named person]
Souriel, Gabriel, Raphael, Michael, Sabaōth	43	A2	27	*PGM* XLIII. 1-27	Amulet against fever, with twelve angel names	[n/h] [amulet format] [named person]
Sabaōth, Michaēl, Abraham, Isaac, Jacob, Elōei, Ele	83	A2	20	*PGM* LXXXIII. 1-20 *SM* 29	Amulet against fever with shivering fits.[1]	πρὸς [named person]
				PGM LXXXIV. 1-21	*See L2* [2]	
	86	A2	2	*PGM* LXXXVI. 1-2 *SM* 80 a	Amulet, as it mentions an attachment round the neck	[n/h] [named persons]
	86	A2	5	*PGM* LXXXVI. 3-7 *SM* 80 b	Rite on 10th day of Didymon (Gemini)[3]	[n/h]
Samousoum Souma	87	A2	11	*PGM* LXXXVII. 1-11 *SM* 14	Fever amulet	[n/h] [named person]
Zagourē Pagourē	88	A2	19	*PGM* LXXXVIII. 1-19 *SM* 11	Fever amulet with V-shaped wing layout	[n/h] [amulet format] [named person]
Abrasax	89	A2	27	*PGM* LXXXIX. 1-27 *SM* 13	Amulet against fever, phantoms and daimones	[n/h] [named person]
Ablanathanalba	91	A2	14	*PGM* XCI. 1-14 *SM* 9	Fever amulet with V-shaped wing layout	[n/h] [amulet format] [named person]

[1] Christianised Jewish formula.

[2] V-shaped amulet format for attracting a named person, so also L2.

[3] Possibly a timing instruction for the previous two line amulet.

Gods, Angels, Daimones, names of magicians, *nomina magica*	Non-Roman PGM Nos.	Category	No. of lines	Betz Papyrus *PGM/PDM/SM* Reference number	Objective/ Technique	Greek Headwords
Ablatnathamala (*sic*), Akrammachamari, Jesus Christ	100	A2	7	*PGM* C. 1-7 *SM* 20	Christian amulet for healing	[n/h] [amulet format] [named person]
Aeōth	104	A2	8	*PGM* CIV. 1-8 *SM* 4	Amulet against fever	[n/h] [named person]
Adōnai Eloai Sabaōth Ablanathanabla, Adōnaei Akrammachamari Sesenger bar Pharanges Iaō Phrē, Ouriēl, Michaēl, Gabriēl, Souriēl, Raphaēl, Adōnias, Seme-silam	106	A2	10	*PGM* CVI. 1-10 *SM* 10	Elaborate amulet against fever with triple-bar 'Z,' triple-bar 'S' Chnoubis sign, and an ouroboros[1]	[n/h] [amulet format] [named person]
Hekate	114	A2	14	*PGM* CXIV. 1-14 *SM* 84	Amulet against attacks by daimones and against epilepsy	[n/h] [name facility]
Zarachthō, Necessity, Maskeli, Maskelō, Phnoukentabaōth	115	A2	7	*PGM* CXV. 1-7 *SM* 12	Fever amulet	[n/h] [named person]
Jesus Christ, son of IAŌ	128	A2	11	*PGM* CXXVIII. 1-11 *SM* 28	Christian amulet against fever	φυλακτήριον πρὸς[2] [amulet format] [named person]
Iarbath	130	A2	13	*PGM* CXXX. 1-13 *SM* 3	Amulet against fever with shivering fits	[n/h] [amulet format] [named person]
ΘΚΠ		A2	11	*SM* 8	Amulet[3]	[n/h] [amulet format] [named person]
Ablanathanalba		A2	20	*SM* 18	Fever amulet, with *charaktēres*	[n/h] [amulet format] [named person]
Damnameneus, Akramachamari, Cherubim, Seraphim		A2	28	*SM* 19	Fever amulet, with *charaktēres*	[n/h] [amulet format] [named person]

1 Illustration in Betz (1996), p. 311. See Figure 31.

2 Not a 'phylactery' because it is against fever and for a named person. This is an example of 5th century Christian confusion over the difference between an amulet and a phylactery.

3 Illustration in *SM*, p. 22. It is possible that this is a phylactery for use in a rite involving water.

Gods, Angels, Daimones, names of magicians, *nomina magica*	Non-Roman PGM Nos.	Category	No. of lines	Betz Papyrus *PGM/PDM/SM* Reference number	Objective/ Technique	Greek Headwords
Father, Holy Ghost, Ablanathanabla		A2	20	*SM* 21	Christian fever amulet	[n/h] [amulet format] [named person]
Jesus Christ		A2	20	*SM* 22	Christian fever amulet	[n/h] [amulet format] [named person]
Christ		A2	17	*SM* 23	Christian amulet against fever and shivering.	[amulet format] [named person] φυλ[α]κτήριον – line 8[1]
Jesus Christ		A2	10	*SM* 25	Christian amulet against fever	[n/h] [named person]
		A2	9	*SM* 26	Christian amulet against eye disease	[n/h] [named person]
Jesus Christ, Erichthonios		A2	13	*SM* 34	Christian amulet against fever – V shaped	[amulet format] [named person] φυλακτήριον – line 10[2]
Christ		A2	15	*SM* 35[3]	Christian amulet against fever.	[n/h] [amulet format] [named person]
Akrachamiphōnchō ōth-psaus	-	A2 L2	21	*SM* 40	Love amulet to which was attached *ousia* (hair).	[n/h] [amulet format] [named person]
	-	A2 L5	13	*SM* 41	Lead tablet for love.[4]	[n/h] [amulet format] [named person]
[Many god and angel names. See Appendix 3]		A2	121	Kotansky 52	Large personalised amulet with detailed angelic hierarchy.[5]	[n/h] [amulet format] [named person]
Total A2		**32**	**591**			

Table A2: Personalised Amulets for Named Clients.

[1] Not a phylactery, despite the use of the word φυλακτήριον Typically 5th century Christian usage begins to blur the distinction between amulet and phylactery.

[2] An amulet despite the Christian use of the word φυλακτήριον.

[3] *SM* 36 has been omitted as it is a Latin Psalm.

[4] Despite being made of lead, as it was not found in a tomb or watercourse this is not likely to be a *defixio*.

[5] Kotansky (1994), No. 52, pp. 270-300. See Appendix 3 for the complete hierarchy.

Talismans - τέλεσμα (*telesma*)

The word talisman is derived from the Byzantine Greek τέλεσμα *telesma* ("religious rite or consecration ceremony") and not from either τελειόω *teleioō* ("to bring to perfection or completion")[1] or from the Classical Greek τέλεσμα *telesma* ("money paid").[2] This word may however be related to an Arabic loan word, *tilsām*. Talismans are designed to be consecrated or charged in order to embody specific magical objectives, and are not designed for generalised protection or health like an amulet. In the *PGM* talismans are often referred to as στήλη (*stēlē*) which in this context refers to a lamella or to the text written upon a lamella, metal plate or foil.

Talismans have been here divided according to their intent, as embodied in their headword:

T: Talismans, general - στήλη (*stēlē*)

T2: Victory Talismans - νικητικὸν (*nikētikon*)

T3: Restraining Anger Talismans – θυμοκάτοχον (*thymokatochon*)

T4: Binding or Coercion Talismans – κάτοχος (*katochos*)

Talismans are drawn, painted, engraved or carved designs made on paper, parchment, metal or occasionally stone. Their objectives are proactive and very specific, such as winning the love of a specific woman, winning a specific chariot race, etc, and not for general protection from sundry ills, disease or bad luck. In contrast amulets are just a passive form of protection against a more generalized threat, whereas talismans are designed to *cause* a specific change.

For example a Venus talisman might be designed to accumulate the qualities of that planet/goddess to act for the magician in an operation to secure the love of a specific woman. Talismans are not usually worn (as are amulets), but can be simply created, charged, and then left to do their work. Unlike amulets, talismans do not need to be in close physical proximity with their owner.[3]

A talisman is designed to achieve one particular magical objective. The process of making such a talisman consists of invoking a particular power or specific spiritual creature into an inscribed parchment or engraved on a metal disk at

---

[1] Johnston (2008), p. 155 associates τελειόω, in the sense of 'perfection,' with the Greek words for initiate and initiation. See *PGM* IV. 26-51 for this usage.

[2] This shows that the word came into use via Byzantine Greek magical texts, rather than necessarily being part of Classical Greek religion. If the term was a transliteration from Arabic, then it may *possibly* be derived from the separate Astral Magic tradition.

[3] A pentacle is a specific type of talisman, which perhaps originally incorporated the figure of a pentagram inscribed within a circle. Now the term is often used interchangeably with 'talisman.'

the correct time.

As one 17th century writer succinctly put it:

> A talisman is nothing else than the seal, figure, character, or image of a celestial omen, planet, or constellation; impressed, engraved, or sculptured upon a sympathetic stone or upon a metal corresponding to the planet; by a workman whose mind is settled and fixed upon his work and the end of his work without being distracted or dissipated in other unrelated thoughts; on the day and at the hour of the planet; in a fortunate place; during fair, calm weather, and when the planet is in the best aspect that may be in the heavens, the more strongly to attract the influences proper to an effect depending upon the power of the same and on the virtues of its influences.[1]

One particularly interesting *stēlē* can be seen in Figure 34. This incorporates several *charaktēres* and the names Damnameneus and Akrammachamarei (the same as in the talisman in Figure 36). Both are 'gods of the hour:' Damnameneus being a goddess of the 4th hour and Akrammachamarei a god of the 3rd hour.

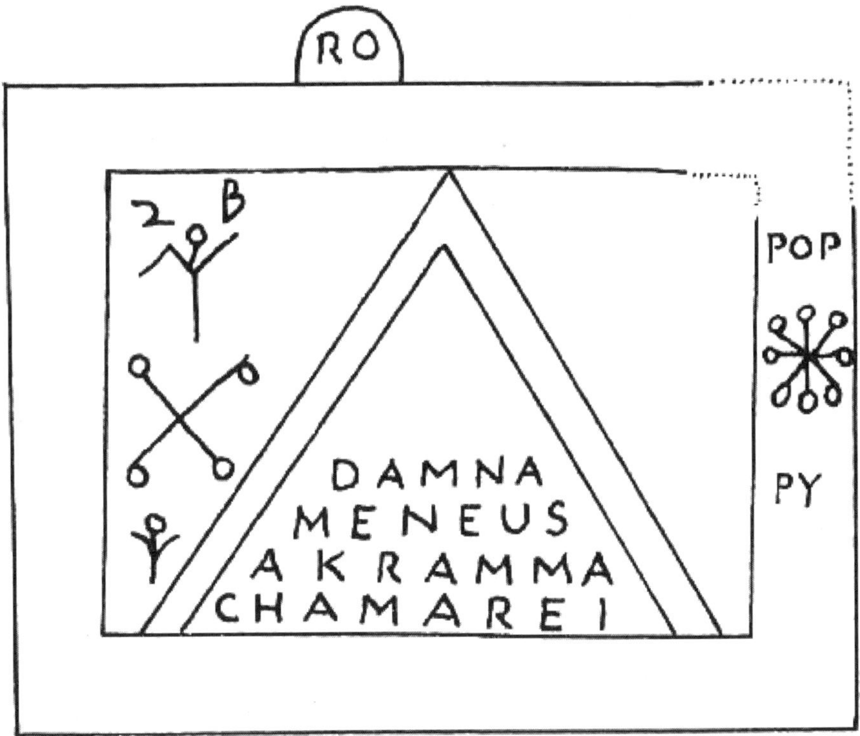

Figure 34: A tin *stēlē* of Aphrodite designed to gain friendship and favour.[2] It includes the name of two 'hour gods.'[3]

---

[1] de Bresche (1671).

[2] *PGM* VII. 215-218. Redrawn in Betz (1996), p. 122.

[3] See Table 04.

Talismans for victory in court, the games, or the arena 'T2' are a specialised subset of talismans, easily recognisable by the presence of the headword νικητικὸν, victory.[1] These mostly occur in *PGM* VII. An excellent example of this type of talisman (Figure 35) is designed for victory, probably in a courtroom setting, where it is desirable for some witnesses not to be able to speak.

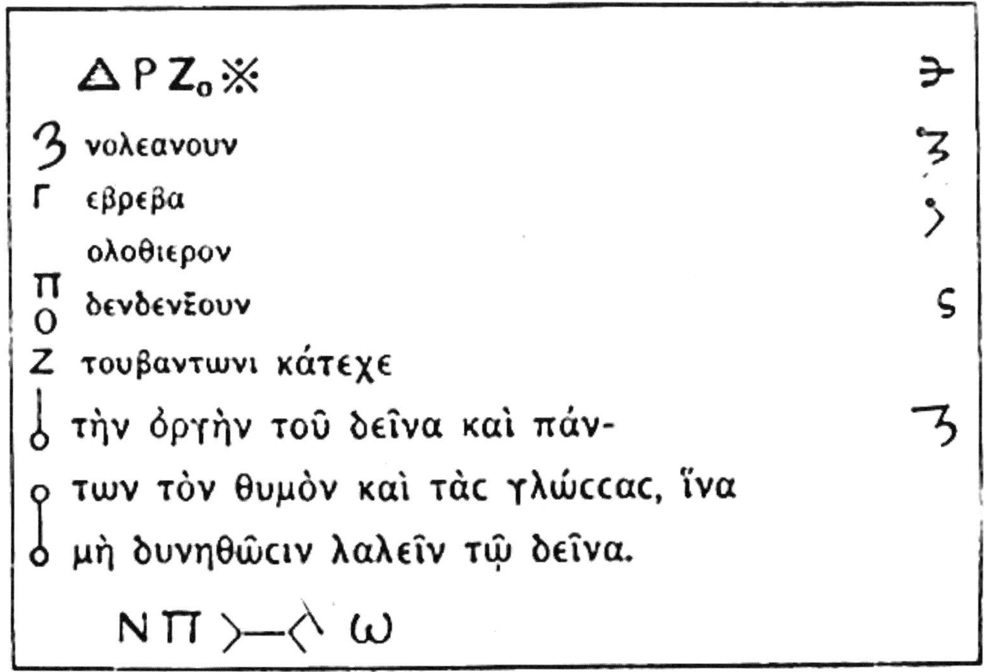

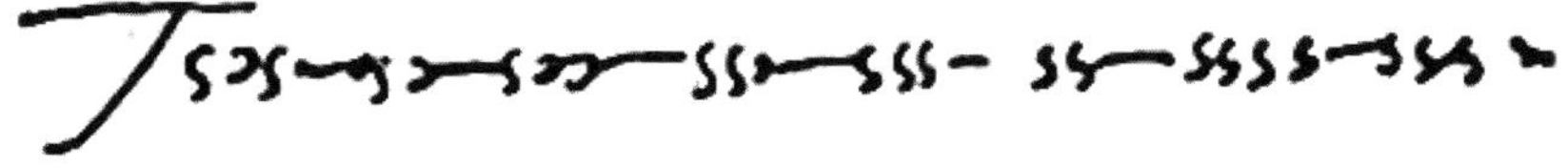

Figure 35: A lead talisman for victory (νικητικὸν) and subjection (ὑποτακτικόν).[2] "Restrain the wrath of him, NN, and the anger and tongues of everybody, in order that they might not be able to speak to him, NN."

Talismans for restraining anger (T3) or binding an opponent or enemy (T4) are also quite common in the *PGM*. They are here listed separately, as they form a distinct group with distinct headwords. Binding formulae κάτοχος (*katochos*) are categorised as 'T4.' These are used for general binding or restraining, not just anger. They could be used to bind the tongue of a hostile witness or advocate in a court trial. Hence these quite often cross over with procedures designed to secure victory in court ('T2').

---

[1] In this case ἄλλο [νικητικὸν], και ὑποτακτικόν.

[2] *PGM* VII. 925-935. From Preisandanz (1931), Vol. 2, p. 41.

Although some talismans fulfil several of the four main objectives listed above, there will be no cross referencing between the various types of talisman, as that would really serve no purpose.

The manufacture of talismans for specific magical purposes (T-T4) makes up 8.1% of all the *PGM* rites, or 5.2% by lineage.

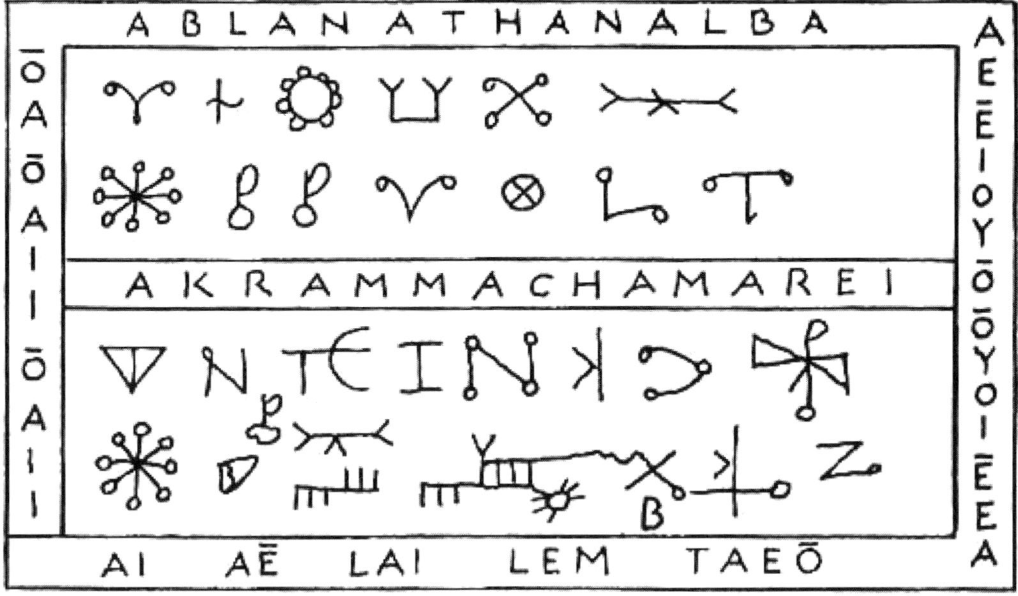

Figure 36: Talisman for restraining the anger of enemies and accusers (in court) to be made of a gold or silver lamella.[1] Note that the side panels are filled with combinations of the seven Greek vowels. The horizontal *nomina magica* are the usual Ablanathanalba, Akrammachamarei, and on the bottom bar the less common Ai Aē Lai Lem Taeō.

[1] *PGM* X. 24-35. Transliterated and redrawn in Betz (1996), p. 149.

Talismans - στήλη (*stēlē*) (T)

Gods, Angels, Daimones, names of magicians, *nomina magica*	Non-Roman *PGM* Nos.	Category	No. of lines	Betz Papyrus *PGM/PDM* Reference number	Objective/ Technique	Greek Headword
Aion	4	T	52	*PGM* IV. 1115-1166	Secret *Stēlē*:[1] all-embracing prayer to the four Elements, aerial spirits, etc	Στήλη ἀπόκρυφος[2]
Helios, [Aiōn]	4	T	60	*PGM* IV. 1167-1226	*Stēlē* (talisman) for all things, addressed to Aion, the four Elements and the aerial spirits.[3] Uses a gold leaf *stēlē*.	[σ]τήλη πρὸ πάντα εὔχρηστος[4]
				PGM IV. 1716-1840	*See L2*	
				PGM IV. 2145-2240	*See Ω*	
Aphrodite, Damnameneus, Akrammachammarei	7	T	4	*PGM* VII. 215-218	Tin *stēlē* of Aphrodite. Talisman for favour and friends.[5]	Ἀφροδίτης στήλη.[6]
	7	T	12	*PGM* VII. 260-271	Conjuration preventing the ascent of the uterus. With Jewish overtones. Written on a tin *stēlē*.[7]	πρὸς μήτρα ἀναδρομήν[8]
Chōnsou	7	T	1	*PGM* VII. 300	Spiral shaped talisman containing an ibis	σαχμουοζοζ
				PGM VII. 459-461 *PGM* VII. 462-466	*See L3*	

[1] *Stēlē* is used here in the sense of an invocation or prayer copied from a stone *stēlē* or from a standard text.

[2] Secret *stēlē*. Here it means an invocation copied from a *stēlē* rather than the *stēlē* itself.

[3] This is clearly marked as a *stēlē* (talisman), not a 'prayer' as suggested by Dieleman (2005), p. 271.

[4] *Stēlē* useful for all things.

[5] Includes part of the *Ephesian Grammata*. The text specifies that it must only "to be carried when pure," so it is a talisman not a day-to-day use amulet. See Figure 34.

[6] Aphrodite's *stēlē* [talisman].

[7] This example of medical conjuration is categorized as an exorcism in Kotansky (1995, 201), pp. 266-268, although its prime purpose is not to eject the womb, but to anchor it.

[8] To control a 'wandering womb.'

[9] *Sachmouozozo*. Possibly the name of a daimon. Maybe connected with Thoth as the talisman is inscribed with the image of an ibis.

Gods, Angels, Daimones, names of magicians, *nomina magica*	Non-Roman *PGM* Nos.	Category	No. of lines	Betz Papyrus *PGM/PDM* Reference number	Objective/ Technique	Greek Headwords
Bainchōōōch, Sabaōth, Abrasax, Maskelli Maskellō	9	T	14	*PGM* IX. 1-14	Talisman and invocation of the daimon Bainchōōōch to enslave all people and suppress anger.[1]	[n/h]
	14	T	12	*PDM* xiv. 1003-1014	Described as an amulet against gout. But as it is made of silver or tin, it is probably a talisman	[Demotic] [n/h]
Abraham, Isaac, Jacob, Iaō, Eloē, Sabaōth, Adōnai, Albanathanalba, Akramachamari, Sarachael, Biliam[2]	35	T	42	*PGM* XXXV. 1-42	Elaborate Hebrew influenced talisman for favour and power.[3] Includes details of the rulers of the heavens.[4]	ἐπικαλοῦμαι[5] [named persons] [amulet format]
	36	T	10	*PGM* XXXVI. 178-187	Lead talisman to break spells	Λυσιφάρμακον[6]
Senseggen bar Pharggēs Maskelli Maskellō	36	T	25	*PGM* XXXVI. 231-255	Talisman to inflict harm. Large drawing of a lead lamella with a female figure cutting off a head	[n/h] [name facility] [amulet format]
	36	T	9	*PGM* XXXVI. 256-264	Talisman to dissolve enchantments	[n/h]
	36	T	11	*PGM* XXXVI. 264-274	Talisman on papyrus	[n/h]
	36	T	9	*PGM* XXXVI. 275-283	Silver lamella (talisman) for gaining favour. Also used to repel daimones	χαριτήσιν μέγα πρὸς παρόντας και πρὸς ὄχλους,[7]
Iō Erbēth, Pakerbēth, Bolchosēth, Abrasax	58	T	25	*PGM* LVlll. 15-39	Lunar rite. List of *nomina magica* probably to be inscribed on a *stēlē.*	[n/h]

[1] See Figure 19.
[2] A magician.
[3] It invokes the 'gods' Abraham, Isaac and Jacob.
[4] See Table 18, and Kotansky (1994), No. 52, pp. 270-300.
[5] Summon.
[6] Remedy against spells.
[7] Formula for winning favour great for all and for crowds.

Gods, Angels, Daimones, names of magicians, *nomina magica*	Non-Roman PGM Nos.	Category	No. of lines	Betz Papyrus *PGM/PDM* Reference number	Objective/ Technique	Greek Headword
Typhon, Osiris, Maskelli Maskellō Phnoun Kentabaōth, Hippochthōn, Iaō	78	T L7	14	*PGM* LXXVIII. 1-14	Love talisman of lead to be nailed up in a house or workshop, therefore not an amulet. 3rd century.[1]	[n/h] [name facility]
	94	T H	3	*PGM* XCIV. 36-38 *SM* 94 g	Tin lamella against strangury (a urinary condition)	πρ[ὸς]
	94	T H	20	*PGM* XCIV. 39-60 *SM* 94 h *SM* 94 i	h. Another tin *stēlē* to protect against migraine.[2] i. Formula to be said to prevent a wound getting gangrene.	ἄλλο πρ[ὸς]
Erōtylos, Brimō, Chōnoutha, Zazeas	123	T H	14	*PGM* CXXIIIa. 24-47 *SM* 96A 24-47	Erotylos. Talisman to ease periods. Same as *PGM* CXXIIIe	[n/h] [amulet format]
Erōtylos, Brimō, Chōnoutha, Zazeas	123	T H	1	*PGM* CXXIIIe. *SM* 96E	Talisman related to periods. Duplicate of *PGM* CXXIIIa. 24-47	[n/h] [amulet format]
Total T		**19**	**338**			

Table T: Talismans.

[1] Illustration of the multi-breasted Artemis. See Betz (1996), p. 299.
[2] Arguably an amulet, but as it is described as a *stēlē* it is a talisman.

Talismans for Victory νικητικὸν (*nikētikon*) (T2)

Gods, Angels, Daimones, names of magicians, *nomina magica*	**Non-Roman *PGM* Nos.**	**Category**	**No. of lines**	**Betz Papyrus *PGM/PDM* Reference number**	**Objective/ Technique**	**Greek Headwords**
	7	T2	5	*PGM* VII. 186-190	Talisman for favour & victory, using a gecko	Χαριτήσιον καὶ νικητικόν[1]
	7	T2	4	*PGM* VII. 390-393	Victory talisman for a runner	νικητικὸν δρομέως[2]
Ielios	7	T2	12	*PGM* VII. 528-539	Victory talisman for the races	νικητικὸν[3]
Iermes, Thōouth	7	T2	6	*PGM* VII. 919-924	Hermes' wondrous victory talisman.	νικητικὸν θαυμαστόν τοῦ Ἑρμοῦ[4]
	7	T2	15	*PGM* VII. 925-939	To subject a person, talisman for victory	ἄλλο [νικητικὸν], και ὑποτακτικόν[5]
abriel, Raphael, Iichael, Sabaōth, Iaō, Ielios, Ablanathanalba, Iarpon Chnouphi, krammachamarei	7	T2	10	*PGM* VII. 1017-1026	Victory talisman. Includes the 59-letter name IAEŌ.	νικητικὸν
	27	T2	5	*PGM* XXVII. 1-5	Victory talisman/rite for stadium wins	Νεικητικὸν (*sic*) [named person]
olomon, kryskylos, uonos, Abrasax, dōnios	92	T2	16	*PGM* XCII. 1-16 *SM* 63	To win favour or victory	[n/h] [named persons]
erapis	98	T2	7	*PGM* XCVIII. 1-7 *SM* 7	Against fever, for victory	[n/h] [amulet format] [named person]
	-	T2	7	*SM* 79 e	Victory in court	νεικητικ[όν]
		T2	45	Kotansky 58 [6]	Victory in court	νίκην – lines 13, 43 νίκητὴν - line 22-23 [named persons]
otal T2		**11**	**132**			

Table T2: Talismans for Victory.

[1] For winning favour and victory.
[2] Victory for the races.
[3] Victory [talisman].
[4] Hermes' wonderful victory.
[5] Another [victory] and subjugation [talisman].
[6] Kotansky (1994), No. 58, pp. 331-346. This is a classic example of a victory charm for use in court with a detailed record of all the persons involved.

Restraining Anger Talismans – θυμοκάτοχον (*thymokatochon*) (T3)

Gods, Angels, Daimones, names of magicians, *nomina magica*	Non-Roman *PGM Nos.*	Category	No. of lines	Betz Papyrus *PGM/PDM* Reference number	Objective/ Technique	Greek Headwords
Iō Erbēth, Pakerbēth, Seth	7	T3	29	*PGM* VII. 940-968	Talisman to restrain anger. Its image is referred to as a στήλη.	θυμοκάτοχον καὶ ὑποτακτικόν.[1] στήλη[2] – line 941 [name facility]
Ablanathanalba,	10	T3	12	*PGM* X. 24-35	Gold or silver talisman to restrain anger, enemies, phobias accusers, nightmares and brigands. Illustration.[3]	θυμοκάτοχον[4]
Apollo, Abrasax, Michaēl, Raphaēl, Gabriēl, Souriēl, Zaziēl, Badakiēl, Syliēl, Iaō, Sabaōth, Adōnai	10	T3	15	*PGM* X. 36-50	Apollo's lamella talisman to subject an enemy	ἄλλως ὑποτακτικὸν Ἀπόλλωνος.[5]
Chneōm	12	T3	3	*PGM* XII. 179-181	Restrain anger	…τινὰ ὀργιζόμενόν σοι καταπαῦσαι[6]
Ablanathanalba, Akrannachamari, Iaō, Sabaōth, Adōnai, Elōai, Abrasax	36	T3 T2 L	34	*PGM* XXXVI. 35-68	Silver lamella to restrain anger and secure favour and victory in courts. With large figure illustration.[7]	θυμοκάτοχον καὶ ὑποτακτικόν καὶ νικητικὸν[8] ἀγωγή[9] - line 68 [name facility]

1 Binding anger & submission talisman.

2 *Stēlē.* The description of '*stēlē*' in many of the following clearly marks them as talismans rather than amulets.

3 See Figure 36.

4 Restraining anger.

5 Another way: Apollo's [talisman] to cause submission.

6 To stop someone's anger.

7 See Figure 36.

8 Binding anger, submission and victory [rite].

9 Love rite.

Gods, Angels, Daimones, names of magicians, *nomina magica*	Non-Roman *PGM Nos.*	Category	No. of lines	Betz Papyrus *PGM/PDM* Reference number	Objective/ Technique	Greek Headwords
Chphyris [Khepri], Michaēl, Raphaēl, Roubēl, Souriēl, Azaēl, Aziēl	36	T3 T2	17	*PGM* XXXVI. 161-177	Talisman to restrain anger and give success.	θυμοκάτοχον καὶ νικητικὸν[1]
Helios, Good Daimon, Harpen Knouphi, Ablanathanalba, Akrammachamari	36	T3 T2	20	*PGM* XXXVI. 211-230	Prayer to Helios plus talisman to restrain anger, for victory and favour.	θυμοκάτοχον καὶ νικητικὸν
Abrasax, Michaēl, Thōouth, Neouphneiōth	79	T3	7	*PGM* LXXIX. 1-7	Talisman to restrain anger	θυμοκάτοχον λεγόμ[ε]νον[2] [name facility]
Abrasax, Michael, Thoouth, Neouphneiōth	80	T3	5	*PGM* LXXX. 1-5	Talisman to restrain anger	θυμοκάτοκον λε[γόμενον]
Iaō, Erbēl, Iō, Pakerbēk, Abrasax, IaSabaōth, Adōnai	-	T3 T2	11	*SM* 58	Ostracon for restraining anger, and speech, for victory in court.	θυμοκάτοχον και νικητικών
Aphphouach, Abras[a]x	-	T3	7	*SM* 79 d	Restrainer of wrath	θυμοκατοχον [name facility]
Total T3		11	**160**			

Table T3: Restraining and Binding Anger.

1 Binding anger & victory [rite].

2 Anger binding words.

Binding or Coercion Talismans – κάτοχος (*katochos*) (T4)

Gods, Angels, Daimones, names of magicians, *nomina magica*	**Non-Roman *PGM* Nos.**	**Category**	**No. of lines**	**Betz Papyrus *PGM/PDM* Reference number**	**Objective/ Technique**	**Greek Headwords**
				PGM III. 1-164	*See Ω*	
	7	T4	2	*PGM* VII. 394-395	Restraining, coercive talisman.	Κατόχων ἐπαναγκαστικοί [1]
Bainchōōōch	7	T4 D	9	*PGM* VII. 396-404	Restraining, silencing, and subjecting using a lead lamella talisman	φιμωτικὸν και ὑποτακτικόν γενναῖον καὶ κάτοχος[2]
Maskelli	7	T4 D	6	*PGM* VII. 417-422	Restraining talisman written on a tin lamella	κάτοχος[3]
Osiris, Mnevis, Isis, Amen, Ch[n]oum, "Askei Kai Taskei", Selene	7	T4 D	30	*PGM* VII. 429-458	Restraining talisman for anything, also for illness, chariots, destruction, etc, on a lead lamella. It also conjures daimones and makes them enter (objects or people).[4]	κάτοχ[ος παντ]ὸς[5] κατάδεσμοι - line 454[6]
Typhon, Iō Erbēth, Seth, Pakerbēth, Bolchosēth, Apomps, Aberramenthō,	36	T4	34	*PGM* XXXVI. 1-34	Lead lamella talisman to restrain. With large elaborate illustration of a figure.	κάτοχος[7]
	119	T4 L7	4	*PGM* CXIXa. 7-11 *SM* 82 c	Rite/talisman of (sexual) subjection. Aphrodisiac?	ὑποτακτικόν[8]
Total T4		**6**	**85**			

Table T4: Binding or Coercion Talismans.

---

1 Restraining and coercive rite.
2 An excellent rite for silencing and restraining.
3 Restraining.
4 To be written on a lead plate and thrown into a watercourse, hence it has some of the qualities of a *defixio*.
5 For restraining anything.
6 *Defixio*.
7 Restraining.
8 For subjection.

Phylacteries

Phylactery is a Greek word which may be derived from the Greek φυλακτικός *phylaktikos*, which means 'a safeguard or preservative.'[1] In Latin texts the word is usually rendered as *phylacterium*.[2]

Phylactery strips of papyrus or parchment (often black and white sheepskin)[3] appear in a number of places in the *PGM*. They are almost always specified at the end of the rite where the ritual equipment is listed separately, rather than in a free-standing section of their own. The reason for this is that phylacteries are specific to the rite to which they are attached. In the *PGM*, phylacteries are designed to be worn by the magician during the rite to protect himself from the specific spiritual creature, even including a god, which he was evoking or invoking.

The phylactery was usually worn over the heart or on the forearms of the Graeco-Egyptian magician, to save him from being overpowered by the spiritual creatures he was invoking:

> ...for I have your name as a unique phylactery in my heart, and no flesh, although moved, will overpower me; no spirit will stand against me - neither daimon nor visitation nor any other of the evil beings of Hades, because of your name, which I have in my soul and invoke. Also [be] with me always for good, a good [god dwelling] in a good [man], yourself immune to magic...[4]

Phylacteries were an important item of protection for the magician during the Graeco-Egyptian period. By convention in the *PGM*, the preparations such as the incense, ink, or manufacture and consecration of the phylactery, were written at the end after the description of the rite itself (*praxis*) and the text of the invocation (*logos*). It is remarkable how many scholars simply treat the details of phylactery manufacture as if they were almost accidental jottings or even a separate passage at the end of the text of the main rite.

If you look at Table U2 you will see that in each case they are located at the end of the rite in which they are to be used. It is therefore very hard to understand why Roy Kotansky could write:

> A phylactery...is a type of amulet used more specifically to protect an individual or community from some impending calamity or plague.[5]

---

[1] The word 'phylactery' only appears once in the New Testament (*Matthew* 23:5) where it is just used as a slighting reference to the *tefillin* of the rabbis, a confusion that has been preserved into modern times.

[2] See Betz (1996), pp. 51, 54, 68.

[3] In "Mithras Liturgy" in *PGM* IV. 814-820.

[4] *PGM* XIII. 795-805. This is more of a 'metaphorical' phylactery.

[5] Kotansky (1997), p. 107.

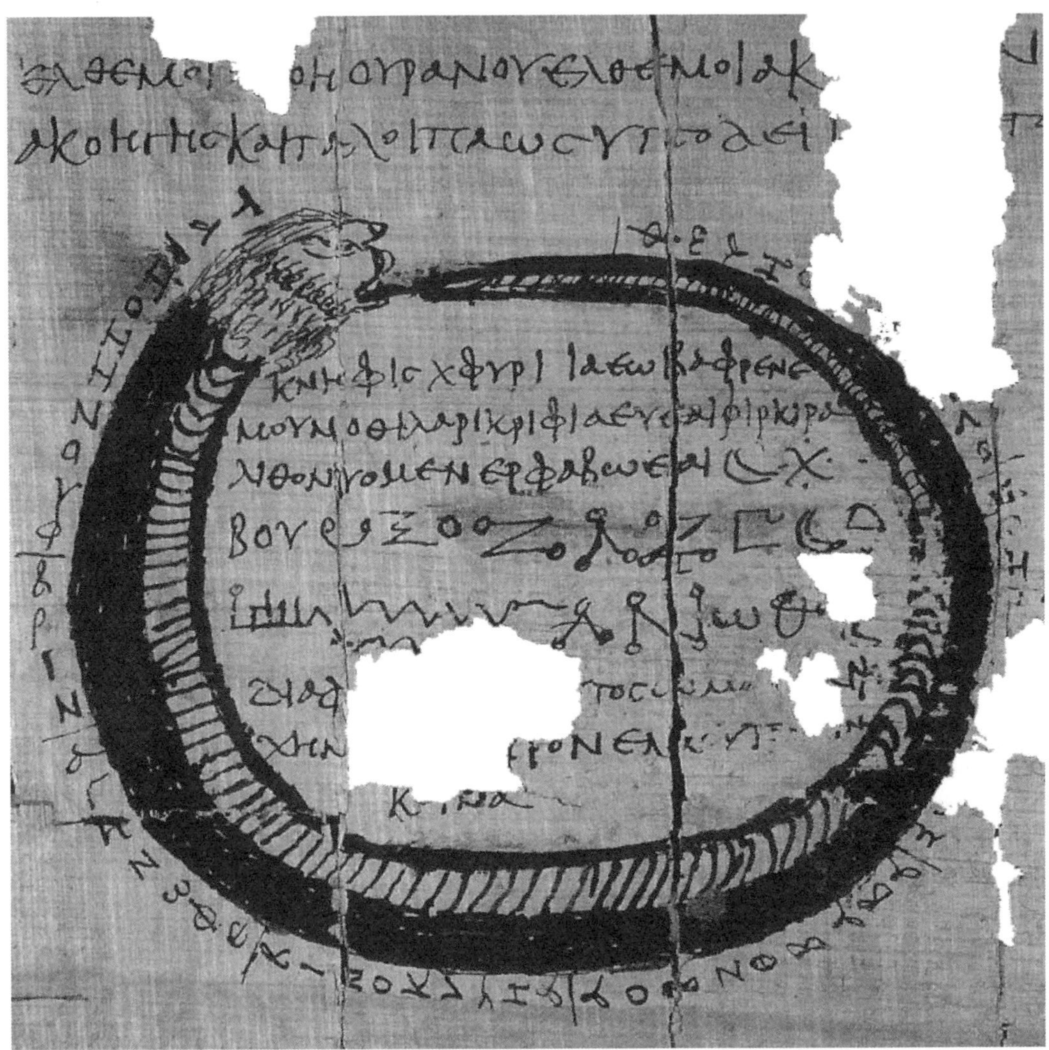

Figure 37: A Graeco-Egyptian phylactery, designed to protect the magician.[1]

One rite which has the clearest drawing of a phylactery also describes its purpose in detail:

> **A phylactery**, a bodyguard against daimones, against phantasms, against every sickness and suffering,[2] [is] to be written on a leaf of gold or silver or tin or on hieratic papyrus. When worn it works mightily for it is the name of power of the great god and [his] seal, and it is as follows:
>
> "KMĒPHIS CHPHYRIS..."[3] These are the names; the figure is like this: let the Snake be biting its tail,[4] the names being written inside [the circle made by] the

---

[1] *PGM* VII. 579-590. Reproduced in colour in Parsons (2007), plate 35.

[2] Sickness or suffering caused by the invoked entity.

[3] Κμῆφις χφυρις. Kheperi.

[4] The ouroboros.

> snake, and the characters thus…[1]
>
> The whole figure is [drawn] thus, as given below, [and put on] with [the invocation], "Protect my body, [and] the entire soul of me, NN."[2] And when you have consecrated [it], wear [it].[3]

Note that significantly this phylactery also features the protective ouroboros as a central part of its design. The phylactery, and its description, shown in Figure 37, is significant for a number of reasons:

i) It confirms that the phylactery was used to protect the magician, body and soul against daimones and phantasms (rather than against physical world injury or disease).

ii) It is referred to as the great god's seal, which is later echoed by the Byzantine description of such a phylactery as a 'heavenly seal,' which is called an οὐρανία σφραγίς (*ourania sphragis*),[4] a 'heavenly seal' or an οὐρανία αλωαφς Σολομῶντος (*ourania alōaphs Solomōntos*) in the *Hygromanteia*.

iii) It is made in the shape of an ouroboros, a shape which echoes the protective circle which was also inscribed on the ground.

iv) It is one of the few extant illustrations of an actual Graeco-Egyptian phylactery, as these would normally have been kept privately by the magician, and possibly destroyed after the rite, unlike amulets, thousands of which survive.

The great god referred to is Khepera. The connection between phylacteries and Khepera is later to surface in Latin grimoires in the word '*candariis*' the obscure Latin word for talisman.[5] The origin of this word comes from the Khepera scarab-shaped carvings made by the thousands and brought from Egypt to Europe where they were identified as talismans.[6]

Some phylacteries also have images incorporated in their design. One such example is a phylactery[7] that is to be used during the invocation of Selene:

> Take a lodestone and on it have carved a three-faced Hekate. And let the middle

---

[1] See Figure 37 for these Celestial *charaktēres*.

[2] The protection for the *entire* soul is mentioned because the Egyptians visualized the soul as constituted of a number of parts, like the *ba, ka,* etc., some being immortal parts, some semi-immortal.

[3] *PGM* VII. 579-590.

[4] The word σφραγίς, *sphragis* is also used in *PGM* IV. 2126 to describe a restraining seal.

[5] See the *Catholicon,* a 13th century lexicon compiled by Johannes Balbus (specifically in the edition dated 1460).

[6] The likely derivation of *candariis* is: Khepera = κάνθαρος = *Kantharos* = *Cantharos* = *Candariis*. Κάνθαρος is the *Scarabaeus pilularius,* or dung beetle.

[7] This is rather weakly translated as 'charm.'

face be that of a maiden wearing horns, and the left face that of a dog, and the one on the right that of a goat. After the carving is done, clean with natron and water, and dip in the blood of one who has died a violent death. Then make a food offering to it, and say the same spell at the time of the ritual.[1]

A phylactery used in another rite to Selene also uses a 'breathing' lodestone, which relies upon the magical powers of that stone. The lodestone remained in use as a stone of attraction by magicians through to at least the 18th century:

> ***Preparation of the procedure's protective charm [phylactery]:***[2] Take a magnet that is breathing and fashion it in the form of a heart, and let there be engraved on it Hekate lying about the heart, like a little crescent. Then carve the twenty-lettered spell that is all vowels, and wear it around [on] your body.
>
> The following name is what is written: "AEYŌ ĒIE ŌA EŌĒ EŌA ŌI EŌI." For this spell is completely capable of everything. But perform this ritual in a holy manner, not frequently or lightly, especially to [invoke] Selene.[3]

Another example made of wood is simplistically translated as a 'charm' but which is called a φυλακτήριον, *phylaktērion* in the original text. As it is used for the magician's protection during a rite it is obviously a phylactery:

> ***The protective charm [phylactery] which you must wear:*** Onto lime wood write with vermilion this name: EPO-KŌPT KŌPTO BAI BAITO-KARA-KŌPTO KARA-KŌPTO CHILO-KŌPTO[4] (50 letters). [Over it say] "Guard me from every daimon of the air, on the earth, and under the earth, and from every angel and phantom and ghostly visitation and enchantment,[5] me NN." Enclose it in a purple skin, hang it around your neck and wear it.[6]

To confirm how important an item the phylactery was as a protection for the magician, one of the all-purpose 'slander spells,'[7] explains that the *unprotected* magician may expect dire retaliation from the goddess, who will presumably be in an evil mood, after having been purportedly slandered:

> Do not therefore perform the rite rashly. And do not perform it unless some dire necessity arises for you. It [the rite] also possesses a protective charm [phylactery][8] against your falling, for the goddess is accustomed to make

---

[1] *PGM* IV. 2880-2890.

[2] The original Greek is φυλακτήριον, 'phylactery' not 'charm' as in the English translation.

[3] *PGM* IV. 2630-2640. This helps to underline that the phylactery was only worn when evoking or invoking.

[4] Hyphens introduced to clarify the structure.

[5] This form of words, via the Griffith and Thompson (1974) translation, appears again in late 19th century Golden Dawn practice.

[6] *PGM* IV. 2695-2705.

[7] A slander spell deliberately sets out to annoy the goddess, in order that she may do what is asked of her to the victim of the spell.

[8] The original Greek is φυλακτήριον, 'phylactery,' not 'charm.'

> airborne those who perform this rite unprotected by a charm [phylactery] and to hurl them from aloft down to the ground. So consequently I have also thought it necessary to take the precaution of [providing] a protective charm [phylactery] so that you may perform the rite with[out] hesitation [or fear]. Keep it secret.[1]

The construction of the phylactery is as follows:

> Take a hieratic papyrus roll and wear it around your right arm with which you make the offering. And these are the things written on it: "MOULATHI CHERNOUTH AMARŌ MOULIANDRON, guard me from every evil daimon, whether an evil male or female."[2]

It is interesting that the goddess is treated in exactly the same way as an evil daimon. It does not seem as if it was necessary to wait for Christianity to demote the ancient gods and goddesses to the level of daimones in 392 CE, for it seems the Graeco-Egyptian magicians had in practice already done so.[3]

In the same rite, Hecate/Aktiōphis is described as "bull-shaped, horse-faced goddess, who howl[s] doglike," and various sacrilegious acts are heaped upon her, to annoy her, and make her act. This confrontational style of magic was very Egyptian and did not translate at all into the later Latin grimoires.

One of the best known phylactery descriptions occurs in the so-called "Mithras Liturgy:"[4]

> Then the phylacteries are of this kind. Copy the [text of the phylactery][5] for the right [arm] onto the skin of a black sheep, with myrrh ink, and after tying it with the sinews of the same animal, put it on; and [copy] that for the left [arm] onto the skin of a white sheep, and use the same method. The [magical word] for the left [arm] is: "PROSTHYMĒRI," and has this memorandum:... [6]
>
> "Let go of what you have, and then you will receive, [from] PSINŌTHER NŌPSITHER THERNŌPSI" (add the usual).[7]

The craft of phylactery making is not above using one god to neutralize another. A love rite which invokes Aphrodite uses a Typhonian phylactery to keep the magician safe:

---

1 *PGM* IV. 2505-2511.

2 *PGM* IV. 2512-2519.

3 This is further reason for using the term 'spiritual creature' when referring to these gods, daimones, demons, or spirits, as to a large extent they were all treated in the same way by the Graeco-Egyptian magician.

4 See chapter 7.2.

5 Betz mistakenly uses the word 'amulet' here.

6 The six line quote from Homer which occurs at this point, and which both Meyer and Betz see as part of the 'Liturgy,' just frames the 'Liturgy' at both the beginning (lines 467-474) and the end (lines 830-834) rather than being part of it.

7 *PGM* IV. 813-820, 828-829. Note the text is taken from Betz (2003) rather than Betz (1996).

> And also have as a protective charm [phylactery][1] a tooth from the upper right jawbone of a female ass or of a tawny sacrificial heifer, tied to your left arm with Anubian thread.[2]

A phylactery to protect against the anger of Kronos, father of the gods, uses the myth that Zeus castrated Kronos with a sickle in order to create a protective phylactery that threatens Kronos:

> On the rib of a young pig carve Zeus holding fast a sickle and this name: "CHTHOUMILON." Or let it be the rib of a black, scaly, castrated boar.[3]

Phibechis, a legendary Egyptian magician, whose name in Egyptian literally means 'falcon,' is supposedly responsible for a rite which exorcises daimones. The most interesting part of his rite is the phylactery that would have been hung on the possessed patient to protect him from the daimon:

> ***The phylactery***: On a tin lamella write "IAĒO ABRAŌTH IŌCH PHTHA MESENPSIN IAŌ PHEŌCH IAĒŌ CHARSOK," and hang it on the patient [the possessed].[4]

The phylactery is described as "terrifying to every daimon, a thing he fears." The conjuration, "by the seal which Solomon placed on the tongue of Jeremiah" to determine the truth, is applied to force the spirit to:

> Also tell whatever sort you may be, heavenly or aerial, whether terrestrial or subterranean, or netherworldly or Ebousaeus or Chersus or Pharisaeus, tell whatever sort you may be..."[5]

It was of course considered necessary that the magician should know the name and station of the spirit, in order to be able to control it. In another rite which utilises the threat of harm to a beetle,[6] a phylactery is used by the magician to protect himself from the daimon being invoked:

> ***The phylactery for the foregoing:*** With the blood from the hand or foot of a pregnant woman, write the name given below on a clean piece of papyrus; then tie it about your left arm by a linen cord and wear it. ***Here is what is to be written:*** "SHTĒIT CHIEN TENHA, I bind and loose [you]."

A more informal phylactery is made from a strip of tin and uses the names of the Egyptian directional angels to protect the magician from his own conjured personal angel:

---

[1] The original Greek is φυλακτήριον, 'phylactery' not 'charm' as the English translation.

[2] *PGM* IV. 2896-2900.

[3] *PGM* IV. 3115-3124.

[4] *PGM* IV. 3014-3017.

[5] This refers to the type of daimon. It has always been an objective during exorcism to determine the spirit's name, and its type, so that the appropriate words can be used to eject it.

[6] Thereby compromising the god Kheperi.

> ***The phylactery for this***: Write these names on a strip of tin: "ACHACHAĒL CHACHOU [MERIOUT] MARMARIOUTI." Then wear it around your neck.[1]

A phylactery designed to protect the magician against Bainchōōch (the spirit of darkness) is designed as follows:

> ***Phylactery for the rite,*** which you must wear wrapped around you for the protection of your whole body: On [a strip] from linen cloth taken from a marble statue of Harpokrates in any temple [whatever] write with myrrh these things:
>
> "I am HOROS ALKIB HARSAMŌSIS IAŌ AI DAGRNNOUTH RARACHARAI ABRAIAŌTH, son of ISIS ATHTHA BATHTHA and of OSIRIS OSOR[ON]NŌPHRIS; keep me healthy, unharmed, not plagued by ghosts and without terror during my lifetime."
> Place inside the strip of cloth an ever living plant; roll it up and tie it 7 times with threads of Anubis. Wear it around your neck whenever you perform the rite.[2]

Some phylacteries just rely upon a string of *nomina magica*:

> ***There is also the protective charm [phylactery] itself*** which you wear while performing, even while standing: onto a silver leaf inscribe this name of 100 letters with a bronze stylus, and wear it strung on a thong [made] from the hide of an ass.[3]

The prescribed name is:[4]

> ANCHCHŌR ACHCHŌR ACHACHACH PTOUMI CHACHCHŌ CHARACHŌCH CHAPTOUMĒ CHŌRACHARACHŌCH APTOUMI MĒCHŌCHAPTOU CHARACHPTOU CHACHCHŌ CHARACHŌ PTENACHŌCHEU (a hundred letters).[5]

A more elaborate and probably earlier Egyptian version of a phylactery to be used by the skryer rather than the magician is described in Demotic:

> A amulet [phylactery][6] to be bound to the body of the one [skryer] who is carrying the vessel [to] enchant [him] quickly: You should bring a band of linen of sixteen threads, four of white, four of [green], four of blue, four of red, and make them into one band and stain them with the blood of the hoopoe. You

---

[1] *PGM* VII. 478-490.
[2] *PGM* IV. 1071-1084. Note the confirmation that it should only be worn "whenever you perform the rite."
[3] *PGM* IV. 256-260. The ass is associated with Typhon/Set.
[4] *PGM* IV. 239-241.
[5] Of course as the original is in Greek, such combinations as 'CH' count as only one Greek letter. The count of how many letters is meant as a scribal check to make sure these names have been copied correctly by the practitioner.
[6] Translated as "amulet" by Griffith and Thompson, as reproduced in Betz (1996), p. 200, but actually a phylactery.

> should bind it [the hoopoe][1] to a scarab in its attitude of the sun god, drowned,[2] being wrapped in byssus.[3] You should bind it to the body of the youth who is carrying the vessel [for skrying]. It enchants [him] quickly…[4]

Here we have an example of a phylactery that not only protects the skryer but also enchants the skryer, or enhances their readiness to skry.

Apollonius of Tyana is credited in the *PGM* with securing a spirit servant from the goddess Nephthys in the form of an old woman. This rite requires that the magician wears a protective phylactery during the course of the invocation which deals with both the goddess Nephthys and the spirit familiar granted to the magician by that goddess. The phylactery is made from the skull of an ass because that is the animal sacred to Seth who was Nephthys' husband. Two teeth from the skull have been given to the magician by the goddess as a pledge of the servitude of the spirit servant, and from these he makes the phylactery:

> ***The phylactery to be used throughout the rite:*** The skull of the ass. Fasten the ass's tooth with silver and the old lady's tooth with gold, and wear them always; for if you do this, it will be impossible for the old woman [the spirit servant] to leave you. The rite has been tested.[5]

This particular phylactery is different from the usual run of phylacteries, and unique inasmuch as it is to be worn all the time, afterwards, rather than just during the rite because its functions are those of binding as well as protection, and the magic is ongoing.

---

1 The hoopoe bird was sacred in ancient Egypt. In Leviticus 11:13–19, hoopoes were categorised as detestable and were banned from being eaten, perhaps because of their magical status in Egypt. In Deuteronomy 14:18 they were listed as not kosher. This bird has a long history of appearing in books of Arabic magic, the *PGM* and later European grimoires, where it is primarily valued for its blood. It is *epops* in Greek. Strangely it has been Israel's national bird since 2008. In Estonia the hoopoe are connected with death and the Underworld, but are symbols of virtue in traditional Persia. The hoopoe is the king of the birds in Aristophanes' play *The Birds*. The bird also has a reputation as a messenger in the Middle East, and was legendarily used that way by King Solomon. It may be that reputation as Solomon's messenger more than any other which contributed to its use in magic.

2 The scarab beetle is the animal/insect of Kheperi, a version of the sun god Phre/Ra. The deification of a scarab by drowning is central to many of the Demotic spells of Egyptian origin.

3 Flax or linen.

4 *PDM* xiv. 90-92. It puts him into a trance quickly.

5 *PGM* XI.a. 1-40.

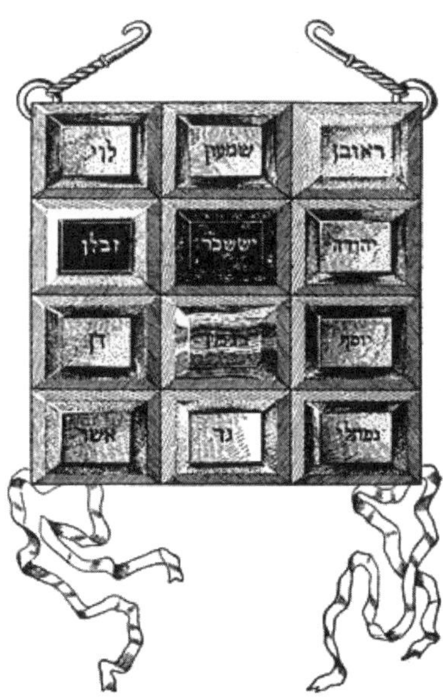

Figure 38: The High Priest's breastplate, made of precious stones engraved with the names of the 12 tribes of Israel. This acted as a phylactery to protect the High Priest from Yahweh.[1]

[1] *Jewish Encyclopedia*, 1904.

The phylactery protects even against gods that have been invoked, especially as the gods in the *PGM* behave rather more like capricious daimones than gods. Even the Jewish god, Yahweh, had been known to kill his followers for minor infractions against his laws. It is therefore not surprising that even Moses was reputed to have needed a phylactery to protect him in his dealings with that god. I am not saying that in fact Moses actually used a phylactery to protect himself against "the one true god", just that it was conventionally though so. In fact the practice of the High Priest protecting himself against Yahweh when he entered the Holy of Holies in the Temple in Jerusalem has been preserved in the form of the High Priest's Breastplate which was none other than an elaborate phylactery (see Figure 38).

Surprisingly there was also a tradition of a simpler phylactery thought to have been worn by Moses, one example of which dating from the 2nd -3rd century CE and made of copper,[1] was found near Akrae (near Syracuse) in Sicily (see Figure 39).[2]

Figure 39: A late 2nd century version of Moses' phylactery designed to protect him from Yahweh. Note that it was folded in half, and not split into two columns.[3]

There have been many scholarly discussions of this phylactery, most of which agree that it contains jumbled Greek quotes from *Deuteronomy,* and possibly an older no longer extant Moses narrative based on the Bible.

Its headword is very clearly [φυλα]κτήριον, and further down (line 8 and 23) the words Φυλακτήριον Μωσέως, the Phylactery of Moses. The first line makes the

---

[1] The phylactery itself (on line 6) suggests that it should have been made out of gold.

[2] Kotansky (1994), No. 32, pp. 126-154.

[3] Kotansky (1994), p. 131, Figure 32.

connection between Moses' phylactery and the High Priest's Breastplate: "a phylactery which Moses used to [protect] him[self] in the Holy of Holies." Line 8 further confirms that it is also the "phylactery of Moses when he went up on mountain Sinai." Line 12-13 confirms that such a phylactery is not meant for a client, but should be carefully kept pure by the magician and handed on only to his children: "But carry it in purity - it is something that you should not hand over to anyone except your offspring."[1]

On line 30 the text adds in protection against fever or the evil eye that read like an after-thought. In fact it is marked off by the standard word which introduces amulets, πρὸς. It is therefore very clear that this last passage has been copied in from another amulet source and had nothing initially to do with the phylactery's function in the Holy of Holies and on Mount Sinai. Kotansky points up the difference:

> The 'Phylactery of Moses' is no ordinary protective amulet, but an initiate's privileged 'membership card' which he (or she) was to carry throughout life and hand down to fellow-initiates. It derives its authority from the fact that it is [supposed to be] the very phylactery that Moses was given and used in his encounters with the divine.[2]

I would just like to refine this comment by adding that the phylactery would only have been worn in the Holy or Holies, or during an encounter with the god. Kotansky also confirms the similarity to *PGM* material:[3]

> Like the Akrai (*sic*) phylactery [Moses' phylactery], two places in the Greek magical papyri also describe Moses and his reception of divine knowledge from God; in both instances this knowledge is described in the language of initiation and of the mysteries: ..."I am Moses your prophet to whom you have handed over your mysteries that Israel commemorates;"[4]..."I am he whom you met [upon?] the sacred mountain and gave the knowledge of your great name that I shall keep holy, imparting it to no one except the fellow holy initiates of your sacred mysteries."[5]

The manufacture of phylacteries makes up only 1.2% of all *PGM* rites, or 1.3% by lineage. This figure is low however, as there are at least 16 other phylacteries imbedded at the end of other rites (as part of the equipment section of those rites). These imbedded phylacteries have been listed separately as 'U2', but are not consolidated into the line count statistics, as they are constituent parts of already tallied rites. If these are taken into account then the figures rise to 6.0% by rite or 2.8% by lineage.

---

[1] Line 13.
[2] Kotansky (1994), No. 32, p. 134.
[3] Kotansky (1994), No. 32, pp. 133-134.
[4] *PGM* V. 108-117.
[5] *PGM* XII. 92-94.

Phylacteries - φυλακτήριον (*phylaktērion*) (U)

Gods, Angels, Daimones, names of magicians, *nomina magica*	Non-Roman PGM Nos.	Category	No. of lines	Betz Papyrus *PGM/PDM* Reference number	Objective/ Technique	Greek Headwords
Kouriēl, Iaphēl	4	U	2	*PGM* IV. 86-87[1]	A phylactery to be worn by the magician as protection against daimones	φυλακτήριον πρὸς δαιμόνια[2]
Helios, Agathos Daimon, Zeus, Serapis	4	U R	120	*PGM* IV. 1596-1715	Consecration of a phylactery, a stone and a ring utilising the 12 gods of the hours, via a Helios invocation.	μυστήρια…πάντ ων τελετὴ[3] φυλακτηρίῳ τελουμένῳ[4] - line 1620 [name facility]
Sabaōth, Adonai, Akrammacham-marei, Abraxas	7	U	4	*PGM* VII. 218-221	The indented lines 220-221 are definitely a φυλακτήριον, but line 218 appears to describe the functions of an amulet (for daily fever with shivering fits)	φυλακτήριον πρὸς[5]
Iao Sabaōth, Adonai, Ablanathanalba, Sesengen bar [Pharanges], Bainchōōch, Bes	7	U	6	*PGM* VII. 311-316	A phylactery to protect from frightful dreams and all demons of the air.[6]	φυλακτήριον[7] [named person]
Ereschigal, Sabaōth	7	U	2	*PGM* VII. 317-318	Phylactery of the Moon	ἄλλο φυλακτήρ[ι]ον[8]

[1] This phylactery probably belongs as part of PGM IV. 52-85, despite the presence of another phylactery at lines 78-82.
[2] Phylactery against daimons.
[3] Mystery…for all initiations [consecrations].
[4] Completion (consecration) of a phylactery.
[5] Phylactery for…
[6] This phylactery is very unusual for having a facility for adding the name of a specific person "NN, whom NN bore." But its function of protecting the magician from demons is specified in the text.
[7] Phylactery.
[8] Another phylactery

Gods, Angels, Daimones, names of magicians, *nomina magica*	**Non-Roman *PGM* Nos.**	**Category**	**No. of lines**	**Betz Papyrus *PGM/PDM* Reference number**	**Objective/ Technique**	**Greek Headwords**
Kmēphis (*sic*), Chphyris, Iao, Ouroboros	7	U	12	*PGM* VII. 579-590	A classic phylactery against daimones, and phantasms, with illustration.[1]	φυλακτήριον σωματοφύλαξ πρὸς δαίμονας[2]
Sesegges bar Pharagges, Atikhis, Cherubim, Pantokrator	48	U	21	*PGM* XLVIII. 1-21	Coptic 6th-7th century. Phylactery?	[n/h] νεφυλακτήριον[3] - line 11
Iao, Ablanathanalba	71	U	8	*PGM* LXXI. 1-8	A detached phylactery	φυλακτήριον[4] [named facility]
		U	36	Kotansky 32 [5]	Phylactery of Moses	[φυλα]κτήριον. Φυλακτήριον Μωσέως[6] – lines 8, 23
		U	32	Kotansky 33 [7]	Possibly a Jewish phylactery.[8]	[n/h]
Total U		**10**	**243**			

Table U: Phylacteries.

[1] The best example of a phylactery in the *PGM*. See Figure 37.

[2] Phylactery, a bodyguard against daimons.

[3] Phylacteries. Coptic.

[4] Arktikē rite phylactery.

[5] Kotansky (1994), No. 32, pp. 126-154.

[6] Moses' phylactery.

[7] Kotansky (1994), No. 33, pp. 155-166.

[8] As it does not name a client nor does it have a specific purpose except the display of many protective angelic names. 'Judah' is more likely to be part of a historiola, and not an amuletic client name.

Phylacteries as integral parts of another Rite - φυλακτήριον (*phylaktērion*) (U2)

Gods, Angels, Daimones, names of magicians, *nomina magica*	Non-Roman *PGM Nos.*	Category	No. of lines	Betz Papyrus *PGM/PDM* Reference number	Objective/ Technique	Greek Headwords
	1	U2	15	*PGM* I. 262-276[1]	Phylactery on a sprig of laurel[2]	...φυλακτήριον - line 276[3]
	3	U2	1	*PGM* III. 95-96	Whiskers of a cat used as a phylactery	...φυλακτήριον .
	3	U2	1	*PGM* III. 125-129	Phylactery (cat's whiskers)	φυλακτήριον
	4	U2	7	*PGM* IV. 78-82	Phylactery on papyrus with blood of a pregnant woman	φυλακτήριον
	4	U2	4	*PGM* IV. 257-260	Phylactery on silver leaf, strung on an ass hide thong	φυλακτήριον
	4	U2	25	*PGM* IV. 410-434	Possible phylactery on the reverse of the binding tablet	[n/h]
	4	U2	9	*PGM* IV. 812-820	Phylactery on the skins of a black and a white sheep	φυλακτήρια[4]
	4	U2	14	*PGM* IV. 1071-1084	Phylactery on linen written with myrrh	φυλακτήριον
	4	U2	13	*PGM* IV. 1252-1264	Phylactery on tin leaf	φυλακτήριον
	4	U2	7	*PGM* IV. 1316-1322	Phylactery of a wolf knucklebone	φυλακτήριον
	4	U2	7	*PGM* IV. 1335-1339	Phylactery of plaited hairs from ass, she-goat and bull	φυλακτήριον
	4	U2	14	*PGM* IV. 2505-2519	Phylactery of hieratic papyrus	φυλακτηρίου
	4	U2	11	*PGM* IV. 2630-2640	Phylactery on an engraved magnet	φυλακτηρίου

1 The U2 are phylacteries that occur as an integral part of a rite type already identified and listed.

2 The word φυλακτήριον is here mistranslated three times as 'charm.' This error occurs in most of the following phylactery passages. This device is not a general 'charm' or 'amulet' but a phylactery, a very specific item of the magician's protective equipment.

3 Phylactery.

4 Phylacteries.

Gods, Angels, Daimones, names of magicians, *nomina magica*	**Non-Roman *PGM Nos***	**Category**	**No. of lines**	**Betz Papyrus *PGM/PDM* Reference number**	**Objective/ Technique**	**Greek Headwords**
	4	U2	10	*PGM* IV. 2695-2704	Phylactery on lime wood written with vermilion	φυλακτήριον
	4	U2	3	*PGM* IV. 2705-2708	Phylactery on silver leaf consisting of *charaktēres*	φυλακτήριον
	4	U2	11	*PGM* IV. 2880-2890	Phylactery on a carved loadstone dipped in blood	φυλακτήριον
	4	U2	5	*PGM* IV. 2896-2900	Phylactery made of a female ass tooth	φυλακτήριον
	4	U2	6	*PGM* IV. 3014-3019	Phylactery on a tin lamella	φυλακτήριον
	4	U2	5	*PGM* IV. 3115-3119	Phylactery on the rib of a young pig	φυλακτήριον
	7	U2	4	*PGM* VII. 487-490	Phylactery on a strip of tin	φυλακτήριον
	7	U2	4	*PGM* VII. 858-861	Phylactery made with *charaktēres*	φυλακτήριον
	11	U2	4	*PGM* XI. a 37-40	Phylactery made of two teeth	φυλακτήριον
	12	U2	2	*PGM* XII. 13-14	Phylactery	φυλακτήριον
	13	U2	13	*PGM* XIII. 899-911	Phylactery on a gold/silver lamella	φυλακτήριον
	14	U2	4	*PDM* xiv. 90-92	Phylactery made of a band of linen	[Demotic] phylactery
	21	U2	5	*PGM* XXI. 24-29	Phylactery	φυλακτ[ήριον]
	62	U2	1	*PGM* LXII. 24	Phylactery made of three peonies[1]	φυλακτήριον – line 24
	70	U2	5	*PGM* LXX. 1-4	A name used as a phylactery	φυλακτήρ[ι]ον
Total U2		28	210			

Table U2: Phylacteries integral parts of another rite.

[1] Not a "protective spell" as suggested by O'Neil.

6.3 Magical Methods for Specific Objectives

Health (H)

There are a plethora of health rites in the *PGM*, most of them too short to establish much in the way of detailed methods, some extending for no more than a few lines. With the exception of advice to cure a snake bite (27 lines) and a cure for insomnia and sciatica (21 lines) no health passage is longer than 13 lines. The range of illnesses catered for include fever, shivering, coughs, bones stuck in the throat, insomnia, sciatica, tumours, headache, migraine, gout, eye and ear problems, strangury, snake bites, scorpion stings, dog bites, various women's problems, contraception, swollen testicles and even hardening of the breasts.

The bulk of the health formulae are in Demotic and occur in just two papyri: *PDM* xiv. 554-1227 and *PDM* lxi. 43-62, interleaved with other rites. By contrast the Greek health formulae are scattered through a number of papyri.

These and love spells are two of the rite types defined primarily by their objective rather than by their method. Where a health spell has a clear method (such as being prescribed as an amulet, 'A' or 'A2'), it is listed under that method rather than in this section. The bulk of the health related passages in Demotic are usually headed by *mt.t a* (magical formula) or *pḫre.t* (medical recipe or prescription) but where they are in Greek, they are only a few lines in length and have no headwords. This is probably because the Greeks had a parallel system of medicine represented by such luminaries as the physicians Hippocrates[1] and Galen of Pergamon.[2] Galen wrote a number of medical texts which remained influential from the 2nd century CE for 1300 years through to the late Middle Ages.

Egyptian medicine developed on other lines, with the earliest medical papyrus dating from 1800 BCE. That papyrus mostly relates to women's diseases but not to either magic or surgery. Life was precarious and plague regularly made its appearance. It was believed, for example, that in one episode around 250 CE half the population of Alexandria died of plague.

A number of other rites in other categories have a reference to health, but these are not cross-referenced here, as Health is an objective rather than a technique.

Health spells are one of the most popular categories, making up 7.6% of the *PGM* by rite, but only 2.4% by lineage.

---

[1] 460-370 BCE.

[2] 129-216 CE.

Gods, Angels, Daimones, names of magicians, *nomina magica*	**Non-Roman *PGM* Nos.**	**Category**	**No. of lines**	**Betz Papyrus *PGM/PDM* Reference number**	**Objective/ Technique**	**Greek Headwords**
Anubis	14	H	9	*PDM* xiv. 554-562	Dog bite cure	*mt.t a*[1]
Osiris, Horus Agathadaimon	14	H	12	*PDM* xiv. 563-574	For removal of poison	*mt.t a*
Osiris	14	H	12	*PDM* xiv. 574-585	Removal of bone stuck in the throat	*mt.t a*
Anubis, Isis, Seth, Osiris, Apophis, Amoun, Triphis, Horus	14	H	9	*PDM* xiv. 585-593	Dog bite cure	*mt.t a*
Anubis, Sekhmet-Isis, Osiris, Atum, Agathadaimon, Geb, Horus	14	H	27	*PDM* xiv. 594-620	To cure a sting (probably a snake bite). Historiola of Isis advising the king's son how to deal with the bite.	*mt.t a*
	14	H	7	*PDM* xiv. 620-626	Removal of a bone stuck in the throat	*mt.t a*
	14	H	5	*PDM* xiv. 935-939	Prescription for a watery ear	*pḫre.t*[2]
	14	H	13	*PDM* xiv. 940-952	Herbs and salamander cure for a wound	[Demotic] [n/h]
	14	H	3	*PDM* xiv. 953-955	To stop blood flow	*pḫre.t*
	14	H	5	*PDM* xiv. 956-960	Pregnancy test	[Demotic] [n/h]
	14	H	5	*PDM* xiv. 961-965	To stop bleeding during sex	*pḫre.t*
	14	H	4	*PDM* xiv. 966-969	Herbal cure	[Demotic] [n/h]
	14	H	8	*PDM* xiv. 970-977	Prescription to stop liquid in a woman	*pḫre.t*
	14	H	3	*PDM* xiv. 978-980	Another prescription to stop liquid in a woman	*k.t* [*pḫre.t*][3]
	14	H	4	*PDM* xiv. 981-984	Another prescription to stop liquid in a woman	[Demotic] Another

1 Magical formula.
2 Prescription.
3 Another [prescription].

Gods, Angels, Daimones, names of magicians, *nomina magica*	Non-Roman PGM Nos.	Category	No. of lines	Betz Papyrus *PGM/PDM* Reference number	Objective/ Technique	Greek Headwords
	14	H	8	*PDM* xiv. 985-992	Gout, prescription for	ποδάκραν [ποδάγρα][1]
	14	H	10	*PDM* xiv. 993-1002	Gout, prescription for	*k.t*
	14	H	6	*PDM* xiv. 1015-1020	Gout remedy?	*pḫre.t*
	14	H	3	*PDM* xiv. 1021-1023	Prescription for a stiff foot	[*pḫre.t*]
	14	H	2	*PDM* xiv. 1024-1025	Another prescription for a stiff foot	*k.t* [*pḫre.t*]
Amoun, Horus	14	H	7	*PDM* xiv. 1097-1103	Eye disease/ophthalmia	[Demotic] [n/h]
	14	H	6	*PDM* xiv. 1104-1109	Eye ointment recipe	[Demotic] [n/h]
Horus, Isis, Nephthys	14	H	9	*PDM* xiv. 1219-1227	Fever	[Demotic] [n/h] [name facility]
Syrian woman of Gadara	20	H	9	*PGM* XX. 4-12	Incantation of the Syrian woman of Gadara against inflammation, cast in the form of a hymn	πρὸς
Philinna (Thessalian)	20	H	7	*PGM* XX. 13-20	Incantation against headache, in the form of a hymn	[n/h] [named person
Phōr, Sabaōth, Adōne, Salama, Tarchei, Abrasax	28	H	7	*PGM* XXVIIIa. 1-7	Binding the Artemesian Scorpion [sting]	[n/h]
Phōr, Iaō, Adōnaei, Sabaōth, Salaman [Solomon], Tarchchei, Artemisos	28	H	9	*PGM* XXVIIIb. 1-9	Binding the Artemesian Scorpion [sting]	[n/h]
Phōr, Iaō, Adōnai, Salama, R Thachi	28	H	11	*PGM* XXVIIIc. 1-11	Binding the Artemesian Scorpion [sting]	[n/h] [amulet format
	36	H	13	*PGM* XXXVI. 320-332	Contraceptive spell. Bitter vetch and henbane.	[n/h]
	61	H	6	*PDM* lxi. 43-48 [*PGM* LXI. i-v]	Ulcer (?) of the head, remedy for	[Demotic]

[1] Gout.

Gods, Angels, Daimones, names of magicians, *nomina magica*	Non-Roman PGM Nos.	Category	No. of lines	Betz Papyrus *PGM/PDM* Reference number	Objective/ Technique	Greek Headwords
	61	H	9	*PDM* lxi. 49-57	Headache, herbal remedy.[1]	[Demotic]
	61	H	5	*PDM* lxi. 58-62 [*PGM* LXI. vi.x]	Erection, to improve	[Demotic]
	94	H	6	*PGM* XCIV 1-6 *SM* 94 a	Eyesight, Drying powder made with saffron for sharp eyes	[n/h]
	95	H	6	*PGM* XCV. 1-6 *SM* 99 a	Cure using the skin of a mouse	[n/h]
	95	H	7	*PGM* XCV. 7-13 *SM* 99 b	Epilepsy, remedy for	[n/h]
	95	H	5	*PGM* XCV. 14-18 *SM* 99 c	Epilepsy, remedy for	[n/h]
	97	H	6	*PGM* XCVII. 1-6	Against eye disease (?)	[n/h]
	97	H	3	*PGM* XCVII. 7-9	Remedy for epilepsy using a mole-rat	[n/h]
	97	H	3	*PGM* XCVII. 15-17	Against every disease	[n/h]
	119	H	5	*PGM* CXIXb. 1-5 *SM* 82 d	Remedy for fever with shivering fits	[n/h]
Osiris, Ammon, Isis-Nephthys	122	H	5	*PGM* CXXII. 51-55[2] *SM* 72 b	Against headache (1st century CE)	[n/h]
Bōeai	-	H	21	*SM* 74	Cure for insomnia, sciatica	[n/h]
	-	H	5	*SM* 78	Six medico-magical prescriptions, each introduced by ἄλλο	[n/h]
	-	H	2	*SM* 79 f	Against fever	[n/h]
Total H		**44**	**327**			

Table H: Health.

[1] Using palm, persea, cypress, mulberry, laurel, black poplar and pine.

[2] Part of *PGM* CXXII. 1-55, but a separate spell.

Invisibility - ἀμαύρωσις (*amaurōsis*) (I)

Invisibility is one boon that has been asked of magic in every time and place by magicians from King Gyges,[1] the prophet Elisha,[2] and Apollonius of Tyana to Aleister Crowley. The Greek word ἀμαύρωσις literally means 'darkening.'

One rite specifies an ointment with which to smear oneself when asking Helios for invisibility. Presumably the logic of this request is that as Helios is responsible for making everything visible, so it is within his power to deny this favour, and make something invisible:

> **Indispensable invisibility spell**: Take fat or an eye of a night owl and a ball of dung rolled by a beetle[3] and oil of an unripe olive and grind them all together until smooth, and smear your whole body with it and say to Helios..."Make me invisible, lord Helios...in the presence of any man until sunset..."[4]

A few lines further on, another invisibility ointment is recommended:

> Take an eye of an ape or of a corpse that has died a violent death and a plant of peony (he means the rose). Rub these with oil of lily, and as you are rubbing them from the right to the left, say the spell... And if you wish to become invisible, rub just your face with the concoction, and you will be invisible for as long as you wish.[5]

The most detailed study of the invisibility rites in the *PGM* was done by Phillips.[6] Note that *PGM* I. 102; V. 459-489; XII. 162 mention invisibility in passing, but are not specifically invisibility spells. Phillips adds Papyrus Oxy. LVIII 3931 to the tally of invisibility spells, where the headword is ἀμαύρωτικὸν, *amaurōtikon.*

In several of these passages the explicitly named "infernal daimon" is called upon using the Erbēth Pakerbēth formula, but the primary object of invocation is Helios who is conjured to turn out that which makes the magician visible.

Although there are only four rites for invisibility, making up 0.7% of the rites in the *PGM* (or 0.3% by lineage), this objective occurs in almost all later grimoires, both Byzantine and Latin, and so is an important link between the magic of Egypt and the later grimoires.

---

1 See Marathakis (2007) for a detailed survey of that invisibility spell.

2 *2 Kings* 6:8-23; Josephus, *Jewish Antiquities* 9.56.

3 The beetle Kheperi symbolises the setting sun. The night owl confers darkness, and the eye obviously connects to visibility. So the ingredients of the ointment are not just random, but follow an internal logic, a physical paste corresponding to the nature of the request to the lord of the darkening Sun.

4 *PGM* I. 222-231.

5 *PGM* I. 247-262.

6 Phillips (2009).

Gods, Angels, Daimones, names of magicians, *nomina magica*	**Non-Roman *PGM* Nos.**	**Category**	**No. of lines**	**Betz Papyrus *PGM/PDM* Reference number**	**Objective/ Technique**	**Greek Headwords**
Helios, Iō Lailam Zizia Ieō	1	I	10	*PGM* I. 222-231	Invisibility	ἀμαύρωσις ἀναγκαῖα[1]
Anubis Osir-Phre Osiris Iō Erbēth Phobēth Pakerbēth Marmariaōth Marmaripheggē	1	I	16	*PGM* I. 247-262	Invisibility	ἀμαύρωσι[ς] δοκίμη.[2]
Moses, IAŌ Sabaōth, Adōnai	7	I L	9	*PGM* VII. 619-627	Invisibility and love, from the *Diadem of Moses.*	ἐκ τοῦ Διαδήματος Μουσέως[3] ἀθεώρητος – line 622[4]
	13	I	0	*PGM* XIII, 234-237, 267-269, 270-277	Minor invisibility rites embedded within other rites.[5]	ἀμαυρά[6] ἀβλεψία[7]
Total I		**4**	**35**			

Table I: Invisibility.

[1] Darkening constraint.

[2] Darkening proved/tested.

[3] From the *Diadem of Moses.* This was obviously extracted from a collection of spells under that title.

[4] Invisible, not seen.

[5] These have already been added into the line count, so they will not be tallied here. See Phillips (2009) for a detailed account of invisibility procedures in the *PGM.*

[6] Dark, obscure.

[7] Blindness, invisibility.

Love Rites (L-L7)

There are seven different subcategories, separated according to the exact method as embodied in the shade of meaning of the headword, but all related to love. The differences depend upon the technique used, be it leading, fetching, potions, binding, torturing, or separating of two lovers, and each has its own specialised Greek term and method.

L: ἀγωγή (*agōgē*), Love Rites of Attraction or 'Love's Leash', literally leading or drawing the 'victim' to the client.

L2: ἀγώγιμον (*agōgimon*) Fetching or delivering the 'victim' into the bondage of love: making a love tie.

L3: φίλτρον (*philtron*) love magic worked at close quarters, via potions, etc;

L4: φιλτροκατάδεσμος (*philtrokatadesmos*)[1] love binding the 'victim;'

L5: ἀγρυπνητικόν (*agrupnētikon*) love enforced by torturing the 'victim' with hunger or insomnia;

L6: διάκοπος (*diakopos)* literally 'breach' or separation between two lovers or friends;

L7: other love rites.

As you can see there were at least seven different approaches, with differing degrees of severity. Love spells are a common objective of magic in every culture, but in Graeco-Egyptian magic specifically, there is a twist. The unique feature of Graeco-Egyptian love spells (not replicated in any other culture as far as I know) is that instead of merely attempting to make the object of the rite fall in love with the magician or his client, the god/goddess invoked is in many cases ordered to torment the object of the rite neither allowing him/her to eat or sleep till he/she comes and declare his/her love to the magician or his client.

Slander Spell

An even more extreme version of the love rite is the addition of a 'slander spell,' in which the magician accuses the object of his love/lust of some form of sacrilegious behaviour, and enjoins the god/goddess to take revenge on the object of the rite, until they relent and submit to him (or his client) sexually.

Many examples of love spells use slander in order to stir up the god/goddess into action,[2] the magician being all the while very careful not to attract the goddesses' wrath onto his own head:

> For I come announcing the slander of NN [the love object of the spell], a defiled

[1] This word seems to be unique to the *PGM*.

[2] Slander spells are more often used with a goddess than with a god.

> and unholy woman, for she has slanderously brought your holy mysteries to the knowledge of men. She, NN, is the one, [not] I, who says, 'I have seen the greatest goddess, after leaving the heavenly vault, on earth without sandals, sword in hand, and [speaking] a foul name.' It is she, NN, who said, 'I saw [the goddess] drinking blood.' She, NN, said it, not I...[1]

The slander spell[2] is unique to Graeco-Egyptian magic, and did not migrate to either the *Hygromanteia* or to later Solomonic grimoires. Perhaps as a procedure it was considered far too risky. In fact the magician is instructed specifically "Do not therefore perform the rite rashly, and do not perform it unless some dire necessity arises for you."[3]

The instructions for 'love' spells are often explicitly sexual rather than loving, for example:

> Let her be in love with me, NN whom she, NN bore. Let her not be had in a promiscuous way, let her not be had in her ass, nor let her do anything with another man for pleasure, just with me alone...[4]
>
> and do not allow her, NN, to accept for pleasure the attempt of another man, not even that of her own husband, just that of mine...[5]

Most of the love spells are small and fragmentary, but a few are given in much greater detail. The essence of one such rite is the drowning (and therefore deification),[6] of very specific type of scarab. A scarab of Mars is used in another method.[7]

Spells for separating lovers or friends, διάκοπος (*diakopos*), are the reverse of this category but are also included here under 'L6'. An interesting turn of events, at the end of one rite is the procedure for getting rid of the lover when she is no longer wanted:

> If, however, you should wish her to stop [desiring you], take a sun scarab and place it in the middle of her head and say to it: "Gulp down my love charm, image of Helios; he himself orders you to do so." And pick up the scarab and release it alive. Then take the [iron] ring and give it to her to wear, and immediately she will depart.[8]

Iron in later periods was considered to be anathema to spirits. Love spells are the most popular category, making up 15.9% of the *PGM* by rite, or 12.3% by lineage.

---

[1] *PGM* IV. 2475-2481.

[2] Διαβολῇ, *diabolē.*

[3] *PGM* IV. 2505.

[4] *PGM* IV. 350-354.

[5] *PGM* IV. 374-376.

[6] A field mouse is deified by drowning it in spring water, and two 'moon beetles' in river water, in *PGM* IV. 2456-2457.

[7] *PDM* xiv. 636-669, especially 636-637.

[8] *PDM* lxi. 175-180 *aka PGM* LXI. 33-37.

Love Rites of Attraction or 'Love's Leash' - ἀγωγή (*agōgē*) (L)

Gods, Angels, Daimones, names of magicians, *nomina magica*	Non-Roman *PGM* Nos.	Category	No. of lines	Betz Papyrus *PGM/PDM* Reference number	Objective/ Technique	Greek Headwo
				PGM IV. 1390-1495	*See D*	
Eros, Babylon, Abrasax, Iaō Sabaōth Adōnai, Maskelli, Maskellō, Anoch	4	L	100	*PGM* IV. 1496-1595	Love rite of attraction over myrrh	ἀγωγή – line 14
				PGM IV. 1872-1927	*See S*	
				PGM IV. 2006-2125 *PGM* IV. 2441-2621	*See Ω*	
Selene, Hekate, Dione, [Aphrodite], Korē, Artemis, Persephone, Aktiōphi[s], Iō, Ereshkigal, Maskelli Maskellō, Ōriōn, Michaēl, Adōnai, Zeus, Damnameneus,	4	L	77	*PGM* IV. 2708-2784	Love rite of attraction	ἀγωγή – line 27
Aphrodite, Adonis, Aktiōphi[s], Ereshkigal, Kythereia	4	L	52	*PGM* IV. 2891-2942	Love rite of attraction	ἀγωγή - line 2891, 293
Iao, Adonai, Sabaōth, Pagoure, Marmorouth, Iaeo, Michael	7	L	27	*PGM* VII. 593-619	A slander spell used for fetching an unmanageable woman. [Hermonthis archive]	ἀγωγή ἀσχέτου[1] - line 593
				PGM VII. 619-627	*See I*	
				PGM VII. 862-918 *PDM* xiv. 376-394	*See Ω*	
	19	L	3	*PGM* XIXb. 1-3	Love rite of attraction	[n/h]

[1] Literally a leash for an ungovernable [woman]. Not L7.

Gods, Angels, Daimones, names of magicians, ***nomina magica***	**Non-Roman *PGM* Nos.**	**Category**	**No. of lines**	**Betz Papyrus *PGM/PDM* Reference number**	**Objective/ Technique**	**Greek Headwords**
Senakōtho, Anoch, etc	19	L	15	*PGM* XIXb. 4-18	Love rite of attraction written with blood and myrrh on flax	ἀγωγή – line 4
				PGM XXXVI. 35-68	*See T3*	
Typhon, [Ptah], Iō Erbēth Pakerbēth, Balchosēth,	36	L	33	*PGM* XXXVI. 69-101	Love rite of burning attraction. [Fayum archive]	ἀγωγή ἔμπυρον[1]
Ablanathanalba, Iaō, Salaioth, [Sabaōth], Adōnai, (Min of Koptos)	36	L	32	*PGM* XXXVI. 102-133	Love rite of burning attraction. With illustration. [Fayum archive]	ἄλλο ἔμπυρον[2] [amulet format]
Isis, Osiris, Abrasax, Maskelli Maskellō	36	L	27	*PGM* XXXVI. 134-160	Wonderful love rite of attraction. [Fayum archive]	ἀγωγή θαυμαστή[3] - line 134
Hekate, Ablanathana[lba], Iaō, Sabaōth, Adōnai	36	L	24	*PGM* XXXVI. 187-210	Love rite of attraction. [Fayum archive]	ἀγωγή – line 189
Aphrodite, Sabaōth, Michaēl, Gabriēl, Sesengen bar Pharangēs, Abraam	36	L	17	*PGM* XXXVI. 295-311	Love rite of attraction. Jewish influenced.[4] [Fayum archive]	ἀγωγή – line 295
Typhon, Horos, Anubis, Isis, Maskelli Maskellō, Iaō, Sabaōth, Adōnai, Abrasax	36	L	28	*PGM* XXXVI. 333-360	Love rite of attraction using myrrh. [Fayum archive]	ἀγωγή – line 333
[Typhon]	36	L	11	*PGM* XXXVI. 361-371	Love rite of attraction. [Fayum archive]	ἀγωγή – line 361
Helios Oseronnōphrios Phaprō Ousiris Typhon Abrasax Iaō Sarxana	61	L	20	*PDM* lxi. 197-216 [*PGM* LXI. 39-71]	Love rite of attraction using a cooked lizard	ἀγω[γή]
				PGM CVII. 1-19 *SM* 44	*See D*	

[1] Love rite of burning attraction.
[2] Another love rite of burning attraction. Mis-translated as "divination by fire."
[3] Wonderful love rite of attraction.
[4] Because it mentions Sodom and Gomorrah.

Gods, Angels, Daimones, names of magicians, *nomina magica*	Non-Roman *PGM* Nos.	Category	No. of lines	Betz Papyrus *PGM/PDM* Reference number	Objective/ Technique	Greek Headword
Hermes, Ammon, Aphrodite, Isis, Nephthys, Osiris, Helios	122	L	55	*PGM* CXXII. 1-50 *SM* 72 a	Enchantment using apples. From the holy *Book of Hermes*.[1]	ἐξαγωγὴ ἐπῳδῶν[2] [name facility]
				SM 37 *SM* 51	*See D*	
Total L		**15**	**521**			

Table L: Love Rites of Attraction or 'Love's Leash.'

[1] This is a form of love enchantment using apples. It is not a whole "Magic handbook" as described by Dieleman (2005), p. 272.
PGM CXXII. 51-55 is a headache remedy, and is obviously an addition, and so it has been separated. 1st century CE.

[2] Invocation drawing/leading of love, therefore an αγωγή.

Love Fetching - ἀγώγιμον (*agōgimon*) (L2)

Gods, Angels, Daimones, names of magicians, *nomina magica*	Non-Roman PGM Nos.	Category	No. of lines	Betz Papyrus *PGM/PDM* Reference number	Objective/ Technique	Greek Headwords
[Typhon], Necessity	7	L2	10	*PGM* VII. 300a-310	Love tie. [Hermonthis archive]	ἀγώγιμον[1] - line 300a
Michaēl Osiris Phor Phorba Abriēl Seseggen bar Pharaggēs Iaō Sabaōth Adōnai Lailam	7	L2	8	*PGM* VII. 973-980	Love rite of attraction by touch. [Hermonthis archive]	ἀγώγιμον – line 937
Helios Aktiōphis Ereshkigal Persephonē Helios	7	L2	13	*PGM* VII. 981-993	Love incantation of attraction. [Hermonthis archive]	[ἀ]γώ[γιμον] - line 981
Anubis	12	L2	16	*PDM* xii. 119-134 [*PGM* XII. 469-473]	Fetching love spell.	[Demotic] A [fetching] spell
				PDM xiv. 1070-1077	*See V2*	
				PDM xiv. 1090-1096	*See R*	
	84	L2 A2	21	*PGM* LXXXIV. 1-21	Fetching amulet	[amulet format] [named person]
Bolsak	119	L2	3	*PGM* CXIXa. 4-6 *SM* 82 b	Fetching charm on an ostracon	ἀγώγ[ιμον]
				SM 39	*See D*	
				SM 40	*See A2*	
Total L2		**6**	**71**			

Table L2: Love Fetching.

[1] Love binding.

Love Potions - φίλτρον (*philtron*) (L3)

Gods, Angels, Daimones, names of magicians, *nomina magica*	Non-Roman *PGM* Nos.	Category	No. of lines	Betz Papyrus *PGM/PDM* Reference number	Objective/ Technique	Greek Headwords
				PGM IV. 2145-2240	*See Ω*	
Boubasti, Cypris	7	L3	5	*PGM* VII. 385-389	Love cup rite	ποτήριον καλόν[1]
	7	L3	2	*PGM* VII. 405-406	Love rite	φίλτρον[2]
Bacchios	7	L3 T	3	*PGM* VII. 459-461	Love rite using a tin lamella	φίλτρον κάλλιστον[3]
	7	L3 T	5	*PGM* VII. 462-466	Love rite using a tin lamella	φίλτρον κάλλιστον
Athena Osiris Iaō Pakerbēth Semesilam Patachna Ablanathanalba Akrammachamarei Sabaōth, Adōnai Abrasax	7	L3	9	*PGM* VII. 643-651	Love, cup rite	ποτήριον, λίαν θαυμαστόν[4]
	7	L3	3	*PGM* VII. 661-663	Love rite	φίλτρον
IAŌ	7	L3	4	*PGM* VII. 969-972	Love rite	πότισμα καλόν[5]
Shu, Ra	14	L3	21	*PDM* xiv. 335-355	To make a woman love a man using an embalmed Nile fish	[Demotic] [Love spell]
Ra, Pre, Sakhmet	14	L3	11	*PDM* xiv. 355-365	To gain favour from a woman or man using an embalmed Nile fish	[Demotic] Another love spell
				PDM xiv. 376-394	*See Ω*	

1 Beautiful [wine] cup [rite].
2 Love rite (potion).
3 Beautiful love rite.
4 Very wonderful [drinking] cup [rite].
5 Beautiful potion.

Gods, Angels, Daimones, names of magicians, *nomina magica*	**Non-Roman *PGM* Nos.**	**Category**	**No. of lines**	**Betz Papyrus *PGM/PDM* Reference number**	**Objective/ Technique**	**Greek Headwords**
Isis, Osiris (as the drowned one), Horus of Edfu, Agathadaimon	14	L3	23	*PDM* xiv. 428-450	Potion to seduce a woman	[Demotic] [Two love potions]
Pre, Shu, Osiris, Atum, Nun, Horus, Isis	14	L3	34	*PDM* xiv. 636-669	A detailed Demotic love rite using wine and the deification of a scarab	[Demotic] [n/h]
	14	L3	33	*PDM* xiv. 772-804	Elaborate love rite involving a swallow and a hoopoe ointment	[Demotic] A method
	14	L3	3	*PDM* xiv. 930-32	Love rite based on the anointing of the phallus	*pḫre.t*
Hathor, Moses, IAHO Sabaho[th], Abrasaks, Geb, Horus, Arbanthala, Mut	14	L3	20	*PDM* xiv. 1026-1045	To inflame love using a mixture to anoint the phallus.	[Demotic] [n/h]
	14	L3	2	*PDM* xiv. 1046-1047	Love rite based on the anointing of the phallus	[Demotic] [n/h]
	14	L3	2	*PDM* xiv. 1047-1048	Love rite based on the anointing of the phallus	[Demotic] [n/h]
	14	L3	7	*PDM* xiv. 1049-1055	Love rite based on the anointing of the phallus	[Demotic] [n/h]
	14	L3	11	*PDM* xiv. 1130-1140	Love rite based on the anointing of the phallus	[Demotic] [n/h]
	14	L3	8	*PDM* xiv. 1155-1162	Love rite based on the anointing of the phallus	[Demotic] [n/h]
	14	L3	2	*PDM* xiv. 1188-1189	Love rite based on the anointing of the phallus	[Demotic] [n/h]
	14	L3	4	*PDM* xiv. 1190-1193	Love rite based on the anointing of the phallus	[Demotic] Another
	14	L3	2	*PDM* xiv. 1194-1195	Love rite based on the anointing of the phallus	[Demotic] Another
	14	L3	2	*PDM* xiv. 1196-1198	To stop menstruation when making love	[Demotic] Another

Gods, Angels, Daimones, names of magicians, *nomina magica*	**Non-Roman *PGM* Nos.**	**Category**	**No. of lines**	**Betz Papyrus *PGM/PDM* Reference number**	**Objective/ Technique**	**Greek Headwords**
	24	L3	15	*PGM* XXIVb. 1-15	Love rite. 2nd/3rd century	[n/h] καθεύδο[- line 15[1]
Isis Osiris Akarnachthas	36	L3	12	*PGM* XXXVI. 283-294	Pudenda key rite. A salve to be put on genital before sex	φυσικλειδιον.[2]
	52	L3	11	*PGM* LII. 9-19	Love potion	[n/h] [amulet format]
	61	L3	5	*PDM* lxi. 95-99	Praise and love (in Nubian)	[Demotic]
	61	L3	20	*PDM* lxi. 128-147	Love rite with phallus anointment	[Demotic]
Agathdaimon, Helios, Osiris, Thōth, Necessity	61	L3	38	*PDM* lxi. 159-196 [*PGM* LXI. 1-38]	Love rite using olive oil	φίλτρον
	-	L3	9	*SM* 83	Two recipes for improving intercourse	[n/h]
Total L3		**30**	**326**			

Table L3: Love Potions.[3]

[1] Sleeping [potion].

[2] Pudenda key.

[3] These may be more the province of the φαρμακὸς (*pharmakos*) rather than the magician.

Love Binding - φιλτροκατάδεσμος (*philtrokatadesmos*) (L4)

Gods, Angels, Daimones, names of magicians, *nomina magica*	**Non-Roman *PGM* Nos.**	**Category**	**No. of lines**	**Betz Papyrus *PGM/PDM* Reference number**	**Objective/ Technique**	**Greek Headwords**
				PGM III. 1-164	*See Ω*	
				PGM IV. 296-466	*See D*	
	7	L4	2	*PGM* VII. 191-192	Binding a lover based on anointing of the phallus before intercourse	φ[ιλ]τοκατάδεσμος αἰώνιος[1]
Hermes, Astrapsoukos (a magician)	8	L4 G	63	*PGM* VIII. 1-63	Invocation of Hermes. Binding love rite of Astrampsychos.[2]	φιλτροκατάδεσμος Ἀστραψούκου.[3]
Lampsourē, Isis	-	L4 D	14	*SM* 38	Binding love spell on a lead tablet, binding the beloved in turn to a snake, crocodile, horns of the ram, poison of an asp, whiskers of a cat, and the forepart of a god to prevent her having intercourse with anyone else.	καταδεσμεύω[4] φιλτροκαταδεσμος[5] - line 8
				SM 49	*See D*	
Total L4		**3**	**79**			

Table L4: Love Binding.

1 Eternal binding [for a lover]

2 This is definitely not a "Business spell to attract customers" as suggested by Dieleman (2005), p. 271.

3 Binding love rite of Astrampsychos.

4 I bind you.

5 Binding love rite.

Love Enforced by Hunger or Insomnia - ἀγρυπνητικόν (*agrupnētikon*) (L5)

Gods, Angels, Daimones, names of magicians, *nomina magica*	**Non-Roman *PGM* Nos.**	**Category**	**No. of lines**	**Betz Papyrus *PGM/PDM* Reference number**	**Objective/ Technique**	**Greek Headwords**
Hekate, Korē	4	L5	24	*PGM* IV. 2943-2966	Love rite through insomnia	ἀγωγή ἀγρυπνητική[1] - line 2943
	7	L5	3	*PGM* VII. 374-376	Love by inducing insomnia	ἀγρυπνητικόν[2]
Hestia, Hephaistos	7	L5	9	*PGM* VII. 376-384	Love by inducing insomnia	ἄλλο [ἀγρυπνητικόν][3]
Typhon	7	L5	9	*PGM* VII. 652-660	Insomnia induced using a living bat as part of a love rite	ἀγρυπνη[τι]κὸν.
	12	L5	21	*PGM* XII. 376-396	Love and death via insomnia using a living bat,[4]	ἀγρυπνητικόν.
Eros	52	L5	7	*PGM* LII. 20-26	Insomnia based love rite	ἀγρυπ[ν]ητικόν [amulet format]
				PGM CI. 1-53 *SM* 45	*See D*	
	103	L5	18	*PGM* CIII. 1-18 *SM* 73	Love rite dependant upon prevention of eating or sleeping.	[n/h] [name facility]
Thōbarabau	108	L5	12	*PGM* CVIII. 1-12 *SM* 43	Love rite to prevent the beloved eating or drinking until he/she relents	[n/h] [named person]
				SM 41	*See A2*	
				SM 42 *SM* 46 *SM* 47 *SM* 48 *SM* 50	*See D*	

1 Love drawing via insomnia.

2 Love via insomnia.

3 Another [love via insomnia].

4 Illustration of a crowned Egyptian holding a handle and plumbob (?).

Gods, Angels, Daimones, names of magicians, *nomina magica*	Non-Roman *PGM* Nos.	Category	No. of lines	Betz Papyrus *PGM/PDM* Reference number	Objective/ Technique	Greek Headwords
Total L5		**8**	**103**			

Table L5: Love Enforced by Hunger or Insomnia.

Love Separation - διάκοπος (*diakopos*) (L6)

Gods, Angels, Daimones, names of magicians, *nomina magica*	Non-Roman *PGM* Nos.	Category	No. of lines	Betz Papyrus *PGM/PDM* Reference number	Objective/ Technique	Greek Headwords
				PGM III. 1-164	*See Ω*	
Iō-Erbēth, Iō Pakerbēth, Iō Bolchosēth, Isis, Osiris, Typhon	12	L6	11	*PGM* XII. 365-375	Separation of lovers, for causing	Διάκοπος.[1]
Io-Erbēth Io-Sēth, Isis	12	L6	12	*PDM* xii. 50-61 *PGM* XII. 445-448	For separating one person/lover from another	[Demotic] For separating one person from another
Io-Erbēth, Bolchosēth	12	L6	14	*PDM* xii. 62-75 *PGM* XII. 449-452	For separating one person/lover from another	[Demotic] Another
Iō Pakerbēth, Iaō	12	L6	32	*PDM* xii. 76-107 *PGM* XII. 453-465	For separating one person/lover from another	[Demotic] Another
IAŌ	12	L6	11	*PDM* xii. 108-118 [*PGM* XII. 466-68]	To cause a woman to hate a man	[Demotic] To cause a woman to hate a man
Geb, Tefnut	14	L6	10	*PDM* xiv. 366-375	For separating man and woman, and encouraging quarrelling	[Demotic] The method [for separating man and woman]
	66	L6	11	*PGM* LXVI. 1-11	For separating two persons, and causing arguments. Illustration.	[n/h] [named persons]
Iō Erbēth, Iō Pakerbēth, Iō Bolchosēth, Apomps, Brabo, Typhon, Sēth, Aion, Apis, Aberamenthō	126	L6	21	*PGM* CXXVIa. 1-21 *SM* 95 a	To cause separation. Invocation using mustard.[2]	[n/h] διάκοψον – line 14
Adōnai, Osiris	126	L6	17	*PGM* CXXVIb. 1-17 *SM* 95 b	To cause separation	[n/h]
Total L6		**9**	**139**			

Table L6: Love Separation.[3]

---

[1] Separation [of lovers].

[2] This rite is listed as a λόγος Τυφῶν, a *logos Typhon,* or an irresistible invocation.

[3] No headword but an unmistakable description.

Other Love Rites (L7)

Gods, Angels, Daimones, names of magicians, *nomina magica*	Non-Roman PGM Nos.	Category	No. of lines	Betz Papyrus *PGM/PDM* Reference number	Objective/ Technique	Greek Headwords
sis, Ape of Thoth, Nephthys, Osiris Onnophris, Belf, Anubis, Re, Hapi, Mnervis	4	L7	60	*PGM* IV. 94-153	Love rite full of Egyptian myth about Osiris, Isis and Nephthys	[n/h]
Aphrodite	4	L7	10	*PGM* IV. 1265-1274	Love rite using Aphrodite's name	Ἀφροδίτης ὄνομα[1]
Eros, Psyche, Aphrodite, Dardanos [2]	4	L7 T	125	*PGM* IV. 1716-1840[3]	Love rite, called the 'Sword of Dardanos.'[4] uses a magnetic stone talisman	Ξίφος Δαρδάνου[5] πάρεδρος[6] - line 1838
Typhon Osiri[s] Iō	7	L7	11	*PGM* VII. 467-477	Love rite	[n/h]
IAŌ Sabaōth, Sothis [Sathis]	10	L7	23	*PGM* X. 1-23	Love rite	[n/h]
Ablanathanalba, Abrasax	11	L7	19	*PGM* XIc. 1-19	Love rite "to obtain intercourse." 2nd/3rd century.	[n/h] [name facility]
Anubis, Abraham	12	L7	12	*PDM* xii. 135-146 [*PGM* XII. 474-479]	Love rite.[7]	[Demotic] [n/h]
Balsames, Anubis	12	L7	18	*PDM* xii. 147-164 [*PGM* XII. 480-495]	Love rite	[Demotic] Another
	14	L7	7	*PDM* xiv. 1063-1069	Love rite utilising the hair of the woman in a lamp wick	[Demotic] [n/h]
	14	L7	13	*PDM* xiv. 1206-1218	Love rite using of a shrew-mouse drowned in wine	[Demotic] [n/h]

---

[1] Aphrodite's name.

[2] The founder of the Mysteries of Samothrace.

[3] Lines 1841-1870 have been separated out as a separate rite under 'P.'

[4] See Gaster, *The Sword of Moses*. This rite is designed to bind a soul to the magician's purposes. It utilises the angels Thouriēl, Michaēl, Gabriēl, Ouriēl, Misaēl Irraēl Istraēl (see *PGM* IV. 1815). An iron sword is often used to constrain spirits, especially in European grimoires. Lines 1841-1870 have been split off as a separate operation to acquire an assistant daimon.

[5] Sword of Dardanos.

[6] *Paredros*, familiar spirit. This is a separate procedure, so it has been moved to a separate rite.

[7] With drawing of Anubis dealing with a mummy on an embalming lion couch.

Gods, Angels, Daimones, names of magicians, *nomina magica*	Non-Roman PGM Nos.	Category	No. of lines	Betz Papyrus *PGM/PDM* Reference number	Objective/ Technique	Greek Headwords
				PGM XV. 1-21 *PGM* XVI. 1-75 *PGM* XIXa. 1-54	*See D*	
Anubis, Hermes	32	L7	19	*PGM* XXXII. 1-19	Lesbian love rite of attraction. 2nd/3rd century	[n/h] [named persons]
Typhon, Helios, Adōnai, Abrasax, Pinouti, Sabaōs	32	L7	25	*PGM* XXXIIa. 1-25	Love rite of attraction. 2nd/3rd century	[n/h] [named persons]
Phnouthi, Pharakounēth, Thōuth	38	L7 C	26	*PGM* XXXVIII. 1-26	Love rite, with details of the rulers of the hours, and their animal form	[n/h] [name facility]
				PDM lxi. 112-127	*See S*	
	61	L7	11	*PDM* lxi. 148-158	Love rite	[Demotic] [n/h]
Osornōphriosor[nōphri] Helios, Senephthys, Selene, Adōne	62	L7	24	*PGM* LXII. 1-24	Love rite which threatens to shake the foundations of world.[1]	[n/h] [name facility]
	64	L7	12	*PGM* LXIV. 1-12	To make her "writhe at my feet." Atypical sigil	[n/h]
Typhon, Helios, Abrasax, Adōnai	68	L7	20	*PGM* LXVIII. 1-20	Love rite	[n/h] [named persons]
				PGM LXXVIII. 1-14	*See T*	
Hermes	109	L7	8	*PGM* CIX. 1- 8 *SM* 56	Love rite	[n/h] [named person]
Anoubis, Osiris Esiēs, Dioskouroi, Hades	117	L7	1	*PGM* CXVII *SM* 71	Love rites: 22 fragments.[2]	[n/h]
	119	L7	3	*PGM* CXIXa. 1-3 *SM* 82 a	Love rite through touch using milk	[n/h]
				PGM CXIXa. 7-11 *SM* 82 c	*See T4*	
Abrathiaou	-	L7	5	*SM* 79 a	For conception	[n/h]
Babraōth	-	L7	6	*SM* 79 b	For conception	ἄλλο

[1] Uses an unusual phylactery made of three peonies.

[2] Supposed 1st century BCE. Sometimes claimed to be a forgery.

Gods, Angels, Daimones, names of magicians, *nomina magica*	Non-Roman *PGM* Nos.	Category	No. of lines	Betz Papyrus *PGM/PDM* Reference number	Objective/ Technique	Greek Headwords
Total L7		**22**	**458**			

Table L7: Other Love Rites.

Homeric magic and divination - ὁμηρομαντεῖον (*homēromanteion*) (O)

These passages consist of texts drawn from Homer which were given a special magical and divinatory significance. The *Illiad* and the *Odyssey* were for the ancient Greeks much more than just stories of gods and heroes, and held a special place in their hearts. Homer was thought of as a god in Alexandria where he was worshipped in a temple called the Homereion. Reading Homer may well have been the route taken by some Egyptians to learn Greek, so it is not surprising to find such passages in a magical handbook that may have been owned by an Egyptian magician.

The association of Homer not just with Greek religion but also with magic was strengthened by his stories about the sorceress Circe in the *Odyssey*. It is a traditional part of Greek culture to claim that its poetry was more than just manmade, so that quoting Homer for magical reasons for the ancient Greeks, was rather like Christians or Jews quoting passages from the Bible for magical reasons.

Aside from their religious significance passages from Homer were used in divination. The Homeric divinatory method was as follows. First the correct time for divination is determined: for example at noon on the second day of the month, or at dawn on the fourth or fifth day of the month.[1] Some days were considered not suitable at all for this type of divination, such as the 16th or 25th day. Then a set prayer or invocation was said inwardly, after which three dice (or knucklebones with 6 faces) were thrown giving three numbers. All of the possible dice combinations of three numbers are shown,[2] and the oracle's answer can thus be looked up. For example a dice throw of 4-5-3 gives the reading "alone to have intelligence, but they are flitting shades"[3] a typically ambiguous divinatory result.

The largest Homeric section in the *PGM* consists of 148 such apparently very random lines, and falls right at the beginning of *PGM* VII. Such passages have no headwords, but are immediately identifiable by being quotations from the *Illiad* or the *Odyssey*. It therefore seems that the magician who owned or penned this particular papyrus often resorted to this method of divination.

It is therefore possible that where such lines are scattered through the *PGM*,[4] that they may have been the results of a divination done before a particular rite was embarked up.

---

1 The times are also been included in this papyrus: *PGM* VII. 155-167.

2 *PGM* VII. 1-148.

3 *Odyssey* 10. 495.

4 See Table O for all such examples.

Homer and the 'Mithras Liturgy'

One fascinating use of quotes from Homer in the *PGM* was to mark off the beginning and end of one of the main Mystery rites, the so-called *Mithras Liturgy* in *PGM* IV. The Homeric verses at lines 467-474 and those at lines 831-832 deliberately bracket the 'Mithras Liturgy,' which is inserted in between them. In each case these passages, which form a header and footer for the Mystery rite, are separated from the rest of the text by a clear paragraph mark.

The content of each of these bracketing quotes from Homer is an apparently random selection of lines drawn from the 8th and 10th book of the *Illiad,* no two lines being adjacent. The lines chosen in both sets are the same, but written in a different line order. The 'opening bracket' has six Homeric lines in order: 123456. The 'closing bracket' has exactly the same lines but written in a different order: 3451612. This is probably done for a deliberate magical reason rather than a case of scribal carelessness. These lines are probably the result of a divination undertaken before the rite.

However the verse has been dissected by Betz into several short "spells." To appreciate the structure it is necessary to look at the layout of the original Greek. The Greek phrase θυμοκάτοχον πρὸς φίλους, *thymokatochon pros philous* or "binding the anger directed at friends/beloved ones" occurs at this point. It is clearly separated from the Homeric quotes by deep indenting in the papyrus, and by setting in a different fount size in Preisendanz.[1]

Although θυμοκάτοχον is used in *PGM* to indicate a procedure for binding anger,[2] here in the context of θυμοκάτοχον πρὸς φίλους it performs a different function, that of bracketing the *Mithras Liturgy*. The emphasis on the phrase θυμοκάτοχον πρὸς φίλους is quite different from that placed on the Homeric lines. I believe it is therefore pointless to try to split the lines up into two one-line "charms."[3]

The theme that these apparently random Homeric lines have in common is a challenge to the gods, especially Zeus. For example the mention of Oros and Ephialtes brings to mind their threat to pile mountain upon mountain and storm Olympus itself.[4] Other lines talk about raising a spear against Zeus. Both these actions look to offend the gods.

Therefore I surmise that "binding the anger directed at friends/beloved ones"

---

[1] Preisendanz (1928), pp. 88, 100.

[2] Talismans of type 'T3' for binding anger.

[3] Betz has arranged the translation of θυμοκάτοχον πρὸς φίλους as two different headings, despite the layout of the papyrus and Preisendanz's typography which both clearly indicate this should be read as one.

[4] *PGM* IV. 474, 830. Zeus was so angered at their presumption that he had both Oros and Ephialtes killed by Apollo.

is a request to Zeus to bind his anger against any initiates who attempt to reach the highest heaven, or storm Olympus, utilising the Mystery rite of the '*Mithras Liturgy*'. That then makes sense of these passages being used to 'bracket' the Mystery rite, both top and bottom.

Pseudo-Plutarch in his *Life of Homer* remarked:

> How could we fail to attribute all good things to Homer, when even things which he did not intend, later men have found in his poems. Some use Homer's words as an oracle, like the prophetic utterances of a god.[1]

One thing which the ancient oracles (like that at Delphi) and Homer's lines had in common is that both were delivered in verse, which the ancient Greeks venerated above prose. It is therefore not surprising that after the 199 CE edict in Egypt outlawing temple oracles, that book oracles, especially those based on Homer became more popular.

Rites which utilise Homeric texts make up only 1.7% of the *PGM* by rite and 2.1% by lineage.

---

[1] Pseudo-Plutarch, *Vita Homeri,* 218, section 4.

Gods, Angels, Daimones, names of magicians, *nomina magica*	Non-Roman *PGM* Nos.	Category	No. of lines	Betz Papyrus *PGM/PDM* Reference number	Objective/ Technique	Greek Headwords
Homer	4	O	8	*PGM* IV. 467-474[1]	Homeric verses (*Il.* 8.424).[2] These bracket the *Mithras Liturgy* – opening.	θυμοκάτοχον πρὸς φίλους[3] - line 469-470
Homer	4	O	6	*PGM* IV. 821-826, 830-834[4]	Homeric verses (*Il.* 5: 385; 6:424; 8: 424; 10: 193, 521, 564, 572). These verses bracket the *Mithras Liturgy* – closing.	θυμοκάτοχον πρὸς φίλους[5] - line 831-832
				PGM IV. 2145-2240	*See Ω*	
Homer	7	O	148	*PGM* VII. 1-148	Oracle drawn from 216 lines of Homer's *Illiad* and *Odyssey* [Hermonthis]	ὁμηρομαντεῖον[6] - line 148a
				PGM VII. 155-167	*See C*	Times for Homeric divination.
	22	O H	1	*PGM* XXIIa. 1	Extract from Homer (*Il.* 17. 714)	[n/h]
Apollo, Zeus	22	O H	8	PGM XXIIa. 2-9	Magico-medical amulet against bloody flux, using a passage from Homer (*Il.* 1.96).	ἄλλο [πρὸς][7] περιάμματα[8] - line 6
Zeus	22	O H	3	*PGM* XXIIa. 9-10	Magico-medical recipe against pain in the breast and uterus, using a quote from Homer (*Il.* 2.548; 8.486).	[n/h]

1 Unecessarily split into four separate sections in Betz (1996), p. 54. It does not appear to be so split in the papyrus, or in Preisendanz (1928), Vol. 2, p. 88.

2 The Homeric verses at lines 467-474 and 831-832 bracket the "Mithras Liturgy," maybe as a preliminary divination or maybe to highlight its special quality as a Mystery rite.

3 Binding the anger [against] the beloved. I believe this is a plea to Zeus to moderate his anger against the intiate of the Mysteries attempting to ascend to the heavens.

4 Unecessarily split into four separate sections in Betz (1996), p. 54. See Preisendanz (1928), p. 100.

5 Binding the anger [against] the beloved.

6 Divination via the verses of Homer.

7 Another [for].

8 Amulet.

Gods, Angels, Daimones, names of magicians, *nomina magica*	**Non-Roman *PGM* Nos.**	**Category**	**No. of lines**	**Betz Papyrus *PGM/PDM* Reference number**	**Objective/ Technique**	**Greek Headwords**
	22	O H	4	*PGM* XXIIa. 11-14	Magico-medical recipe for contraception from Homer (*Il.* 3.40.)	[n/h]
	22	O H	3	*PGM* XXIIa. 15-17	Magico-medical recipe against elephantiasis, using a quote from Homer (*Il.* 4.141).	[n/h]
Anubis, Osiris, Zeus, Hades, Titan Helios, Iaweh, Phthas, Phre, Nepho. Ablanatho, Abraxas, Phren, B[r]i[ar]eus, Ph[r]asios, Circe, etc.	23	O	70	*PGM* XXIII. 1-70	Poetry of Homer and Julius Africanus. About raising the spirits of the dead, sacrificing sheep, etc.[1]	[n/h]
	-	O	35	*SM* 77	Homeric oracle	[n/h]
Total O		**10**	**286**			

Table O: Homeric magic and divination.

[1] Using Homer, *Od.* 11.34-43, 48-50; *Il.* 3.278-80 and other fragments. Followed by the *Kestoi* of Julius Africanus.

Foreknowledge and Memory - πρόγνωσις (*prognōsis*), μνημονική (*mnēmonikē*) (K)

There are only a few operations for memory and foreknowledge. In one case these are both present in the same rite so these categories have been amalgamated. With one exception, these rites all appear in *PGM* III. Memory and foreknowledge formulae together make up just 1.5% of the *PGM* by rite, or 1.8% by lineage.

Gods, Angels, Daimones, names of magicians, *nomina magica*	Non-Roman PGM Nos.	Category	No. of lines	Betz Papyrus *PGM/PDM* Reference number	Objective/ Technique	Greek Headwords
	1	K	16	*PGM* I. 232-247	Memory rite	μνημονική[1]
Iao Sabaōth,	3	K	13	*PGM* III. 263-275	Foreknowledge rite	πρόγνωσις[2]
Phoibos, Gabriel, Michael	3	K	128	*PGM* III. 282-409	Foreknowledge operation which uses a Magical Table of Practice for invocation, a floor circle and a tripod, gold lamella. With hour attributions	...[προ]γνωστικὴ πρᾶξις[3] αὔτοπτον – line 292
[Helios]	3	K	14	*PGM* III. 410-423	Memory rite	[n/h] μνήμην[4] - line 416
Moses, Helios, Mithras, Lailam, Amoun, Harpon, Chnouphi, Sesengen bar Pharaggēs, Osiris, Abrasax, Iaō Sabaō[th], Helios. Manethon [Manetho]	3	K G	43	*PGM* III. 424-466	Invocation of the goddess of the Moon for foreknowledge and memory, using a holy book. By eating a raw heart mixed with honey.	ἀντίγραφον ἀπὸ ἱερᾶς βιβ[λο]υ.[5] πρόγνω[σ]ις καὶ μνημον[ική][6] – line 424
	3	K	12	*PGM* III. 467-478	Memory rite	μνημονική[7]
Helios	3	K	5	*PGM* III. 479-483	Rite to detect a thief (foreknowledge)	πρόγνωσις[8]
	3	K	6	*PGM* III. 483-488	Another rite to detect a thief (foreknowledge)	ἄλλη [πρόγνωσις] [9]
	3	K	7	*PGM* III. 488-494	Another rite to detect a thief (foreknowledge)	ἄλλη [πρόγνωσις]
Total K		**9**	**244**			

Table K: Foreknowledge and Memory.

1 Memory [rite].
2 Foreknowledge [rite].
3 Foreknowledge practice.
4 Memory.
5 Copy of a sacred book.
6 Foreknowledge and memory.
7 Memory [rite].
8 Foreknowledge.
9 Another [foreknowledge].

Other Magical Procedures (X)

There are usually only one or two examples of each of these procedures. This category contains a number of rites that are not numerous enough to warrant their own category, and which are therefore of less use for comparative examination of specific techniques. These procedures include:

- Using a naked boy as a vehicle for Helios;
- To catch a thief (4);[1]
- To eject fleas from a house;
- Natural magic;[2]
- Eliciting secrets by cause a woman to talk whilst asleep (2);
- Winning at dice;
- Enchantment or casting a glamour;
- Business success in a premises;
- Releasing prisoners and opening doors (2);
- Obtaining eloquence or favour (2);
- Alchemy: about tincture of gold and stones (2);
- Vision of shadows and spirits (2);
- Fighting with, and speaking to a superior;
- To cause madness;
- Using an oracle of lots or leaves (2);
- Slander spell;
- To move a stubborn donkey;
- An adjuration which may be a *defixio*;
- Protection of a house (?);
- Sundry prescriptions and fragments (2);
- Finding a house;
- Christian curses (4);

None of these categories form a large corpus like, for example, love spells or the arrival of a god. All of these passages are relatively small. These single example operations and minor magical procedures make up a significant 6.0% of the *PGM* by rite numbers, or 3.1% by lineage.

[1] Procedures for catching a thief re-appear in later Latin grimoires.

[2] A batch of 'Book of Secrets' formulae.

Gods, Angels, Daimones, names of magicians, *nomina magica*	Non-Roman PGM Nos.	Category	No. of lines	Betz Papyrus *PGM/PDM* Reference number	Objective/ Technique	Greek Headwords
Helios, Adōnai, Sabaōth, Barbarioth	4	X	6	*PGM* IV. 88-93	To Helios. Uses a naked boy as medium inviting obsession by, or communication with, Helios	ἄλλη πρὸς[1]
	5	X	26	*PGM* V. 70-95	To catch a thief, using a hammer to strike an image of the Eye of Horus. (See also *SM* 86.)	[n/h]
Hermes, Iao, Helios, Themis, Erinys, Ammon, Parammon	5	X	41	*PGM* V. 172-212	Invocation of Hermes, to catch a thief, using a food ordeal for the suspects	ἄλλως κλέπτην πιάσαι[2]
	7	X	6	*PGM* VII. 149-154	Bugs, kept out of the house	[n/h]
Demokritos	7	X	20	*PGM* VII. 167-186	Natural magic. Demokritos' dinner table game.[3]	Δημοκρίτου παίγνια[4]
	7	X	6	*PGM* VII. 411-416	Rite for causing a woman to talk while asleep	Νυκτολάλημα[5]
Adriel	7	X	6	*PGM* VII. 423-428	Dice, to win and throw what you want	Κυβεύοντα νικᾶν[6]
	11	X	5	*PGM* XIb. 1-5	Enchantment: to make men who have been drinking appear to have donkey's snouts.[7]	[ἀνθρ]ώπους πίνοντα[ς][8]

1 Another for.

2 Another way to press upon a thief. The 'another way' refers to *PGM* V. 70-95, not the immediately preceeding passage.

3 'Book of Secrets' a type of magical text very much in vogue in the 18th century.

4 Demokritos' 'games,' or simple formulae.

5 Rite for causing a woman to sleep-talk [about her secrets].

6 To win at dice

7 "Book of Secrets" style rite.

8 Men drinking.

Gods, Angels, Daimones, names of magicians, *nomina magica*	Non-Roman *PGM* Nos.	Category	No. of lines	Betz Papyrus *PGM/PDM* Reference number	Objective/ Technique	Greek Headwords
Typhon, Nousi Amoun, Ammon Thōuth, Iaō, Good Daimon, Himerios	12	X	11	*PGM* XII. 96-106	A rite for business success. Himerios' recipe.	[τ]ὰ παρὰ Ἡμερίου[1] εὐχὴ[2] - line 104
Aiōth, Adōnai, Thōth, Sesengen bar Pharaggēs, "daimon of the great god," Zeus, Helios, Hephaistos	12	X	19	*PGM* XII. 160-178	To release prisoners from bonds or danger, or "to do something spectacular"	[Δεσμόλυτον][3] [name facility]
Ablanathanalba, Akrammachamarei Marmaraōth	12	X	8	*PGM* XII. 182-189	Invocation for gaining eloquence and favour	[n/h]
	12	X	9	*PGM* XII. 193-201	Gold, chemical operation to make tincture of gold using salt, vinegar, vitriol, alum, etc. Alchemy.	ἴωσις χρυσοῦ.[4]
	14	X	1	*PDM* xiv. 115	Securing vision of shadows	[Demotic] [n/h]
	14	X	1	*PDM* xiv. 116	To see spirits	[Demotic] Another
				PDM xiv. 376-394	*See Ω*	
	14	X	8	*PDM* xiv. 451-458 [*PGM* XIVb. 12-15]	For fighting a superior, and for going to speak him	[Demotic] For going before a superior
	14	X	10	*PDM* xiv. 920-929	About stones	[Demotic] Lees of wine
Dioscorus, Adonai	14	X	7	*PDM* xiv. 1056-1062	To find a thief	[Demotic] [n/h]
	14	X	6	*PDM* xiv. 1182-1187	Madness, to cause	[Demotic] [n/h]
Helios, Iaō, Sabaōth, Lailam, Barbaras, Michaēl, Gabriēl	22	X	10	*PGM* XXIIa. 18-27	Request to Helios to be loved, beautiful, honoured and famous	[n/h]

1 Himerios' 'recipes.'

2 Prayer.

3 To release from a binding spell.

4 Refine a tincture of gold.

Gods, Angels, Daimones, names of magicians, *nomina magica*	Non-Roman PGM Nos.	Category	No. of lines	Betz Papyrus *PGM/PDM* Reference number	Objective/ Technique	Greek Headwords
Isis, Hermes, Osiris, Helios	24	X	25	*PGM* XXIVa. 1-25	Oracle, based on a *Book of Hermes*, using 29 leaves. 2nd/3rd century.	Μεγάλη Ἶσις ἡ κυρία[1]
Horos, Osiris, Isis, Typhon	37	X	9	*PGM* XXXVI. 312-320	To open a door	ἄνοιξις θύρας [2]
Tyche	50	X	18	*PGM* L. 1-18	Oracle by Lots of Tyche	[n/h]
Nephthys, Phrē	61	X	6	*PDM* lxi. 100-105	A spell of destruction of the "impious one."[3]	[Demotic] [name facility]
Horus, Geb, Isis. Horus	61	X	6	*PDM* lxi. 106-111	Remedy for a donkey not moving	[Demotic]
	63	X	6	*PGM* LXIII. 7-12	To make a woman confess the name of the man she loves using a bird's tongue	[n/h]
Adonaiōs, Sabaōth, Abrasax chthonic Hermes-Thouoth, Sesengen bar Pharaggēs	67	X	24	*PGM* LXVII. 1-24	Adjuration.[4]	[n/h] [name facility]
Helios, Sapeiphnēp, Abrasakx(*sic*)	81	X	10	*PGM* LXXXI. 1-10	Greetings to deities for protection of a house	[n/h]
	127	X H	12	*PGM* CXXVII. 1-12 *SM* 76	Magico-medical prescriptions relating to erections, causing fights and souring wine.	[n/h]
	-	X	7	*PDM* Supp. 162-168	Procedure to find a house to live in	[Demotic]
Mithra, Horus, Anubis, Isis, Osiris, Harsiese	-	X	23	*PDM* Supp. 185-208	Fragments of rites	[Demotic]
Emmanuel	-	X	18	*SM* 59	Christian papyrus curse asking for judgement by god	[n/h] [named persons]

[1] Great is the Lady Isis.
[2] Door opening.
[3] Categorised as a "Spell of attraction" by Dieleman (2005), p. 262.
[4] May be a *defixio* as it refers to "those who have died] in an [untimely] death.

Gods, Angels, Daimones, names of magicians, *nomina magica*	**Non-Roman *PGM* Nos.**	**Category**	**No. of lines**	**Betz Papyrus *PGM/PDM* Reference number**	**Objective/ Technique**	**Greek Headwords**
	-	X	7	*SM* 60	Christian papyrus curse	στήλη[1] [named persons]
God, Gabriel, Michael, Jesus Christ	-	X	4	*SM* 61	Christian papyrus curse	[n/h] [named persons]
	-	X	8	*SM* 62	Christian papyrus curse	[n/h] [named person]
	-	X	34	*SM* 86	Five spells for identifying a thief.	[n/h]
Total X		**35**	**423**			

Table X: Other Magical Procedures.

[1] *Stēlē.*

'Evil Sleep,' Blindness and Death - *nktk bin* (Z)

These formulae are the province of the φαρμακὸς (*pharmakos*) rather than the magician as they are concerned with the use of drugs, herbs and poisons. These formulae are solely Demotic and therefore entirely of Egyptian provenance. The only magical part involves the harnessing of the destructive forces of Seth/Typhon using the Iō Erbēth Iō Pakerbēth formula and a touch of slander. The process is progressive, so that for example with four days of repetitions of one formula, he sleeps.[1] With seven more days of repetition, the victim dies.

The ingredients include relatively harmless items like flour of wild dates, milk, honey, oil and wine used as a base for the active ingredients: [poison] western apple seeds,[2] henbane, [poison] ivy,[3] mandrake root, scammony root, 'poisonous herbs' and opium. The animal ingredients include gall of a horned viper, gall of an Alexandrian weasel, gall of a shrew-mouse, a beetle burned with styrax(?), a camel's blood, blood of a man, a two tailed lizard,[4] a drowned shrew-mouse, a drowned hawk, and a nightjar's or bat's blood for blinding, all relatively poisonous. Needless to say, the victim is encouraged to eat or drink the mixture.

'Evil sleep' has been translated as catalepsy, which seems appropriate. With one exception all are designed to cause catalepsy, death or blindness. The exception is designed to counter these effects.[5] The whole corpus is confined to just two series of contiguous passages,[6] from just one Demotic papyrus (*PDM* xiv). They make up 2.2% of all the *PGM/PDM* rites in number, but only a very small proportion of lines of text (0.5%).

---

[1] *PDM* xiv. 675-694.

[2] *Datura*?

[3] "It grows in gardens; its leaf is like the leaf of a *shekam* plant, being divided into three lobes like a grape leaf. It is one palm in measurement; its blossom is like silver…[or] gold."

[4] Geckos are quite poisonous.

[5] *PDM* xiv. 706-710.

[6] Plus *PDM* xiv. 675-694 which has more magical content.

Gods, Angels, Daimones, names of magicians, *nomina magica*	Non-Roman *PGM* Nos.	Category	No. of lines	Betz Papyrus *PGM/PDM* Reference number	Objective/ Technique	Greek Headwords
				PDM xiv. 376-394	*See Ω*	
Typhon, Seth, Pakerbēth, Erishkigal	14	Z	20	*PDM* xiv. 675-694 [*PGM* XIVc.16-27]	To cause "evil sleep" or death	ἐπικαλοῦμαι[1] [name facility]
	14	Z	5	*PDM* xiv. 706-710	Against "evil sleep"	[Demotic] [n/h]
	14	Z	5	*PDM* xiv. 711-715	To cause "evil sleep"	*nktk bin*[2]
	14	Z	9	*PDM* xiv. 716-724	To cause "evil sleep" for two days	*nktk bin*
	14	Z	3	*PDM* xiv. 724-726	To cause "evil sleep"	*nktk bin*
	14	Z	10	*PDM* xiv. 727-736	To cause "[evil] sleep"	*nktk bin*
	14	Z	2	*PDM* xiv. 737-738	To cause "evil sleep"	*nktk bin*
	14	Z	2	*PDM* xiv. 739-740	To cause death	[Demotic] Another
	14	Z	1	*PDM* xiv. 741	To cause blindness	[Demotic] Another
	14	Z	1	*PDM* xiv. 742	To cause blindness	[Demotic] Another
	14	Z	7	*PDM* xiv. 743-749	To cause "evil sleep" or death	*nktk bin*
	14	Z	6	*PDM* xiv. 911-916	To cause "evil sleep"	*nktk bin*
	14	Z	3	*PDM* xiv. 917-919	Against "evil sleep"	*nktk bin*
Total Z		**13**	**74**			

Table Z: 'Evil Sleep,' Blindness and Death.

---

1 Summon.

2 Evil sleep, or catalepsy.

6.4 Skrying and Dreams

Evocationary Bowl Skrying - λεκανομαντεία (*lekanomanteia*), *šn-hne (shen ben)* (B)

Unlike the Greek lexicon definition of *manteiai* as simple divination, in the *PGM manteiai* are a form of evocation of a daimon or spirit who speaks through a skryer. In each case the magician evokes a spirit and a virgin child skryer states what he or she hears or sees. The method covers a number of variations in equipment, including water, oil, bowl and saucer:[1]

> ***Inquiry of bowl divination and necromancy:*** Whenever you want to inquire about matters, take a bronze vessel, either a bowl or a saucer, whatever kind you wish. Pour water [into it]... Holding the vessel on your knees, pour out green olive oil [onto the water], bend over the vessel and speak the prescribed spell. And address whatever god you want and ask about whatever you wish...[2]

In the *PGM* they are all referred to as a 'vessel inquiry,' often translated into English as 'bowl divination.' Vessel inquiry has a long history which clearly extends from the *PDM* and *PGM* period through the Byzantine Greek *Hygromanteia,* and beyond. In fact *lekanomanteia*[3] is still practised in many Muslim areas today. The original demotic word for this practice is *šn-hne (shen ben)* or 'vessel inquiry.' Because this skrying involves evocation, and is not just a passive process, it is more precise to refer to it as Evocationary Bowl Skrying rather than bowl divination.

This practice does *not* however relate to the Aramaic, Hebrew and Babylonian bowls which were found buried (usually inverted) in Mesopotamia, Syria and Palestine, which appear to occur only in the 5th and 6th centuries, and which serve a totally different purpose as 'demon traps.'[4] These Mesopotamian bowls have been found buried under houses or near graves. They do not have a corresponding textual record, but are fairly obviously apotropaic, specifically for the binding of demons, a totally different objective to the bowls considered here. Furthermore they bear no trace of ever having contained liquids, an essential part of *lekanomanteia.* However they do attest many god and angel names in common with other *PGM* texts (but not specifically those of Evocationary Bowl Skrying/vessel inquiry): and this simply demonstrates that

---

[1] Water and oil skrying methods, which also appear later in the Byzantine *Hygromanteia* all derive from the *PGM,* as confirmed by the remark made in the *PGM* at the beginning of one bowl skrying procedure.

[2] *PGM* IV. 221-232. This passage is actually abruptly inserted into a letter supposedly written by Nephōtēs to Psammetichos, so it comes highly recommended.

[3] Λεκάνη, *lekanē,* simply means 'pot or pan,' referring to the vessel that holds the liquid.

[4] For which see Montgomery (1913) and Naveh and Shaked (1985).

they are part of shared Middle Eastern magical conventions.[1]

The bowls used in *lekanomanteia* were used specifically by a virgin boy skryer gazing into the bowl of liquid,[2] accompanied by the magician's invocations of the god, daimon or spirit involved.[3] On the whole, the god most often called upon in the *PDM/PGM* for vessel inquiry was Anubis, lord of the Underworld, which helps to confirm the rite's Egyptian origin.[4] These operations are found mainly in the Demotic papyri, specifically *PDM* xiv.

Usually oil would be poured onto the surface of water. Or, more sophisticatedly, the flame from a lamp might be reflected in the surface of the liquid providing a suitably animated skrying surface.

Lecanomancy is first recorded in the Babylonian Ritual Tablets (7th century BCE):

> Cypress, *fine* flour he shall pour out, oil on the libation he shall put, an offering he shall pour out, oil on the water of the vessel he shall put, of Šamaš and Hadad, the great gods, he shall inquire. When the omen and the oil [divination] are faultless the great gods come near and judge a judgement of justice and righteousness…the diviner shall look upon oil in water…[5]

An early *baraitha*[6] on the *Babylonian Talmud* (200 CE) shows that Jews living there also adopted the same practices. In it the vessel was referred to as a *makalta/makultu*,[7] which was used for mixed oil and water skrying.

In one example of this practice in the *PGM* a boy skryer looks into olive oil in a

---

[1] These names include *Gnostic*: Ablanathanalba, Abrasax, Ialdabaot, Iao Zouka; *Hebrew*: Akatriel, Anqatam, Azriel, Barqiel, Dalqiel, Dfuniel, El, Gabriel, Hadriel, Hafkiel, Halusiel, Haniel, I-am-who-I-am, Kadutiel, Kariel, Kouriel, Lilith, Masagiel, Metatron, Michael, Moriath, Nuriel, Paspasim, Pastam, Payumiel, Puriel, Qoriel, Raphael, Sabaot, Samael, Samarel, Sandalphon, Sarafiel, Selah, Shakniel, Shamish, Shamriel, Shamshiel, Soutiel, Suriahel, Suriel, Tetragrammaton, 'Uziel, Yah, Yahu, Yehoel, Yequtiel, Zebuth, Zotiel; *Greek*: Ares, Bar-Theon, Diyonisim, Eros, Gyllou, Helios, Hermes, Morphous, Pelagia, Sideros; *Egyptian*: Horus, *ntrws syh*, Ptah, *tinyt, twinyt*; *Mesopotamian and sundry*: Labartu, Bagdana, Danahish, Dlibat, Iabezebut, Iurba, Musagaoth, Sanoy, Sansanoy, Samangalaf, Sesegen bar Pherenges (*sic*), Smamit, Thraphiari. These names are predominantly a mixture of Greek and Hebrew names, which one would expect by the 5th and 6th centuries.

[2] The vessel is also referred to as an ἄγγος.

[3] See Ogden (2002), pp. 205-206 for his comment on *PGM* IV. 222-260.

[4] There are only three *PGM* examples in Greek as opposed to more than eight Demotic *PDM* examples of *lekanomanteia*.

[5] Ritual Tablets 15-25 quoted in Daiches (1913), pp. 8-9. Daiches contends that the Babylonians practised oil divination "as long back as 2000 BCE." The Babylonians in turn ascribed these practices to the Sumerians, so the practice has a long history.

[6] Commentary.

[7] מכל is simply a container for oil.

saucer.[1] This rite is quite revealing as it gives the rubric, or ritual instructions, in detail. The saucer or bowl is placed on a 'brick.' The word translated as a 'brick' throughout the *PGM* is, I think, more adequately rendered as a clay tablet. The magician is instructed to "carve these characters on a magnet that is 'breathing.'"[2] In addition the afterbirth of a white dog should be added to the bowl, and KARBAŌTH[3] should be written with myrrh ink on a phylactery, for protection of the skryer, and hung on his chest.

A skrying with a more Greek flavour is affected via Aphrodite and uses a mixture of water and oil in a bronze drinking cup. Typically the bowl is written on with myrrh ink.[4] Here it is recommended that the magician waxes over the writing on the bowl, presumably to prevent this writing being washed off by the skrying medium.[5]

Another bowl skrying is inserted as part of a rite of divine encounter. It utilises a bronze bowl or saucer, with water and green olive oil, but it makes a distinction between the different types of water used.[6] This bowl skrying also advises using a phylactery for protection.[7]

In the *London and Leiden Papyrus* a similar rite begins with an invocation of the gods of the Underworld.[8] It utilises a boy ("a pure youth who has not yet gone with a woman") as a skryer, a dish filled with oasis oil (presumably palm oil), and seven clay tablets[9] representing the planets, seven loaves of bread, and seven lumps of salt, as offerings.[10] The invocation is designed to be spoken down into the head of the boy who must wear a phylactery for his own protection.

In yet another rite the god invoked is Khonsu (in Thebes Nefer-hotep) the Moon god described as "the noble child who came forth from the lotus,"

---

[1] *PGM* LXII. 24-46.

[2] The point of 'breathing' is that the magnet should still be able to 'inhale' or attract other metal to it.

[3] Probably a corruption of Sabaōth.

[4] It is an interesting assumption that writing which is meant to be taken notice of by spiritual creatures should always be scented in one way or another. Myrrh is the preferred incense for ink in *PGM*.

[5] *PGM* IV. 3209-3254.

[6] Rainwater = the heavenly gods; seawater = earthly [chthonic?] gods; river water = Sarapis or Osiris; and spring water = the dead.

[7] *PGM* IV. 221-260.

[8] *PDM* xiv. 1-92.

[9] As before, this is translated as 'bricks.'

[10] Dr. John Dee in 1583 arrayed seven tablets (one for each of the planets) on his 'Holy Table' which supported his skrying stone. His procedures are not far distant from those of the *PGM*.

thereby clearly identifying him with Harpocrates.[1] The standard Egyptian gods Anubis, Isis, Horus, Nephthys and Osiris also appear. This rite calls upon the souls of the dead for answers to the divinatory questions. The vessel is either a clean copper beaker or a new pottery vessel, used with an equal measure of water and oil (or oil alone) with a stone *qs-'nh,* which is probably magnetic haematite, and a plant associated with embalming. The usual array of three clay tablets under and four around, with offering loaves, is prescribed. Both the magician and skryer sit on a clay tablet.

Another rite utilises a copper cup with the figure of Anubis engraved upon it,[2] with an oil/water mixture, and the usual clay tablet arrangement. A lobe of an Anubis plant[3] is to be put on the lamp. The incense is to be frankincense, oil, ammoniac, incense and dates pounded with wine.

There is also a method which can be used by the magician without a skryer.[4] In it the magician commands Anubis to bring the god of the day and the gods of whatever town the magician is currently residing in (in order to approve his operation). Anubis acts like a psychopomp, introducing the magician in turn to the gods that he needs to answer his questions.

One passage gives the correct facing directions in cases where a skryer is used: in this case the skryer should face east, while the magician faces west.[5]

Another bowl auto-skrying in Demotic relies upon an ointment placed on the magician's eyes to give him the ability to skry.[6] Ingredients include the blood of a Nile goose, a hoopoe, a nightjar, myrrh, lapis-lazuli, plus several plants.

It may be possible to re-create what was said seven times into the skryer's ear from later Jewish sources. One mediaeval German source claims the words to be said in the boy's right ear are: "Adam Chavah Abton Absalom Sarfiel Nuriel Daniel" followed nine times by:

> *Gerte,* I conjure you with these seven names which I have mentioned, to appear in the wax of this candle, carefully prepared and designated for this purpose, and to answer truthfully concerning that which I shall question you.[7]

Vessel inquiry makes up 3.1% of the *PGM* by rite, or 3.2% by lineage.

---

[1] *PDM* xiv. 239-295.

[2] *PDM* xiv. 395-427. The procedure of using a copper cup for skrying appears later in chapter 53 of the *Hygromanteia* as *chalkomanteia.*

[3] The text explains, "it grows in millions of places. Its leaf is like the leaf of a Syrian [plant] which grows white; its flower is like the flower of conyza." Deines and Grapow (1959) identified this plant as *mentha aquatica.*

[4] *PDM* xiv. 528-553.

[5] *PDM* xiv. 627-635

[6] *PDM* xiv. 295-308.

[7] Trachtenberg (2004), p. 220.

Evocationary Bowl Skrying - λεκανομαντεία (*lekanomanteia*), *šn-hne (shen ben)* (B)

Gods, Angels, Daimones, names of magicians, *nomina magica*	**Non-Roman PGM Nos.**	**Category**	**No. of lines**	**Betz Papyrus *PGM/PDM* Reference number**	**Objective/ Technique**	**Greek Headwor**
				PGM IV. 154-220, 261-285.[1]	*See G*	
Typhon	4	B	0	*PGM* IV. 221-260 [2]	Evocationary Bowl Skrying/vessel inquiry.	ἰσοθέου φύσε κυριεύσας[3] ...λεκανομαν
Aphrodite	4	B	46	*PGM* IV. 3209-3254	Evocationary Bowl Skrying/ vessel inquiry of Aphrodite, using a copper vessel	Ἀφροδίτης φι[α]λομαντεῖ
				PGM VII. 319-334	*See F*	
				PGM VII. 335-347	*See V*	
Anubis, Ram-Lion-Lotus, Ablanathanalba, Hor-Amoun, Marighari, Horus, Isis, Osiris, Sobek, Agathdaimon	14	B	92	*PDM* xiv. 1-92	Demotic Evocationary Bowl Skrying/vessel inquiry via Anubis, using a virgin boy as skryer	*šn-hne (shen b* - line 9
Khonsu, Ram-Lion-Lotus	14	B	57	*PDM* xiv. 239-295	Demotic Evocationary Bowl Skrying/vessel inquiry	[Demotic] *šn-hn[e]* – lin Vessel inquiry Khonsu
Anubis, Thoth	14	B	14	*PDM* xiv. 295-308	Demotic Evocationary Bowl Skrying/vessel inquiry using eye ointment	[Demotic] [*šn-hn*]*e* – line Vessel [inquir
Anubis	14	B	33	*PDM* xiv. 395-427	Demotic Evocationary Bowl Skrying/vessel inquiry	[Demotic] [*šn-hne*] – line *šn-hne* - line
				PDM xiv. 489-515	*See E*	*šn-hne* - line

[1] Betz lists *PGM* IV. 154-285 as one procedure of bowl skrying/vessel inquiry, whereas lines 154-220 and 261-285 is a rite of Divine Encounter, with a bowl skrying/vessel inquiry (lines 221-260) inserted in the middle of it. See under 'B' for the latter section.
[2] See also *PGM*. 154-220, 261-285 which bracket this passage. The line number tally is shown as zero because they are already included in the tally of the bracketing passage.
[3] Make equal to the original gods in power.
[4] *Lekanomanteia.*
[5] Aphrodite's Bowl divination.

Gods, Angels, Daimones, names of magicians, *nomina magica*	**Non-Roman *PGM* Nos.**	**Category**	**No. of lines**	**Betz Papyrus *PGM/PDM* Reference number**	**Objective/ Technique**	**Greek Headwords**
Anubis	14	B	26	*PDM* xiv. 528-553	Demotic Evocationary Bowl Skrying/vessel inquiry	[Demotic] *šn-hne* – lines 528, 537, 539 Vessel inquiry
Osiris, Iaho, Sabaho, Mikhael, Anubis	14	B	9	*PDM* xiv. 627-635	Demotic Evocationary Bowl Skrying/vessel inquiry through Osiris.	[Demotic] *šn-hn[e]* – line 627 Vessel inquiry of Osiris
Moon, Amoun, Abrasaks	14	B	6	*PDM* xiv. 695-700	Demotic Evocationary Bowl Skrying/vessel inquiry	[Demotic] *šn-hn*[*e*] – line 695
Moon	14	B	5	*PDM* xiv. 701-705	Demotic Evocationary Bowl Skrying/vessel inquiry, another	[Demotic] *ke* [*šn-hne*]
				PDM xiv. 805-840	*See Ω*	*šn-hne* – line 805, 817 *šn-n* – line 837 *šn-hn* – line 838
Isis, Iaho, Nephar	14	B G	10	*PDM* xiv. 841-850	Demotic Evocationary Bowl Skrying/vessel inquiry	[Demotic] *šn-hne* – line 841 Another method
Hamst	14	B	5	*PDM* xiv. 851-855	Demotic Evocationary Bowl Skrying/vessel inquiry	[Demotic] *šn-hne* – line 851 Another
	14	B	20	*PDM* xiv. 856-875	Demotic Evocationary Bowl Skrying/vessel inquiry	[Demotic] *šn*[*-hne*] – line 856
	14	B	11	*PDM* xiv. 875-885	Demotic Evocationary Bowl Skrying/vessel inquiry	[Demotic] Here is another *šn-hne* - line 880
Sabaōth, Osiris Ablanathanalba, Agathodaimon,	14	B	20	*PDM* xiv. 1110-1129	Demotic Evocationary Bowl Skrying/vessel inquiry to open the skryer's eyes, if working without a skryer	[Demotic] *hn n šn* - line 1111
IAŌ, Ablanathanalba	14	B	17	*PDM* xiv. 1163-1179	Demotic Evocationary Bowl Skrying/vessel inquiry	[Demotic] [*šn-*]*hne*
	62	B	22	*PGM* LXII. 24-46	Greek Evocationary Bowl Skrying/vessel inquiry with boy skryer	[n/h]
	-	B	37	*SM* 65	Terracotta bowl probably for skrying incised with a large wing format formula.	[n/h]
Total B		**18**	**430**			

Table B: Evocationary Bowl Skrying/Vessel Inquiry.

Evocationary Lamp Skrying - λυχνομαντεία (*lychnomanteia*), *wᶜ šn / qmꜣ tꜣ* (E)

Just as *lekanomanteia* involves a skryer looking into the water or oil in a bowl, so λυχνομαντεία, *lychnomanteia,* or Evocationary Lamp Skrying begins with the skryer concentrating on the flame of a lamp (λύχνος, *lychnos*) whilst listening to the invocations of the magician. These rites occur predominantly in *PGM* VII and *PDM* xiv.[1] This procedure also sometimes features in Vision ('V') rites where the lamp is used to request later answers in a dream. Evocationary Lamp Skrying or *wᶜ šn* or *qmꜣ tꜣ* in Demotic, is primarily an Egyptian practice,[2] and makes up 2.6% of the *PGM/PDM* by rite, and 3.5% by lineage.

The procedure usually involves the calling of a god to give verbal answers to particular questions posed by the magician. Integral to the practice is the use of the virgin boy skryer, although sometimes the magician also asks for a direct vision of the god himself. The magician is instructed to put his hand, or finger, on the head of his skryer, or alternatively whisper the invocation directly "down into his head."

There are frequent references in the *PGM* to not using lamps coloured red, or more specifically tainted with red lead (*prš*).[3] This might apply to lamps coloured with red ochre (*miltos).* The reason apparently is to avoid the symbolism of or calling Seth-Typhon.[4]

Typical offerings to be made during this rite are frankincense and grape-vine wood[5] or myrrh and willow leaf.[6] The brazier should be placed upon a clay tablet (referred to as a 'brick') and the boy upon another. Interestingly, in one passage, the spirit being conjured is referred to as the "spirit that flies in the air, [and is] called with secret codes." The wick is conjured by the hand of Anubis and by the "blood of the Drowned One," Osiris. According to the nature of the entity called, or of the question, so the wick and the oil are changed.[7]

---

[1] This technique is confined to the *PGM/PDM* and was not transmitted onwards to either the *Hygromanteia,* the *Clavicula Salomonis* or later vernacular grimoires.

[2] See Gee (1999) for details of the procedure.

[3] Such lamps are mentioned in *PGM* I. 277, 293; II. 57; IV. 2373, 3191; VII. 542, 594; VIII. 87; XII. 27, 131; and LXII. 1.

[4] Red has a well known association with 'demonic' gods like Seth and Apophis. Red is the preferred ink colour for writing the names of demons or enemies. The avoidance of the colour in *PGM* is based on the same symbolism, especially in the case of skrying lamps.

[5] *PGM* VII. 540-544.

[6] *PDM* xiv. 766.

[7] For a daimonic spirit, a wick of sailcloth and butter is used; to seduce a woman oil of roses is recommended; in other matters a clean wick and pure genuine oil, probably olive oil. For an Apollonian invocation use either rose oil or oil of spikenard. See *PGM* I. 279.

Other accoutrements occasionally used for Evocationary Lamp Skrying include a wolf's head on which the lamp is to be balanced.[1] An altar is sometimes used to give a surface on which to sacrifice to this particular god when he arrives. In that case the offering will consist of:

> ...a wolf's eye, storax gum, cassia, balsam gum and whatever is valued among the spices, and pour a libation of wine and honey and milk and rainwater, [and make] 7 flat cakes and 7 round cakes.[2]

One of the names conjured many times in various operations of Evocationary Lamp Skrying is a daimon or spirit called BOEL, who is described as "the first servant of the great god, he who gives light exceedingly, the companion of the flame."[3] This name is repeatedly mentioned in a number of Evocationary Lamp Skrying invocations,[4] and seems to be integral to this method:

> Bring in BOEL! Bring BOEL in! Bring BOEL in! ARBETH-BAI YTSIO, O doubly great god, bring BOEL in! TAT TAT,[5] bring BOEL in! Bring BOEL in! Bring BOEL in! TAGR TAT, he of Eternity, bring BOEL in! Bring BOEL in! Bring BOEL in! BEYTSI, O great god, bring BOEL in! Bring BOEL in! Bring BOEL IN![6]

This same spirit name appears over a thousand years later in 1623, when a magician called Jean Michel Menuisier, who had learnt magic in Toledo, claimed that:

> During a visit to Vienna he had purchased a magic phial containing a spirit named Boël, which he consulted to know occult secrets and therefore help his clients.[7]

One of the standard inducements offered to the daimones/spirits to perform in an Evocationary Lamp Skrying is that the magician will praise them before the senior gods:

> I shall praise you in heaven before Pre;[8] I shall praise you before the moon; I shall praise you on earth; I shall praise you before the one who is on the throne...[9]

Several examples of Evocationary Lamp Skrying assumes that the evocation will cause the boy skryer to see the king of the spirits, who can then be cross examined by the magician, via the boy. This procedure is sometimes extended

---

[1] *PGM* I. 282.
[2] *PGM* I. 285-289.
[3] *PDM* xiv. 195, 489-490.
[4] Mentioned in more than 12 Demotic Evocationary Lamp Skrying rites.
[5] Thoth.
[6] *PDM* xiv. 470-473.
[7] Davies (2009), pp. 64-65.
[8] Ra, the sun god.
[9] *PDM* xiv. 493.

to making the king of the spirits more comfortable before cross examining him, by either bringing him a throne to sit on, or laying a feast for him to eat, in both cases this is done in the spirit vision rather than physically.[1] An example:

> If he [the god] says, "I [will] prophesy," say: "Let the throne of god enter, THRONOUZATERA KYMA KYMA LYAGEU APSITADRYS GĒ MOLIANDRON BONBLILON PEUCHRĒ, let the throne be brought in." If it then is carried by 4 men, [say to the boy] as, "With what are they crowned, and what goes before the throne?" If he says, "They are crowned with olive branches, and a censer precedes," [then the] boy speaks the truth.[2]

One extension of the use of an olive oil lamp in Evocationary Lamp Skrying, is the "Maskelli" formula. Elsewhere Maskellei Maskellō is referred to as "the all-powerful queen.[3] After consecrating three reeds to the four quarters, a clean lamp is placed facing east, and the same invocations are both said seven times and written on a cloth strip. Frankincense is offered and the three reeds are bound together with date palm fibre into a tripod which holds the lamp. The use of a tripod in divination is typically Greek, something which is further underlined by the magician being crowned with olive branches rather than laurel. The desired outcome is that the answers are shown to the magician in his sleep:

> I conjure you by the sleep releaser [of dreams] because I want you to enter into me and to show me concerning the NN matter…[4]

This request also relates to Visions and Dream Revelation ('V'). Strangely, one of the experiments of Evocationary Lamp Skrying contains a passage which was later to become a classic recipe for the production of a homunculus.

> You bring some flowers of the Greek bean plant.[5] You find them in the place of the garland seller (also called the lupine seller).[6] You should bring them while they are fresh; you should put them in a glass bowl; you should seal its mouth with clay very well for twenty days in a hidden, dark place. After twenty days, if you bring it up and open it, you find some testicles in it together with a phallus. If you leave it for forty days and [then] bring it up and open it, you find that it

---

1 This procedure of making the spirit comfortable, especially with food, is carried through from the *PGM* to both the *Hygromanteia* and later Latin and vernacular grimoires.

2 *PGM* V. 31-40.

3 *SM* 54. The Maskellei Maskellō formula is a specific invocation rather than a *nomina magica*, a fact that is revealed by the $^{\lambda}{}_{o}$ that is often written immediately after it. The 'λο' is an abbreviation for λογος, *logos,* or invocation.

4 *PGM* IV. 3190-3209.

5 Literally "eye of raven" plant. Beans have a long history of being considered magical, beginning before the Pythagorean prohibition against eating them.

6 Such 'shopping hints' confirm that these texts are written by working magicians who went to some lengths to secure their ingredients.

> has already become bloody. In a place which is hidden at all times, you put it in a glass object, and you put the glass object into a pottery object.[1]

One interesting *PGM* procedure (one of the few directly attributed to Solomon) explains how the magician should throw the skryer into a trance before he begins skrying, a trance so deep that the skryer will actually fall down as if in a faint.[2] This rite which is described by Betz as a "charm of Solomon that produces a trance," is also a good example of the lax use of words like "charm." The Greek is Σολομῶντος κατάπτωσις, *Solomōntos kataptōsis,* which Preisendanz translates more accurately as 'Solomon's fall.'[3] In fact, the extended meaning is "Solomon's invocation which causes the skryer to fall down in a trance." This interpretation is confirmed by a passage further on in the same rite:

> Then say the formula 7 times just into the ear of the NN man or little boy [skryer], and right away he will fall down [in a trance].[4]

The passage states, with a touch of pride, that it "works both on boys and on adults." The magician planning to use this procedure is specifically made to swear not to disclose it to anyone else.

Evocationary Lamp Skrying 'E' has a lot of cross references, because it is a technique which is often used as a jumping off point for other techniques, especially for Visions and Dream Revelation .

---

[1] This is repeated almost word-for-word in several other papyri. This example comes from *PDM* xiv. 141-145.

[2] *PGM* IV. 850-929.

[3] *Salomon's Niederfallen*. Interestingly, this is one of the few mentions of Solomon in the *PGM.*

[4] *PGM* IV. 910-911.

Gods, Angels, Daimones, names of magicians, *nomina magica*	Non-Roman PGM Nos.	Category	No. of lines	Betz Papyrus *PGM/PDM* Reference number	Objective/ Technique	Greek Headwords
Apollo, Zeus, IAŌ, Michael, Gabriel, Abrasax, Adōnai, Aiōn, Pakerbēth, Adōnaios, Thōthō, Elōaios, Moirai, Hades	1	E	86	*PGM* I. 262-347	Apollonian invocation in an Evocationary Lamp Skrying, with a touch of necromancy.	Ἀπολλωνιακὴ ἐπίκλησις.[1] λυχνον - lines 283, 289
Solomon, Hermes Trismegistos	4	E	80	*PGM* IV. 850-929	"Solomon's Seizure." Solomon's invocation that makes the boy skryer fall into a trance.[2] With dismissal.	Σολομῶνος κατάπτωσις, καὶ ἐπὶ παίδων καὶ τελείων ποιοῦσα[3]
				PGM IV. 930-1114	*See F*	
				PGM IV. 3172-3208	*See V*	
Zeus, Helios, Mitra [Mithras], Sarapis, Iaō, Meliouchos, Bainchōōōch	5	E	53	*PGM* V. 1-53	Evocationary Lamp Skrying, but called an 'oracle' of Sarapis. With dismissal.	μαντεῖον Σαραπιακὸν [ἐπὶ] παιδός, ἐπὶ λύχνου[4]
				PGM V. 370-446	*See S*	
				PGM VII. 222-249 *PGM* VII. 250-254 *PGM* VII. 255-259 *PGM* VII. 359-369 *PGM* VII. 407-410	*See V* [5]	

1 Apollonian invocation.

2 Although this is not an Evocationary Lamp Skrying *per se*, but it is related to the preparation of the skryer for this procedure, and it occurs between two other lamp skrying rites. It is incorrectly identified by Dieleman (2005), pp. 262, 271, 274 as an 'exorcism.'

3 Solomon's [trance] seizure of a boy skryer made perfect.

4 Skrying of Sarapis [via] a boy and lamp.

5 This block of procedures for obtaining a dream revelation or vision utilise the lamp.

Gods, Angels, Daimones, names of magicians, *nomina magica*	Non-Roman PGM Nos.	Category	No. of lines	Betz Papyrus *PGM/PDM* Reference number	Objective/ Technique	Greek Headwords
Chaos, Erebos	7	E	11	*PGM* VII. 348-358	Evocationary Lamp Skrying by means of a boy. [Hermonthis archive]	Μαντεῖον ἐπὶ παίδός[1] - line 348
Anoubis, Hermes Trismegistus, Bainchōōōch	7	E	39	*PGM* VII. 540-578	Evocationary Lamp Skrying using a boy skryer. [Hermonthis archive]	λυχνομαντεῖον[2] - line 540
				PDM xiv. 117-149	*See G*	
Anubis, the Drowned One, Osiris, Re-Kepre-Atum, Amoun, Isis, Nephthys, Pre, Sakhmet, Hike [i.e. Heka], Horus, Aniel, Sisihyt, Eresgshingal, Lion-Ram	14	E G	82	*PDM* xiv. 150-231	Evocationary Lamp Skrying, which can also be used to compel a god's arrival	*wᶜ šn* An inquiry of the lamp *pḥ-nṯr* – lines 170, 176
Boel, Tat	14	E	17	*PDM* xiv. 459-475	Evocationary Lamp Skrying by Boel	[Demotic] *wᶜ*
	14	E	14	*PDM* xiv. 475-488	Evocationary Lamp Skrying - another	[Demotic] [n/h]
Boel, Tat, Aniel, Zeus	14	E	27	*PDM* xiv. 489-515	Evocationary Lamp Skrying by Boel - another	[Demotic] Another [lamp skrying] *šn-hne* – line 509
Boel, Tat, Aniel, Sabaōth	14	E	12	*PDM* xiv. 516-527	Evocationary Lamp Skrying - another	[Demotic] Another [lamp skrying]
Harpokrates, Isis	14	E	22	*PDM* xiv. 750-771	Evocationary Lamp Skrying	[Demotic] *šn* Lamp skrying
				PDM xiv. 805-840	*See Ω*	
	14	E	14	*PDM* xiv. 1141-1154	Evocationary Lamp Skrying	[Demotic] [n/h]

1 Skrying using a boy.

2 *Lychnomanteion,* skrying by lamp.

Gods, Angels, Daimones, names of magicians, *nomina magica*	Non-Roman *PGM Nos.*	Category	No. of lines	Betz Papyrus *PGM/PDM* Reference number	Objective/ Technique	Greek Headwords
	14	E	7	*PDM* xiv. 1199-1205	Evocationary Lamp Skrying	[Demotic] [n/h]
				PGM XXIIb. 27-31 *PGM* XXIIb. 32-35 *PDM* lxi. 63-78 *PGM* CII. 1-17 *SM* 90	*See V* [1]	
				PDM Supp. 28-40	*See V2*	
Isis, Nephthys, Re, Amun, Osiris, Anubis	-	E	12	*PDM* Supp. 138-149	Evocationary Lamp Skrying using a copper vessel	[Demotic] [n/h]
Osiris, Michaēl	-	E	7	*SM* 93	Evocationary Lamp Skrying	λ[ύ]χνε[2] λύχνε –line 2
Total E		**15**	**483**			

Table E: Evocationary Lamp Skrying.

[1] This block of procedures for obtaining a dream revelation or vision utilise the lamp.

[2] Lamp.

Visions and Dreams (V and V2)

Invocations to secure relevant or prophetic dreams of a god are a common practice in the *PGM*. Apart from ὀνειραιτητόν,[1] *oneiraitēton*, the main Greek words used to describe this procedure include: ὀνειρετησία,[2] *oneiretēsia*; ὀνειροθαυπτάνη,[3] *oneirothauptanē*; ὀνειρομαντεῖον,[4] *oneiromanteion*; ὄνειρον,[5] *oneiron*; ὀνειροπομπὸς,[6] *oneiropompos* and ὀνείρου αἴτησις,[7] *oneirou aitēsis*.

These procedures often involve other subsidiary techniques, like invocation or the methods of Evocationary Lamp Skrying ('E'). There is considerable overlap between the previous chapter Evocationary Lamp Skrying ('E') and Visions and Dream Revelation ('V'). These procedures are often translated as 'oracles' by Betz and his editors, but as they have little relationship to the classical oracles of the ancient world, such as Delphi, I have preferred the term 'revelation,' as the aim of these procedures is to reveal things to the magician in a dream.

Oneiropompos or 'dream sending' was an art also practised by Graeco-Egyptian magicians to insert ideas into the minds of a target sleeper ('V2'). Often the dream would be structured round the appearance to the target sleeper of an image of their favourite god/goddess giving them advice, which would be easily accepted. However this would in fact be derived from the instructions of the magician, or his client. The early Christians were well aware of the practice, which was common enough for St. Peter to comment on it. As Faraone explains:

> A general, detailed discussion on the value of visions and dreams takes place in Pseudo-Clement (*Hom.* 17.13f.) between Peter and Simon Magus. Here the dream as a source of truth and spiritual enlightenment is emphatically denied by Peter: an evil daemon had in this [situation] the best opportunity to pass himself off as a being sent by God. Previously Peter had expounded to his listeners that it was precisely in dreams that the daemons assumed the likeness of gods, in order to receive the adoration and offerings accruing to those same gods (9.15)...On the other hand Christians were convinced that God could reveal his will and his counsel to men in dreams.[8]

Dream sending remained a popular technique from Graeco-Egyptian right up

---

[1] Revelation obtained in a dream.
[2] Request for a dream.
[3] Dream producing [rite].
[4] Rite for a divine revelation.
[5] Dream.
[6] The sending of dreams.
[7] Request for a dream.
[8] Faraone (1997), p. 182. For Christians this was an extension of the same problem as that encountered in trying to distinguish between a miracle and an act of magic.

to the 16th century, and beyond. Not only did the technique remain popular but the exact same procedure, calling upon the same Egyptian god survived over the same time period. This Egyptian request for a dream revelation utilises a drawing of the Dynastic Egyptian god Bes made with a specially prepared ink:

> ***Request for a dream oracle [revelation] from Besas*:** Take red ochre [and the blood] of a white dove, likewise of a crow, also sap of the mulberry, juice of single-stemmed wormwood, cinnabar, and rainwater; blend all together, put aside and write with it and with black writing ink, and recite the formula to the lamp at evening.[1] Take a black [cloth] of Isis and put it around your hand. When you are almost awake the god will come and speak to you, and he will not go away unless you wipe off your hand with spikenard or something of roses and smear the picture with the black [cloth] of Isis. But the strip of cloth put around your neck,[2] so that he will not smite you.
>
> "I conjure you, daimon, by your two [dual] names ANOUTH ANOUTH.[3] You are the headless god, the one who has a head and his face on his feet, dim-sighted Besas. We are not ignorant. You are the one whose mouth [continually] burns. I conjure [you by] your two names ANOUTH ANOUTH M... ORA PHĒSARA Ē... Come, lord, reveal to me concerning the NN matter, without deceit, without treachery, immediately, immediately; quickly, quickly..."[4]

More than 1300 years later, almost exactly the same *PGM* rite appears in a 16th century manuscript in the British Library:

> Make a drawing of Besa (Bes) on your left hand, and envelop your hand in a strip of black cloth that has been consecrated to Isis, and lie down to sleep without speaking a word, even to answer a question. Wind the remainder of the cloth round your neck.
>
> The ink with which you write must be composed of the blood of a cow, the blood of a white dove (fresh), frankincense, myrrh, black ink, cinnabar, mulberry juice, rain water, and the juices of wormwood and vetch.[5] With this write your petition before the setting sun (saying), "Send the truthful seer out of the holy shrine, I beseech thee, Lampsuer, Sumarta, Baribas, Dardalam, Iorlex. O Lord send the sacred deity Anuth Anuth, Salbana, Chambré, Breïth, now, now, quickly, quickly. Come in this very night."[6]

This extraordinary survival is more than just evidence of the retention of a

---

[1] This procedure appears to also incorporate a lamp skrying.

[2] The cloth is used as a phylactery.

[3] Although Anouth appears here to be a name for the Headless God, the usual scholarly interpretation equates it with Osiris.

[4] *PGM* VII. 222-249.

[5] The blood of a cow, and of a white dove, frankincense, myrrh, cinnabar and sun vetch all appear as incenses in *PGM*.

[6] 16th century BL Sloane manuscript quoted by Thompson (1973), p. 57.

method. It is almost a word-for-word copy, allowing for a little bit of variation between the two different translations from the Greek. In fact, the 16th century translation is, in some places, more detailed than the modern translation of the Graeco-Egyptian text.[1] For example, the modern translation by Grese says "Take a black of Isis" whilst the 16th century translation supplies the missing noun: "a strip of black cloth that has been consecrated to Isis." The *PGM* versions mentions "smear the picture" but does not say what picture that is. The 16th century text supplies that deficiency with "Make a drawing of Besa on your left hand," a crucial detail left out of the *PGM* text.

A chunk of the invocation is missing from the 16th century text, but on the other hand key *nomina magica* are missing from the *PGM,* but supplied by the 16th century text. It can only be conjectured that both versions come from an older more complete text. One wonders how many other *PGM* formulae were available in 16th century Europe, long before the present magical papyri were recovered by Anastasi in Thebes in the 19th century, or translated by modern scholars from 1853 onwards.

One of the most interesting rites designed to produce visions involved the Headless or Akephalos god.[2] In case anyone thought that this was a metaphorical description, the papyrus includes a drawing of the god with various vowel combinations written on his torso, arms and legs, and Sabaōth written along his neckline (see Figure 40).[3]

The invocation of a god to appear in a dream and the sending of dreams to third parties make up 6.5% of the *PGM* by rite, and 5.7% by lineage.

---

[1] Hutton raises the question as to whether this was composed by a 16th century magician or if it was a survival of a specific text (Hutton (2003), p. 186). The first quotation above answers this query and confirms that indeed it was a survival from a specific papyrus.

[2] *PGM* 64-184.

[3] The Headless god survives till at least the 15th century when Georg Midiates (who produced a copy of the *Hygromanteia*) prescribed an amulet against fever on which he recommends that you "inscribe on it an erect headless spirit with its hands and feet bound behind." The binding of hands and feet is also closely connected with the methods of ancient Egyptian magic. See Gager (1992), p. 28.

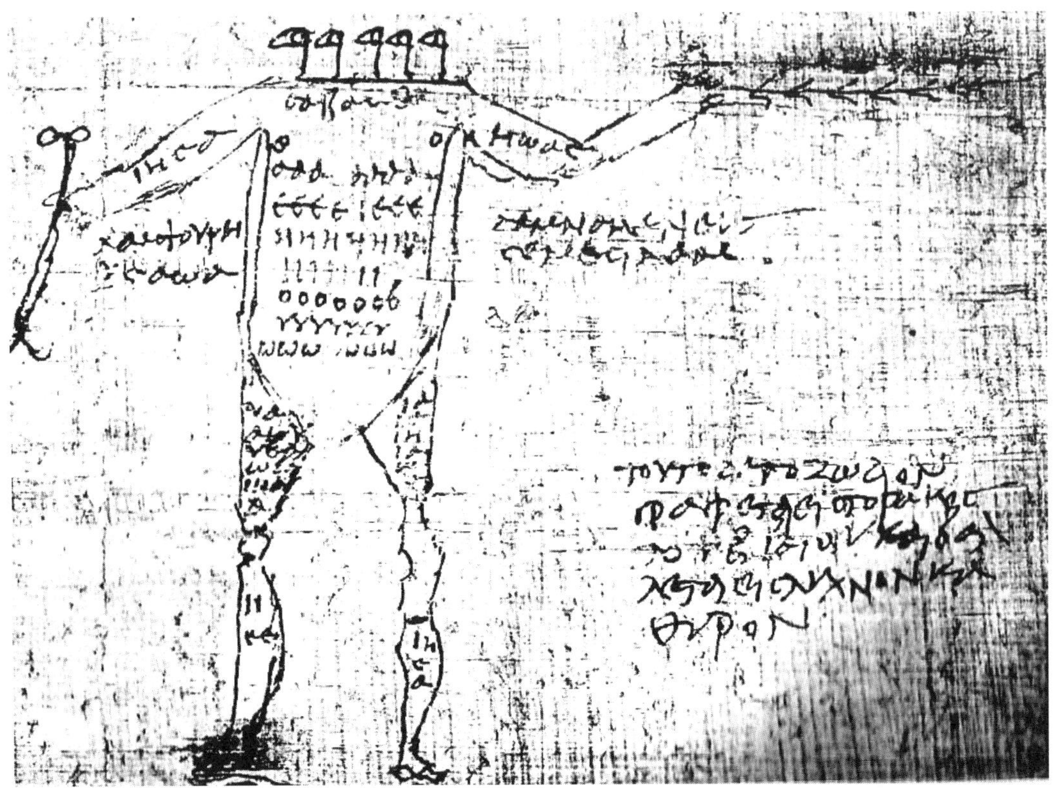

Figure 40: The Headless god.[1]

[1] *PGM* II. 170-175.

Visions and Dream Revelation - ὀνειραιτητόν (*oneiraitēton*) (V)

Gods, Angels, Daimones, names of magicians, *nomina magica*	**Non-Roman *PGM* Nos.**	**Category**	**No. of lines**	**Betz Papyrus *PGM/PDM* Reference number**	**Objective/ Technique**	**Greek Headwords**
Phoibos, Leto, Apollo Paian, Zeus, Erishkigal,	2	V	64	*PGM* II. 1-64	Dream revelation via the daimon the Headless One, using compulsive formulae.[1]	[n/h] εὐχῆς[2] - lines 9, 13
Apollo Paian, Titan, Zeus, Muses, Phoibos, Moirai (Klotho, Atropos, Lachis), Sesengen bar Pharangēs, Iō Erbēth, Sabaōth, Adōnai, Kommes, Apollo of Klaros, Abraxas, Michaēl, Damnameneus	2	V	121	*PGM* II. 64-184	Dream revelation compulsive formulae, with consecration of the doorposts, and the figure of the Headless One, with Dismissal formula.[3]	ἄλλως ποίησις[4]
				PGM IV. 2006-2125	*See Ω*	
				PGM IV. 2441-2621	*See Ω*	
Maskelli, Thrōbeia	4	V E	37	*PGM* IV. 3172-3208	Dream producing rite using three reeds and lamp. The Maskelli formula.	ὀνειροθαυπτάνη[5]
				PGM V. 447-458	*See R*	
				PGM V. 459-489	*See G2*	
Besas, the Headless god [Akephalos], Necessity, Arbathiaō, Anouth	7	V E	28	*PGM* VII. 222-249	Request for a dream or revelation from Besas.[6]	ὀνειραιτητὸν Βησᾶς[7]
	7	V E	5	*PGM* VII. 250-254	Divination by a dream spoken to the lamp. Not an 'oracle.'	ὀνειραιτητόν

[1] This rite is divided into eight sections, respectively beginning at lines: 1 – Invocation (incomplete); 16 – Recipe; 21 – Preparation; 34 – twelve names; 35 - ink; 40 – memory formula; 44 – compulsive formula; 51 – alternative formulae.

[2] Prayer, as a constituent of the rite.

[3] See Figure 40.

[4] Alternative method/procedure.

[5] Dream producing [rite].

[6] This also uses Evocationary Lamp Skrying.

[7] Dream revelation of Besas.

Gods, Angels, Daimones, names of magicians, *nomina magica*	Non-Roman PGM Nos.	Category	No. of lines	Betz Papyrus *PGM/PDM* Reference number	Objective/ Technique	Greek Headwords
Osiris, Michael, Osirchentecha,	7	V E	5	*PGM* VII. 255-259	Dream using an Evocationary Lamp Skrying to see if usable.	ἄλλο [ὀνειραιτητόν][1]
	7	V	13	*PGM* VII. 335-347	For direct vision. [Hermonthis archive]	αὐτοπτκή - line 335
	7	V E	11	*PGM* VII. 359-369	Evocationary Lamp Skrying for a dream revelation.	ὀνειραιτητόν
	7	V E	4	*PGM* VII. 407-410	To appear in someone else's dream using a lamp.	[n/h] ὀνείροις[2] - line 407
Eros, Bear asterism	7	V G3	13	*PGM* VII. 478-490	A request to Eros for a personal angel[3] to provide information in a dream.[4] Phylactery on tin.	[n/h]
Besas, Hermes, Selene, the Moirai	7	V	22	*PGM* VII. 664-685	Request for a dream revelation from Besas.[5]	ὀνειραιτητόν
Phrē	7	V	24	*PGM* VII. 703-726	Request for a dream revelation (not an oracle)	ὀνειραιτητόν
Iaō, Adōnai	7	V	16	*PGM* VII. 740-755	Request for a dream revelation (not an oracle)	[ὀνειραιτητόν]
Pythagoras, Demokritos, Zizaubiō	7	V	51	*PGM* VII. 795-845	Pythagoras' request for a dream revelation and Demokritos' dream divination.[6]	ὀνειραιτητὸν
				PGM VII. 862-918	*See Ω*	
Sabaōth, Michael, Raphael, Gabriel, Iaō	7	V	8	*PGM* VII. 1009-1016	Dream revelation	ὀνε[ιρομαντ]-εῖ[ον]
Besas, Isis, Helios, Anouth, Headless god, Necessity, Sabaōth, Adōnai, Osiris	8	V S	46	*PGM* VIII. 64-110	Dream revelation from Besas.[7] [Hermonthis archive]	ὀνειραιτητόν στοιχεῖα - line 78[8]

1 Another [dream revelation].

2 Dream.

3 Not a *paredros*, as is sometimes maintained.

4 Uses the Egyptian version of the four angels of the four directions. Prescribes a phylactery at line 487. Includes an offering to the goddess of the Bear asterism.

5 See *PGM* V. 400-420 for an identical invocatory poem.

6 Using the secret names of the zodiac and the angel Zizaubiō from the Pleiades.

7 With a clear drawing of a crowned man with plant stem wand and sword See Figure 18.

8 Magical statue.

Gods, Angels, Daimones, names of magicians, *nomina magica*	Non-Roman PGM Nos.	Category	No. of lines	Betz Papyrus *PGM/PDM* Reference number	Objective/ Technique	Greek Headwords
Hermes, [Thoth], Osiris, Isis	12	V	9	*PGM* XII. 144-152	Dream revelation	ὀνείρου αἴτησις[1]
Iaō, Ra, Ablanathanalba	12	V	8	*PGM* XII. 153-160	Divine revelation from the serpent-faced god	θεομαντεῖον[2]
Iēsous	12	V G3	3	*PGM* XII. 190-192	Dream revelation request with invocation to the Bear asterism	ὀνειραιτητὸν λεγόμενον πρὸς Ἀρ[κτον][3]
				PDM xiv. 93-114 [*PGM* XIVa. 1-11]	*See G*	
	14	V G3	12	*PDM* xiv. 1078-1089	Revelation in a dream. Request to the Bear goddess.	[Demotic] [n/h]
Osiris, Michael	22	V E	5	*PGM* XXIIb. 27-31	Request for a dream revelation, using a lamp.	ὀνειραιτητὸν
	22	V E	4	*PGM* XXIIb. 32-35	Request for a dream revelation, using a lamp.	ἄλλο ὀνειραιτητόν
Har-Thoth, Re, Atum, Tatenen,	61	V E	16	*PDM* lxi. 63-78	Evocationary Lamp Skrying for a dream revelation.	[Demotic] [n/h]
Iou	77	V	24	*PGM* LXXVII. 1-24	Dream revelation. 2nd century.	[n/h]
Necessity, Bēsas, Headless One, Anouth, Osiris, Iaeō, Sabaōth, Adōnai	10 2	V E	17	*PGM* CII. 1-17 *SM* 90	Dream revelation, using a lamp, involving the Headless god.	[n/h]
Neith, Neieth	-	V	7	*SM* 79 c	For a true dream revelation	ὄνειρον[4]
	-	V	4	*SM* 85	Request for a dream	ὀνειρετησία
Total V		**26**	**577**			

Table V: Visions and Dream Revelation.

[1] Request for a dream.
[2] Rite for a divine revelation.
[3] Request for a dream revelation spoken to the goddess of the Bear asterism.
[4] Dream.

Sending Dreams - ὀνειροπομπὸς (*oneiropompos*) (V2)

Gods, Angels, Daimones, names of magicians, *nomina magica*	**Non-Roman *PGM* Nos.**	**Category**	**No. of lines**	**Betz Papyrus *PGM/PDM* Reference number**	**Objective/ Technique**	**Greek Headwords**
				PGM III. 1-164	*See Ω*	
Agathokles, Thōth, Iaou, Ablanathanalba, Akrammachamari, Thēouris, Amēn, Aōth, Apollobex[1]	12	V2	15	*PGM* XII. 107-121	Talisman of Agathokles[2] for sending dreams, using a deified cat	ὀνειροπο[μπὸ]ς Ἀγαθοκλεύς[3]
Zminis of Tentyra, Ostanes, Sēith	12	V2	23	*PGM* XII. 121-143	Zminis of Tentyra's[4] rite for sending dreams to other people	ὀνειροπομπὸς[5] Ζμίνιος Τεντυρίτου[6]
	14	V2 L2	8	*PDM* xiv. 1070-1077	To send dreams to make a woman love you	[Demotic] [n/h]
	-	V2	6	*PDM* Supp. 1-6	Sending a dream	[Demotic]
	-	V2	12	*PDM* Supp. 7-18	Sending a dream	[Demotic]
	-	V2	24	*PDM* Supp. 19-27	Sending a dream	[Demotic]
	-	V2 E	13	*PDM* Supp. 28-40	Sending a dream, using a lamp, lizard and brick.	[Demotic]
Nun	-	V2	21	*PDM* Supp. 40-60	Sending a dream, using a mummy spirit from Abydos	[Demotic]
Osiris, Alkhah, Khephri, Amoun, Pre, Shu, Horus, Seth, Apophis	-	V2	42	*PDM* Supp. 60-101	Sending a dream, using a mummy spirit	[Demotic]

[1] Apollobex was a relatively famous magician. The Egyptian version of his name was probably 'Horus-the-falcon' as Horus was often equated with Apollo.

[2] Agathokles' name may be derived from ἀγαθός 'good' as in the Agathos Daimon.

[3] Dream revelation of Agathokles.

[4] Zminis of Dendera on the Nile (a devotee of the god Min). This and the previous rite are obviously 'signature rites.'

[5] The sending of dreams.

[6] Dream revelation of Zminis of Tentyra. Tentyra = Dendera, 60 kilometres north of Thebes, so Zminis lived relatively close to where this papyrus was found. His name indicates that he was a devotee of the god Min.

Gods, Angels, Daimones, names of magicians, *nomina magica*	Non-Roman PGM Nos.	Category	No. of lines	Betz Papyrus *PGM/PDM* Reference number	Objective/ Technique	Greek Headwords
Anubis, Osiris, Isis	-	V2	16	*PDM* Supp. 101-116	Sending a 'breathing spirit' disguised as a god to influence someone's dream	[Demotic]
Osiris, Anubis	-	V2	29	*PDM* Supp. 117-130	Sending a spirit to influence the content of a dream	[Demotic]
Total V2		**11**	**209**			

Table V2: Sending Dreams.

6.5 Dealing with Divinity

Face-to-Face Encounter with a God – αὔτοπτος (*autoptos*) (F)

The gods of ancient Egypt, especially Anubis, Isis, Osiris, Harpocrates and Thoth frequently feature in the rites of both *PDM* and the *PGM*. Interaction with the god or goddess was considered by the magician as one of the most valuable outcomes of his craft. The god may simply answer some pressing questions, or it may be constrained to remain a permanent helpmate or sponsor.[1] The arrival of the god or goddess may be achieved in several different manners. These experiments, in order of increasing intimacy, are categorised as Visions and Dream Revelation ὀνειραιτητόν (*oneiraitēton*) ('V'); direct vision of the god αὔτοπτος (*autoptos*) ('F'); and the close association or conversation with the god συστάσις (*systasis*) ('G').

The most common occurrence was the first category or the god's intervention in the practitioner's dreams. Such dreams were reputedly very lucid and not at all like ordinary dreams (which was the touchstone of their nature). In addition, the divinity might appear in the context of a skrying operation and be seen in a bowl of water or oil, or in the reflected flame of a lamp. These techniques are categorised as 'B' or 'E.'

The direct vision of a god is αὔτοπτος (*autoptos*), a rite designed to enable the magician to *see* the gods face-to-face with his own eyes, but not to communicate with him. 'Αὔτοπτος' only occurs as a word in *PGM,* and as far as I can tell occurs nowhere else in Greek literature. It literally means the god is 'self-revealed,' resulting in an encounter with the god face to face. See also rite type 'G,' which involves more complex interaction and conversation with the god as well as just seeing it face-to-face. Type 'F' makes up 0.9% of the *PGM* by rite, but 1.7% by lineage.

[1] Rather like the classical Greek gods or goddesses who often assisted a chosen mortal.

Gods, Angels, Daimones, names of magicians, *nomina magica*	Non-Roman PGM Nos.	Category	No. of lines	Betz Papyrus *PGM/PDM* Reference number	Objective/ Technique	Greek Headwords
Lailam, Iaō, Sabaōth, Bainchōōōch, Albalal, Sesengen bar Pharaggēs, Ablanathanalba, Akrammachamari, Hōros, Harpokratēs, Abraiaōth, Balsamēs, Barbariēl	4	F G E	185	*PGM* IV. 930-1114	Evocationary Lamp Skrying, for a direct vision of a god, with an encounter of the god face-to-face.	αὔτοπτος – line 930 σύστασεις[1] - line 930 αὐτόπτου λυχνομαντίας - line 950, 951
Ablamathanalba (*sic*), Tabaōth, Akrammachamarei	5	F	16	*PGM* V. 54-69	Direct vision for a god to prophesy	αὔτοπτος λόγος[2] - line 53
Helios	5	F	3	*PGM* Va. 1-3	Direct vision of a god.	...αὐτοπτήσεις[3] - line 1
Osiris, Anubis, Belphenō	7	F B	16	*PGM* VII. 319-334	Using a copper vessel to invoke Anubis face-to-face. [Hermonthis archive]	αὔτοπτος[4] - line 319
Apollo, Helios	7	F G	13	*PGM* VII. 727-739	Invocation for a direct vision of Apollo face-to-face. [Hermonthis archive]	Ἀπόλλωνος αὔτοπτος[5] - line 727
Total F		**5**	**232**			

Table F: Face-to-Face Encounter with a God.

1 *Autoptos. Systasis.* Both 'F' and 'G.'
2 Direct vision invocation
3 Direct vision.
4 Direct vision [of Anubis].
5 Direct vision of Apollo.

The God's Arrival - συστάσις (*systasis*), *pḥ-nṯr* (G)

The invocation of the gods and goddesses has formed an integral part of magic from ancient times up to the late 19th century revival of magic by the Hermetic Order of the Golden Dawn. The arrival of the god was referred to in the *PGM* as συστάσις (*systasis*). '*Systasis*' literally means 'introduction or bringing together,' and indicates a conversational familiarity greater than the god simply revealing himself to the magician in a vision. The 'god's arrival' is called *pḥ-nṯr* (*peh-netjer*) in Demotic.[1]

Systasis is defined as communication between man and god in some Greek lexicons, but it has a more dramatic meaning which is better captured by "a god's arrival." However, the most impressive epiphany of the god or goddess was their physical appearance in front of the magician ('G'), during which the magician may be able to ask questions and receive answers. Under these circumstances the usual injunction to the magician (just as in Biblical accounts of Yahweh appearing to Moses, or to the other Hebrew prophets) was not to look directly at the face of the divinity, but to "look at their feet."[2] Likewise, both gods and spirits were constrained to tell the plain truth and to appear in a human-like form in many of the conjurations:[3]

> I, N, son of N, present my supplication before you, that you appear to me [without] causing fear, and you be revealed to me without causing terror, and you conceal nothing from me and tell me truthfully all that I desire.[4]

Apparently even the gods could be tricky and not always reliable. A typical Apollonian invocation from the *PGM* also makes a similar request.

> I adjure these holy and divine names that
> They send me the divine spirit and that it
> Fulfil what I have in my heart and soul...
> Send me this daimon at my sacred chants...
> And send him gentle, gracious, pondering
> No thoughts opposed to me. And may you not
> Be angry at my sacred chants. But guard
> That my whole body come to [the] light intact.[5]

---

[1] Ritner (2008), p. 214-220.

[2] Yahweh reputedly showed Moses his hind-quarters, to protect that worthy from the probably fatal outcome of a direct glance. In the Greek context, Medusa also provided similarly disastrous outcomes for those that looked her straight in the face.

[3] These requirements are repeated in many of the later grimoires.

[4] *Sepher ha-Razim,* 4: 63-65.

[5] *PGM* I. 312-323.

One divine encounter, recounted in the form of a letter from Νεφώτης, Nephōtēs (Nepher-hotep) to Psammetichos, King of Egypt, is designed to question Helios.[1] As both the actors in this are Egyptian, it is a fairly safe assumption that the original Sun god so conjured would have been Phre/Ra, or less likely Horus. This rite explains that, although the god may not be visible, there will (always) be a sign of his presence:

> After you have said this three times, there will be this sign of divine encounter, but you, armed by having this magical soul,[2] be not alarmed. For a sea falcon flies down and strikes you on the body with its wings, signifying this: that [the god has arrived, and so] you should arise.[3]

One of the most detailed accounts of a god's arrival is recounted by Thessalos of Tralles, a doctor (in a letter to the Emperor Claudius):

> Now, he [the priest][4] had prepared a pure room (*oikos*) and the other things that were necessary for the visitation… (22) The high-priest asked me whether I would want to converse with the soul of some dead person or with a god. I said, 'Asklepios.'
>
> …Now when he had shut me in the room and commanded me to sit opposite the throne upon which the god was about to sit, he led me through the [pronunciation of the] god's secret names and he shut the door as he left. (24) Once I sat down, I was being released from body and soul by the incredible nature of the spectacle. For neither the facial features of Asklepios nor the beauty of the surrounding decoration can be expressed clearly in human speech. Then, reaching out his right hand, Asklepios began to say: (25)
>
> "Oh blessed Thessalos, attaining honour in the presence of the god. As time passes, when your successes become known, men will worship you as a god. Ask freely, then, about what you want and I will readily grant you everything." (26)
>
> I scarcely heard anything, for I had been struck with amazement and overwhelmed by seeing the form of the god. Nevertheless, I was inquiring why I had failed when trying the prescriptions of Nechepso. To this the god said: (27)
>
> "King Nechepso, a man of most sound mind and all honourable forms of excellence, did not obtain from an utterance of the gods what you are seeking to learn. Since he had a good natural ability, he [just] observed the sympathy of stones and plants with the stars, but he did not know the correct times and places one must pick the plants. (28) For the produce of every season grows and withers

---

[1] *PGM* IV. 154-220.

[2] I believe this is a mis-translation, and ψυχὴν should be translated as 'spirit,' in the sense of an assistant spirit. It makes more sense to be armed with an external assistant spirit rather than your own soul.

[3] *PGM* IV. 207-212.

[4] The priest incidentally was a Theban, which is particularly interesting as the techniques used in this account are preserved in the *PGM* which was found in a Theban tomb.

> under the influence of the stars. That divine spirit, which is most refined, pervades throughout all substance and most of all throughout those places where the influences of the stars are produced upon the cosmic foundation."[1]

Thessalos was neither a priest nor a magician, but due to persistence he was granted the privilege of meeting the god Asklepios face to face, courtesy of a priest who gave him the correct *nomina magica.* One of the prime requirements of ritual magic, in all periods, is to know the correct names, not only of the god being invoked and the names of his superiors (if applicable), but also of his secret names. This passage also affords us confirmation of the importance of right times in magic. G' deals specifically with the God's Arrival whilst 'G2' deals just with the invocation of a god.

Invocation of a God (G2)

One of the rites in the *PGM* affords us a contemporary view of the key god names across various cultures in Egypt used in the first few centuries CE. These are listed in Table 14.

According to	God name – original Greek	Translation/transliteration
Egyptians	Φνω εαι Ἰαβωκ	PHNŌ EAI IABŌK
Jews	Ἀδωναῖε Σαβαώθ	ADŌNAIE SABAŌTH, Lord of Hosts
Greeks	ὁ πάντων μόναρχος βασιλεύς	"the king of all, ruling alone"
[Egyptian] High priests	κρυπτέ, ἀόρατε, πάντας ἐφορῶν	"hidden, invisible, overseer of all"[2]
Parthians	Οὐερτω παντοδυνάστα	OUERTŌ (great one of the earth) master of all
[Gnostics][3]	Ἰάω Σαβαὼθ Ἀβρασάξ	IAŌ SABAŌTH ABRASAX[4]

Table 14: God names derived from the various contributory cultures as recorded in one particular *PGM* rite.[5]

---

[1] Codex Matritensis Bibliotheque Nationale MS 4631, published by Graux in 1878. English translation by Philip Harland.

[2] *Ogdoas*. See the *PGM* XIII. 741-747 for a justification of this interpretation.

[3] The Gnostic names inscribed on the back of the stone.

[4] This is followed by an illustration which appears in Preisendanz Vol. 2, p. 76, but not in the corresponding translation in Betz (1996), p. 163. The illustration is of poorly presented hieroglyphics, of which only '*ankh*' and '*neter*' are easily recognizable.

[5] *PGM* XII. 264-269.

Of these names, Iaō, Sabaōth, Adōnaie and to a lesser extent Abrasax, have endured through to the later European grimoires. These were not necessarily the gods of religion but the god names the magician used to enforce his control over lesser spirits. The same passage concludes:

> Yea, lord, for to you, the god in heaven, all things are subject, and none of the daimones or spirits will oppose me because I have called on your great name for the consecration.[1]

Another passage which neatly sums up the gods important to the magician comes from Homer but is embedded in the Graeco-Egyptian texts, as if it were a valued reference for the magician.[2] The list of gods in this passage is very much a mixture of each of the cultures that have contributed to the *PGM*. It opens with Anubis (Egyptian), and lists Gnostic gods (Abraxas, Ablantho), Greek gods (Circe, infernal Zeus, Hermes, Hades, Titan), gods of the firmament (the Bear asterism[3] and Sirius) and even the Jewish god (Iaweh or Yahweh).

In another passage,[4] apart from the usual gods/goddesses there are the Greek gods of personified qualities, like Famine, Jealousy, the Destinies, the Malignities and the Punishments. This rite has the longest roll-call of Greek mythology of any *PGM* rite: the Erinys, Orgogorgoniotrian; many chthonic forms of Persephone (Persephassa), Hermes, Hekate, Acheron, Amphiaros, Ariste, Tartaros, Charon, Chaos, Erebos, Styx, Lethe, Hades, Pluto, Aiakos and Zeus. There is also a long string of rather unusual *nomina magica*. Korē is one of the few classical Greek goddesses that persisted through to the European grimoires, usually appearing as a demon, right up to her appearance in the 15th century *Sacred Magic of Abramelin the Mage*.[5]

Invocation of the Goddess of the Bear asterism - (G3)

Type G3 rites involve invocation of the goddess of the Bear or Dipper asterism (Ursa Major), which was held to be a significant asterism by the ancient Egyptians because it is a set of stars that turn around the Pole star, and so never set below the horizon. This asterism was seen by the ancient Egyptians as the polar 'handle' which turns the vault of heaven (Nikaroplēx), and allows the stars to move across the sky. The Egyptians associated the soul of Typhon with the Bear asterism. Hence the mention of the 100-lettered name of Typhon.[6]

---

[1] *PGM* XII. 261-263.
[2] *PGM* XXIII. 26-50.
[3] This is the constellation of Ursa Major or the Plough. The Egyptians considered this asterism to be very important and female (*PGM* LXXII. 36).
[4] *PGM* IV. 1390-1595.
[5] Mathers (1900).
[6] *PGM* IV. 1380.

The Greeks often identified the Bear goddess with Callisto, the huntress who was transformed by Zeus into the constellation Ursa Major. She is sometimes seen as a manifestation of her fellow huntress Artemis.

The same asterism is held in awe by other cultures, for example the Taoist Chinese who use it as a time and season marker.

The God's Arrival - συστάσις (*systastis*), *pḥ-nṯr* (G)

Gods, Angels, Daimones, names of magicians, *nomina magica*	Non-Roman *PGM* Nos.	Category	No. of lines	Betz Papyrus *PGM/PDM* Reference number	Objective/ Technique	Greek Headwords
Helios, [King] Semea, Abrasax, Scarab [Khepera], Zeus, [Raphaēl], [Michaēl], Sese[ngen b]ar Pharaggēs, Sabaōth, Adōnai, Akrammach[ari], Apollo, Phoibos	3	G	76	*PGM* III. 187-262	Revelation by invocation of Helios and use of the tripod. With illustration of two snakes (?). Contains a hymn to Helios, and a dismissal formula (ἀπόλυσις).	[n/h] συστάσις - line 197
				PGM III. 424-466	*See K*	
Helios	3	G	118	*PGM* III. 494-611	Rite to establish a relationship with Helios.	σύστασις[1] εὐχῆς[2] - lines 498, 590
	3	G	21	*PGM* III. 612-632	Gaining control of one's shadow as part of a divine encounter	[n/h][3]
Sabaōth, Adōnai, Lotus-Lion-Ram, Horus, Re, Helios, Harpokrates, Abrasax, Ablanathanalba	3	G	99	*PGM* III. 633-731	A god's arrival	...σύστασ[ιν τὴ]ν τοῦ θεοῦ[4] - line 696 Λόγον αὔτοπτον – line 699
Helios, Typhon, Moirai, Pakerbēth. Nepher-hotep (priest), Psammetichos (King)	4	G B	97	*PGM* IV. 154-220, 261-285.[5]	Letter from Nephōtēs (the priest Nefer-hotep) to King Psammetichos about a divine encounter, plus a Vessel Inquiry.	αὔτοπτου – line 162 συστάσεως - line 210 σύστασις - line 260
				PGM IV. 930-1114	*See F*	

[1] *Systasis.* Divine encounter.

[2] Prayers.

[3] No headword, but linked to the previous σύστασις above. It looks like a continuation.

[4] Encounter with the god.

[5] Betz lists *PGM* IV. 154-285 as one procedure of bowl skrying/vessel inquiry, whereas lines 154-220 and 261-285 is a rite of Divine Encounter, with a bowl skrying/vessel inquiry (lines 221-260) inserted in the middle of it. See under 'B' for the latter section.

Gods, Angels, Daimones, names of magicians, *nomina magica*	Non-Roman *PGM* Nos.	Category	No. of lines	Betz Papyrus *PGM/PDM* Reference number	Objective/ Technique	Greek Headwords
Helios, Apollo, Phoebus, Paian, Leto, IAŌ, Sabaōth, Nomios, Seseggen bar Pharaggēs, Arbēthō, Selene	6	G	47	*PGM* VI. 1-47	Invocation for an encounter with Helios. 2nd/3rd century.	[σ]ύστάσις σύστασις - line 39
	7	G	24	*PGM* VII. 505-528	Meeting with your own Daimon. A form of initiation.	σύστασις ἰδίου δαίμονος.[1]
				PGM VII. 727-739	*See F*	
				PGM VIII. 1-63	*See L4*	
Barzan, Agathos Daimon, Phōx, Imhotep	14	G V	22	*PDM* xiv. 93-114 [*PGM* XIVa. 1-11]	A god's arrival to reveal answers in a dream.[2]	[Demotic] *pḥ-nṯr* - line 95
Agathodaimon, Moses, Peteri	14	G G3 E	33	*PDM* xiv. 117-149	Invocation of the Invocation of the Bear goddess, using Evocationary Lamp Skrying.	*pḥ-nṯr* - line 117, 145 *šn…n ẖbs* - line 140
				PDM xiv. 150-231	*See E*	*pḥ-nṯr* - line 169, 175
Pekhe. Paysakh priest of Cusae.[3]	14	G G3	7	*PDM* xiv. 232-238	God's arrival of the Bear goddess.[4]	*pḥ-nṯr* - line 232
	14	G	5	*PDM* xiv. 670-674	God's arrival. Introduction to the Great One of Five.[5]	[Demotic] [n/h]
				PDM xiv. 805-840	*See B*	*pḥ-nṯr* - line 828, 833, 836, 837

[1] Meeting with your own daimon. As a form of initiation, this could have been included under 'M.' If the daimon was considered to be a *paredros,* then this passage might have been included under 'P.' But neither of these categorisations seem appropriate, as the headword is very clearly σύστασις (*systasis*). Hence it is listed under 'G.'
[2] Identified by Dieleman (2005), p. 262 simply as a divination.
[3] Cusae was about 200 kilometres north of Thebes.
[4] This is a God's Arrival, not simply a divination as suggested by Dieleman (2005), p. 265.
[5] An introduction to a collection of rites.

Gods, Angels, Daimones, names of magicians, *nomina magica*	**Non-Roman *PGM* Nos.**	**Category**	**No. of lines**	**Betz Papyrus *PGM/PDM* Reference number**	**Objective/ Technique**	**Greek Headwords**
				PDM xiv. 841-850	*See B*	
Osiris, Osiris Wennefer, Nephthys, Horus	-	G	9	*PDM* Supp. 130-138	God's arrival of Osiris	[Demotic] *pḥ-nṯr* (?) - line 130
Thoth	-	G	14	*PDM* Supp. 149-162	God's arrival of Thoth	[Demotic] *pḥ-nṯr* - line 149, 155
Imhotep, Ptah, Osiris Wennefer, Thoth, Horus	-	G	17	*PDM* Supp. 168-184	God's arrival. Invocation of Imhotep, son of the god Ptah.	[Demotic] *pḥ-nṯr* - line 169, 183
Total G		**14**	**589**			

Table G: The God's Arrival.

Invocation of a God (G2)

Gods, Angels, Daimones, names of magicians, *nomina magica*	Non-Roman *PGM* Nos.	Category	No. of lines	Betz Papyrus *PGM/PDM* Reference number	Objective/ Technique	Greek Headwords
Helios	1	G2	28	*PGM* I. 195-222	Invocation (not prayer) of Helios.[1]	[n/h]
Zeus, Osiris, Athabot, Sabaōth, Althonai, Eou, Michael, Anubis, Thoth, Akshha Shha, Sabasha, Shlot	4	G2	25	*PGM* IV. 1- 25	Opening and dedication to the gods of the *Great Magical Papyrus of Paris*	[n/h]
	4	G2	34	*PGM* IV. 52-85	Summoning by threatening harm to a beetle, with phylactery.	[n/h]
Selene, Klotho, Kerberos, Mene, Brimo, Alkyone, Hermes the Elder, Mare, Korē, Helios, Tethys, Aiōn, Kronos, Helios-Osiris, Isis, Michael, Harken-techtha.[2]	4	G2	118	*PGM* IV. 2241-2358	Invocation to the waning Moon (Selene).[3]	δέλτος ἀποκρουστική πρὸς Σελήνην.[4]
				PGM IV. 2441-2621	*See Ω*	
Selene, Hecate, Pan, Aktiōphis	4	G2	86	*PGM* IV. 2622-2707	'Slander spell' against Selene, "which works for everything and every rite."	διαβολὴ πρὸς Σελήνην[5]

[1] Mentions, but does not list, angels (Δόξαι), the Decans and archangels.

[2] Also many other gods and goddesses mentioned by allusion, such as Isis' father, the Nile goddess, the goddesses of Dodona and Ida, or Hekate ("O dog in maiden form").

[3] The last line (2359) mentions, but does not provide, a phylactery for this procedure.

[4] 'Written tablet for the waning Moon [Selene]' or more likely 'Dismissal tablet for Selene.'

[5] Slander [spell] against Selene.

Gods, Angels, Daimones, names of magicians, *nomina magica*	Non-Roman PGM Nos.	Category	No. of lines	Betz Papyrus *PGM/PDM* Reference number	Objective/ Technique	Greek Headwords
Kronos, Helios, Zeus	4	G2	39	*PGM* IV. 3086-3124	Although called "Oracle of Kronos," or the "Little Mill," it is an invocation of the god Kronos	Μαντία Κρονικὴ[1]
Aiōn, Zeus, Adōnai, Iaō, Sabaōth, Iaōth Ablanathanalba, Lailam	5	G2 V	31	*PGM* V. 459-489	All-purpose invocation of Zeus to loosen shackles, grant invisibility, send dreams and gain favour	ἄλλως[2]
Isis, Agathos Daimon, Sothis, Boubastis, Amon (of Pelusium), Nemesis, Adrasteia, Horus	7	G2	15	*PGM* VII. 490-504	Invocation of Isis as goddess of the Moon.	[n/h][3]
Erbēth, [Helios]	7	G2	16	*PGM* VII. 846-861	Shadow on the sun, an evocation of the daimon of the 5th hour (i.e. just before midday).[4]	εἰς τὸν ἥλιον[5]
Horus, Imhotep[6] Nephthys, Osiris, Shu, Sokar, Ptah, Thoth	12	G2 H	29	*PDM* xii. 21-49	Request for a revelation of a prescription from various gods	[Demotic]
Korē, [Hekate]	12	G2	13	*PGM* XII. 1-13	Rite to produce an epiphany of Korē, and to kill someone.	πρᾶξις
Thoth, Hapy, Ra-Khepri-Atum, Sakhmet, Lotus-Lion-Ram	14	G2	26	*PDM* xiv. 309-334	Thoth invocation. Plus an anointing oil to win favour in public places	[Demotic] For causing favour
				PDM xiv. 805-840	*See Ω*	

[1] Kronos oracle [invocation].

[2] Another way. This does not appear to refer to the immediately preceeding passage, but may apply to *PGM* V. 370-446.

[3] Preisendanz (1931), p. 22 incorrectly inserts <φυλακτήριον> as a headword.

[4] Using a cat's tail, a phylactery and a protective chalk circle on the ground. This is important because it gives a clear indication of the use of the protective floor circle.

[5] Shadow on the sun.

[6] Iymhotep, the Egyptian Asklepios.

Gods, Angels, Daimones, names of magicians, *nomina magica*	Non-Roman *PGM* Nos.	Category	No. of lines	Betz Papyrus *PGM/PDM* Reference number	Objective/ Technique	Greek Headwords
Muses, Amoun, Io, Agathos Daimon	21	G2	29	*PGM* XXI. 1-29	Invocation to a lord whose name consists of 7 letters	[n/h]
Adonai, Osiris, Typhon, Kronos Ammon, Isis, the Bear, Pronoia, Chaithrai	57	G2	37	*PGM* LVII. 1-37	Meeting the goddess Isis with a compulsive passage	[n/h]
Hekate Ereshkigal, Brimō	70	G2	22	*PGM* LXX. 4-25	Invocation of Hekate Ereshkigal against a punishment daimon in the Underworld.[1]	πρὸς φόβον κολασιος[2]
Zeus-Iao-Zen-Helios, Isaac, Sabaōth, Abraham, Jacōb	105	G2	15	*PGM* CV. 1-15 *SM* 87	Invocation of Zeus-Iao-Zen-Helios	[n/h]
Erbēth, Pakerbēth, Abrasax, [Typhon-Seth]	116	G2	17	*PGM* CXVI. 1-17	The Pakerbēth formula. Probably an invocation of Seth-Typhon.	[n/h]
Total G2		**17**	**481**			

Table G2: Invocation of a God.

[1] Has *Ephesian Grammata* and magical gestures.
[2] Against fear of [post mortem] chastisement.

Invocation of the Goddess of the Bear asterism - Ἀρκτικὴ (*Arktikē*) (G3)

Gods, Angels, Daimones, names of magicians, *nomina magica*	**Non-Roman PGM Nos.**	**Category**	**No. of lines**	**Betz Papyrus *PGM/PDM* Reference number**	**Objective/ Technique**	**Greek Headwords**
Bear (Ursa Major), Helios, Phre [Ra]	4	G3	145	*PGM* IV. 1275-1322	Bear asterism invocation	Ἀρκτικὴ πάντα οιοῦσα.[1] - line 1275
	4	G3	8	*PGM* IV. 1323-1330	Bear asterism invocation	ἄλλη [Ἀρκτικὴ][2] - line 1323
(Autochthons)	4	G3	59	*PGM* IV. 1331-1389	Bear asterism invocation	Ἀρκτικὴ δύναμις πάντα ποιοῦσα.[3] - line 1331
				PGM VII. 478-490	*See V*	
Brimo	7	G3	17	*PGM* VII. 686-702	Bear asterism invocation. [Hermonthis archive]	Ἀρκτικὴ.[4] - line 686
				PGM VII. 862-918	*See Ω*	
				PGM XII. 190-192 *PDM* xiv. 1078-1089	*See V*	
				PDM xiv. 117-149 *PDM* xiv. 232-238	*See G*	
	72	G3	36	*PGM* LXXII. 1-36	Bear asterism invocation. Part of LVII [5]	Ἀρκτικὴ πρᾶξις[6] - line 1
Total G3		**5**	**265**			

Table G3: Invocation of the Bear goddess.

1 Bear [rite] which creates/works in all directions.
2 Another [Bear rite].
3 Powerful Bear [rite] which creates [spreads] in all directions.
4 Bear [rite].
5 According to Brashear (1995), p. 3495.
6 Bear rite.

Prayers - εὐχή (*euchē*) (W)

There is a considerable difference between an invocation, a prayer and a hymn. The simplistic but valid explanation (which harks back to one of the popular distinctions between religion and magic) is that prayers are supplications whilst invocations are expressed as commands. Specifically invocations are commands to appear, whereas prayers do not have that requirement.

Prayer, although not usually associated with magic, is in an important element when dealing with the gods, as distinct from daimones or spirits. In the course of making an argument against the Frazerian view of magic and religion, Fritz Graf makes some interesting points about prayer:

> To the Greeks, a magician not only uttered spells, he also prayed to the gods: Plato, for one, connects the ἐπωιδαί (spells)[1] and the εὐχαί (prayers) of the magician, both of which helped him to persuade (πείθειν) the gods.[2] In the magical papyri themselves, the usual term for the spoken part of the magical action [the invocation] is λόγος (formula),[3] but the word εὐχή (prayer) occurs several times, as do the verb εὔχομαι and kindred terms.[4]

These prayers are not submissive.[5] As in later grimoire magic, prayer is seen as a useful protection and preparation before a ritual, but more importantly in the *PGM* prayer is part of the method of hierarchical threatening, where a high god is invoked to command the actions of lesser spiritual creatures.

Graf identifies a three-fold structure for these prayers (patterning them after Sappho's prayer to Aphrodite:

i) Invocation of the god to call the god's attention – *invocatio;*
ii) Commemoration of the god's qualities, epithets, exploits and myths, designed to flatter the god and put them under an obligation to come and listen – *pars epica* or *argumentum;*
iii) The actual request for a boon from the god, sometimes with a recitation of the magician's credentials and *nomina magica*[6] – *preces.*

Prayers make up 0.9% of the *PGM* by rite or 1.6% by lineage.

---

[1] 'Sung incantations' is perhaps a bit more precise.

[2] Plato, *Laws,* 10.909b. Plato also includes 'sacrifices', omitted by Graf.

[3] The word λόγος, *logos* is used often used to mark the beginning of an invocation, like a headword. Its use can be seen in the discussion of the so-called 'Mithras Liturgy' in chapter 7.2.

[4] Graf (1997), pp. 188-189.

[5] The presence of sacrifices (as a trade for the boon) and a phylactery (for protection from the god) confirm that 'submission' is not part of the deal. See *PGM* IV. 2871-2890.

[6] Graf suggests that the recitation of the nomina magica was also a kind of credential, displaying the magician's knowledge to the god.

Gods, Angels, Daimones, names of magicians, *nomina magica*	**Non-Roman *PGM* Nos.**	**Category**	**No. of lines**	**Betz Papyrus *PGM/PDM* Reference number**	**Objective/ Technique**	**Greek Headwords**
	3	W	22	*PGM* III. 165-186	Prayer and offering to consecrate a papyrus talisman.	[n/h] εὐχῆς - lines 176, 177
Selene, Helios, Klotho, Hekate, Lachesis, Mene, Atropos, Allekto Kerberos, Artemis, Erinys, Kronos, Ra, Persephone, Megaira	4	W	106	*PGM* IV. 2785-2890	Prayer to Selene with offerings. This is an invocation, not just a prayer, because of the presence of offerings and the phylactery	Εὐχὴ πρὸς Σελήνην[1]
Mene, IAŌ,	7	W	39	*PGM* VII. 756-794	Prayer to Mene. With the 14 magical sounds like popping (crocodile) and hissing (snake).	εὐχή[2]
Hermes, Selene, Moirai	17	W	23	*PGM* XVIIb. 1-23	Prayer to Hermes asking for mantic skill. Literary	Ἑρμῆ
Jacob, Abraam, Abaōth, Sabaōth, IAŌ, Adōnai, Aōth, "God of the Hebrews"	22	W	26	*PGM* XXIIb. 1-26	Prayer of Jacob[3]	προσευχὴ Ἰακώβ[4] εὐχήν - line 18 εὐχὴν - line 19
Total W		**5**	**216**			

Table W: Prayers.

[1] Prayer to Selene.

[2] Prayer.

[3] Excluded by Graf (1997), p. 208 from his discussion of Greek prayers in the *PGM*, as he sees it as a Jewish spell which requires submission to the one God anyway.

[4] Prayer of Jakob

Hymns

Hymns are part of the background pagan religious culture of the period and have been co-opted in some of the invocations, as they are designed to praise or flatter the god/goddess concerned. As such they are supplementary rather than central. In the *PGM* hymns are always part of other rites, and do not stand alone, and so they are not here separately tallied.[1] Preisendanz was careful to make as complete a list as possible, and this list was incorporated in the second edition of his *Papyri Graecae Magicae*.[2] In most cases the identification as a hymn correlates with poetic format,[3] or identification with known Greek hymns.

I have followed Preisendanz's identification in the following Table J, and his hymn numbers, which group together specific gods, are listed in the last column.

Hymns make up 6.2% by lineage, but as they are constituent parts of other rites are not counted separately. They are to be found predominantly in *PGM* IV.

[1] The 26 hymns are listed in Preisendanz and Henrichs (2001), Vol. II, pp. xxiii, 237-266.
[2] Preisendanz (2001), Vol. 2, pp. 237-266.
[3] Most of the hymns are written in Dactylic hexameter, with Hymns 6, 17 and 25 in Iambic trimeter. Hymn 19 is in Iambic tetrameter acatalectic. Hymn 8, although apparently just one line, is written in Iambic pentameter.

Hymns - ὕμνος (*hymnos*) (J)

Gods, Angels, Daimones, names of magicians, *nomina magica*	**Non-Roman *PGM* Nos**	**Category**	**No. of lines**	**Betz Papyrus *PGM/PDM* Reference number**	**Primary god**	**Preisendanz Hymn number**
Apollo, Zeus, IAŌ, Michaēl, Gabriêl, Abrasax, Adōnai, Pakerbēth, Aiōn, Adōnaios, Elōaios, Chaos, Hades, Moirai	1	J	32	*PGM* I. 296-327	Apollo	23[1]
	1	J	11	*PGM* I. 315-325	Helios	4
Hades	1	J	4	*PGM* I. 342-345	Primal god	23
Apollo, Phoibos	2	J	6	*PGM* II. 2-7, 10	Apollo, Phoibos	9
Apollo, Zeus, Muses, Phoibos, Moirai (Klotho, Atropos, Lachis)	2	J	21	*PGM* II. 81-101	Apollo	11
	2	J	8	*PGM* II. 133-140	Apollo, Apollo-Helios	11
	2	J	4	*PGM* II. 163-166	Apollo, Apollo-Helios	11
Helios, Zeus, IAŌ, Raphaēl, Abrasax, Michaēl, Sese[ngen b]ar Pharaggēs, Sabaōth, Adōnai, Akrammach[ari], Apollo	3	J	32	*PGM* III. 198-229	Helios and all gods	5
Phoibos, Muses, Daphne	3	J	25	*PGM* III. 234-258	Apollo, Daphne	12
	3	J	9	*PGM* III. 550-558	The stars	2
Typhon, Osiris Aberamenthōou	4	J	23	*PGM* IV. 179-201	Typhon	6
Typhon, Moirai	4	J	13	*PGM* IV. 261-273	Typhon	7
Helios, Chaos, Hades, Moirai, Horus	4	J	26	*PGM* IV. 436-461	Helios	4

[1] Line 296 f. listed by Preisendanz (2001), Vol. 2, p.244, as Hymn 8.

Gods, Angels, Daimones, names of magicians, *nomina magica*	Non-Roman *PGM Nos*	Category	No. of lines	Betz Papyrus *PGM/PDM* Reference number	Primary god	Preisendanz Hymn number
Helios, Lailam	4	J	10	*PGM* IV. 939-948	Helios	3
Moirai, Destinies, Malignities, Hekate, Persephassa [Persephone], Korē, Erinys	4	J	36	*PGM* IV. 1399-1434	Moirai, Destinies, Malignities	25
Chaos, Erebos, chthonic Hermes, Moirai, Anubis	4	J	11	*PGM* IV. 1459-1469	Underworld gods	26
Helios, Chaos, Hades, Lailam, Iaō, Horus, Moirai	4	J	35	*PGM* IV. 1957-1989	Helios	4
Hekate, Selene, Artemis, Klotho, [Hekate], Brimo, Alkyone, Hermes the elder, Isis, Korē, Pan, Helios, Aion, Kronos, Moirai, Osiris	4	J	105	*PGM* IV. 2242-2346[1]	Hekate-Selene-Artemis	17
Zeus, Artemis, Persephone, Selene, [Hekate], Chaos, Aphrodite	4	J	46	*PGM* IV. 2522-2567	Hekate	20
Hekate, Selene, Pan, Aktiōphis, Mene, Hermes, Brimo, Dardania	4	J	37	*PGM* IV. 2574-2610	Hekate-Selene	19
Hekate, Selene, Pan, Aktiōphis	4	J	32	*PGM* IV. 2643-2674	Hekate-Selene	19
Hekate, Dione, Baubo Phroune, Korē, Artemis, Ereschigal	4	J	51	*PGM* IV. 2714-2783	Hekate	21
Hekate, Selene, Artemis, Helios, Moirai (Klotho, Lachesis, Atropos), Persephone, Megaira, Allekto, Kronos, Chaos, Zeus, Necessity, Kerberos	4	J	85	*PGM* IV. 2786-2870	Hekate, Selene, Artemis	18

[1] Not 2242-2417 as listed by Preisendanz (1974), Vol. 2, p. 250.

Gods, Angels, Daimones, names of magicians, *nomina magica*	Non-Roman *PGM Nos*	Category	No. of lines	Betz Papyrus *PGM/PDM* Reference number	Primary god	Preisendanz Hymn number
Aphrodite, Adonis, Hades, Ereschigal, Neboutosoualēth	4	J	14	*PGM* IV. 2902-2939	Aphrodite	22
Hermes, Selene, Helios	5	J	21	*PGM* V. 400-420	Hermes	15/16
Apollo, Phoebus, Phoibos, Leto	6	J	18	*PGM* VI. 6-21	Daphne	13
	6	J	17	*PGM* VI. 22-38	Apollo	10
Apollo, Phoibos, Sabaōth, Delios, Nomios, Leto, Zeus	6	J	8	*PGM* VI. 40-47	Apollo	14
Hermes, Selene, Moirai	7	J	13	*PGM* VII. 668-680	Hermes	15/16
Helios	8	J	8	*PGM* VIII. 74-81	Helios (as setting sun)	4
	12	J	9	*PGM* XII. 244-252	All gods	1
Hermes, Selene, Moirai	17	J	23	*PGM* XVIIb. 1-23	Hermes	15/16
Hermes, infernal Zeus, Titan Helios, Iaweh, Phthas, Phre, Nephtho, Ablanatho, Abrazas, the Bear, Sirius, Circe	23	J	53	*PGM* XXIII. 1-53	Evocation of the spirit of Elpenor	24
Total J		**33**	**846**			

Table J: Hymns.

6.6 Dealing with Daimones

Familiar Spirit or Assistant Daimon – πάρεδρος (*paredros*) (P)

A *paredros* (πάρεδρος) is a magical servant.[1] The acquisition of a *paredros,* 'familiar' or 'assistant daimon' is a procedure which has always been part of magic, and continues to be so. The rationale for this was that, in dealing with spirits, it was always helpful to have one who is 'tame' and can act as a guide or intermediary with the denizens of the other world. This theme appears first in the *Testament of Solomon* and the Graeco-Egyptian texts, then in the *Hygromanteia* and later in the Latin and vernacular Solomonic grimoires.

In the 1st/2nd century *Testament of Solomon,* Solomon has first to tame Ornias (which he does with the help of God, a consecrated ring and the archangel Michael), after which Ornias acts as a magical assistant and introduces him to, and helps him bind, the other 59 spirits listed in that text. In many later European grimoires, specific demons (such as Paimon in the *Goetia*) are said to "grant good familiars."

The concept of a spirit familiar is a long enduring idea. Although witchcraft is not part of this book it is worth noting that many 16th and 17th century witchcraft confessions involved the admission that the witch had a familiar spirit in the form of a cat, toad or similar, and searching for the 'witch's mark' became a standard procedure for witch-finders like Matthew Hopkins.[2] This mark was reputedly the bodily point where the witch suckled her familiars or imps.[3] In the late 19th century, the Golden Dawn and some of its offshoots taught methods of creating an artificial Elemental, which was effectively a 'designer' familiar.

Hence this technique is one of enduring importance, and a technique used by magicians in almost every culture. In fact this procedure is not coincidently the subject of the very first two sections in *PGM* I. 1-195, as it was often considered an indispensable first step to magical practice. The opening line of the first procedure explains that "A [daimon comes] as an assistant who will reveal everything to you clearly and will be your [companion and] will eat and sleep with you." This description seems to be of a very concrete entity.[4]

---

[1] The derivation of πάρεδρος is supposed to be from *para,* 'near,' and *hedros,* 'sided.'

[2] He was a self-appointed 'Witchfinder General' born in 1620, and active 1645-1647.

[3] Whether true or not, this re-confirms the common perception of the very physical nature of such familiars.

[4] The theme of eating and drinking with spirits is repeated in the *Hygromanteia,* and again in later European grimoires, such as the *Grimorium Verum,* where the magician is enjoined to lay out a physical table with choice foods in preparation for the arrival of the spirits.

Obtaining a Paredros

The theory is that, in many ways, the acquisition of a familiar spirit is the most important part of a magician's initial development, as a familiar gives him direct help from the spiritual world and advice on how to deal with other spiritual creatures.

A rite designed to provide a spirit servant is to be found in one of the most interesting sections of the *PGM* which is rather ambiguously titled in English "Apollonius of Tyana's old serving woman." A more descriptive rendering might have been "Apollonius of Tyana's [method for securing a spirit] servant [in the form of] an old woman."[1]

The method involves invoking the goddess Nephthys, who manifests first as a beautiful woman then as an old serving woman. When Nephthys attempts to depart, the magician must restrain her and reply "No, lady! I will use you until I get her."[2] The goddess then binds the old woman spirit servant to the service of the magician, by giving a tooth from an ass, and one from the old woman, to the magician, who then has complete control over this spirit servant.

A more sinister magical assistant is offered by King Pitys (already mentioned under 'N'), in two separate rites. In the first rite this assistant turns out to be the soul of a dead man (who has died a violent death). In the second rite the assistant is simply described as a chthonic daimon. In both cases a skull cup is used, and in the second case the skin of an ass is also used, indicating the Typhon/Seth related nature of the ritual.

The second rite is more complex and requires three writing surfaces:

i) The hide of an ass inscribed with an ink made of the heart blood of an ass which has been sacrificed, mixed with coppersmiths' soot. The figure drawn also incorporates the qualities of Chnoubis:

> ...a lion-faced form of man wearing a sash, holding in his right hand a staff, and on it let there be [drawn] a serpent. And around all his left hand let an asp be entwined, from the mouth of the lion let fire breath forth.[3]

ii) Drawn on a leaf of flax, using an ink made of falcon's blood mixed with goldsmiths' soot:

> Hekate with three heads and six hands, holding torches in her hands, on the right sides of her face having the head of a cow; and on the left sides the head of a dog; and in the middle the head of a maiden with sandals bound on her feet.[4]

---

[1] *PGM* XI.a 1-40.
[2] *PGM* XI. a 20.
[3] *PGM* IV. 1928-2005.
[4] *PGM* IV. 2006-2125.

iii) On a piece of papyrus, with ink made from eel's blood mixed with acacia [ashes] is drawn the figure of Osiris "clothed as the Egyptians show him."

The whole rite therefore involves three gods of the Underworld: one Gnostic, one Greek and one Egyptian. As the Egyptian gods are spoken about in the third person, the rite has probably been assembled by a Greek magician.

The rite was allegedly sent from King Pitys to Ostanes. One Ostanes was mentioned by Hermodōrus, a disciple of Plato. Another Ostanes accompanied Xerxes on his expedition to Greece, where he reputedly taught Demokritos magic. Pliny identified that Ostanes with the Persian magi, but also suggested that this Ostanes dealt in magic and necromancy, making him a much more likely candidate. His fame survived through the Byzantine period, mainly in connection with alchemy, and Ostanes' name was often associated with magic right up till the late Middle Ages.

Pachoumi[1] identifies two of the above rites,[2] but also suggests two other rites (*PGM* LVII. 1-37 and *PGM* VII. 862-918). *PGM* VII. 862-918 includes a request for an angel of the hour or a *paredros,* but is primarily a love rite using a statue of Selene (see 'S'), rather than a *paredros* invocation *per se*. *PGM* LVII. 1-37 is a straight invocation of the goddess Isis, using a compulsive formula, with no relation to the *paredros*.

On the other hand Pachoumi has omitted to mention the three *paredros* rites at *PGM* I. 1-42, *PGM* IV. 1840-1870, and *PGM* XII. 14-95, and she seems to have difficulty in distinguishing between 'god' and '*paredros*,' even suggesting a confusion between 'god' and 'angel' as the explanation.

---

[1] Pachoumi (2011), p. 164.

[2] *PGM* I. 42-195 including I. 147 ff and *PGM* XIa. 1-40.

Gods, Angels, Daimones, names of magicians, *nomina magica*	Non-Roman PGM Nos.	Category	No. of lines	Betz Papyrus *PGM/PDM* Reference number	Objective/ Technique	Greek Headwords
	1	P	42	*PGM* I. 1-42	Assistant daimon rite	[πρᾶξις] παρεδρικῶς προσ[γίνεται δαί]μων
Pnouthis, the Keryx[1]	1	P	154	*PGM* I. 42-195	Rite of Pnouthis, the temple scribe, for acquiring an assistant daimon.[2]	[Πνού]θεως ἱερογραμματέως πάρεδρος[3] πάρεδρος - lines 128, 192
	4	P	31	*PGM* IV. 1840-1870[4]	Sword of Dardanos.[5]	…πάρεδρον[6]
				PGM IV. 2006-2125	*See Ω*	
				PGM VII. 862-918	*See Ω*	
Nephthys, Typhon, Apollonius of Tyana (magician)	11	P	40	*PGM* XIa. 1-40	Apollonius of Tyana's method for a binding a spirit servant, in the form of an old woman, via an invocation of Nephthys	γραύς Ἀπολλωνίου Τυανέως ὑπηρετίς[7]
Eros	12	P S	82	*PGM* XII. 14-95	Statue of Eros as assistant daimon, which gives dreams. Sacrifice to animate a statue.	π[ά]ρεδρος ἔρως[8] τελετή - lines 15, 36[9]
Total P		**5**	**349**			

Table P: Familiar Spirit or Assistant Daimon.

[1] This letter is addressed to a Keryx, which is a messenger or herald.

[2] This rite is divided into six sections, respectively beginning at lines: 42 – Introduction; 55 – Preliminaries; 96 – Functions of the *paredros*; 134 - *logos* or Invocation; 144 – image to be engraved; 149 - *logos* or Invocation to Selene.

[3] Pnouthis the temple scribe's method for [obtaining] a *paredros*. 'Temple scribe' equates with Temple priest.

[4] This section has been separated out from *PGM* 1716-1840 as it is clearly a separate rite.

[5] The text appears at the end of the Sword of Dardanos, but it is actually a separate procedure for acquiring an assistant daimon.

[6] *Paredros* (adjective), i.e. helpful.

[7] Apollonius of Tyana's old woman [spirit] assistant.

[8] Eros as a *paredros*.

[9] Mystery.

Daimonic Possession and Exorcism - δαιμονία-ζομένους (*daimonia-zomenous*) (Q)

Exorcistic formulae are not common in the *PGM,* but they do occur. Three out of four however are heavily Jewish or Christianised.[1] The first exorcism hails the God of Abraham, Isaac and Jacob, but also Jesus Chrestos, the Holy Spirit, and the Son of the Father, confirming its Christian pedigree.[2] It also refers to "this unclean daimon Satan." This rite uses a tin phylactery for hanging on the patient after a successful exorcism which does not use Christian terms, focussing on variations on the word 'phorba' instead.[3]

It is probable that the idea of the invasion of the human body by an external entity, and the methods designed to drive it out are probably all Jewish rather than Graeco-Egyptian, as Kotansky notes:

> Scholars have long recognized that the concept of an unfamiliar spirit possessing a human being by somehow infiltrating the body and securing control over the faculties is Semitic; it is largely foreign to Greek thought in classical and Hellenistic times.[4]

Smith also confirms that Palestine is the source of the earliest Latin/Greek mention of exorcism:

> ...there is no description of exorcism in pagan literature before Lucian, who in the *Philopseudes* describes a Syrian exorcist from Palestine.[5]

This helps explain why there is very little in the way of Jewish magic apart from exorcism before the 2nd century CE, as noted in chapter 2.2.

The second rite listed in Table Q is one reputed to have been invented by Pibechis as a cure for those possessed by demons.[6] Like the first example in Table Q, this rite abounds in Jewish references like "the tongue of Jeremiah," and conjures:

> by the god of the Hebrews, Jesus... by the one who appeared to Osrael [Israel] in a shinning pillar and a cloud by day, who saved his people from the Pharaoh and brought upon the Pharaoh the ten plagues...

---

1 The fifth example *PGM* XCIV. 17-21 is too fragmentary to judge, but as it references Solomon is likely to have been Jewish.

2 *PGM* IV. 1227-1264.

3 Amongst the many men called Phorbas, one was reputed to have driven out all the snakes (or dragons) from the island of Rhodes. The association is tenuous, but Satan was often linked with the serpent.

4 Kotansky (1995, 2001), p. 246.

5 Smith (1965), p. 409.

6 *PGM* IV. 3007-3086. Pibechis was reputed to be a famous Egyptian magician, but the contents of the rite are not particularly Egyptian.

This rite calls on Ammōn and uses Egyptian *nomina magica,* but it concludes unequivocally with the statement that the invocation is Hebraic. It prescribes a tin phylactery for the preservation of the patient.

This section also includes the famous *Stēlē* of Jeu the 'hieroglyphist'.[1] As already remarked a *stēlē* in this context can simply mean the text of something to be written or engraved. Jeu's profession is likely to have been an illustrator of texts, rather than the rather cumbersome 'hieroglyphist.' Therefore we can deduce that this text was probably a standard one utilised a number of times because of its association with a professional illustrator of *stelae*. It also has a strong literary flavour, with lines like:

> I summon you, Headless One,[2] who created earth and heaven, who created night and day, you who created light and darkness... you have distinguished the just and the unjust; you have made female and male; you have revealed seed and fruits; you have made men love each other and hate each other...
>
> I am the one who begets and destroys; I am the Favor of the Aion; my name is a heart encircled by a serpent; come forth and follow.[3]

Part of the fame of this passage comes from it having been first translated by Griffith and Thompson,[4] in the late 19th century, and then having been adopted by the founders of the Hermetic Order of the Golden Dawn as a rather stirring invocation. Certainly the words are rather elegant. However the Greek of the last part clearly indicates that its function is as a demon binding:

> Subject to me all daimones...And all daimones will be obedient to you...[5]

The text also requests Akephalos, the "mighty Headless One," to deliver a specific person (NN) "from the daimon that restrains him" confirming its exorcistic quality.[6]

Ironically Aleister Crowley chose this passage to preface his edition of the *Goetia,* although whether he chose it as simply an initial conjuration (which is how most 20th century practitioners used it) or whether he was fully aware that it was meant to restrain daimones/demons cannot be confirmed.

The fourth rite is too fragmentary to judge, but its mention of Solomon suggests a Jewish provenance.[7] These rites make up only 0.7% of the *PGM* by rite but 1.5% by lineage.

---

[1] *PGM* V. 96-172.

[2] The Akephalos god.

[3] *PGM* V. 97-106, 150-156. the last phrase "the heart girt with a serpent" was later used by Aleister Crowley in his book *Liber Samekh.*

[4] Griffith and Thompson (1904).

[5] *PGM* V. 165-172.

[6] *PGM* V. 129-130.

[7] *PGM* XCIV. 17-21.

Gods, Angels, Daimones, names of magicians, *nomina magica*	Non-Roman PGM Nos.	Category	No. of lines	Betz Papyrus *PGM/PDM* Reference number	Objective/ Technique	Greek Headwords
Jesus Christ, Satan, Abraham, etc	4	Q	38	*PGM* IV. 1227-1264	Driving out daimones, a rite for Judaeo-Christians.[1] Involves a tin lamella	πρᾶξις γενναία ἐκβάλλουσα δαίμονας[2]
Jesus, 'the god of the Hebrews,' Ammōn, Sabaōth. Pibechis	4	Q	80	*PGM* IV. 3007-3086	Exorcism. Possession by daimones, phylactery of Pibechis for exorcism.[3] Uses a tin lamella	πρός δαιμονία-ζομένους Πιβήχεως δόκιμον[4]
Headless daimon, Jeu, Moses Pharaoh Osoronnophris, Iabas, Iapos, Favour of the Aiōn, Iao, Ibaoth, Abrasax, Abraōth, Adonaie	5	Q	77	*PGM* V. 96-172	*Stēlē* of Jeu the 'hieroglyphist'. Invocation of the Headless daimon. A daimon binding rite.[5]	στήλη τοῦ Ἰέου τοῦ ζωγρ[άφου] εἰς τὴν ἐπιστολήν[6] μυστήρια[7] - line 109
Solomon	94	Q	5	*PGM* XCIV. 17-21 *SM* 94 d	Amulet against possession by daimones.	πρ[ὸς] δαιμονιαζομενους[8]
Total Q		**4**	**200**			

Table Q: Daimonic Possession and Exorcism.

[1] See Kotansky (1995, 2001), pp. 261-266.
[2] Excellent practice for driving out daimons.
[3] See Kotansky (1995, 2001), pp. 262-266. The phylactery strangely occurs at lines 3014-3019 rather than at the end as usual. See U2.
[4] Pibechis' trusted [method] for those possessed by daimons. Pibechis was allegedly an Egyptian magician.
[5] See lines 165-172.
[6] *Stēlē* of Jeu the illustrator of epistles.
[7] Mystery.
[8] Against daimonic possession.

6.7 Dealing with the Dead

Necromancy – νεκρομαντεία (*nekromanteia*) (N)

Necromancy is divination by the dead, or the temporary raising of the dead in order for them to answer questions put by the magician. Quite often this operation will be associated with bodies and/or grave goods. Such practices were very popular in classical Greek times, and have endured also from dynastic Egyptian times, through Hellenic culture and European grimoires right up to the modern practice of spiritualism. Johnston identifies eight *PGM* necromantic rites,[1] but these do not exactly map onto the list in Table N. For example, *PGM* I. 262-347 is placed under Evocationary Lamp Skrying in category 'E,' as Evocationary Lamp Skrying is more prominent in that passage than any mentions of the dead. Johnston herself concedes that *PGM* IV. 154-285 is "actually part of an elaborate type of lecanomancy," and it has therefore been so categorized here. In addition two 'drowned animal' rites have been included under necromancy, as they use the spirits of dead animals.

Necromancy is a procedure that has fascinated people from time immemorial. The word 'necromancy' has had a chequered history. Despite the obvious Greek derivation, in Mediaeval Europe, this term became identified with 'nigromancy,' and hence with the evocation of demons. Jean-Patrice Boudet suggested that 'necromancy' should be used in its original meaning of Evocationary divination by the dead, whilst 'nigromancy' should refer just to evocation of demons.[2] Kieckhefer does not accept this logical division but sees 'nigromancy' as a relatively modern term.[3]

Conventionally according to modern scholars and standard Greek lexicons '*manteia*' indicated a form of divination. In the case of necromancy, the literal meaning is clearly divination by questioning the dead. But nigromancy is usually glossed as 'the black art' or 'black magic.' How can this be as 'nigro-' simply means 'black' so logically 'nigromancy' should mean something like 'black divination,' but it doesn't. Elsewhere I have made the case for broadening the definition of '*-manteia*' to mean a magical procedure, rather than just a divination. If this is not the case, then how can the conflation of nigromancy and necromancy have occurred if only one was a method of divination and the other a method of magic? Robert Ritner discusses the (mis)use of 'necromancy' to mean a magical operation rather than its original Greek meaning of divination by questioning the dead.[4] According to the *OED* the use of 'necromancy' to mean any kind of magical operation only came to

---

[1] Johnston (2008), pp. 171-175.

[2] As noted by Benedek Lang (2008), p. 41.

[3] Kieckhefer (1997), p. 19. See also Kieckhefer (2003), pp. 152-153.

[4] Ritner (2008), pp. 236-249; Ciraolo and Seidel (2002), p. 96.

full fruition in about 1550,[1] but I believe this usage occurred at least a century earlier, because of this kind of reference to necromancy in the *Hygromanteia.*

A unique and rather strange Jewish interpretation of the meaning of 'nigromancy' is voiced by Menahem Ziyuni:

> 'Nigromancia' is a combination of two words, *nigar* [Hebrew], 'gathered together, collected,' like water that has been stored up, and *mancia,* the name of the incense that magicians burn to [attract] the demons.[2]

The Hebrew meaning of *nigar* is closer to "to draw in or invoke," rather than "to gather." The most interesting part of this definition is the equation of *mancia,* and hence possibly of μαντεία, *manteia* with a specific incense used in evocation. However this seems to be an isolated usage and it is not clear how this might advance the argument.

Dating from before the questioning of the spirit of Samuel by King Saul (mediated by the witch of Endor) there has always been a Jewish tradition of necromancy. In the Talmud it says:

> There are two kinds of necromancy (**בעל אוב**. Baal Aib [Aub]), the one where the dead is raised by naming him, the other where he is asked by means of a skull (**הנשאל בגלגלת**).[3]

The first kind of necromancy has survived through to the modern era.[4] The second type where a head, or skull, has been kept as a sort of oracle to answer questions also has a long but separate history. The most famous oracular skull was that reputed to have been owned and used by Roger Bacon.[5]

One such skull (which came from an archaeological dig in Nippur) was kept in the museum of the University of Pennsylvania.[6] The inscription across the top of the skull includes the word **ללתא**, Lilita, a clear reference in Hebew to the female Babylonian demon Lilitu. Other words on the skull make it clear that it was used as a focus for an address to that spirit.[7]

The Sabians of Harran were also reputed to use 'speaking skulls' for oracular

---

[1] *OED*, Vol. VII, p. 67.

[2] Quoted in Trachtenberg (2004), p. 22.

[3] *Sanhedrin*, 65b.

[4] See the famous engraving of Edward Kelley and Paul Waring questioning the ghost of a woman besides a newly opened grave. The incident dates from the late 16th century, but the engraving comes from Sibley (1784 – 1792). More recent cases of this type of necromancy were reported in the 1980s relating to Highgate Cemetery in London.

[5] Even in more modern times the skulls of famous men, especially magicians and mystics, have become collectors' items. As recently as 1978 the skull of Emanuel Swedenborg (1688-1772) went on sale at Sotheby's in London for 2,500 pounds.

[6] Exhibit No. 41 (CBS 179).

[7] As an aside, the Arabic words for the skull and the soul are almost identical.

purposes[1] and in Roman times Lucius Apuleius mentioned the use of skulls in magic in his *Apology*. Classical Greek references to the use of the dead in magic, such as the re-animation of corpses by Erichtho in the *Pharsalia* have very little in common with Graeco-Egyptian magic, and even less in common with later grimoire magic.[2]

The use of mortuary remains in magic also leads to the use of *defixiones*, which attempt to compel the aid of the dead in a magical operation. *Defixiones* are a common part of Graeco-Egyptian magic, and are treated separately in chapter 6.7 section 'D.'

The shortest necromantic rite for questioning corpses in the *PGM* is credited to King Pitys the Thessalian. In this a flax leaf[3] has AZĒL BALEMACHŌ written on it, and no invocation is mentioned, but the writing as usual must be done with a special ink.[4]

Another rite, although captioned as a "Spell of Attraction of King Pitys" is obviously an example of necromancy, for the caption continues with "over any skull cup."[5] The operation requires the skull of a dead man who died prematurely or violently. Surprisingly the invocation is not addressed to one of the chthonic gods, but to Helios himself, and his "holy angels on this day, in this very hour."[6] Here Helios is addressed as a supreme god, rather than as god of the Sun.[7] A second version of King Pitys' necromantic rite occurs a few lines before in the same papyrus.[8]

Pitys may be related to the priest Bitys, who Iamblichus praised for having translated hieroglyphic texts into Greek, as the letters 'p' and 'b' were often switched in Egyptian/Arabic transliteration.

Homer and the Kestoi

A much more concrete version of necromancy occurs in a papyrus[9] which Betz's Table of Spells[10] credits to the *Kestoi* of Julius Africanus. However, the

---

[1] Chwolson (1965), Vol. ii, p. 150.
[2] *Pharsalia*, VI. 447-830.
[3] Flax was always associated by the Greeks with the dead, as a consequence of which flax is often used as a writing material in necromantic operations.
[4] *PGM* IV. 2140-2144.
[5] *PGM* IV. 1928-2005.
[6] The importance of choosing the correct day and hour is stressed (although the rite does not identify which specific hour was to be used).
[7] *PGM* IV. 2140-44. One strange facet of this passage is the use of the word 'tent' to describe the dead man's grave.
[8] *PGM* IV. 2006-2125.
[9] *PGM* XXIII. 1-70.
[10] Betz (1996), pp. xi-xxii.

passage appears to be sourced from Homer and is therefore much older than Julius Africanus, with only a short commentary section inserted by the latter.[1] The passage very clearly describes the sacrifice of sheep and the pouring of their blood into a trench:

> [when with vows] and prayers [I had appealed]
> [To them], the tribes of dead, I took [the] sheep
> And slit their throats [beside the trough, and down]
> The dark blood [flowed. From out of Ere]bos
> Came gathering [the spirits] of the dead…
> [These many] thronged from ev'ry side around
> The trough [of blood] with [awful] cry. Pale fear seized me.
> [But] having drawn the sharp sword at my thigh,
> [I sat,] allowing not the flitting heads
> Of the dead to draw nearer to [the blood]…[2]

Here there are two magical techniques explicitly mentioned. The first is the shedding of blood to attract the spirits, a procedure that carries on through to the later Latin European grimoires. The second is the use of a sword to control the spirits and keep them at bay. Although it is contra-intuitive that a sharp sword should strike fear into a spirit that is already dead, it is a recurrent motive in both the Byzantine magical handbooks and the later Latin grimoires that a sharp sword, specifically made of iron, is an effective threat to spirits, as if they reputedly fear being cut.

One extraordinary rite in the *PGM* is designed to restrain a divinatory skull that has got out of hand. The idea that a skull might 'get out of hand' is in itself extraordinary, but it demonstrates the continuing use of necromantic skulls that answer questions:

> **A restraining seal** for skulls that are not satisfactory [for use in divination], and also to prevent [them] from speaking or doing anything whatever of this [sort]:
>
> Seal the mouth of the skull with dirt from the doors of [a temple] of Osiris and from a mound [covering] graves. Taking iron[3] from a leg fetter, work it cold and make a ring on which a headless lion [is] engraved. Let him [the lion] have, instead of his head, a crown of Isis, and let him trample with his feet a skeleton (the right foot should trample the skull of the skeleton). In the middle of these [images] should be an owl-eyed cat with its paw on a gorgon's head; in a circle

[1] Julius Africanus c.160-c.240 CE. The *Kestoi* was an encyclopaedic work on various sciences: mathematics, botany, medicine, divination and magic. The Greek word κεστοί literally means 'embroidery.' Although Betz's Table of Spells lists this as a *Kestoi* extract, the first 54 lines of the fragment are from Homer *Od.* 11. 34-43, 48-50; *Il.* 3. 278-80; *Il.* 15. 412; *Il.* 7.741; *Od.* 10. 513-14; *Od.* 11.51.

[2] *PGM* XXIII. 1-14.

[3] Iron occurs here as it threatens the spirit operating through the skull.

> around [all of them?], these names: IADŌR INBA NICHAIOPLĒX BRITH.[1]

The visual threat of the skull being crushed by the Headless One plus the iron fetter and a mouth full of sacred dirt should presumably have restrained any wayward skull. The point of quoting this is to show that Graeco-Egyptian necromantic procedures were quite detailed, and had an internal logic of their own.

Necromancy makes up 0.9% of all the *PGM* rites.

[1] *PGM* IV. 2125-39.

Gods, Angels, Daimones, names of magicians, *nomina magica*	Non-Roman PGM Nos.	Category	No. of lines	Betz Papyrus *PGM/PDM* Reference number	Objective/ Technique	Greek Headwords
Adōnai, Helios, IAŌ, Horus, the Moirai. Pitys, the Thessalian (King),	4	N	78	*PGM* IV. 1928-2005	King Pitys' first rite of attraction[1] via necromancy using a dead man's spirit as a familiar.[2]	ἀγωγὴ Πίτυος βασιλέως[3] - lir 1928-1929 [name facility]
				PGM IV. 2006-2125	*See Ω*	
Osiris	4	N	15	*PGM* IV. 2125-2139	A restraining seal ring to bind a divinatory skull from speaking or doing wrong things	ὡς Αἰγύπτιοι μηνύουσιν.[4] κάτοχος σφραγίς[5] πάρεδρος[6] - line 2138
Pitys, the Thessalian King and magician	4	N	5	*PGM* IV. 2140-2144	Corpse revelation. [King] Pitys the Thessalian's rite for questioning corpses.	Πίτυος θεσσαλοῦ ἀνάκρισις σκήνους[7]
Isis, Asklepios Osiris, Hebe, Seseggen bar Pharaggēs, Sabaōth	7	N	17	*PGM* VII. 993-1009	Conjuration of a *nekudaimon.*	[n/h] νεκυδαιμον[8] - line 1006 [στή]λην [9] – line 1009
				PGM XVI. 1-75	*See D*	
Khu, Geb, Isis, Thoth, Shu, Buto, Horus	61	N	15	*PDM* lxi. 79-94	Necromantic method for finding a thief using the head of a drowned man and flax.	[Demotic]
Total N		**5**	**130**			

Table N: Necromancy.

[1] 'Attraction' here refers to attracting the spirit rather than in the sense of sexual attraction. See Composite rites, chapter 6.8 for King Pitys' second method.

[2] Prayer to Helios lines 1957-1989.

[3] King Pitys rite of attraction (in the sense of drawing the spirit to the magician. It is not a love rite ('L').

[4] An Egyptian secret revealed.

[5] Restraining seal.

[6] Assistant daimon.

[7] [King] Pitys' trick [literaly 'shoe'] for examining corpses.

[8] *Nekudaimōn,* ghost of a dead man.

[9] *Stēlē.* If the reconstruction is correct, it probably refers to a text rather than a lamella.

Defixiones - κατάδεσμος (*katadesmos*) (D)

Defixiones are orders to the dead (or *nekudaimōnes*) to affect a particular desired magical result. There is no equivalent English word. The theory behind them is that the spirits of the dead can be constrained by the evocation and words on the *defixio,* to carry out the specific orders of the magician who created the *defixio,* or for the spirits of the dead to communicate with daimones or gods who can so do. The restless dead (especially the victims of murder or premature death) are thought to be constrained by the *defixio,* to carry out the wishes of the magician.[1]

A *desmos* is a 'bond or fetter,' whilst *kata* means 'down' (amongst other things). It is therefore not surprising that *katadesmos* refers to the practice of binding *nekudaimōnes* down in the tomb. Faraone states that *katadesmos* is derived from the verb καταδέω, *katadeō* meaning 'to bind down.'[2] Given the importance of 'tomb culture' in ancient Egypt, *defixiones* have a long history of use there. Examples of *defixiones* have also been found in Greece and many of its colonies as far back as the late 6th century BCE.[3] *Defixiones* may originally have been an Egyptian practice, having been attested in the Old Kingdom, despite Faraone's contention that they are of Greek origin.[4]

This practice was designed to utilise the dead to carry the instructions of the magician to the appropriate Underworld god (typically chthonic Hermes, Ge, Hekate and Persephone) or daimon to carry out. As such *defixiones* were often inserted into the mouth of the cadaver, or at the very least buried alongside the coffin. *Defixiones* were not meant to benefit the occupant of the tomb, but the magician (or his client) who placed them there. The hieratic phrase for a tomb used in this way is "the noble (mail)-box of Osiris," or πυξις, *pyxis* in Greek. Such practices were exported to other parts of the Graeco-Roman world with examples being found in Rome, Athens and even Autun in Burgundy, as well as being popular amongst local magicians in Alexandria.[5]

The oldest *defixio* in the *PGM* is *PGM* XL which dates from soon after Alexander the Great's death in 323 BCE. Despite the fact that Betz, in his Table of Spells, labels it as a 'curse,' it is more than that, and is in fact a *defixio,* designed to act

---

[1] This practice resurfaces again in Europe where beans are buried in churchyards and subsequently dug up to help confer invisibility. Food and drink offerings to the dead are a part of many cultures, but the binding of specifically restless spirits with a *defixio,* to carry out magical acts appears to be unique to Egypt and the Hellenic world.

[2] Faraone (1997), p. 21. Whereas the Latin *defixio,* means 'to nail down,' reflecting the common occurrence of nails or nail holes in *defixiones,* but missing the more subtle and accurate sense of binding embodied in the Greek term.

[3] Johnston (2002), p. 42, but Faraone and Obbink (1991), p. 3 suggest 5th century BC.

[4] See Ritner (2008), pp. 179-183.

[5] Marcillet-Jaubert (1979).

against someone who robbed a tomb of its funeral gifts. This is confirmed by the phrase "my cry for help is *deposited* here [in the tomb]."

Defixiones, or to use the more accurate Greek name, *katadesmoi,* date back to, and before, Plato. In his *Republic* he confirms that:

> Begging priests and soothsayers go to the doors of the wealthy and convince them that if you want to harm an enemy, at very little expense, whether he deserves it or not, they will persuade the gods through *epōdai* [incantations] and *katadesmoi* [*defixiones*] to do your bidding.[1]

The objective was to bind the speech or actions of the 'target person' and only in some more extreme cases to kill them. One such *defixio* was meant to compel the love of a specific woman, with the aim of binding "her brain and her hands and her intestines and her genitals, and her heart to love me." To this end it conjures "boys here who have died prematurely," as their spirits are presumably still free to roam the Earth till their appointed time. As might be expected, the papyrus was found folded up in a clay vessel and deposited in a cemetery. As if to further charge the magic, the vessel also contained two clay figures configured as if having intercourse.[2]

The material usually used to make *defixiones* was lead.[3] A typical *defixio* text can also be recognised by the form of its words, even if the material written on is not lead. The giveaway line is, "I adjure you, daimon of the dead..."[4] which in one instance is repeated no less than eight times.[5]

Some academic texts refer to all magical inscriptions on metal plates as *defixiones.* I have applied this description only to lead plates which have definitely been left in graves or cast into a watercourse. Metal plates are also used for talismans (T-T4) which are not treated in the same way, as they do not rely upon *nekudaimōnes* to function, and so these have been separated.

One very clear example of instructions to make a typical *defixio* has the full procedure of using a *defixio* to secure the love/lust of a specific woman. This sequence of procedures is:

- making clay images of both the magician and the woman of his desire;
- binding to them a lead plate;
- burying it near/in a grave;
- constraining the untimely dead occupants of the grave to carry out the

---

[1] Plato, *Republic,* book 2 (364C), c. 375 BCE. The original translation rendered *epōdai* and *katadesmoi* as "charms and binding spells."

[2] *PGM* CI. 1-53.

[3] At least 60 were made on sheets of selenite. See Gager (1992), p. 132.

[4] *Nekudaimōn.*

[5] *PGM* XVI. 1-75.

magician's orders;

- invoking the chthonic gods/goddesses;
- taking back a remnant from the grave to establish a magical link back to the magician;
- and finally saying over this link another invocation.
- The magician has thoughtfully added two other versions of the *nomina magica*.[1]

In the invocation, the magician equates Horus with the Moirai (μοῖραι) using isopsephy.[2] The Moirai are often translated as the Fates, but the meaning is closer to "they who apportion your just desserts," rather than just arbitrary fates. The Moirai are especially relevant as, according to Caius Julius Hyginus, they invented the seven Greek vowels. These vowels appear in long strings in many of the invocations in the *PGM*, each vowel representing a planet. The addition of vowels is what distinguished Greek from its predecessor (primarily consonantal) languages like Phoenician or Hebrew. To take that line of thought a bit further, it is the disposition of these planets (in astrology) which determines the fate (Moirai) of every individual.

An ancient figure, which had been treated exactly in this way as described in the rite, was found near Antinoopolis[3] in a clay vase, together with a lead *defixio*.[4] Both the treatment of the figure, (which has her arms bound, with her knees drawn up, and pierced by 13 copper needles) and the Greek inscription, correspond almost exactly to the instructions in *PGM* IV, 296-466. Strange as it may seem, the needles are not meant to harm the 'victim' like a voodoo doll, but simply to obsess her with love for the client for whom the magic was done. The text and figure date to the 3rd or 4th centuries CE. Ritner confirms that the procedure with the copper needles is of ancient Egyptian origin.[5] The description of these dolls by some scholars as "voodoo dolls" is however both

---

[1] *PGM* IV. 296-466.

[2] Lines 455-456. Isosephy calculates values for each word from the numerical equivalents of the letters making up each name. Using the Greek spelling μοιρῶν = 1170 and Ὦρος = 1170 (not Ὦρ as it appears abbreviated in the papyri).

[3] Antinoopolis is a Roman city founded on the Nile by Hadrian in 130 CE. This city commemorates Hadrian's companion Antinoös who had earlier drowned in the Nile nearby after a journey to Hermopolis. The Egyptians explained to Hadrian that the mysterious drowning effectively deified Antinoös, who had, by this, been taken to the bosom of Osiris. This reasoning is also behind the use of actively drowned animals in many Egyptian and *PGM* magical rites, and their later mummification (see chapter 6.8). Antinoopolis was a resolutely pagan city during its heyday, and actively welcomed magicians as residents. I would not be surprised if the tombs amongst its ruins were at some future time found to contain many magical papyri.

[4] Louvre, Paris, inventory E.27145. See Figure 20.

[5] Ritner (2008), p. 113.

anachronistic and misleading in terms of function.[1]

At the level of popular practice, *defixiones* spread from Egypt across the Roman Empire, but *defixiones* do not appear as a method in either the *Hygromanteia* or later Latin grimoires.

Graf divides *defixiones* into five types (which I have expanded to six types):[2]

a) *Defixiones judicariae* designed to silence one's adversaries at a trial.

b) *Defixiones amatoriae* designed to force the love or lust of beloved.

c) *Defixiones agonisticae* designed to prejudice the outcome of a chariot race or other athletic competition.

d) *Defixiones* against slanderers, in order to silence them.

e) *Defixiones* against thieves, to compel them to confess or return the stolen property.

f) *Defixiones* against economic competitors.

Although there are talismans designed to meet most of the above objectives (these will be found in sections like L-L7, and T-T4) the defining quality of a *defixio* is its final deposit in a grave, coffin, burial site or less often a cistern, river, or the sea, in order to utilise the dead or daimones occupying these locations. If such a deposit is not made then the inscribed metal disk or tablet is a talisman, and the link with the daimones or gods is not made via the *nekudaimōnes* or that part of the soul of the dead that still occupied the grave. The requirement was preferably the grave of someone who had died violently or prematurely as their souls were thought to be still connected with the grave.

The first two varieties are by far the most common in the *PGM*. This practice was so common than Greek graves made during the Roman period even had pipes leading down to them, down which *defixiones* could be dropped.[3] These were indeed a very popular magical technique. According to John Gager, who refers to them as "a dark little secret of Mediterranean culture," the number of discovered *defixiones* exceeds 1500.[4] As a method *defixiones* has died out, although Gager records a tablet which may have been a *defixio* found in 17th

[1] Faraone in *Classical Antiquity* (1991), pp. 165-220. Faraone later qualifies this, in Faraone & Obbink (1991), p. 25, as "without implying any connection whatsoever to the Afro-Carribean religious practices of the island of Haiti," thereby admitting the complete inappropriateness of his original comparison. Why then, if there is no connection, use the term?

[2] Graf (1999), pp. 120-121.

[3] Gager (1992), p. 215 for illustrations of this arrangement.

[4] Gager (1992), p. 3.

century England in Wilton Place.[1] Gager ascribes the lack of academic interest in these very concrete examples of magical technique to "the potential harm to the entrenched reputation of classical Greece and Rome, not to mention Judaism and Christianity, as bastions of pure philosophy and true religion," which might be caused by such interest.[2]

The method of manufacturing *defixiones* recorded in the *PGM*, makes up 4.5% of the *PGM* by rite, but 9.4% by lineage, as they are substantial procedures. They also have the largest number of *nomina magica* and god or daimon names per rite than any other category.

Figure 41: A defixio meant to be written on hieratic papyrus (as above) or on a lead lamella and iron ring, designed to prevent a specific woman from ever getting married. Apart from the *nomina magica* the text states "let whatever I wish not take place; let her NN, not get married forever."[3]

[1] Gager (1992), p. 29, Figure 5. This tablet looks as if it was made of lead, although this is not confirmed by Gager. It is inscribed in a flowing hand and inscribed with the planetary spirit sigils which can be found in Agrippa's *De Occulta Philosophia,* and the number '369.'

[2] *Ibid.*

[3] *PGM* V. 304-369.

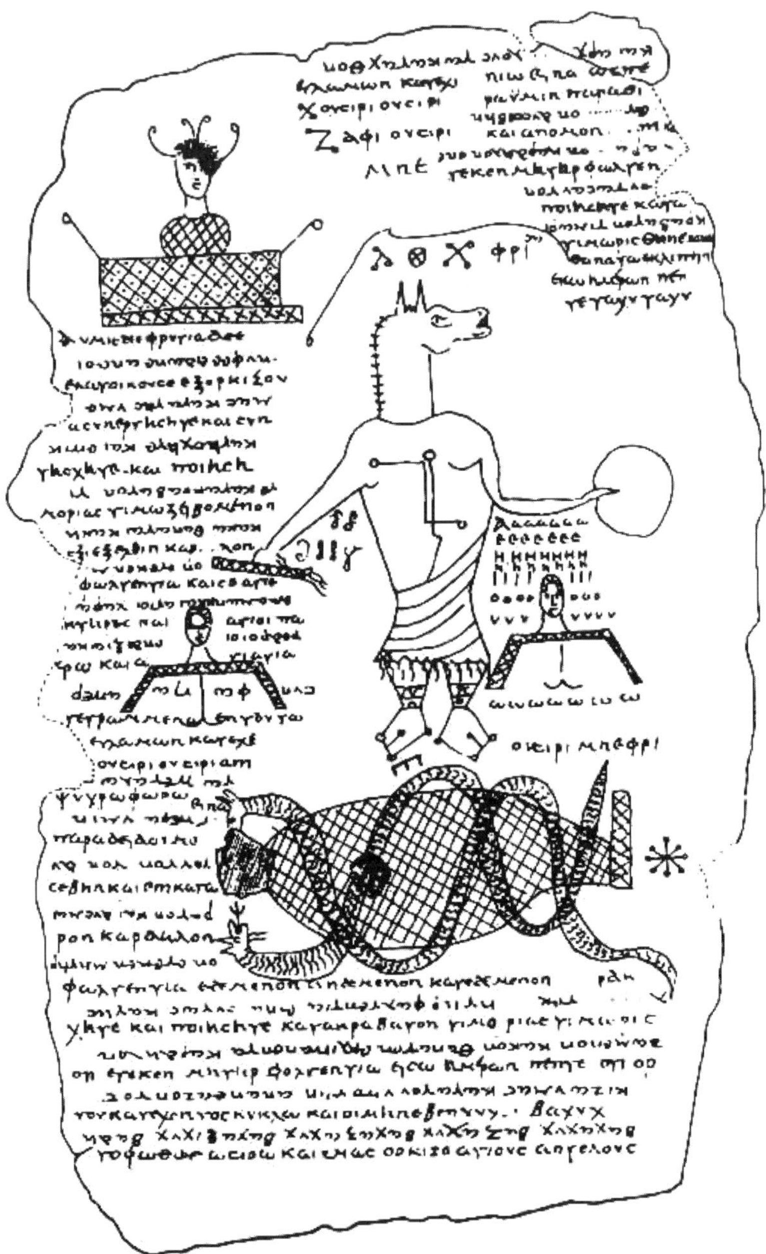

Figure 42: A late fourth century *defixio,* meant to restrain (or kill) a rival jockey, found in a terra-cotta sarcophagus inside a tomb in Rome.[1] The wrapped figure at the bottom is probably the target jockey mummified and bound by two snakes, one Kardēlos, son of Pholgentia (or to give him his Latin name, Cardelus son of Fulgentia). It is surmised that the two heads on little platforms are two *paredroi* mentioned in the text, who are to assist in this binding operation.

[1] From Gager (1992), No. 13, p. 68.

Gods, Angels, Daimones, names of magicians, *nomina magica*	Non-Roman *PGM* Nos.	Category	No. of lines	Betz Papyrus *PGM/PDM* Reference number	Objective/ Technique	Greek Headwords
Korē, Persephone, Erishkigal, Anubis, Anubis Psirinth, Adonis, Hermes, Thōoth, Abrasax, Sensengen bar Pharanggēs, Marmareōth, Adōnai, Aōth, Sabaōth, Horus, the Moirai.[1]	4	D L4	171	*PGM* IV. 296-466	Love rite of attraction, for binding a lover, in the form of two clay images tied to a complex lead *defixio*, followed by a long prayer said whilst holding a grave body remnant from the tomb where the *defixio* was buried.	φιλτροκατάδεσμος θαυμαστός[2] κατάδεσμοι[3] - line 336 νεκυδαιμον[4] – lines 368, 397 στοιχεῖα[5] - line 441
Moirai, Hekate, Korē, Abaōth, Arbathiaō, Morka, Ereshkigal, Neboutosoualēth, Phorba, Anubis, Iaō, Sabaōth, Adōnai, Sesengen	4	D L	206	*PGM* IV. 1390-1595	Poetic love spells of attraction to be performed with the help of those who died a violent death. Seven bread fragments are used rather than a lead tablet.[6]	ἀγωγή – line 1390, 1457
				PGM IV. 2145-2240	*See Ω*	
IAŌ, Ereschigalch (*sic*), Phrē, Sabaōth, Lailam, Osornōphri, Abrasax	5	D	66	*PGM* V. 304-369	*Defixio* using a lead lamella and iron ring	[n/h]
				PGM VII. 396-404 *PGM* VII. 417-422 *PGM* VII. 429-458	*See T4*	
IAŌ Sabaō[th], Osornōphri, Agathos Daimon	15	D L7	21	*PGM* XV. 1-21	Binding a lover using a *defixio*	[n/h] [named person]
Adōnaios Sabaōth, Kronos	16	D N L7	75	*PGM* XVI. 1-75	Binding a lover using a *defixio*	ὁρκίζω σε νεκύ[δαιμον][7] νεκυδαιμον[8] [named person]

[1] Plus many unique *nomina magica.*
[2] A wonderful love procedure.
[3] *defixio.*
[4] *Nekudaimōn,* ghost of a dead man.
[5] Magical statue.
[6] This rite could have been categorised under 'L', but the method is the same as a *defixio,* hence it is listed under 'D.'
[7] I adjure you *nekudaimōn.*
[8] *Nekudaimōn,* ghost of a dead man. See lines 1, 9, 18, 43, 53, 61, 67, 73.

Gods, Angels, Daimones, names of magicians, *nomina magica*	Non-Roman *PGM* Nos.	Category	No. of lines	Betz Papyrus *PGM/PDM* Reference number	Objective/ Technique	Greek Headwords
Tenoch, Anoch, Nouthi, Phrē, Abaōth, Iaō, Osor nōphris, Amoun, Bolchosēth, Ereshkigal, Phrax, Maskelli, Maskellō, Phnoukentabaōth, Samas, Thouri, etc	19	D L7	54	*PGM* XIXa. 1-54	Love rite of attraction primarily made of a long string of *nomina magica.* These are written presumably on a lead tablet, and inserted into the mouth of a dead man as a *defixio.*[1]	[n/h]
	40	D	18	*PGM* XL. 1-18	*Defixio* against a tomb robber	[n/h] [named person]
	51	D	27	*PGM* LI. 1-27	Necromantic use of a daimon of the dead (*nekudaimōn*). Revenge for bringing court charges.	[π]αρακαλῶ σε νεκυδαιμον[2] νεκυδαιμον – line 22 κατάδεσμοι - line 6 [3] [named persons]
Typhon, Osiris	58	D	14	*PGM* LVIII. 1-14	Rite to bind a wicked man by a slander spell and a lead *defixio.*	[n/h] [name facility]
Ablanathanalba, Akrammachamarei, Abrasax, Adonai	59	D	15	*PGM* LIX. 1-15	*Defixio* to protect a grave, to be affixed to the grave.[4]	[n/h] [named person]
Fates, Necessity, Iaō, Brimiaō, Barbathiaō, Osiris Nophriōth, Isis, Eōnebyōth, Adōnai, Hades, Iōthath, Akrammachamari, Psychopompoiaps, Maskelli, Maskellō, Chmouōr, Abrasax	10 1	D L5	53	*PGM* CI. 1-53 *SM* 45	Papyrus *defixio,* as it conjures "boys who have died prematurely" and which was found in pot in a cemetery, with two wax dolls	[n/h] [named persons]
Phnou, Biou, Bibiou, Ousiri, [*not* Bainchōōch], Eulamo	10 7	D L	19	*PGM* CVII. 1-19 *SM* 44	Linen *defixio* to fetch a lover - part of a mummy wrapping.[5]	[n/h] [named person]
	-	D L	18	*SM* 37	Two lead tablets pierced by nails and placed in a grave	[n/h] [named person]

[1] Lines 6-9 were copied onto a mass produced amulet produced for a specific person. See Heintz (1996).

[2] Summoning a *nekudaimōn.*

[3] *Defixiones.*

[4] Not a phylactery as suggested by Betz's Table of Spells in Betz (1996), p. xix.

[5] Probably of an untimely dead man or Βακαξιχυχ, *Bakaxichuch,* 'son of darkness.'

Gods, Angels, Daimones, names of magicians, *nomina magica*	Non-Roman *PGM Nos.*	Category	No. of lines	Betz Papyrus *PGM/PDM* Reference number	Objective/ Technique	Greek Headwords
				SM 38	*See L4*	
Iaō, Teilouteilou, Iatabaōth	-	D L2	17	*SM* 39	Lead tablet invoking a corpse-demon to provoke love.	[n/h] [named person]
Erinyes, Harmachimeneus, Azaēl, Lykaēl, Beliam, Belenēa, Kerberos, Persephone, Sarapis, Osiris, Anoubis, Ereschigal, Azēl, Thōbarabau, Semeseilamps, Sōth, Phrē, Sesengen Barpharaggēs, Chmouōr, Harouēr Abrasax, Phnounoboēl, Thēnōrthsi, Marmaraōth, Mithra, Arsenophrē, Iaō, Iabōth, Ablanathanalba, Akrammachammari, Sesengen Barpharaggēs	-	D L5	66	*SM* 42	Oval lead *defixio* tablet, descriptive of the Greek entrance to the Underworld with Greek and Egyptian chthonic gods. Evokes a corpse-demon. Includes two hymns.	[n/h] [named person]
Plouton, Yes[em]m[e]igadōth, Koure, Persephone, Ereschigal, Adonis, Barbaritha, chthonic Hermes, Thoth, Anoubis Psēriphtha, Barbaratham cheloumbra, Adōnaios, Abrath, Abrasax, Sesengen Barpharaggē, Iaō, Marmaraiōth, Marmaraōth, Marmarauōth	-	D L5	27	*SM* 46	Lead *defixio,* designed to be fixed to a tablet figurine. Utilises a corpse-daimon.	[n/h] [named persons]

Gods, Angels, Daimones, names of magicians, *nomina magica*	Non-Roman *PGM* Nos.	Category	No. of lines	Betz Papyrus *PGM/PDM* Reference number	Objective/ Technique	Greek Headwords
Plouton, Korē, Persephone, Ereschigal, Adonis, Barbaritha, chthonic Hermes, Thoth, Anoubis Psēriphtha, Barbaratham Cheloumbra, Adōnai, Abrasax, Iaō, Marmaraouōth, Marmarachtha	-	D L5	28	*SM* 47	Lead *defixio*, folded and found in an earthenware pot with a clay model of a nude kneeling and bound female figure, pierced with 13 pins. Utilises a corpse-daimon called Antinoos.[1] See Figure 20.	κατάδεσμον[2] νεκυδαιμον[3] - lines, 11, 14, 18 [named persons]
Plouton, Korē, Yesemmeigadōn, Koure, Persephone, Ereschigal, Adonis, Barbaritha, chthonic Hermes, Thoth, Phōkensepseu, Anoubis Psēriphtha, Barbaritham, Barbarithaam, Chelombra, Adōnaios, Ambrath, Abrasax, Sesengen Barpharaggēs, Iaō, Sabaōth, Iaeō, Marmaraōth, Marmarauōth, Barbadōnaiai, Barbadōnai, Aōth, Zeus	-	D L5	47	*SM* 48	Lead *defixio*, with elaborate multi-wing structure. Found in an earthenware pot with a clay model of a female figure.	κατάδεσμον[4] νεκυδαιμον - line 6 [named persons] [wing format]

[1] Maybe the same as the drowned and deified lover of the Emperor Hadrian. Almost the same formula as *SM* 46.
[2] A binding.
[3] *Nekudaimōn,* ghost of a dead man.
[4] A binding.

Gods, Angels, Daimones, names of magicians, *nomina magica*	Non-Roman *PGM Nos.*	Category	No. of lines	Betz Papyrus *PGM/PDM* Reference number	Objective/ Technique	Greek Headwords
Iaō, Adōnai, Elōe, Plouton, Yessemigadōn, Orthō, Baubo, Korē, Persephone, Ereschigal, Adonis, Barbariōnēth, chthonic Hermes, Thoth, Phōkentazepseu, Anoubis Psērichtha, Barbaratham, Chaloumbra, Adōnaios, Abrasax, Babarbariaōth, Sesenge Barbarapharaggēs, Marmarachtha, Hekate, Artemis, Arsenophrē, Aktiōphi, Neboutosoualēth, Orthō, Baubō, Demeter, Erebos, Aphrodite	-	D L4	83	*SM* 49	Lead *defixio* written on both sides. Uses hair from the intended woman.	[n/h] [named persons] κατάδεζμον[1] - lines 4, 61-62, 74.
Plouton, Korē, Persephone, Obach, Barbaratham, Adōnaios, Adōnaiios (*sic*), Abrasax, Sesenge [Bar]Pharaggēs, Iaō, Iarbatiaō, Arbatiaoth, Akrammachamarei, Mamaraōth	-	D L5	72	*SM* 50	Lead *defixio* written on both sides. With *ousia*. Uses the corpse-daimon Kames.	[n/h] [named persons] κατάδε[σ]μον[2] – lines 5-6
Barbaratham, Adōnaios, Sesengen [Bar] Pharaggēs Iaō, Marmaraōth, Isis, Osiris, Sabaōth, Adōnai, Abrasax	-	D L	12	*SM* 51	Clay vessel with spiral writing, using hairs.	[named persons] κατάδε[σ]μον - line 6
Hades, Osiris	-	D	39	*SM* 52	Wooden tablet *defixio*, cursing a woman who has not buried someone properly	[n/h] [named persons]
Eulamō, Abrasax	-	D	32	*SM* 53	Lead *defixio* designed to bind athletes, body and mind, and to darken their eyes	[n/h] [named persons]

1 A binding. The scribe wrote ζ instead of σ.

2 A binding (with the suggested editorial insertion of ζ replaced by σ).

Gods, Angels, Daimones, names of magicians, *nomina magica*	Non-Roman PGM Nos.	Category	No. of lines	Betz Papyrus *PGM/PDM* Reference number	Objective/ Technique	Greek Headwords
Hekate, chthonic Hermes, Pluto Yesemmigadōn, Korē, Ereschigal, Persephone, Maskellei Maskellō, chthonic Gē, Hermes	-	D	39	*SM* 54	Lead *defixio* for victory to win a court case, plus a love issue.	[n/h] [named persons] κατάδεσμον[1] - line 31
Akrammachamarei	-	D	38	*SM* 55	Lead *defixio* with elaborate wing formations. Designed to make a witness mute in a court case.	[n/h] [named persons] [wing format]
Brimo, Baubo, Maskellei, Maskellō, Phnoukentabaōth, Chnouōr, Abrasax, Phnounoboēl, Iōbezebyth, Zeus, Eulamō, Iaō, Harouēl, Chmouch, Iabor, Sabaōth	-	D	43	*SM* 57	Made of lead with nail holes, therefore most likely to be a *defixio.* Restrainer of wrath, to prevent 'speaking against' in court. With an interesting sigil.	[n/h] [named persons] κατάδησον – line 34
Total D		**26**	**1300**			

Table D: *Defixiones.*

[1] A binding.

6.8 Composite Rites (Ω)

There are seven rites which involve four or more methods and so have been classified here as Composite rites. All of these rites achieve multiple results and use a combination of methods.

The first Composite Rite listed in Table Ω is also the first rite in *PGM* III.[1] It is structured around the concept that death by drowning in the Nile effectively deifies the creature so drowned, in this case a cat.[2] If one assumes that there were other instances of the magical use of drowned animals, this may help to explain the large finds of carefully mummified cats, birds, crocodiles and other animals found in Egypt, rather than simply assuming this was to simply allow beloved pets a passage to the afterlife (as has sometimes been suggested), or to provide food in the afterlife, or to act as offerings to a particular god.

The cat is made into an ἐσίην,[3] an embassy or ambassador to send the magician's instructions to the goddess. The spirit of the cat is addressed as the 'cat-faced god,' almost certainly Bestet.[4] Bestet (or Bastet) was one of the magicians' favourite gods, as can be seen in chapter 5 and Figure 14. Lamellae (or talismans) inscribed with 'IAEŌ' and 'TREBA…' are then inserted into the three orifices of its body (anus, ears and throat). The formula is then written out on a papyrus with cinnabar ink,[5] along with the names of the chariots and charioteers the magician desires to bind. This is then wrapped around the cat. An offering is made in payment to the goddess. The mummified cat is then buried in a tomb.[6] The connection with the stadium where the race is to be performed is made by sprinkling there the water in which the cat was deified (drowned), during which the formula is also spoken. This is reinforced with a

---

[1] *PGM* III. 1-164.

[2] This applied to drowned humans as well as animals. The most famous example of this form of deification is the story of the founding of Antinoopolis on the Nile by Hadrian in 130 CE. This city was constructed to commemorate Hadrian's favourite Antinoös, a Greek youth who had earlier drowned in the Nile. The Egyptian priests explained to Hadrian that the drowning had effectively deified Antinoös.

[3] More usually translated as 'to send in' or 'betaking themselves into their own roost.'

[4] As recently as 2010 a temple to Bastet dating from the Ptolemaic period was uncovered in Alexandria. It was attached to a royal palace and was of considerable size, having dimensions of 60m x 15m. Herodotus identified Bestet with Artemis, a goddess who appears also in the *PGM*.

[5] Betz restores the name as PHŌKENSEPSEUARE, but it is possible that this name should be PHARAKOUNĒTH, as the latter was the secret name appropriate to Bast and the first hour of the day. See Table 04.

[6] Probably buried in a cat cemetery rather than in a human grave. In excess of 300,000 mumified cats were discovered in her temple at Per-Bast, aqnd many more elsewhere. It would be interesting to ascertain if any of these had been treated in the same was as the cat in *PGM* III. 1-164, or were they simply offerings, or buried in a devotional fashion.

slander spell spoken against Meliouchos, the helmsman of the bark of Ra. Yet another invocation to the sun-god is added. Furthermore the magician adds an identification with Adam followed logically by a clutch of Jewish *nomina magica*: Iaō, Abaōth, Adōnai, Gabriēl, Raphaēl, Michaēl and Souriēl.[1] The rite specifies a very unique phylactery for the protection of the magician: the left and right whiskers of the cat.

Amongst the techniques used in this Composite Rite are: deification by drowning; creation of lamellae; formulae written in perfumed ink on papyrus; *defixiones*; offerings to the goddess; the use of a phylactery; a slander spell; invocation of the sun-god, identification with Adam and the use of Jewish *nomina magica*. This rite uses most of the main *nomina magica* in the *PGM*,[2] and by its grouping of them, acts as a useful compendium of these formulae, and an indication of their origins. This all contributes to why this rite is given pride of place at the beginning of *PGM* III. At the end of the rite are a list of the other applications to which this technique can be put (lines 161-164):

κάτοχος (*katochos*) – for binding (the charioteers) (T4)

ὀνειροπομπὸς (*oneiropompos*) – for sending dreams (to other people) (V2)

φιλτροκατάδεσμος (*philtrokatadesmos*) – love binding (L4)

διάκοπος (*diakopos*) – for the separation of lovers (L6)

μίσηθρον (*misēthron*) – for the production of hatred (L6)

See the following Table for the other Composite Rites to be found in the *PGM*.

---

[1] Each of these angels is identified as a god.

[2] Not all of these are tabulated in Table Ω.

Gods, Angels, Daimones, names of magicians, *nomina magica*	Non-Roman PGM Nos.	Categories	No. of lines	Betz Papyrus *PGM/PDM* Reference number	Objective/ Technique	Greek Headwords
[Bastet], Helios/ Meliouchos, Abrasax, Adam, Adōnai, Gabriēl, Raphaēl, Michaēl, Souriēl, Mithra, Erbēth, Pakerbēth, Bolchosēth, Sēth, Typhon, Iaō, Sabaōth, Adōnai, Abrasax, Iaeō, Ablannathanalba	3	Ω T4 L4 L6 V2	164	*PGM* III. 1-164	Ritual of the (embalmed) Cat: a multi-purpose invocation that requires the deification of a cat by drowning, making it an ambassador to the goddess for the main purpose of restraining charioteers. But it is also offered with subsidiary objectives such as sending dreams; binding a lover; causing separation and enmity. With drawings of charioteers.	ἐσιῆς[1] κάτοχος - line 162[2]
Osiris. Pitys, the Thessalian King, Ostanes (King)	4	Ω N L V P	120	*PGM* IV. 2006-2125	King Pitys' necromancy rite (version 2)[3] given to Ostanes.[4] Gives dreams revelations. A chthonic daimon acts as an assistant.	νεκυδαίμων[5] – lines 2027, 2054 Πίτυος ἀγωγή[6] - line 2006 κάτοχος[7] - line 2118 [name facility]
Erbēth, Iō Pakerbēth, Bolchosēth, Ra, Pan, Phorba, Maskelli	4	Ω T O D L3	96	*PGM* IV. 2145-2240	Multi-use iron talisman for divine assistance utilising three Homeric verses (*Il.* 10: 521, 564, 572), inscribed large, with formulae of consecration. Uses a tin lamella.	τριστιχος ὁμήρου πάρεδρος[8] τελετή - line 2199[9] φίλτρον - line 2222[10] καταδέσμου - line 2169[11] ἀγωγιμων - line 2231

[1] Ambassador. [Creation of] a [cat daimon as] an ambassador [to the gods].

[2] Binding.

[3] See chapter 6.7 Necromancy ('N') for the first version.

[4] Dieleman (2005), p. 269 just sees this as the acquisition of an assistant, whereas the mention of flax and buried bodies, confirms that it is definitely an operation of necromancy (in the original meaning of the word) with a love objective (ἀγωγή).

[5] *Nekudaimōn,* a daimon of the dead.

[6] [King] Pitys' rite of attraction. It uses the spirit of a dead person to compel the attention of the one loved or lusted after.

[7] Binding.

[8] Assistance from 3 Homeric verses. Not relevant to πάρεδρος in the sense of 'P.'

[9] Mystery.

[10] *Philtron*.

[11] *Defixio*.

Gods, Angels, Daimones, names of magicians, *nomina magica*	Non-Roman PGM Nos.	Categories	No. of lines	Betz Papyrus *PGM/PDM* Reference number	Objective/ Technique	Greek Headwords
Aktiōphis, Ereshkigal, Selene, Hermes, Hecate, Brimo, Zeus, Artemis, Persephone. Pachrates/Pankrates,[1] Hadrian	4	Ω L G2 V	181	*PGM* IV. 2441-2621	Invocation of various goddesses, with three invocations. General all-purpose rite for: love; attracting the uncontrollable; inflicting illness; destruction; sending dreams; accomplishes revelations. Includes hymns.	ἀγωγή – lines 2441, 2539 ἀγωγής - line 2543
Selene, Aphrodite Urania, Ereshkigal. Klaudianos (a magician)	7	Ω S L P G3 V	57	*PGM* VII. 862-918	Lunar rite of Klaudianos invoking Selene and the goddess of the Bear asterism, with a clay statue, in order to secure the love of a woman.[2]	Κλαυδιανοῦ σεληνιακὸν.[3] τελετή - lines 862, 872[4] πάρεδρον – line 885[5] [name facility]
	14	Ω X Z L L3 R	18	*PDM* xiv. 376-394	Various recipes using a drowned shrew-mouse	[Demotic] [n/h]
Pre, Geb, Heknet, the Rishtret, Nun, Nut, Anepo [Anubis], Maat, Iaho,	14	Ω B G2 E	36	*PDM* xiv. 805-840	Demotic Evocationary Bowl Skrying/vessel inquiry using eye paint for clairvoyance and the creation of a homunculus.	*šn-hne* *šn-hne…w*ᶜ - line 817 *šn… šn… šn* - line 827 *pḥ-nṯr* – lines 828, 833, 836
Total Ω		**7**	**672**			

Table Ω: Composite Rites utilising a number of different techniques.

---

[1] Pankrates was a prophet of Heliopolis who allegedly learnt magic from Isis herself during a 23 year sojourn in an underground *aduton*. See Fowden (1986), p. 166f.

[2] This complex rite includes the sending of dreams, and a catalogue of the daimones of each of the 12 hours. It is also a *paredros* rite, as suggested by Ciraolo (1995, 2001), p. 283, although here the assistant is referred to as an angel. It is identified by Dieleman (2005), pp. 262 and 271 as a simple 'Lunar spell (of attraction)' but it is so much more than that.

[3] Klaudianus' lunar rite.

[4] Mystery rite.

[5] Magical assistant.

7.0 The Mysteries and Initiation Rites - μυστήρια (*mystēria*), τελετή (*teletē*) (M)

These rites form six important sections in the *PGM*, and they include the three largest self-contained books in the *PGM* collection of papyri. However these are initiation rituals, Mystery rituals, designed to invoke one of the gods/goddesses for the benefit of the soul of the candidate, and are therefore not strictly magic. Although several gods are mentioned in the "Mithras Liturgy" they are essentially part of the ladder to the supreme, unnamed, god. Mithras is *not* part of the process, merely named as part of a backward looking reference to a previous experience had by the initiator.

The essential quality offered by the Mysteries is spiritual immortality, through an intimate association with one god/goddess, rather than immediate gratification of more worldly objectives (as in magic). The fact of their inclusion in the *PGM* simply points up the fact that pre-5th century CE magicians were often also initiates of the Mysteries. One of the stated objectives was to make the initiate conscious after death, rather than leaving him as just a wandering shade with no memory of his previous life. Part of the Mystery process may have included a descent into Hades/Amentet with a god/goddess such as Hermes as the psychopomp.[1]

The Mystery rituals are the missing link which has almost always been left out of the modern arguments concerning the relationship between religion and magic. The Mysteries, and specifically these passages in the *PGM*, were *not* transferred to the magic of Byzantium or the Latin West, and form no part of later magical practice in either of these cultures, because indeed they were not magic in the first place.

It should be remembered that the whole corpus of the *PGM* is a collection of many different papyri, of which the longest is *PGM* IV. Even within each papyrus are a number of other texts brought together by the magician who owned them. The three 'books' examined in this chapter were certainly separate books, with a separate existence, before being copied into these collections. The three Mystery rites found in three completely separate books within the *PGM* are:

1. The so-called "*Mithras Liturgy*" - *PGM* IV 475-820.
2. The *Monas* or *Eighth Hidden Book of Moses* - *PGM* XIII. 1-734.
3. The *Tenth Hidden Book of Moses* - *PGM* XXX, 734-1077.

[1] This is suggested by the tradition that Nero suddenly refused to be initiated at Eleusis after he was told this was what to expect, and so immediately declined the ordeal. When told, he may well have thought that meeting the shade of his mother, whom he had just recently murdered, was not such a brilliant idea.

There is no *Ninth Hidden Book of Moses* in the *PGM*. However there are seven references to the Κλειδί or *Key of Moses*.[1] Possibly this missing *Key* constituted the *Ninth Hidden Book of Moses*. In each case the reference is to just two things: the names of the Lords of the hours and days and the preparation of the incense referred to as the Egyptian 'bean.' [2]

There are also several smaller *teletai*. These rites are not designed to achieve the many and varied personal objectives of magic (health, love, lust, health, power, money, control, victory, injury, etc) but solely to provide immortality and the companionship of the gods to the candidate, the main function of all Mystery rituals.[3]

Early Christians also co-opted the term μυστήριον, *mystērion* to refer to some of the more esoteric parts of their developing theology. I suspect, but I cannot prove it, that they did this to compete with the surrounding pagan religions who offered various *mystēria*. Betz sums up the later Christian use of this term:

> Expansion of mystery cult terms and ideas is evidenced also by the early Christian literature. Paul frequently employs μυστήριον (mystery) as a term designating the revelation of the transcendental realities of the divine world and of wisdom, prophecy, history, the afterlife and, by implication, the sacraments of baptism and the eucharist as well. Ephesians extends the usage, calling the Gospel itself μυστήριον (mystery), something Paul himself did not do.[4]

Nevertheless the later Christian idea of μυστήριον never approached the original methods of immortalisation.

In the *PGM* these rituals make up just 1.0% of all the *PGM* by rite, but take up 10.5% of the lines. The fact that they are (as Mysteries) quite different from the surrounding magic rites is confirmed by their relative size as well as their contents. The four largest average 303-348 lines per rite, as opposed to between 6 and 64 lines per rite for operations of magic.[5] These Mystery rites are quite different in objective and method from the magical procedures.

---

[1] There are no less than six forward references to it in *PGM* XIII. 21-22, 30-31, 35-36, 59-60, 228-229, 382-383 [erroneously referred to by Betz as 282-83], 431-432 and one backwards looking reference to it in the *Tenth Hidden Book of Moses* XIII. 735-743.

[2] Speculatively, this Κλειδί τῇ Μοὒσέως (*sic*) might later have given its title (and maybe its contents) to the *Key* (a name used in some manuscripts for the *Hygromanteia*), and later to the *Clavicula Salomonis*.

[3] They are not even meant to provide 'enlightenment' in the way that quality is thought of by the current proponents of various New Age movements.

[4] Betz (1997), p. 251.

[5] See Table 13.

7.1 *Teletē* in the Great Magical Papyrus of Paris[1]

This rite comes second in this papyrus, immediately after the hailing and dedication to the gods,[2] and so was considered very important by the magician who owned/wrote this magical handbook. Betz or the translator Hubert Martin make the comment about this rite that "the purpose of this rite is not clear," but the rite is very clearly headed τελετή, *teletē* or 'initiation into the Mysteries.' It was therefore the solitary initiation and sacrifice that the magician undertook before attempting the other procedures in the papyrus.

This rite is not as long or complete as the other *teletai* examined in the rest of this chapter, but it is complete within itself. I surmise that the invocation to be pronounced is the text of the dedication that comes before it (lines 1-25).

The rite includes many of the stipulations already examined in chapter 4, including: a period of purification before the rite ('keep yourself pure for seven days beforehand'); careful selection of a date (the third day of the month after inundation); selection of a virgin place not disturbed by other humans ('before anyone walks on the area'); purification by the Nile waters ('jump into the river'); timing at dawn ('when half of the sun is above the horizon'); digging a trench round the altar to receive the sacrifice;[3] sacrifice of a white cock;[4] sacrifice of an 'unblemished' bird;[5] washing in the Nile; and walking backwards from the scene of the rite.[6]

The requirement to rub the eyes with the bile of an owl or the white of an ibis's egg, is of Egyptian derivation. The reasoning being that the ibis is the bird of Thoth, and the owl was the bird of Athena, the goddess of wisdom. This action will therefore give the initiate the wisdom and vision necessary.[7]

---

[1] *PGM* IV. 26-51.

[2] The first passage (lines 1-25) is not an incomplete request for an oracle, as suggested by the translator, but the dedicatory invocation for the whole papyrus, as well as probably being the invocational text for the following *teletē*. It is addressed to μεγαδαίμων καὶ ὁ ἀπαραίτητος, the "megadaimon, and the one who is not to be moved by prayer." The phrase "bring me news" near its end might be better translated as a request for guidance (in what follows).

[3] Seen in Greek accounts of *chthonic* rituals designed to raise the shades of the dead.

[4] Found in Jewish magical texts, and in later grimoires.

[5] Sacrificing an animal without blemish was a particular stipulation of Jewish religious sacrifice. It was also inherited by later grimoires.

[6] A procedure found later in the *Hygromanteia,* and later grimoires.

[7] Till the present day there is still a trade in owls and their bile for use in magic in India. Maybe this is rooted in the same thinking as the Egyptian practice. The hunting and trade in owls was banned in India in 1972, but the practice continues.

7.2 The Mithras Liturgy[1]

Although there has been some scholarly debate over the exact nature of the so-called Mithras Liturgy, it seems to me that the inclusion of the name of Mithra is no more significant than the inclusion of any one of a number of god names. I agree with Franz Cumont that here Mithra is clearly identified with Helios, the sun god, and not with the religion which so fascinated the Roman army. What is important however is that this rite is formulated with the objective of elevating the soul to the level of the gods, and so is in every sense the ceremonial directions for a Mystery religion, rather than a magical formula designed to achieve rather more petty objectives. William Brashear,[2] a scholar who has written the best overall introduction to the Graeco-Egyptian papyri, clearly states that in his opinion the initiatory rituals in *PGM* (i.e. The Mithras Liturgy, etc) are reminiscent of the procedures of the Mystery religions. This view also reinforces my view that religion, the Mysteries and magic are three distinct practices.

There has been much controversy over the naming of this passage by Dieterich as the 'Mithras Liturgy.' The phrase does not appear in the text itself. Helios Mithras does indeed appear, at the beginning of the text, but only as a backward looking reference to a previous event.[3] The text reads instead like a Mystery rite, which is precisely what it is. Utilizing the definitions of Mysteries and magic in chapter 1.2, this rite can be seen to belong to the former category despite the fact that it is embedded in a collection of magic formulae.

Betz states rather categorically that "the Mithras Liturgy, while using mystery-cult language and concepts, is not as such a mystery-cult text" but immediately shoots down his own assertion by adding "to be sure, however, there are no agreed definitions of what qualifies as a mystery-cult text."[4] I would like to point out that something "using mystery-cult language and concepts" is likely to be part of a Mystery cult, especially as its objectives, to bring the writer's daughter to immortalization, are so clearly laid out in the opening sentences. In the words of the old adage "if it walks like a duck, swims like a duck and quacks like a duck, then it probably is a duck."

It is not in any sense a liturgy to be performed publicly or as part of religious observance. No traditional Egyptian deities are mentioned. No Greek/Gnostic gods are mentioned except for Helios who only stands in for the 8th Heaven rather than as the god of the sun *per se.* Aiōn stands in for time, and hence

[1] *PGM* IV. 475-829.

[2] Brashear (1995), p. 3462.

[3] *PGM* IV. 482.

[4] Betz (2005), p. 33.

immortality, rather than being a god who is taken as an object of worship.[1] Greek abstract qualities such as *pronoia* and *psyche* are also mentioned, but they are clearly not gods in this context. If it had been a Mithraic rite then there would have to have been the standard Mithraic symbols for each grade of the planetary ascension such as crow for *Corax,* cup and wand for Mercury; lamp and diadem for Venus; helmet and spear for Mars, and so on. The present text certainly has a 7-fold planetary structure, but not even one of these well documented Mithraic symbols occurs anywhere in the text.[2]

Some scholars have tried to draw parallels between this text and the *Hermetica,* but this text is a practical instruction whilst the *Hermetica* are theological or philosophical texts, and so quite different.[3] Furthermore there are no traces of either Gnosticism or Christianity in the text, so that it is clearly a pagan Mystery ritual, with no hint of religion or philosophy (except as a theoretical underpinning for the 7 Heavens).

In order to understand exactly what this text is, and how it works, it will be helpful if we break it down into its constituent parts. The whole text is contained in *PGM,* IV 475-829.[4] It is not sufficient to break the text along the broad lines already proposed by Dieterich and Betz,[5] but it is necessary to analyse its parts in much greater detail. In doing this analysis a number of idiosyncrasies in the translation have become apparent, and some of these are discussed below.

Section Markers

The subheading Λόγος γ (*logos* 3) on line 587 has been translated as "the third prayer." Leaving aside the translation of *logos* as 'prayer,'[6] it begs the question as to the location of the first and second prayer/invocation? The first invocation is clearly marked by 'λόγου' in line 485, and begins with the indented text of line 487, but is not so identified in the translation. The second invocation begins at the indented text at line 559. It is only by identifying all three of these invocations that the structure of the textual divisions as used by the scribe can begin to be correctly established.

---

[1] Merkelbach (*Abrasax,* Vol. 3) denies the text has any connection with the Mithras cult, but tries instead to associate it with the Alexandrian god Pschai-Aiōn. But here again Aiōn is specific to the objective of timelessness and immortality rather than being an object of worship, and the Pschai-Agathos-Daimon is not even mentioned.

[2] This is like identifying a rite as Christian without any trace of Jesus Christ, the cross, or any other Christian iconography.

[3] *Vide* Festugière (1981), 4. 203, n. 1.

[4] The revised translation in Betz (2005), pp. 50-59 has been used, rather than the earlier one in Betz (1992). That version has the considerable advantage of much clearer line breaks and a number of key amendments, plus a facsimile of the original papyrus.

[5] Dieterich (1966); Betz (2005), pp. 29-31, 60-87.

[6] It might better have been translated as 'invocation.'

The Seven Invocations

Over the whole rite, the invocation beginnings marked by the use of the word ‘λογος’ can be established as follows:

1. The First invocation is clearly marked by λόγου in line 485 and the following indentation on line 487.[1]
2. The Second invocation beginning Σιγή (‘silence’) is repeated 5 times at:[2]
   a) the indented text at line 559,
   b) marked by the indented λό(γος) at line 573,
   c) in line 577 it is clearly marked as β λόγον (i.e. Second invocation),[3]
   d) in line 582 its repetition is simply indicated again by Σιγή, σιγή,[4]
   e) in line 623 its repetition indicated by ‘σιγή λό(γος).’
3. The Third invocation is marked by ‘Λόγος γ’ which begins on line 587[5]
4. The Fourth invocation begins with the indented line 639.
5. The Fifth invocation begins with the indented line 666.
6. The Sixth invocation begins with the indented line 678.
7. The Seventh invocation begins with the indented line 713.[6]

Following the structure indicated by these seven invocations makes for a much clearer and organic division of the ritual.

---

[1] Not marked by κλῆσις, as suggested by Betz (2005), p. 62. It is marked by λογος, which is then repeated in one form or another at the opening of every one of the seven invocations present in the text. Betz only appears to notice the first and third invocation plus some repetitions of the second. The remainder passes without a comment, whereas in fact they are clearly an important set of seven.

[2] As ‘silence’ is enjoined three times at the beginning of each repetition, and as the initiate is told to “at once put your right finger on your mouth,” it is almost certain that the invocation is an invocation of Harpocrates, the Egyptian god of silence (or at least so the Greeks thought), who is portrayed with his finger to his mouth.

[3] But here the translator unhelpfully translates it as “(the formula)” without being consistent and using “invocation/prayer.” He totally omits to mention the Greek letter *beta* which here represents “second” as in “second invocation.” By being inconsistent in the translation, the clear and useful pattern of seven numbered invocations is totally lost.

[4] “Silence, silence.”

[5] The Greek letter *gamma* is used here as a number 3.

[6] The identification of these seven invocations (not prayers) do *not* match Dieterich’s list of seven stages of ascension at all. To claim that seven stages marks it out as Mithraic, is to overlook the universality of a classification using the seven planets, which is common to many religions and practices. See Betz (2005), p. 138.

Secondary Divisions

Another clear division marker is the consistent use by the scribe of Ταῦτά, *tauta,* meaning a 'tie or magic knot' to mark the opening of a new section (see line 724). However the usefulness of this *as a marker* in the translation is reduced by Betz translating this same word in several different ways, such as 'after' or 'when,' etc, so this second clear pattern does not emerge in the English as it does in the Greek. To a lesser extent, Ἐπεὶ (translated as 'for') performs a similar function, as a marker, in introducing a sub-section. Utilising the above criteria, the text now easily falls into the following natural divisions.

The objective of the ritual is no less than the immortalization (ἀπαθανατισμός , *apathanatismos*) of the initiate carrying it out. The use of 'immortalisation' firmly characterises it as a Mystery rite designed to permanently enhance the spiritual status of the initiate doing it, rather than simply being a magical operation.

The Divisions of the Text

Part A: 475-485.[1] *Purpose and Practitioners.* The ritual opens with an appeal by the author to Providence and Psyche to be gracious to him. This is merely a formal introduction and benediction, and not an indication that these two entities are in any way central to the operation. The author then requests the boon of immortality (via an ascent into the Heavens), for his daughter, an only child, who is also an initiate (μύσται, *mystai*) of "this our power." This passage clearly identifies that the rite was designed by an initiate for the benefit of an initiate, in this case the writer's only daughter. It clearly implies that both have already achieved at least an initial initiation into a Mystery cult, and that this rite is designed to take the daughter to the next level. It is therefore certainly a Mystery rite, rather than either a piece of magic or a passage relating to religion.

There is then an interesting aside and forward reference,[2] about the "juices of herbs and drugs" to be revealed at the end of "my sacred treatise" (the present text), which were given to the author as ordered by Helios-Mithras through the medium of his archangel. The reference to Helios-Mithras is therefore a reference to a past event, not an integral part of the current ritual. This further confirms the complete inappropriateness of the title of *Mithras Liturgy.* The "greatest god" mentioned in line 643 is specifically not named, and there is no certainty as to his identity, despite 'Mithras' being suggested by a number of scholars eager to bolster the "*Mithras Liturgy*" thesis.

These juices and drugs were designed to allow the author to "go to heaven as

[1] Part 1 as per Betz (2005), p. 29.

[2] Probably originally a marginal gloss that has become inserted into the text by a copyist.

an 'eagle' and behold the all."[1] These include the herb *kentritis*[2] and an ointment made from a scarab beetle,[3] which are therefore likely to have both been psychoactive and designed to facilitate the whole immortalization experience. He obviously plans for his daughter to use the same herb and ointment.

***Part B*:**[4] 485-536. *The First Invocation*. This is designed to invoke the four Elements which make up the universe and more specifically the human body of the initiate. The invocation ranges through Spirit, Fire, Water, Earth, Air and Ether.[5]

Lines 516-536 are an appeal for immortality to Aiōn, the god of time or infinity, and therefore very apt for the process of immortalisation. At the end of this section the initiate identifies himself as the son of "PSYCHŌ[N] DEMOY PROCHŌ PRŌA... MACHARPH [.]N MOY PRŌPSYCHŌN PRŌE."[6]

***Part C*:**[7] 537-557. Breathing and Visualisation Instructions. The initiate is told to drawn in his/her breath from the rays of the sun, "drawing in as much as you can."[8] Then the initiate is to then visualise himself rising into

---

1 The Ophite doctrines list Eloaios as an Archon, who mounted to heaven in the form of an eagle. Therefore the reference to the eagle may be a coded acknowledgement of the initiatory degree attained by the author, which is the fourth degree of seven degrees.

2 Elsewhere in *PGM* the "eagle" (see line 485) is listed as a code for wild garlic. It is said that the herb for mounting to heaven like an eagle will be mentioned at the end of the "Liturgy," and *kentritis* is the only herb so mentioned. Scarborough (1991) therefore tentatively suggests 'wild garlic' which might be *Trigonella foenum graecum* or *hellebore*. Hellebore was a herb that remained very popular in Mediaeval magic, and so it might well be equivalent to *kentritis*. The jury is still out over a certain identification of *kentritis*, but if it was proven to be hellebore, then this is an example of the transmission of a herb used for magical purposes that appears in both the *PGM* and mediaeval grimoires. Additionally hellebore does have some psychedelic properties.

3 See lines 750-810.

4 Betz characterises the next section as Part II: 485-732. Part IIa. 487-536 is the invocation. Part IIb. 537-438 is a one line instruction to breathe in the rays of the sun, and Part IIc. 539-544 is simply a visualization instruction. Neither of the latter is significant enough to deserve a section all to itself, as given to them by Betz.

5 The Elements have been here capitalized to indicate the 5 philosophic elements rather than physical water, earth, etc.

6 See the first line (475) of the whole text.

7 Betz considers this part of the text as Part IIb. 537-538; Part IIc. 539-544; Part IId: 544-731. IIb and IIc are only a few lines each, and not worthy of categorisation as a whole section each.

8 This is equivalent to the well documented Chinese Taoist magical practice of breathing in the rays of the Moon, especially at full Moon and the Indian yogic practice of 'sun eating' or 'breathing' the sun at dawn.

midair.[1] There follows a description of what the initiate may expect to see. The gods will appear from the sun disk via a flute (translated by Betz as 'pipe'). The significance of this flute is that as the wind blows through it, it will emit different musical vowel tones, each capable of invoking a different god, at different hours of the day (hence the gods of the hours, a recurrent theme in magic). See chapter 4.3.

Part D: 557-586. *The Second Invocation*. This invocation is repeated twice. As it is prefaced by the command to "put your right finger on your mouth" and its first line is "Silence! Silence! Silence!" it is almost certainly an invocation of Harpocrates the god of silence, and a key magician's god. It reappears at various points in the ritual, as noted above.

In lines 576-586, the Second Invocation is repeated twice more. This section also introduces the hissing and popping sounds reputedly made by snakes and crocodiles, with the intent of subsuming the powers of their associated Egyptian gods.[2]

Part E: 587-616. *The Third Invocation*. Amongst the names invoked here is IAŌ. This is just another magical name, and there is no sense that the writer identified it specifically with the Jewish YHVH.[3] The last 10 lines of this invocation are the various gods identified as the "seven immortal gods of the universe," and called down by the permutations of the 7 Greek vowels that are associated with them.

Part F: 617-638. *The Epiphany of Helios*. The god is described as being "a youthful god, beautiful in appearance, with fiery hair, in a white tunic and a scarlet cloak (χλαμύς, *chlamys*), and wearing a fiery crown," and identified by Betz as Helios.[4] This section incorporates another repetition of the Second Invocation of Harpocrates ("Silence.").

Part G: 639-654. *The Fourth Invocation*. This is a greeting invocation of Helios, whom the initiate asks to "announce me to the greatest god."[5] It is clear

---

[1] This may be equivalent to the practice of Rising on the Planes taught at the end of the 19th century by the Hermetic Order of the Golden Dawn.

[2] Harpocrates is master of snakes and crocodiles, as can be seen for example on the Metternich *Stēlē*.

[3] The "NN" is identified by name as well as by the name of their mother. Despite the common use of patrilineal naming in Egypt and the Levant, identification for purposes of magic was *always* done in terms of the mother, not the father. In Hebrew texts this is usually abbreviated to פ ב פ, *Peloni bar Peloni*, "so-and-so son of so-and-so."

[4] But definitely *not* Mithras. Betz (2005), p. 98, even goes so far as to suggest a deliberate omission, simply because it does not fit his presupposition. "Did the author purposefully omit the name Mithras at l[ine] 696." I think we can safely assume that was not the case in such a carefully written and detailed text.

[5] Again the initiate identifies himself via the name of his mother.

that Helios has assisted in the spiritual rebirth of the initiate ("since he has been born again from you today, [and] has become immortal"). Helios is now able to introduce the initiate to other gods, which would not have been possible whilst he was still human and "born from the mortal womb of NN and from the fluid of semen."

A very interesting thing occurs at this juncture. The initiate is told to take along his Ephemeris so that he may determine which hour is most suitable for this meeting.[1] Even a specific hour is named (*thrapsiari morirok*).

Part H: 655-665. *Introduction to the Fates.* The celestial pole (associated with Harpocrates and Arktikē, the Bear goddess of Ursa Major) is mentioned in passing, and then the vision focuses on the seven virgins who are the Fates.

Part I: 666-677. *The Fifth Invocation.* This is the invocation to the seven Fates which are named in order. Then the Seven Pole Lords come forth, who are responsible for the pivot of the celestial sphere, and are therefore again associated with Harpocrates.

Part J: 678-712. *The Sixth Invocation.* This invocation is directed to the Pole Lords, "warders of the pivot of the celestial sphere...who turn...the revolving axis of the vault of heaven." All seven are named and hailed in turn. The goddess of the Bear asterism (Ἄρκτος, *Arktos*) then descends.[2] At that point the protective phylacteries must be kissed by the initiate, who has greeted this god with a bellowing sound (maybe commemorative of the Apis Bull).

Part K: 713-731. *The Seventh Invocation.* This confirms that the initiation has succeeded and is a form of death, release, and identification with a new immortal body Pheroura Miouri. This invocation will be answered by the god "with a revelation" spoken in verse, like the ancient Greek oracles. The initiate is reassured that even if the revelation contains many lines, he will remember it all infallibly.

---

[1] See chapter 4.2 section C where the hours are discussed at length. The habit of choosing a good hour in which to commence an important project died out in the 17th century Europe, but is very much alive in areas of Chinese culture where such ephemerides are printed annually in printruns exceeding 3 million copies. These are designed specifically to help choose the best hours for marriages, contract signing, moving house, and quite possibly (in the past) for introductions to the gods.

[2] The Bear asterism rotates around the North Pole annually and daily. The Ursa Major constellation is perhaps the most important in Chinese Taoist magic. Its revolution marks out time and the seasons, as well has the release of spiritual forces upon the earth, in a specific order, according to the Taoists.

Rubrics and Instructions:

Part L: 732-750.[1] *Evaluation of Candidates*. These are not 'supplemental rituals' as suggested by Betz,[2] but a description of different ways of doing the main ritual, with or without help. This part explains the procedure for hearing the god (with and without a medium) and the symbols needed in each case.

Part M: 750-812.[3] *Preparation of the Herbs and Drugs*. The translated title 'Instructions for Performance' is rather misleading as it effectively only contains two parts:

i) preparation of the Khepera balm by drowning a scarab (751-771, 792-796)

ii) the use of the plant *kentritis*[4] (772-791, 798-812)

Part N: 813-819. *Preparation of the Phylactery*. It is necessary to produce a protective phylactery to be worn by the initiate.[5] There is a long tradition of magicians wearing a lamen on their chest, which performs a protective function.[6]

The word to be written on the phylactery is προσθυμηρι, *prosthymeri*[7] (on the left arm) and probably *prosthymeri* (on the right). This is the true end of the text.

The Ascension Ritual

This is the sequence of ascent through those 7 Heavens, each marked by a planet, in the ascending order of Luna, Mercury, Venus, Sol, Mars, Jupiter, Saturn, to the 8th Heaven where resides the goddess of the Bear asterism,[8] and

---

[1] Marked by Betz (2005), p. 31 as Part IIIa: 732-750.

[2] Betz (2005), p. 80.

[3] Marked by Betz (2005), p. 31 as Part IIIb (1) (a): 751-778.

[4] Although it is an Egyptian plant, it is named here in Greek. It is similar to verbena with fruit like asparagus tips, but its identification is not certain. The plant is to be picked during a conjunction of the Sun and Moon in the zodiacal sign of Leo. Verbena remained an important herb in later European magic.

[5] In line 820 the ritual instruction concludes, but this one line is not worth a whole new section IV, as given to it by Betz.

[6] This tradition appears again in the *Hygromanteia* through to European grimoires like the *Key of Solomon*, right up to magical evocationary practice in the 21st century.

[7] It is probably just coincidence, but the sum total of the numeric values of these letters isopsephy comes to 1017, which is the same as δεσποσυνη, which means 'the power of the master' or 'absolute power,' a fitting phrase for a protection.

[8] This is the constellation of Ursa Major or the Plough, and it is highly significant in Chinese Taoist and other culture's magic. This asterism is seen either as a huge clock marking both seasons and hours (Chinese) or the polar 'handle' which turns the vault

the Pole Lords, and finally Helios-Mithra, in this instance not a stand-in for the Sun. In each Heaven there is a suitable invocation, and greeting of the resident deities, to ensure that the initiate passes through successfully. The objective is for the initiate to ascend without opposition, and with the blessing of each (planetary) Heaven. If this ritual was performed in a temple of the Mysteries, then the initiators would perform it theatrically, but as a solitary ritual the initiate has to rely upon the presence of the invoked deities to ensure success.

Supplemental Rituals

These are not 'supplemental rituals,' in the sense of adding extra support, but are optional rituals that now may be performed as a result of the initiation described above. This section is therefore an example of a Mystery initiation forming a portal to later magical techniques. It is also a concrete example of the magical principle that once the magician has 'bound' the spirit or god, he can thenceforth use a short-form ritual without going through the whole previously described procedure.

---

of heaven, and allows the stars to move across the sky (Egyptian). The Bear asterism or the Dipper takes a central place in Chinese Taoist magic.

7.3 Monas *or* Eighth Hidden Book of Moses[1]

Another self-contained book which runs to 1077 lines is to be found amongst the magical passages of the *PGM.* This book actually appears in the papyrus three times, each time in a different recension, which gives us plenty of material to explore and compare.

- i) The first version consists of *PGM* XIII. 1-234, with additional less relevant material at lines 235-343.
- ii) The second version of the book occurs at *PGM* XIII. 345-645.
- iii) A third version occurs at *PGM.* 646-720.

The Monad

Collating these versions it will be seen that the book has a number of titles, many of which later appear in the titles of European grimoires. These titles include:

The sacred book called *Monad,* or *Eighth Book of Moses,*[2] concerning the holy Name.
The sacred, *Hidden Book of Moses called Ogdoad,*[3] or 'holy.'[4]
The Eighth, Hidden Book of Moses.
The Hidden Book of Moses concerning the Great Name.[5]

This text is entitled *The Unique* by Betz, but μόνας, *Monas* (which is the title which appears in the papyrus) is in fact a much more apposite title translation. He footnotes that title to mean "by oneself, solitary," but I think it is much more likely that it is here used in the technical sense understood by ancient Greek philosophers, as the 'One.'[6]

---

[1] In *PGM* XIII. 1-734.

[2] *PGM* XIII, 1. Obviously Moses only wrote (or had ascribed to him) five books, the so-called *Pentateuch* or first five books of the Bible. As a magician of some note (along with Aaron) it is not surprising to find later books of magic pseudonymously attributed to him. The 6th to 10th Books of Moses were later used as the titles of predominantly German grimoires, and although the content is not the same, it is conceivable that these titles owed their origin to much earlier books of Moses such as the *8th, 9th* (missing) and *10th Book of Moses* referred to here.

[3] *PGM* XIII, 345. Translated by Betz as "eighth," but better left as Ogdoad, to indicate its technical meaning of the grouping of Eight Gods, rather than just reducing it to the numeral eight.

[4] A well known European grimoire of the 13th century with Greek origins is entitled *Liber Sacer* ('Holy Book') or *Liber Juratus.*

[5] *PGM* XIII, 733.

[6] 'Monas' was also later used by Dr John Dee (who was under-reader in Greek at Cambridge) for the title of one of his books which dealt with magical, geometric and alchemic topics, the *Monas Hieroglyphica.* The appearance of the word *Hieroglyphica* in the title of Dee's book also links his interest in the *Monas* back to Egypt.

The book's title could therefore either be interpreted as the *Eighth Book of Moses*[1] or the *Hidden Book of Moses about the Ogdoad or Eight Gods.* In fact the book is about the 7 gods of the hours, weeks and months, with the Ogdoad being the outermost supreme god, and so the latter title is more true to its contents.

In addition the word *monas* occurs again in other contexts related to magic, such as John Dee's *Hieroglyphic Monad,* a direct and conscious reference by Dee back to Egypt (as in 'hieroglyphic') and the Greek concept of the One, or *monas.* Accordingly I will continue to refer to this Book as the *Monas.* Let us look at the precise makeup of the book. Table 15 tracks the various contents of the *Monas* over its three recensions.

---

[1] There exist Books 6th to 10th supposedly by Moses.

Eighth Book of Moses[1] **(sections and line numbers in all three recensions)**	**Version 1 1-343**	**Version 2 344-645**	**Version 3 646-734**
Title of the *Monas*; timing, purity and ritual requisites (remain pure for 41 days, Moon in Aries, sleep on floor, door facing west, altar, 10 pinecones, sacrifice 2 white roosters, 2 lamps)	1-14	344-353, 363-380	646-652
Incense and flower specifications	15-29	354-362	
Invocation of the gods of the hours and weeks; figures of flour.	30-38	381-383	
Invocation using the square of natron;[2] popping and hissing noises to invoke the falcon-faced crocodile and nine-formed gods.	39-52	384-423	
Great name of 9 names; initiate recognition	53-60	424-432	
Text of invocation to be written on the natron *stēlē*; invocation of Aion, Helios and angels, Selene, in various languages; initiate assertion. Angel BIATHIARBAR…IAŌ. Also CHI CHI CHI…TIP TIP TIP… (See below lines 137-161)	61-90	568-602	
Setup of the tablet; sacrifices and libations; garments olive wreath; canopy of 365 gods, tripod; carved figure of Apollo with Bainchōōōch written forwards and backwards.	91-113	-	653-670
Rite sequencing, purification, performance of the Rite; 8 days of Helios greetings; gods of the week, day and hour called.	114-120	-	671-679
The eighth day; roosters, lamps; invoking from the *stēlē;* scarab talisman; milk and wine offerings; licking natron square	121-136	433-443	680-698
Hermetic invocation – Helios/highest god called in various languages; ALDABIAEIM and ABRASAX called. Also CHI CHI CHI…TIP TIP TIP… (See above lines 61-90)	137-161	444-470	699-703
"The Account of the Making of the World;" making seven gods from his laughs;[3] seven breaths; 1. Phōs-Auge; 2. Eschakleō; 3. Nous (Semesilam); 4. Genna; 5. Moira; 6. Kairos; 7. Psyche (and the Pythian serpent);[4] the seven vowels said.	162-206	471-532	
Pythian serpent, whose name is Ililloui…; Phobos; DANOUP… IAŌ, etc.	-	533-564	
The heptagram – saying the 7 vowels, in imitation of the Lord	207-209		
Asking the god for his secret name personal to the initiate	209-212	564-566	704-718
Technique to determine the current ruling god of the Pole Star	215-224		719-734
Summary address to child; instructions about incense, etc.	225-234		
Practical uses of the Book.; individual applications of the formula: invisibility; fetching a lover; exorcism; health; invoking Helios; killing snakes; resurrection; release from bonds, etc.	235-343		
Calling King of kings, daimon of daimones; angel ANAG BIATHI		603-618	
Ruler of the cosmos; magician names NN; protection from astrological destiny; calling to 4 quarters, earth, moon, water, sky.		619-645	

Table 15: Comparative structure of the three recensions of the *Monas* with line numbers.

[1] *PGM* XIII. 1-734.

[2] Natron was used as a universal purifier by the ancient Egyptians.

[3] Γελάσαντος, *gelasantos*, 'laughed' probably indicates that the god breathed out vigorously, rather than being amused, in order to create the seven following gods from his breath. See line 523 which confirms he was "breathing hard."

[4] See Figure 09.

7.4 The Tenth Hidden Book of Moses[1]

The first instruction in this text is that the magician should be certain that he/she has lists of the gods of the days and hours,[2] but also the rulers of the 12 months.[3] This is to ensure that these gods can be invoked before the main operation, in order to get their blessing but also so the magician can demonstrate that his is an initiate. He must also be equipped with the seven-letter name which "is what brings alive all your books."[4] This secret name is apparently to be found in the *Key* or Κλειδί, a book which has not been identified, but which may have been the missing *Ninth Book of Moses*.[5] This name (which may be the secret name of the ὀγδόας, Ogdoas) is the name of "the god who commands and directs all things, since to him angels, archangels, he-daimones, she-daimones, and [to which] all things under the creation have been subjected."[6] The name of the Ogdoas is probably Ē Ō CHŌ CHOUCH NOUN NAUNI AMOUN AMAUNI.[7] This name is used in the Compulsive formula, to be used when the gods invoked do not come readily. In a system that relies heavily on hierarchical threats (see chapter 4.1) this sounds like the most potent name available. It is therefore not surprising that the book also has an oath to be taken by the magician concerning the secrecy which needed to be maintained about this name and procedure.

Four other names are mentioned: the name of nine letters composed of a vowel sequence (AEĒ EĒI OYŌ); the name of 14 letters (YSAU SIAUE IAŌUS); the name of 26 letters (ARABBAOUARABA-ABARAUOABBARA); and the secret name of Zeus (CHONAI IEMOI CHO ENI KA ABIA SKIBA PHOROUOM EPIERTHAT). These names are referred to as γραμμάτων, *grammaton,* a likely source for the title of later grimoires or 'grammars' books of invocatory names. The text confirms that these names are necessary to assist boy skryers for operations of types 'B' and 'E.'

This initiation (τελεῖτή, *teleitē*) is to be performed at dawn, midday and sunset on the 13th day of the month.[8] The rite consists of a number of invocations and 'intimations.'

---

1 *PGM* XIII. 734-1077.

2 See Table 04 and Table 05.

3 See Table 07.

4 *PGM* XIII. 739.

5 These 'Books of Moses' should not be confused with later grimoires claiming to be the 6th-10th Books of Moses.

6 *PGM* XIII. 745-746.

7 *PGM* XIII. 789.

8 *PGM* XIII. 889.

The First Invocation

The first invocation (or *logos*) is a recitation of the 7 vowels (to get the god's attention. This name is referred to as an επταγραμματων, *heptagrammatōn,* meaning a seven lettered formula.[1] He invokes the secret names of the sun and the moon, the 'eyes of heaven,' the 28 Mansions of the Moon, and the Ogdoas. This is followed by an identification of the magician with the Ogdoas, "For you are I, and I, you."[2]

The Intimation[3]

This section of the rite involves aligning with the four quarters and summoning the 'eternal and unbegotten' good at each quarter with a vowel string. This has already been dealt with in some detail in the Spatial Orientation of chapter 4.3. The four animals of the quarters are the lynx, eagle, snake and phoenix, whilst life, power and necessity correspond to the three planes: above, mid-air and below.[4]

The Phylactery

There are two prescribed lamellae, one for the sun in gold, and one for the moon in silver. The silver (and possibly also the gold) lamella acts as the phylactery. Vowel strings are said six times over these and also written in ink on the lamellae. This writing is to be licked off the gold lamella at the beginning of the rite.[5] The details of the ritual for engraving and consecrating the lamella are outlined further down the text with specific details of timing.[6] Interestingly the archangel Michael is also invoked.

Orpheus and other Authorities

Orpheus is invoked and described as a θεόλογος, *theologos,* that is the revelatory or "one who converses with the gods." A note indicates that this invocation should be accompanied by strenuous breathing, bellowing, howling and hissing, forcing air into and out of the lungs.[7]

---

[1] The translator unhelpfully translates this word as 'heptagram,' which is a seven-sided geometric figure rather than a seven-lettered invocation, adding the comment "More pretentious terminology."

[2] Although this rite is a Mystery rite, the magician adds for good measure "Restrain [κατάσχες, *katasches*] the evil eyes of each and all of my legal opponents, whether men or women." I suspect that this restraining command might have been a later interpolation.

[3] Although rendered as 'instruction' by the translator, ὑπόδειξις is closer in meaning to 'intimation' or 'indication.'

[4] See *PGM* XIII. 880.

[5] See *PGM* XIII. 890-927 for the text of these invocations and inscriptions.

[6] See *PGM* XIII. 1001-1041.

[7] Reminiscent of some of the methods of *pranayama.*

The text then quotes a number of variant *nomina magica* from authorities such as Erotylos, Hieros, Thphes, King Orchos (Artaxerxes III), Zoroaster, Pyrrhus, Moses, and other worthies together with unidentifiable books such the *One and the Whole*. These are meant to provide alternative names, should the main ones fail.

The last three sections look like later additions especially as the fall at the end of the papyrus. They include: a formula for removing fear or anger; a formula to annul it; a secret prayer of Moses to Selene; and a formula for opening doors.

The title of the book, *The Tenth Hidden Book of Moses,* completes the text.

Gods, Angels, Daimones, names of magicians, *nomina magica*	Non-Roman PGM Nos.	Category	No. of lines	Betz Papyrus *PGM/PDM* Reference number	Objective/ Technique	Greek Headwords
	4	M	26	*PGM* IV. 26-51	Initiation and a method of sacrifice	τελετή[1]
Helios, Mithras, Psyche	4	M	348	*PGM* IV. 475-820, 828-829[2]	*Mithras Liturgy* (a Mysteries Initiation ritual)	μυστήρια[3] μύσται - line 477[4] σύστασις - line 779[5]
Zeus, Ares, Helios, Aphrodite, Hermes, Selene, Aion, Iaō, Sabaōth, Zagourē, Adōnai, Lailam, Anoch, Abrasax, Apollo, Achebykrōm, Phōs-Auge, Nous, Phrenes, Semesilam, Moira, Kairos, Psyche, Aphyphis, Christ	13	M	343	*PGM* XIII. 1-343	Initiation ritual: a sacred book called *Monad* or *Eighth Hidden Book of Moses*, version A (343 lines)	ΘΕΟΣ ΘΕΟΙ[6] Βίβλος ἱερὰ ἐπικαλουμένη Μονὰς ἢ Ὀγδόη Μοϋσέως[7] τελετή - lines 27, 230[8] ἀγωγή - line 237[9]
Aries, Moses, Achebykrōm, Zagourē, Iaō, Lailam, Phōs-Auge, Nous, Phrenes, Semesilamps, Moira, Hermes, Kairos, Psyche, Helios, Selene	13	M	303	*PGM* XIII. 343-646	*Monad* or *Eighth Hidden Book of Moses*, version B (303 lines)	Μοϋσέως ἱερὰ Βί[β]λος ἀπόκρυφος ἐπικαλουμένη ὀγδόη ἢ ἁγία[10]
Apollo, Helios, Selene, Ares, Hermes, Zeus, Aphrodite, Kronos	13	M	87	*PGM* XIII. 647-734	*Monad* or *Eighth Hidden Book of Moses*, version C (87 lines)	[n/h]

1 Initiation.

2 Lines 821-826 and 830-834 are misplaced fragments which are not connected to the "Mithras Liturgy," and so have been separated from it.

3 Mysteries.

4 Initiate.

5 Communion with the god.

6 GOD GODS.

7 The Sacred Book called *Monad* or *Eighth Book of Moses.*

8 Mystery.

9 Love rite.

10 Moses' Hidden Sacred Book called *Ogdoad* or *Holy.*

Gods, Angels, Daimones, names of magicians, *nomina magica*	**Non-Roman *PGM* Nos.**	**Category**	**No. of lines**	**Betz Papyrus *PGM/PDM* Reference number**	**Objective/ Technique**	**Greek Headwords**
Agatho Daimon, Ogdoas, IAŌ, Amoun, Anoch, Ieou, Outhro, Ablanathanalba, Ereschigal, Sabaōth, Adōnai, Michael, Abraham, Isaac, Jacob, Aion, Zeus, Aphrodite, Kronos, Ares, Selene.[1]	13	M	344	*PGM* XIII. 734-1077	*Tenth Hidden [Book of] Moses*[2]	[n/h] τελετή - lines 891, 898[3]
Total M		**6**	**1451**			

Table M: Mysteries and Initiation Rites.

[1] Magicians quoted in the *Tenth Book of Moses*: Orpheus; Erotylos in *Orphica*; Hieros; Thphes scribe of King Ochos; Eunos; Zoroaster; Pyrrhus; Moses; Ptolemaeus in the 5th book of the *Ptolemaica*.

[2] There is no *Ninth Hidden Book of Moses.* But see the note on this in chapter 3.2.

[3] Mystery initiation.

Appendix 1 – Main Gnostic Teachers - Magicians & Samaritans

Gnostic Movements and their Founders.				
Founder[1]	Dates	Disciple of	Sect	Origin/Location/Comment/Books
John the Baptist (ben Yahya)	c.6 BCE-30/36 CE	?	Johannites → Mandaeans	*Samaritan*. Johannites still exist as a sect. John is still viewed as the Messiah by the Mandaeans. Buried in *Samaria*.
Dositheos	d. 29 CE	John the Baptist	Dositheans	*Samaritan* magician, sometimes said to have come from Arabia.
Simon Magus aka Faustus	15 BCE-53 CE	Dositheos, Phillip	Simonians	*Samaritan* magician who levitated in front of the Emperor, and attempted to buy magical powers from the apostles.[2]
Jesus of Nazareth	6 BCE – 33 CE	John the Baptist	Nazarenes/ Christians	He was said to be *Samaritan*.[3] Not a Gnostic, but nevertheless the founder of a Jewish heresy that rejected Levite dietary laws, etc., but accepted the idea of a Messiah.
Menander	35-117	Simon	Menandrists/ Menandrians	*Samaritan* from Capparatea and Antioch. Probably a magician. Invented the 'bath of immortality.'
Cleobius	c. 50	Dositheos, Simon	Cleobians	*Samaritan* associate of Simon.
Ebion[4]	c. 70	Cerinthus	Ebionites	Jewish Christians in Pella, in *Samaria*. Arisen at the time of the destruction of the Second Temple (70 CE).
Simon of Gitta	c. 70			*Samaritan* author of *Megale Apophasis*. Sometimes identified with Simon Magus.

1 Benjamin Walker, *Gnosticism*, pp. 133-160.

2 See *Acts* 8:10-19.

3 Jesus was accused of being Samaritan and a magician by the Temple priests: "Then the Jews answered and said to Him, 'Do we not say well [true] that you are a Samaritan, and have a [tame] demon?'" in *John* 8:48. He was definitely pro-Samaritan as shown by the Parable of the Good Samaritan, *Luke* 10:29-37.

4 Maybe Ebion did not exist, but Ebionites simply derived their name from the Hebrew for "poor."

Gnostic Movements and their Founders.

Founder[1]	Dates	Disciple of	Sect	Origin/Location/Comment/Book
Cerinthus	c. 70	Menander?	Cerinthians	In Alexandria and Asia Minor. Predicted Christ's reign of 1000 years. Jewish-Christian.
Saturninus, Satornilus or Satornil	90-150	Menander		Antioch. Founder of Syrian Gnosticism. Urged sexual restraint. Ascetic
Carpocrates	78-138	Cerinthus, Saturninus	Carpocratians, Harpokratianoi	Probably a magician. In Alexandria and Antioch. Called themselves 'Gnostics.' Incorporated Egyptian Mysteries Greek philosophy, reincarnation. Rejected Yahweh. *Secret Gospel of Mark, Gospel according to the Hebrews*
Cerdo	f. 135 d. 143	Simon Magus, Menander	Cerdonians	Syrian. Taught in Rome. Teacher of Marcion
Basilides	85-145	Matthias, Glaucias, Menander	Basilideans	Alexandria, Egypt and southern Europe. Favoured Abraxas. Author of the *Exegetica,* 24 books of commentary on the Gospels.
Isidorus	125 fl.	Basilides	Basilideans	Son of Basilides
Marcellina	145 fl.	Carpocrates	Carpocratians	Established in Rome
Euphrates	d. 160		Peratae	Worshipped the serpent which they identified with the brass serpent fashioned by Moses
Marcion	90-165	Cerdo	Marcionites	Wealthy ship owner who came to Rome in 140 and was excommunicated in 144 CE. Involved with astrology, symptomatic of Chaldaean roots. Rejected the OT and most of the NT. Later absorbed by Manicheans
Theudas/ Theodas		St Paul		A link in the Valentinian chain

Gnostic Movements and their Founders.				
Founder[1]	**Dates**	**Disciple of**	**Sect**	**Origin/Location/Comment/Books**
Montanus	110-172		Montanists / Cataphrygians	Pagan convert to Christianity, castrato from Phrygia. Montanus claimed to be the Paraclete. Sect founded in 156. Puritan, celibate, Adventist, practised baptism for the dead.[1] Tertullian was a Montanist.
Valentinus	110-175	Basilides, Theodas	Valentinians	Alexandria, Rome. The most influential Gnostic teacher. Urged sexual freedom. *Gospel of Truth.* 'Mainstream' Gnosticism.
Theodotus, the currier	Fl. 140-170	Valentinus		Responsible for *Excerpta ex Theodoto*
Marcus of Memphis	f. 150 d. 175	Valentinus	Marcosians / Marcians	Egyptian magician, taught in Asia Minor and Gaul. For him magic, proto-Kabbalah and isopsephy (numerology) were important.
Alexander Abonouteichos the Paphlagonian	c.105-180	Apollonius of Tyana	Cult of Glycon	Alexander from Abonouteichos in Asia Minor, said to be grandson of Asclepius. Maybe an indirect founder of the Ophites
Severus	d. 183	Marcion	Encratites	Theology included Ialdabaoth
Apelles	180 fl.	Marcion	Apelliasts	Taught in Rome and Alexandria. Used a skryer called Philumēnē.[2]
Prodicus	180 fl.	Carpocrates		Persian. Alexandria to Carthage.
Ptolemaeus	180 fl.	Valentinus		Rome. Author of *Letter of Ptolemaeus to Flora.*[3]
Justinus	c. 200		Ophites	Worshipped the serpent (ὄφις, *ophis*) of *Genesis,* and identified it with the brass serpent made by Moses. Justinus was not the founder of the Ophites, but an Ophite teacher. Primal power is Priapus. Author of *Book of Baruch.*

[1] These doctrines may have influenced the modern day Mormons.

[2] See Mead (1960), pp. 250-252.

[3] See Mead (1960), pp. 383-390.

Gnostic Movements and their Founders.				
Founder[1]	**Dates**	**Disciple of**	**Sect**	**Origin/Location/Comment/Boo**
Heracleon	140-200	Valentinus	Valentinians	Wrote commentary on St. John. "The most distinguished Valentinian."[1]
Numenius of Apamea	150-209	Marcion		'Chaldaean' astrologer who influenced the neo-Platonist Plotinus
Axionicus	f. 220	Valentinus		Antioch
Bardesanes	154-222	Valentinus	Bardaisanites	Assyrian from Edessa. Well educated from a wealthy family. Converted from Christianity. *Hymn of the Pearl.* Taught in Egypt, Syria, Asia Minor, Spain, and Gaul. Contributed doctrinal to Manicheans, and probably to the Cathars.[2]
Plotinus	204-270	Numenius		Philosopher and Neoplatonist, not a Gnostic
Priscillian	340-386	Marcus of Memphis		Magician and Bishop of Avila, later excommunicated and executed for heresy, sorcery and studying magic, then later venerated as a martyr.
Eutactus	c. 340	Peter of Capharbarica, near Hebron	**Sethians**	Active in Egypt and Asia Minor. Venerated Seth, son of Adam an Melchizedek. Sometimes linked with the Ophites, Barbelites, etc. *Three Stelae of Seth, Zostrianos, Second Treatise of the Great Seth, Paraphrase of Shem, Allogenes, Trimorphic Protennoia.*

Table 16: The main teachers and development of Gnosticism clearly demonstrating the preponderance of magicians and Samaritans amongst the early founders.

[1] See Mead (1960), pp. 391-392.
[2] See Mead (1960), pp. 392-405.

Appendix 2 - Excluded Fragments

These passages provide too little material to properly identify either their purpose or method. They are listed in full in order that the corpus of Graeco-Egyptian magical material analysed in this book is complete. Although these fragments make up 5.0% of all the *PGM* rites numerically, their actual extent in terms of number of lines is very small, averaging only 5 lines per rite, a total of 1.9% of the whole corpus.

Gods, Angels, Daimones, names of magicians	**Non-Roman *PGM* Nos.**	**No. of lines**	**Betz Papyrus *PGM/PDM/SM* Reference number**	**Objective/ Technique**
	7	2	*PGM* VII. 591-592	[probably misplaced]
	12	5	*PDM* xii. 1-5	Fragmentary
	14	2	*PDM* xiv. 933-934	About stones
	14	2	*PDM* xiv. 1180-1181	Moon in Scorpio fragment
Zabaot, Sabaōth	25	0	*PGM* XXVa-d	(omitted by Betz)
	26	0	*PGM* XXVI. 1- 21	*Sortes Astrampsychi*[1]
	29	10	*PGM* XXIX. 1-10	Literary poem not magic
	30	0	*PGM* XXX a-f	Oracle questions. Omitted by Betz
	31	0	*PGM* XXXI a-c	
	34	24	*PGM* XXXIV. 1-24	Fragment of a Greek romance
	37	26	*PGM* XXXVII. 1-26	Oath about sexual cleanliness
Bainchōōch	41	9	*PGM* XLI. 1-9	Fragment
Abraxas, Adōnaia, Elōe	45	8	*PGM* XLV. 1-8	Invocation
	46	4	*PGM* XLVI. 1-4	Revelation from a god?
Iō-Erbēth, Iō Sēth, Iō	46	5	*PGM* XLVI. 4-8	To subject and silence (an enemy)
Hera, Selene	52	9	*PGM* LII. 1-9	[amulet format]
	53	0	*PGM* LIII	Omitted by Betz. Forgery (according to Brashear). Arabic period
	54	0	*PGM* LIV	
	55	0	*PGM* LV	
	56	0	*PGM* LVI	

[1] The oracle of Astrampsychus first appeared in the 3rd century CE. It contained 91 questions and 910 answers, originally written in Greek. Versions of this oracle were later very popular in the Middle Ages. Omitted by Betz.

Gods, Angels, Daimones, names of magicians	Non-Roman PGM Nos.	No. of lines	Betz Papyrus *PGM/PDM/SM* Reference number	Objective/ Technique
	60	5	*PGM* LX. 1-5	Fragment with *charaktēres*
Anubis	61	30	*PDM* lxi. 1-30	Revelation
	61	12	*PDM* lxi. 30-41	
	61	1	*PDM* lxi. 42	
	63	7	*PGM* LXIII. 1-7	Using the 7 vowels
	63	7	*PGM* LXIII. 13-20	Formula with seven vowels
	63	4	*PGM* LXIII. 21-24	
Iō Abrasax	69	3	*PGM* LXIX. 1-3	
	73-76	0	*PGM* LXXIII - LXXVI	Oracle questions. Omitted by Betz
	82	12	*PGM* LXXXII. 1-12	Formulary including roots
	85	6	*PGM* LXXXV. 1-6	Non-magical fragments
Hekate	93	6	*PGM* XCIII. 1-6 *SM* 100 a	Fragmentary sacrificial rite
	93	15	*PGM* XCIII. 7-21 *SM* 100 b	Fragmentary rite
	98	0	*PGM* CXVIII	Magical scroll. Omitted by Betz
	121	14	*PGM* CXXI. 1-14	List of a variety of evils.[1]
Sabaōth, Adonai	125	1	*PGM* CXXVa-f. *SM* 98	
Barbaratham, Seseggen Barpharangēs	-	22	*SM* 75	Invocation and sacrifice instructions
	-	10	*SM* 89	Fragment
Iaō, Adōnai	-	8	*SM* 91	Fragment
Total -	**29**[2]	**269**		

Table 17: Fragmentary passages in the *PGM* which have insufficient content to identify either a method or an objective, and hence are not categorised. These are listed here for the sake of completeness, so that every scrap of Graeco-Egyptian magical text has been analysed. None of these fragments have a headword.

[1] Because it was enclosed in an ouroboros it was categorised as a phylactery by Betz, but it is not either that, nor is it an amulet. It may not even be a magical papyrus.

[2] The total does not include rites omitted by Betz.

Appendix 3 - An Angelic Hierarchy on a Phylactery

Line number[1]	Angelic function	Angel Name
15	sits upon [in] the first heaven	*Marmaraôth*
17	sits upon [in] the second heaven	*Ouriêl*
20	sits upon [in] the third heaven	*Aêl*
23	sits upon [in] the fourth heaven	*Gabriêl*
26	sits upon [in] the fifth heaven	*Chaêl*
28	sits upon [in] the sixth heaven	*Moriath*
31	sits upon [in] the seventh heaven	*Chachth*
34	in charge of the lightnings	*Riopa*
35	in charge of the thunders	*Bonchar*
37	in charge of the rains	*Tebriêl*
39	in charge of the snows	*Tobriêl*
41	in charge of the Nile waters	*Thadama*
43	in charge of earthquakes	*Sioracha*
45	in charge of the sea	*Souriêl*
47	in charge of serpents	*Eithabira*
49	sits in charge of rivers	*Bêdlia*
52	sits in charge of roads	*Phasousouêl*
54	sits in charge of cities	*Eistochama*
57	in charge of the mountains	*Nochaêl*
58	sits upon the streets	*Apraphês*
60	sits in charge of the…	*Einath, Adônês Dechochtha*
64	sits upon the serpents	*Iathennouian*
66	sitting upon the firmament	*Chrara*
67	sitting upon the … in the midst of the two Cherubim, forever and forever	*[Yahweh]*
71	the God of Abraham and the God of Isaac and the God of Jacob	*[Yahweh]*

Table 18: Angelic hierarchy as found on a fourth century amulet.[2]

[1] Not significant in itself. For the purpose of location on the amulet.

[2] Kotansky (1994), No. 52, pp. 276-281.

Appendix 4 – A Selection of *Nomina Magica*

Nomina Magica	Title/Ascription	Notes
ABERAN NEMANE THŌUTH/ ABERAMEN THŌOU	The god of the 3rd hour of the day, relating to Thoth.	Table 04
ABLANATHANALBA	A common palindrome, probably of Hebrew origin, which might be read as 'ABLA NATHAN ALBA.'	
ABRAŌTH	From Abra ('four') and AŌTH, the four lettered supreme name.	
ABRAXAS/ABRASAX	The 'anguipede.' A solar god with snakes as legs, a cock's head, whip and shield. Numerically equal to 365.	
ACHRAMACHAMAREI	The god of the heavenly firmaments.* See AKRAMMACHAMAREI	
ADŌNAI/ADŌNAEI/ADONAIŌS /ADONAĒL	Hebrew אדני for 'the Lord,' often inflected in its Greek form, which form then assumes the role of a god. Also god of the 12th hour.	Table 03
AERTHOĒ	The god of the 12th hour of the day.	Table 03
AGATHOS DAIMON/ AGATHA DAIMON	'The good daimon' was originally invoked at Greek banquets, but in the *PGM* becomes a god in its own right.	
AIŌN	The god of time or eternity	
AKEPHALOS	The Headless god. Sometimes identified with Besas. See Figure 40.	
AKRAMMACHAMAREI	The god of the 3rd hour of the day. See ACHRAMACHAMAREI	Table 03
AKROUROBORE	The ouroboros.	
AKTIŌPHIS	Goddess related to Hekate.	
AKTIŌPHIS ERESCHEICHAL NEBOUTOSOUANT	The triple form of Hecate.*	
ALDABIAEIM	The magical name of nine (?) letters of the highest god	
AMEKRANEBECHEO THŌYTH	The god of the 3rd hour of the day.	Table 04
ANOCH (ANOK)	"I am" used by magicians when self-proclaiming themselves as a god.	
AŌABAŌTH	The god of this day in which I bind.*[1]	
AŌNKREIPH	The terrestrial…*	

[1] This one was just the day on which the original talismanic binding was done.

Nomina Magica	Title/Ascription	Notes
AŌTH	[The god] before whom every god prostrates himself and every daimon shudders, for whom every angel completes those things which are assigned.	*PGM* XII. 117
ARBATHIAŌ	See ABRAŌTH	
ARBRATHIABRI	The god of the 12th hour of the day.	Table 04
ARCHPHĒSON (?)	The god of the underworld, the god who leads departed souls [like] holy Hermes.*	
AROUROBAARZAGRAN[1]	The god of Necessity.*	
ARPNOPHĒR	Horus the son	II. 118 VII. 362
ARPŌN/AREPO (Latin)	Harpokrates	IV. 2433
BAALSAMĒS	Baal, Sun = Lord Sun	IV. 1019
BACHACHUCH/ BAZACHUCH/BACHUCH	A great daimon in Egypt.*	Lead tablet Carthage
BADĒTOPHŌTH ZŌTHAXATHŌZ	Secret name of Genna & Spora.	XIII. 176
BAINCHŌŌŌCH/ BAINCHOOCH	A daimon sometimes translated as 'Spirit of darkness.' See Figure 19.	
BAISOLBAI	The god of the 6th hour of the day.	Table 04
BAKAXICHUCH	Prince of Daimones.[2]	
BALSAMES	Originally a Phoenician sun god.	
BARBATHIAŌ	See ARBATHIAŌ	
BASMA	In the name of...	IV. 1736
BATHIABĒL	The god of the 11th hour of the day.	Table 04
BAZĒTŌPHŌTH	The god of the 2nd hour of the day.	Table 03
BESBYKI	The god of the 10th hour of the day.	Table 04
BESSYN BERITHEN BERIO	Secret name of Phōs-Auge	XIII. 165
BIAIOTHANATOS	The spirit of one prematurely dead, utilised by *defixiones*.	
BIATHIARBAR BERBIR SILATOUR BOUPHROUMTRŌM (36 letters)	Secret name of Kairos (Time).	XIII. 190
BLABLEISPHTHEIBAL	The firstborn god of the Earth on which you lie.[3]*	
BOLCHOSĒTH	Sacred name of the Egyptian god Seth.	

[1] Variant of OREOBAZAGRA.

[2] Usually glossed as Soul of Darkness or Son of Darkness, but glossed in Greek as ὁ τύραννος τῶν δαιμόνων in an unpublished tablet in the Getty Museum. See Kotansky and Spier (1995), p. 319.

[3] Earth meaning soil rather than the planet.

Nomina Magica	Title/Ascription	Notes
BŌRPHORBABARBOR	A supreme name sometimes associated with Hekate or Selene.	
CHEAUNXIN	[The god] who granted as a favour to men, movement by the joints of the body.*	
CHNOUB/CHNOUBIS	Chnum the Great	XIII. 1058
CHNOUPHI/ CHNOUBIS	Lion-headed serpent god, a combination of Chnoum and Kneph.	
CHŌOICHAREAMŌN	The god who fashioned every kind of human being.* A form or title of Amoun.	
CHŌOUK	Darkness	VII. 361
CHORBORBATH	The god of the 6th hour of the day.	Table 04
DAMNAMENEUS[1]	The goddess of the 4th hour of the day. Mentioned in the *Ephesia Grammata.*	Table 03
DANOUP CHRATOR BERBALI BARBITH	Secret name of the strong man of the god's seventh 'laugh.'	XIII. 197
DIATIPHĒ	The god of the 8th hour of the day.	Table 04
ĒCHETARŌPSIEU	The god who granted vision to all men as a favour.*	
EIAU AKRI LYX…	The god of the 6th hour of the day.	Table 03
ELŌAIOS	The Hebrew god El in Greek guise. One of the Aeons in Gnostic belief.	
ENPHANCHOUPH	The god of the 5th hour of the day.	Table 04
ERBĒTH	Set.[2]	
ERESCHIGAL[3]	Babylonian deity transformed into a daimon in the *PGM.* Often associated with Hekate.	
ESCHAKLEŌ	Name of the second god created.	XIII. 171
ĒSTHANCHOUCHĒN	See ENPHANCHOUPH.	
HARPOKRATES/ HARPOCRATES	The young Horus with side-lock and finger to mouth. Especially significant for magicians.	
HARPON-KNOUPHI	A form of Harpocrates-Chnoubis. [4]	

[1] One of the constituents of the *Ephesia grammata.* See chapter 4.5 for an explanation of her nature, and a new tentative translation of the *Ephesia grammata.*

[2] See IŌ ERBĒTH IŌ PAKERBĒTH.

[3] See AKTI[O]PHI[S] ERESCHEICHAL NEBOUTOSOUANT.

[4] See Harpon-Knouphi in *PGM* III. 435-6, 560-63; IV. 2433; VII. 1023-25; XXXVI. 219-20.

Nomina Magica	Title/Ascription	Notes
HECATE	The tremor-bearing, scourge-bearing, torch-carrying, golden-slippered blood-sucking netherworldly and horse-riding one.*	
HEKA/HIKE	Egyptian god of magic.	
HEKATE	See HECATE.	
IABAŌTH	Combination of IAŌ and Sabaoth	
IAŌ[1]	The god appointed over the giving of soul[s] to everyone.* The Greek transliteration of יהוה, IHVH.	
IAŌ IBOĒA	The god who lords over the heavenly firmaments.*	
IAŌTH	A combination of IAŌ and Sabaoth	
IARBATHA	Related to Helios.	*PGM* I. 142; XII. 94-95
IBAS	A Samaritan form of IAŌ	
ILLOU ILILLOU… ITHŌR MARMARAUGĒ PHŌCHŌ PHŌBŌCH	Secret name of the Pythian serpent that arose after the god's creation of Psyche.	XIII. 195
IŌ ERBĒTH IŌ PAKERBĒTH	Invocation of Set.[2]	
IŌNA[3]	The god who established earth and heaven*	
IPOS	A Samaritan form of IAŌ	
ISOS[4]	The god who has the power of this hour in which I bind you.*[5]	
ITHUAŌ	The god of heaven.*	
KENTABAŌTH	Kenta (torments/rage?) + Sabaoth	
KHNUM (CHNUM)	Egyptian ram god.	
KMEPH (KNEPH/KMĒPHIS)	Egyptian serpent god.	
KORĒ	Proserpine, later a demon	
LAILAM	The god of winds and spirits.*[6]	
LAMPSOURĒ	Sun god	V. 62 LXII. 27
LĒMNEI	The god of the 3rd hour of the day.	Table 04
MARMARIAŌTH	The god of the second firmament who possesses power in himself.*	See also AŌTH.

1 See ŌĒ IAO EEĒAPH.
2 See binding talisman of Sēth in *PGM* XXXVI. 1-34, which has the full formula.
3 Possibly a form of IAŌ, as demiurge.
4 Not Jesus as suggested by Gager (1992), p. 63.
5 Specifically for the hour of the original operation.
6 Not related to the Hebrew *le-olam,* forever.

Nomina Magica	Title/Ascription	Notes
MARMARIPHEGGĒ	MARMARI followed by φέγγη, 'light, splendour and lustre.'	
MARMOROUTH	See MARMARIAŌTH	
MASKELLI MASKELLŌ	A common formula.[1]	
MENCHTHŌTH	Thoth the beneficent	II. 77
MENE	Epithet of the Moon goddess Selene.	
MENEBAIN	The god of the 1st hour of the day.	Table 04
MOIRAI	The Fates.	
MOLTIĒAIŌ	Protector (?).*	
MORMOTH	The god of the 4th hour of the day.	Table 04
MOU RŌPH	The god of the 11th hour of the day.	Table 04
NACHAR	The god who is the master of all tales.*	
NAPUPHERAIŌ	Necessity (?)*	
NEBOUN	The god of the 2nd hour of the day.	Table 04
NEBOUTOSOUALĒTH[2]	Moon goddess.	
NEGEMPSENPUENIPĒ	The god who gives thinking to each person as a favour.*	
NEICHAROPLĒX	The god who holds the power of the places down beneath [Underworld].*	
NETHMOMAŌ	The god who has given you (the corpse [body]), the gift of sleep and freed you from the chains of life.*	
NOUPHIĒR	The god of the 5th hour of the day.	Table 04
ŌĒ IAO EEĒAPH	The god of the air, the sea, the subterranean world, and the heavens, the god who has produced the beginning of the seas, the only-begotten one who appeared out of himself, the one who holds the power of fire, of water, of the earth and of the air.*	
ORBEĒTH	The god of the 7th hour of the day.	Table 04
OREOBA[R]ZAGRA[3]	See MASKELLI MASKELLO.	
OSORNOUPHE	Osiris the good	VII. 444
OSORONNOPHRIS	Osiris the beautiful.	
OUĒR/ OUĒRI	Great	XII. 346 XIII. 1061
OUERTŌ	The great one of earth.	XII. 265
OUMESTHŌTH	The god of the 7th hour of the day.	Table 04

[1] In full it reads MASKELI MASKELLŌ PHNOUKENTABAŌ OREOBAZAGRA RHĒXICHTHŌN HIPPOCHTHŌN PYRIPĒGANYX. Parts of this formula also appear as free-standing *nomina magica*.

[2] See also AKTI[O]PHI[S] ERESCHEICHAL NEBOUTOSOUANT.

[3] See AROUROBAARZAGRAN.

Nomina Magica	Title/Ascription	Notes
OUROBOROS	The serpent that swallows its tail, seen on phylacteries and also used as a protective floor circle.	
PAKERBĒTH	Set.[1]	
PANMŌTH	The god of the 8th hour of the day.	Table 04
PHARAKOUNĒTH	The god of the 1st hour of the day.	Table 04
PHĒOUS PHŌOUTH	The god of the 9th hour of the day.	Table 04
PHNOU	The Abyss	CVII. 1
PHNOUPHOBOĒN	The Father-of-Father god (*sic*).*	
PHŌKENGEPSEUARET-ATHOUMISONKTAIKT	The god of the 5th hour of the day.	Table 03
PHŌOUTH	The great snake	IV. 1683
PHŌR	Short form for next two entries.	
PHORBA	Short form for next entry.	
PHORBABORPHORBABOR-PHORORBA	The true name that shakes Tartarus, earth, the [ocean] deeps and heaven.*	
PHRĒ	Egyptian Sun god Ra.	
PHROUER	The god of the 1st hour of the day.	Table 03
PIBĒCHIS	The falcon.	IV. 3007
PNOUTHIS	He of god.	
PŌPHOPI	Apophis	XIXB. 14
PSINŌTH	Son of the female falcon (?)	VII. 316
PSICHOM	The image/power	VI. 711
PTAH	Egyptian Creator god.	
RABCHLOU	Master of Power, a Samaritan angel	XXXVI. 175
RAPŌKMĒPH	The god who presides over all penalties of every living creature.*	
SABAŌTH	The god who [brought] knowledge of all the magical arts.* Derived from the Hebrew Tzabaoth, the god angelic and spirit hosts, rather than the usual interpretation of armies.	
SABERRA	Anubis	XIa, 3
SALBALACHAŌBRĒ	The god of the underworld who lords over every living creature.*	
SARNOCHOIBAL	The god of the 10th hour of the day.	Table 04
SEMEA	Syrian goddess. Maybe associated with Shamash. Also addressed as a king.	III. 29 V. 429 III. 207
SEMESEILAM	The god who illuminates and darkens the world.* Nous, Phrenes.	XIII. 174

[1] See IŌ ERBĒTH IŌ PAKERBĒTH.

Nomina Magica	Title/Ascription	Notes
SENSEGGEN BAR PHARAGGĒS (PHARANGĒS)	A secret name for Harpocrates.[1]	
SENTHENIPS (SESENIPS)	The god of the 4th hour of the day.	Table 04
SET (SETH)	Egyptian god opposed to Osiris, equated with Typhon by the Greeks.	
SOUARMIMŌOUTH	The god of Solomon.*[2]	
SOUPHI	The god of the 2nd hour of the day.	Table 04
STHOMBLOĒN	The god who is lord over slumber.*	
THŌBARRABAU	The god of rebirth.*	
THORIOBRITITAMMAŌRRANGADŌ	Secret name of Moira	XIII. 184
THYMENPHRI	The god of the 9th hour of the day.	Table 04

Table 19: Selection of *nomina magica* and gods of the hours and days. As one can see the *nomina* are primarily the names of gods or daimones, and not just gibberish.*[3] This list does not include well-know classical gods like Anubis, Aphrodite, Apollo, etc.

This table demonstrates that many of the supposed *nomina magica* are actually names of gods, minor time gods and daimones. This helps to support my contention that many more of the *nomina magica* will turn out to be unidentified proper names of gods or daimones, rather than random nonsense syllables made up by magicians.

* Some of the less common attributions (marked with an asterisk) are derived from a 3rd century lead binding talisman found in Carthage. Although written on lead and invoking a spirit of the dead, this was not secreted in a grave or watercourse, and so may be a talisman and not strictly a *defixio.* Although these meanings are not for the most part supported in the modern scholarly literature, the thorough and logical format of the wording of that particular talisman leads me to believe that these were some of the interpretations accepted by the magicians of that century, even if their original meaning might have been otherwise lost. This talisman is one of the very few sources which bother to gloss meanings that must have been common knowledge for contemporary practitioners.[4]

[1] See chapter 4.5 and *PGM* II. 107. Nothing to do with fig trees in ravines near Baaras.

[2] An interesting attribution, possibly a secret name for the god of the Jews.

[3] The asterisked descriptions are quoted directly from Gager (1992), No. 10, pp. 62-64.

[4] It is conceivable that some of these meanings were later tacked on to the *nomina magica* by practitioners who no longer understood the original meanings (like IAŌ for example) but that nonetheless were considered valid meanings within the *milieu* of the *PGM.*

Appendix 5 – Distribution of Rite Types across Papyri

Code	Category of Rites Procedure/Objective	VII	IV	xiv	XII	III	V	I	XXXVI	VIII	XI	XIII	II	VI	IX	X
	Amulets	X		X	X											
2	Amulets personalised															
	Evocationary Bowl Skrying/ Vessel Inquiry	X	X	X												
	Calendrical Considerations	X	X		X	X										
	Defixiones	X	X				X									
	Evocationary Lamp Skrying	X	X	X			X	X								
	Face-to-Face Encounter with a god	X	X				X									
	God's Arrival	X	X	X		X				X				X		
2	Invocation of a god	X	X	X	X	X	X	X								
3	Invocation of the Bear goddess	X	X	X	X											
I	Health			X	X				X							
	Invisibility	X						X				X				
	Hymns (as integral parts of another rite)	X	X			X	X	X		X			X	X		
	Foreknowledge and Memory					X		X								
	Love Rites of Attraction	X	X	X		X			X							
2	Love Fetching	X		X	X											
3	Love Potions	X	X	X					X							
4	Love Binding	X	X							X						
5	Love Enforced by hunger or insomnia	X	X		X											
6	Love Separation			X	X											
7	Other Love Rites	X	X	X	X						X					X

Code	Category of Rites Procedure/Objective	VII	IV	xiv	XII	III	V	I	XXXVI	VIII	XI	XIII	II	VI	IX	X
M	Mysteries and Initiation Rites		X									X				
N	Necromancy	X	X													
O	Homeric magic and divination	X	X													
P	*Paredros* or Assistant Daimon	X	X		X			X			X					
Q	Daimonic Possession and Exorcism		X				X									
R	Rings & Gemstones, Magical	X	X	X	X		X									
S	Statues, Magical	X	X		X		X			X						
T	Talismans, general	X	X				X		X						X	
T2	Victory Talismans	X														
T3	Restraining Anger Talismans	X			X	X			X						X	X
T4	Binding or Coercion Talismans	X							X							
U	Phylacteries	X	X													
U2	Phylacteries (integral parts of another rite)	X	X	X	X	X		X			X	X				
V	Visions and Dream Revelation	X	X	X	X		X			X			X			
V2	Sending Dreams			X	X	X										
W	Prayers	X	X			X										
X	Other Magical Procedures	X	X	X	X		X		X		X					
Y	Herbs and Plants		X	X	X											
Z	'Evil Sleep,' Blindness and Death			X												
Ω	Composite Rites	X	X	X		X										
-	Excluded Fragments	X		X	X											
	Total Types Present	33	29	21	19	11	11	7	7	5	4	3	2	2	2	2

Table 20: The distribution of all Rite Types over the main Papyri, in descending order from the most to the least representative. Selected from the 15 largest papyri.

Appendix 6 – The Constituent Parts of a Rite

Many of the individual procedures are divided into well defined sections. These are often clearly marked in bold in Betz following a clear titling or indent in the Greek.

a) *Praxis* or method or formula
b) *Logos* or invocation or formula to be spoken
c) Preparation, such as fasting
d) Production and assembly of equipment
e) Compounding Incenses
f) Production of perfumed Inks
g) Words to be engraved or written
h) Salutation to be said upon a god's arrival
i) Characters or signs to be used
j) Compulsive procedure, if the spiritual creature is tardy
k) Any alternative procedures should the main procedure fail
l) Offering or sacrifice
m) Prayer or hymn
n) Phylactery for protection
o) Applications of the main rite to various sub-objectives
p) Dismissal formula

Not every rite has every one of these ingredients, because not every rite needs each of these. For example the manufacture of amulets is simple, and seldom requires more than the text to be used and maybe an invocation to be spoken. However a major invocation of a god will often need most of the above ingredients, especially the *praxis, logos,* phylactery, compulsive formula and dismissal formula.

Glossary

Greek

Term	Transliteration	Meaning
ἅγιος	*hagios*	Holy
ἀγρυπνητικόν	*agrypnētikon*	Love enforced by hunger or insomnia. Operations of type 'L5'
ἀγωγή	*agōgē*	Love rite of attraction. Operations of type 'L'
ἀγώγιμον	*agōgimon*	Love fetching. Operations of type 'L2'
ἀμαύρωσις	*amaurōsis*	Invisibility rite. Operations of type 'I'
ἀπόλυσις	*apolusis*	Dismissal formula used at the end of rites
Ἀποτελεσματικὴ πραγματεία	*Apotelesmatikē Pragmateia*	Greek title of the *Hygromanteia*
ἄγγελος	*angelos*	Angel or messenger
ἀπαθανατισμός	*apathanatismos*	A ritual for immortalization
ἀπόλυσον	*apolyson*	The practice of dissolving or 'loosening' spells
αὐθέντης	*authentēs*	King (of the spirits) that has full power to swear, or to be bound by the magician
αὐτοψία, αὔτοπτος	*autopsia, autoptos*	Face-to-Face Encounter with a God (without the need for a skryer). Operation of the type 'F'
βοτάνη	*botanē*	Herbs, especially as used in magic
γαστήρ	*gastēr*	A bottle designed to imprison the spirit
γαστερομαντεία	*gasteromanteia*	Procedure for capturing a spirit in a (metal) bottle
γόης	*goēs*	A magician who evokes demons/spirits as distinct from gods[1]
γοητεία	*goēteia*	Evocation of demons/spirits
δαίμων	*daimōn*	An entity half way between the human and the divine, or one's personal daimon
δαίμων καταχθόνιος	*daimōn kataxthonios*	Chthonic daimon
δακτύλιος, δακτύλιον	*daktylios, daktulion*	(Magical) ring. Operations of type 'R'
δεσμός	*desmos*	Binding
διαβολή	*diabolē*	Slander spell
διάκοπος	*diakopos*	Separation of lovers or friends. Operations of type 'L6'
εἴδωλον	*eidōlon*	Image, image of a god/goddess, magical figures on a talisman

[1] The meaning of this word, and the next, has been explored in depth in Dickie (2003), pp. 12-16, 29-33. Here the later meaning, as used in the grimoires, has been used.

εἰκών	*eikōn*	An image, of a saint, god, or (in the *Hygromanteia*) a planet.
ἔκλυσις	*eklysis*	Releasing (from a binding)
ἔκστασις	*ekstasis*	Ecstasy or trance
ἐξορκίζω	*exorkizō*	Conjure
ἐπαοιδός, ἐπαοιδήν	*epaoidos*	Incantation
επιβακτορομαντεία	*epibaktoromanteia*	Water-pot evocationary skrying
ἐπικαλοῦμαι	*epikaloymai*	Summon (a god)
εὐχή	*euchē*	Prayer. Operations of type 'W'
θεουργία	*theurgia*	Invocation of the gods
θυμίαμα	*thymiama*	Incense
θυμοκάτοχον	*thymokatochon*	Restraining Anger Talismans. Operations of type 'T3'
ἱερὰ μαγεία	*hiera magia*	Holy magic
κάνθαρος	*kantharos*	Scarab
κατάδεσμος	*katadesmos*	*Defixio.* Operations of type 'D'
κατάδησον	*katadēson*	Bind.
κατακλητικόν	*kataklētikon*	An image or statue that calls or summons customers (for use outside a business premises)
κάτοχος	*katochos*	Binding or coercion talismans. Operations of type 'T4'
Κλεὶς ἡ Μοϋσέως	*Kleis hē Moyseōs*	*Key of Moses*
λαβών	*labōn*	To take (ingredients), as in a recipe. Sometimes loosely translated as 'spell'
λεκανομαντεία	*lekanomanteia*	Evocationary Bowl Skrying/Vessel Inquiry. Operations of type 'B'
λυχνομαντεία	*lychnomanteia*	Evocationary Lamp Skrying. Operations of type 'E.'
μαγεία	*mageia*	Magic
μαγεύματα	*mageumata*	Piece of magical art
μαγικὴ ἐνέργεια	*magikē energeia*	Magical power
μάγος	*magos*	Magician
-μαντεια	*-manteia*	Usually defined as 'divination,' but in the context of a suffix to words like γαστερομαντεία or νεκρομαντεία, it means 'a magical procedure'
μνημονική	*mnēmonikē*	Memory. Part of the operations of type 'K'
μύστης	*mustēs*	An initiate of the Mystery
μυστήρια	*mystēria*	The Mysteries. Operations of type 'M'

μυστοδόκος	*mystodokos*	Receiving the Mysteries. Initiate
νεκρομαντεία	*nekromanteia*	Necromancy, invocation and interrogation of a spirit of the dead. Operations of type 'N'
νυκτολάλημα	*nyktolalēma*	Rite for making a woman talk in her sleep
νικητικόν	*nikētikon*	Talismans for victory in court or the arena. Operations of type 'T2.'
ὁμηρομαντεῖον	*homēromanteion*	Magic by verses of Homer. Operations of type 'O'
ὀνειραιτητόν	*oneiraitēton*	Visions and Dream Revelation. Operation of type 'V'
ὀνειροπομπός	*oneiropompos*	Sending dreams. An operation of type 'V2'
ὁρκισμός	*orkismos*	Conjuration; administration of an oath (to a spirit)
οὐρανία αλωαφς Σολομῶντος	*ourania alōaphs Solomōntos*	Solomonic lamen in the *Hygromanteia,* according to Preisendanz
οὐρανία σφραγίς	*ourania sphragis*	The lamen in the *Hygromanteia*
οὐροβόρος	*ouroboros*	The image of a snake with its tail in its mouth
οὐσία	*ousia*	The essence of a thing or person which is used to establish a magical connection, e.g. hair or nail clippings
πάρεδρος	*paredros*	Familiar Spirit or Assistant Daimon. Operation of type 'P'
περιάμματα	*periammata*	An amulet, i.e. a general personal protection carried around on a day-to-day basis. Operation of type 'A' or 'A2'
πιβακτρομαντεία	*pibaktromanteia*	Skrying using a water pot. Also *epibaktromanteia*
πνεῦμα	*pneuma*	Spirit, breath
πρᾶξις, πραγματεία	*praxis, pragmateia*	Magical operation, rite
πρόγνωσις	*prognōsis*	Foreknowledge. Part of the operations of type 'K'
Σολομωνική	*Solomōnikē*	A Greek book of magic associated with Solomon
στήλη	*stēlē*	A stone tablet carrying an inscription; a rectangle of metal, stone or natron with an inscription; the inscription itself
στοιχεῖα	*stoicheia*	An ensouled talisman or statue
στοιχειοκρατοῦσα	*stoicheiokratousa*	A (female) magician who fixes the spirit or god to the material talisman or statue, to bring it 'alive'

στοιχειωματικός	*stoicheiōmatikos*	A magician who creates *stoicheia* (ensouled statues) or talismans.[1] Partaking of operations of type 'S'
σύμβολα	*symbola*	An item which forms part of the same chain of correspondences, e.g. a lion is a *symbola* of Helios and laurel leaves that of Apollo
σύστασις	*systasis*	God's Arrival. Divine encounter or association with a god. Operations of type 'G'
σφραγίς	*sphragis*	Seal
τέλεσμα	*telesma*	Talisman. Operations of type 'T'
τελετή	*teletē*	Initiation Rite. Operations of type 'M'
ὑγρομαντεία	*hygromanteia*	A method of evocationary skrying using a virgin boy skrying in water, basin, kettle, etc
Ὑγρομαντεία	*Hygromanteia*	The common title of the *Magical Treatise*
ὑδρία	*hydria*	Water pot, which may have been used by Solomon to imprison demons
ὑδρομαντεία	*hydromanteia*	*See* hygromanteia
ὑποτακτικά	*hypotaktika*	Rite for subjugation
φαρμακός	*phamakos*	A dealer in herbs and poisons, and only incidentally one involved in magic
φιαλομαντεία	*phialomanteia*	Saucer divination or skrying
φίλτρον	*philtron*	Love Potions. Operations of type 'L3.'
φιλτροκατάδεσμος	*philtrokatadesmos*	Love binding. Operations of type 'L4.'
φιμωτικὸν	*phimōtikon*	Rite for silencing someone. Operations of type 'T4.'
φυλακτήριον	*phylaktērion*	Phylactery, protection to be worn by the magician during a rite. Operations of type 'U'
χαρακτήρ	*charaktēr*	Characters found on talismans, made of straight and curved lines ending with small circles
χαριτήσιον	*charitēsion*	Winning favour

1 Not the "persons who cast nativities from the signs of the zodiac," as defined by Liddell and Scott.

Demotic

Term	Transliteration	Meaning
bȝ n kky	*bainchōōōch*	The spirit or soul of darkness
bȝ.w		Souls
dbn.phr		The ritual of encircling for purification
ẖbs		Lamp
ḥkȝ	*heka*	Magic
ḥkȝy		Magician
ḥkȝy.t		Sorceress
ḥm nṯr		High priest / the god's servant
hpe n sẖ		Written spell
ẖry-ḥb ḥry-tp		Chief lector priest, the most learned priest in the temple, who wore a leopard skin as insignia
k.t		Another method
mn mn mn		The point where the name of the person against whom the rite is directed should be inserted. Similar to 'NN' in Latin grimoires
mt.t a		Magical formula
nh.t		A 'protection' or amulet
nktk bin		'Evil sleep' and death. Operations of type 'Z'
nsb		The technical term for an ink 'lick off' spell
nṯr	*neter*	Gods
pḥ-nṯr	*peh-netjer*	God's Arrival. Operations of type 'G.' Consultation with an ensouled divine statue, or in a dream
pẖr		Enchant, also "to encircle" or "go around" as in the circle of protection
pẖr.t		Magical/medical recipe/prescription
pr- 'nḫ	*per-ankh*	House of Life, a combined library, scripyorium and college
qmȝ tȝ		Evocationary Lamp Skrying. Operations of type 'E'
rẖ-ẖ.ṯ		Magician
sd m rȝ		Snake eating its tail – the Ouroboros
sẖ pr- 'nḫ		Scribe of the House of Life (sometimes used to describe a magician)
sẖr		To exorcise
šm.w		Oracles
šn		Encircled or enchanted

šn-hne	*shen ben*	Evocationary Bowl Skrying/Vessel Inquiry. Operations of type 'B'
šn.t		Conjuration
šnty		Exorcised
šnw		Conjurations/conjurer
w' gswr		Ring [rite]
wd͟ʒw		Health, a general term for an amulet, confirming their most frequent *raison d'être*. Operations of type 'A'
wdnw		Litany
wp.t-rʒ		Ring
z-mt.t		[Magical] formula

The meanings listed in this Glossary are not the full definition of each term, for which consult a lexicon, but solely their meanings appearing in the context of magic in the *PGM*. The words are not always presented in the lexical form, but in the form encountered in the *PGM*. Some of the Greek words are not directly relevant to the *PGM* but relate to later forms of Greek magic such as is found in the *Hygromanteia*, but are included here because many of these later forms derive from the magic of the *PGM*.

Bibliography

Ancient Egyptian and Mesopotamian Sources. These are in the broadest sense the Pyramid and Coffin texts, as have been edited by R. O. Faulkner (1973-78), followed by some chapters in the *Book of the Dead.*[1] These texts by definition focus on post-mortem magic, and are not for the most part for the use of the living. Specific magical handbooks from the Dynastic period are therefore few. The most significant Demotic texts are from *The Demotic Magical Papyrus of London and Leyden,* which was originally edited and translated by F. L. Griffith and Herbert Thompson (1904). Their translation has however been improved upon and incorporated into Hans Dieter Betz's *The Greek Magical Papyri in Translation, including the Demotic Spells* (1996).

Robert Ritner's *The Mechanics of Ancient Egyptian Magical Practice* (2 Volumes, 2008) is undoubtedly one of the best secondary texts as it concentrates on the mechanics of specific magical techniques. The ten essays in Panagiotis Kousoulis's *Ancient Egyptian Demonology: Studies on the Boundaries between the Demonic and the Divine in Egyptian Magic* (2011) expand Ritner's work, and underline the point that demons/daimones in the Egyptian world do not have the negative connotations that later accreted to them, but act as intermediaries between the gods and man in a ritual context. Otto Neugebauer's *Egyptian Astronomical Texts* III (1969) gives useful background to the selection of auspicious times by Egyptian magicians. Wallis Budge's *Amulets and Talismans* (1970) shows the mass produced nature of many Egyptian amulets as opposed to the 'made for one purpose' talismans. Despite no longer being held in such high regard by academia, the breadth of Budge's research (across a wide range of cultures) and linguistic reach has seldom been matched.

Erica Reiner's *Astral Magic in Babylonia* (1995) is one of the best organised summaries of Mesopotamian magic, a source of some of the techniques examined in this book.

The Graeco-Egyptian Magical Papyri. The Greek Magical Papyri in Translation edited by Betz (1996) is the key text for the Graeco-Egyptian magic in the Ptolemaic period and the first five centuries of the Christian era. To Betz must also be added Robert Daniel and Franco Maltomini's *Supplementum Magicum* (1990/1992). Jacco Dieleman's *Priests, Tongues, and Rites* (2005) supplements this with very useful background material. The original Greek texts, which are essential for checking the exact meanings of key technical words, are to be found in Karl Preisendanz's *Papyri Graecae Magicae, Die Griechischen Zauberpapyri* (1928/1931, revised by Henrichs and reprinted in 1973-74, 2001).

William Brashear's *The Greek Magical Papyri: an Introduction and Survey* (1994),

[1] Budge (1967).

is still the most systematic and well organised summary of the *PGM*. Other important secondary sources include Marvin Meyer and Paul Mirecki, *Ancient Magic and Ritual Power* (1995), and Christopher Faraone and Dirk Obbink, *Magika Hiera: Ancient Greek Magic and Religion* (1991) both of which contain key essays on the topic. John Gager, *Curse Tablets and Binding Spells from the Ancient World* (1992), is a very thorough study of one specific method (the *defixiones*) but also contains useful material on other forms of Graeco-Egyptian magic. Naomi Janowitz's *Magic in the Roman World: Pagans, Jews and Christians* (2001), although a relatively slim volume, makes a number of very useful observations on the intersection of these three cultures, and draws a clear line between learned magic and witchcraft.[1] Matthew Dickie in *Magic and Magicians in the Graeco-Roman World* (2001) provides cogent background on the various shades of meaning of Latin and Greek terms for the different varieties of magic and divination.

Greek and Roman Necromancy by Daniel Ogden (2001) ventures into the mechanics of necromancy and evocation from a classical Greek perspective, with excellent chapters on lecanomancy (bowl skrying) and the technology of necromancy and magic. Ogden takes a linguistic approach carefully distinguishing the different shades of meaning of the original Greek and Latin technical terms of magic, a very necessary approach. His *Magic, Witchcraft, and Ghosts in the Greek and Roman Worlds* (2002) provides an excellent selection of classical sources, with incisive comments.

Theurgy. Undoubtedly the most important source for theurgy is Iamblichus. The most usable editions of the Greek text of *De Mysteriis* are those of Gustav Parthey (1857) and Des Places (1996). The English translations of *De Mysteriis* include the charming but wordy translation by Thomas Taylor (1821), and that of Alexander Wilder (1911), but these have been surpassed by the 2003 translation by Clarke, Dillon and Hershbell. Emma Clarke's *Iamblichus De Mysteriis: a Manifesto of the Miraculous* (2001) and Finamore and Dillon's *Iamblichus, De Anima* (2002) provide useful background material. More recently, work by Ilinca Tanaseanu-Döbler in *Theurgy in Late Antiquity* has provided a window on the development of theurgy after Iamblichus. Algis Uždavinys in *Philosophy & Theurgy in Late Antiquity* (2010) provides useful, if somewhat controversial, links between magic, theurgy and Neoplatonic philosophy in Late Antiquity.

1 "The ancient practitioners [of magic] would have been horrified to be lumped together with "witches" and "warlocks" " – Janowicz (2001), p. 3.

Abbreviations

ANRW	*Aufstieg und Niedergang der römischen Welt*
Goetia	*Goetia* (volume 1 of the *Lemegeton*)
Juratus	*Liber Iuratus Honorii* (ed. Gösta Hedegård)
PDM	*Papyri Demoticae Magicae*
PGM	*Papyri Graecae Magicae: The Greek Magical Papyri in Translation*
SM	*Supplementum Magicum*
SSM	*Summa Sacre Magice*
SWCM	*Sourceworks of Ceremonial Magic*
ZFPE	*Zeitschrift für Papyrologie und Epigraphik*

Mesopotamian Magic Sources

Frantz-Szabó, Gabriella. 'Hittite Witchcraft, Magic, and Divination,' in Jack M. Sasson (ed.), *Civilizations of the Ancient Near East,* III. New York: Scribner, 2007-2012.

Jacobsen, Thorkild. *The Treasures of Darkness; A History of Mesopotamian Religion*. New Haven and London: Yale University Press, 1976.

King, Leonard. *Babylonian Magic and Sorcery,* 1896 rpt. Kessinger 2010.

Thompson, R. Campbell. *The Reports of the Magicians and Astrologers of Nineveh and Babylon*. London: Luzac, 1900.

Thompson, R. Campbell. *The Devils and Evil Spirits of Babylonia…translated from the original cuneiform texts*. 2 Volumes. London: Luzac, 1903; rpt. New York: AMS, 1976.

Oppenheim, A. 'The Golden Garments of the Gods' in *JNES* 8, 1949, pp. 172-93.

Oppenheim, A. Leo. *Letters from Mesopotamia; Official, Business, and Private Letters on Clay from Two Millenia*. Chicago and London: The University of Chicago Press, 1967.

Pingree, David. 'Mesopotamian Astronomy and Astral Omens in Other Civilizations,' in *Mesopotamien und seine Nachbarn*. (ed.) Hans-Jörd Nissen and Johannes Renger. Berlin: Dieterich Reimer, 1982.

Reiner, Erica. *Astral Magic in Babylonia.* Transactions of the American Philosophical Society, New series, Vol. 85, No. 4, 1995.

Van Buren, E. Douglas. *The Symbols of the Gods in Mesopotamian Art*. Rome: Pontifical Biblical Institute, 1945.

Ancient Egyptian Dynastic Magic Sources

Borghouts, J. F. *Ancient Egyptian Magical Texts.* NISABA. Leiden: Brill, 1978.

Breasted, James Henry. *The Edwin Smith Surgical Papyrus.* 2 Vols. Chicago: University of Chicago Press, 1930.

Budge, E. A. Wallis. *Book of the Dead.* New York: Dover, 1967.

Faulkner, R. O. *The Ancient Egyptian Coffin Texts.* 3 Vols. Warminster: Aris and Phillips, 1973-78.

Johnson, Janet H. 'The Demotic Magical Spells of Leiden I 384' in *OMRO* 56, 1975, pp. 29-64.

Griffith, F. L. and Thompson, Herbert (ed. & trans.). *The Leyden Papyrus. An Egyptian Magical Book.* (originally published London: Grevel, 1904 as *The Demotic Magical Papyrus of London and Leyden*); rpt. New York: Dover Publications, 1974.

Lichtheim, M. *Ancient Egyptian Literature,* 3 Vols. Berkeley: University of California, 1973-80.

Neugebauer Otto, and Parker, Richard A. *Egyptian Astronomical Texts,* III. *Decans, Planets, Constellations and Zodiacs.* Providence: Brown University Press; London: Lund Humphries, 1969.

Smith, Mark. *Traversing Eternity: Texts for the Afterlife from Ptolemaic and Roman Egypt.* Oxford: OUP, 2011.

Ancient Egyptian Dynastic Magic Secondary Literature

Andrews, Carol. *Amulets of Ancient Egypt.* London, 1994.

Brier, Bob. *Ancient Egyptian Magic.* New York: Perennial/Harper Collins, 2001.

Budge, E. A. Wallis. *Egyptian Magic.* 1899. rpt. New York: Dover, 1971.

Budge, E. A. Wallis. *Amulets and Talismans.* Originally published as *Amulets and Superstitions;* rpt. New York: University Books, 1961.

D'Auria, Sue, Peter Lacovara and Catharine Roehrig. *Mummies & Magic: the Funerary Arts of Ancient Egypt.* Boston: Museum of Fine Arts, 1992.

Gahlin, Lucia. *Egypt: Gods, Myths and Religions.* London: Hermes, 2007.

Gardiner, A. H. 'Professional Magicians in Ancient Egypt' in *Proceedings of the Society for Biblical Archaeology,* 39.

Kousoulis, Panagiotis. *Ancient Egyptian Demonology. Studies on the Boundaries between the Demonic and the Divine in Egyptian Magic.* Orientalia Lovaniensia Analecta, Leuven: Peeters, 2011.

Lehner, Mark. *The Complete Pyramids.* London: Thames & Hudson, 2008.

Manniche, Lise. *An Ancient Egyptian Herbal.* London: British Museum, 1989.

Morenz, S. *Egyptian Religion.* London: Methuen, 1973.

Pinch, Geraldine. *Egyptian Mythology.* Oxford: OUP, 2002.

Pinch, Geraldine. *Magic in Ancient Egypt.* Austin: University of Texas, 2006.

Quibell, J. E. *The Ramesseum.* London: Quaritch, 1898.

Rankine, David. *Religion and Magic in Ancient Egypt.* London: Avalonia, 2002.

Rankine, David. *Heka: Egyptian Magic.* London: Avalonia, 2006.

Ritner, Robert K. *The Libyan Anarchy.* Leiden: Brill, 2009.

Ritner, Robert K. 'Egyptian Magic: Questions of Legitimacy, Religious Orthodoxy, and Social Deviance' in A. B. Lloyd (ed), *Studies in Pharaonic Religion and Society in Honour of J. Gwyn Griffiths.* London, 1992.

Ritner, Robert K. 'Egyptian Magical Practice under the Roman Empire: the Demotic Spells and their Religious Context,' in *ANRW* II, 18.5, 1995, pp. 3333-3379.

Ritner, Robert K. *The Mechanics of Ancient Egyptian Magical Practice.* [Studies in Ancient Oriental Civilization No. 54.] Illinois: Oriental Institute of the University of Chicago, 2008.

Sauneron, Serge. *The Priests of Ancient Egypt.* New York: Grove Press, 1960.

Sharpe, Samuel. *Egyptian Mythology and Egyptian Christianity.* London: Carter, 1896.

Smith, Mark. 'A New Version of a well-known Egyptian Hymn,' in *Enchoria* 7, pp. 115-49.

Tait, W. J. 'Theban Magic' in S. P. Vleeming (ed.). *Hundred-Gated Thebes.* Leiden and New York, 1995.

Graeco-Egyptian Magic Sources

Bagnall, Roger and Peter Derow. *Historical Sources in Translation: The Hellenistic Period.* Oxford: Blackwell, 2004.

Bell, H. I., A. D. Nock and Herbert Thompson. *Magical Texts from a Bilingual Papyrus in the British Museum.* Oxford: OUP, 1933.

Betz, Hans Dieter (ed). *The Greek Magical Papyri in Translation, Including the Demotic Spells,* Volume One Texts. 2nd edition. Chicago: University of Chicago Press, 1996.

Boeft, J. Den. *Calcidius on Demons (Commentarius Ch. 127-136).* Leiden: Brill, 1977.

Clarke, Emma, John Dillon, Jackson Hershbel. *Iamblichus: On the Mysteries: A manifesto of the miraculous.* Atlanta: Society of Biblical Literature, 2003.

Copenhaver, Brian P. (trans. and ed.). *Hermetica.* Cambridge: Cambridge University Press, 1992.

Daniel, Robert W. and Franco Maltomini. *Supplementum Magicum.* 2 Vols. Opladen: Westdeutscher, 1990 and 1992.

Delatte, A. and Derchain, P. *Les intailles magiques gréco-égyptiennes.* Paris, 1964.

Eitrem, Samson. *Papyri Osloensis,* I: *Magical Papyri.* Oslo: Dybwad, 1925.

Festugière, A.-J. *La Révélation d'Hermès Trismégiste,* 3 Vols. Paris, 1981.

Hand, Robert (ed.). *Hephaisto of Thebes: Apotelesmatics Book I.* Berkeley Springs: Golden Hind, 1994.

McCown, Chester C. *The Testament of Solomon, edited from manuscripts at Mount Athos, Bologna, Holkham Hall, Jerusalem, London, Milan, Paris and Vienna, with Introduction. Untersuchungen zum Neuen Testament,* Heft 9. Leipsig, 1922.

Meyer, Marvin and Smith, Richard (eds). *Ancient Christian Magic: Coptic Texts of Ritual Power.* San Francisco: Harper, 1994 rpt. Princeton 1999.

Meyer, Marvin. *The Ancient Mysteries: A Sourcebook of Sacred Texts.* Philadelphia: University of Pennsylvania, 1987.

Montgomery, James Alan. *Aramaic Incantation Texts from Nippur.* Philadelphia: University of Pennsylvania, 1913, rpt. Cambridge: CUP, 2010.

Paap, A. H. *Nomina Sacra in the Greek Papyri of the First Five Centuries A. D. the Sources and Some Deductions.* Papyrologica Lugduno-Batava 8, Leiden, 1959.

Phillips, Richard L. *In Pursuit of Invisibility: Ritual texts from Late Roman Egypt.* Durham: American Society of Papyrologists, 2009.

Preisendanz, Karl. *Papyri Graecae Magicae. Die Griechischen Zauberpapyri,* 2 Vols. Stuttgart: Teubner, 1928 and 1931, rpt. (revised) Albert Henrichs, 1973-74, rpt. 2001.

Psellus, Michael. (trans.) Marcus Collisson, (ed.) Stephen Skinner. *On the Operations of Daimones.* [Περι Δαιμόνων]. Singapore: Golden Hoard, 2009.

Rice, David and John Stambaugh. *Sources for the Study of Greek Religion.* Corrected edition, Society of Biblical Literature, 1979.

Ronan, Stephen (ed.). *Iamblichus of Chalcis: On the Mysteries (De mysteriis Aegyptiorum).* Hastings: Chthonios, 1989.

Waterfield, Robin (trans.). *The Theology of Arithmetic* (attrib. to Iamblichus). Grand Rapids: Phanes, 1988.

Graeco-Egyptian Magic Secondary Literature

Angus, Samuel. *The Mystery-Religions and Christianity.* 1924, rpt. Kessinger, n.d.

Ankaloo, Bengt and Stuart Clark (eds). *Witchcraft and Magic in Europe: Ancient Greece and Rome.* Philadelphia: University of Pennsylvania, 1999.

Aronen, Jaakko. 'Hecate's Share in the Cosmic Order' in Gothóni, René and Julia Pentikäinen (eds.) [*Studia Fennica, 32*] Helsinki: Suomalaisen, 1987.

Audollent, A. *Defixionum Tabellae.* Paris: Fontemoing, 1904.

Barb, A. A. 'The Survival of Magic Arts' in *The Conflict between Paganism and Christianity in the Fourth Century,* ed. A. Momigliano. Oxford: Clarendon, 1963, pp. 100-125.

Barb, A. A. 'Three Elusive Amulets' in *JWCI*, Vol. 27, 1964.

Barry, Kieren. *The Greek Qabalah.* York Beach: Weiser, 1999.

Barton, Tamsyn. *Ancient Astrology.* London: Routledge, 1994, rpt. Ponting-Green, 2006.

Beck, Roger. *Planetary Gods and Planetary Orders in the Mysteries of Mithras.* Leiden: Brill, 1988.

Betz, Hans Dieter. 'Fragments from a Catabasis Ritual in a Greek Magical Papyrus' in *History of Religions,* 19, 1980, pp. 287-295.

Betz, Hans Dieter. 'The Formation of Authoritative Tradition in the Greek Magical Papyri' in *Jewish and Christian Self-Definition,* ed. B. F. Meyers and E. P. Sanders, Vol. 3. Philadelphia: Fortress, 1982.

Betz, Hans Dieter. 'Magic and Mystery in the Greek Magical Papyri' in *Magika Hiera: Ancient Greek Magic and Religion,* ed. Christopher Faraone and Dirk Obbink. New York: OUP, 1991, pp. 244-259.

Betz, Hans Dieter. 'Secrecy in the Greek Magical Papyri' in *Secrecy and Concealment: Studies in the History of Mediterranean and Near Eastern Religion,* ed. Hans Kippenberg and Guy Stroumsa. (Numen Book Series 64) Leiden: Brill, 1995, pp. 153-75.

Betz, Hans Dieter. *The "Mithras Liturgy."* Tubingen: Mohr Siebeck, 2003.

Blum, C. 'The Meaning of στοιχεῖον [*stoicheion*] and its Derivatives in the Byzantine Age,' in *Eranos-Jahrbuch* XLIV, 1946. pp. 315-325.

Bohak, Gideon. 'Greek, Coptic & Jewish Magic in the Cairo Genizah,' in *Bulletin of the American Society of Papyrologists,* No. 36, 1999, pp. 27-44.

Bohak, Gideon. 'Hebrew, Hebrew Everywhere? Notes on the interpretation of *Voces Magica*' in Scott Noegel (ed.) *Prayer, Magic, and the Stars in the*

Ancient and Late Antique World. Pennsylvania: Pennsylvania State University, 2003, pp. 69-82.

Bohak, Gideon. 'Reconstructing Jewish Magical Recipe Books from the Cairo Genizah,' in *Ginzei Qedem*, No. 1, 2005, pp. 9-29.

Bohak, Gideon. *Ancient Jewish Magic: a History*. Cambridge: CUP, 2008.

Bohak, Gideon. 'Prolegomena to the Study of the Jewish Magical Tradition,' in *Currents in Biblical Research*, 8, 2009, pp. 107-150.

Bohak, Gideon. 'Jewish Magical Traditions from Late Antique Palestine to the Cairo Genizah,' in H. M. Cotton, Wasserstein, *et al* (eds.), *From Hellenism to Islam: Cultural and Linguistic Change in the Roman Near East*. Cambridge, 2009, pp. 321-339.

Bohak, Gideon. 'Towards a Catalogue of the Magical, Astrological, Divinatory, and Alchemical Fragments from the Cambridge Genizah Collections,' in Ben Outhwaite & Bhayro (eds.), *From a Sacred Source*. Leyden: Brill, 2010, pp. 53-80.

Bohak, Gideon. 'Magic and Divination' in Bohak, Gideon, Harari and Shaked, *Continuity and Innovation in the Magical Tradition*. Leiden: Brill, 2011.

Bohak, Gideon, Yuval Harari and Shaul Shaked. *Continuity and Innovation in the Magical Tradition* (Jerusalem Studies in Religion and Culture). Leiden: Brill, 2011.

Bonner, Campbell. 'The Techniques of Exorcism' in *HTR*, Vol. 36, No. 1, Jan 1943, pp. 39-49.

Bonner, Campbell. 'The Violence of Departing Demons,' in *HTR*, Vol. 37, 1944, pp. 334-336.

Bonner, Campbell. *Studies in Magical Amulets Chiefly Graeco-Egyptian*. Ann Arbor: University of Michigan, 1950.

Boustan, Ra'anan and Annette Reed. *Heavenly Realms and Earthly Realities in Late Antique Religions*. Cambridge: CUP, 2004.

Bowden, Hugh. *Mystery Cults of the Ancient World*. Princeton and Oxford: Princeton University Press, 2010.

Brashear, William. 'The Greek Magical Papyri: an Introduction and Survey; Annotated Bibliography (1928-1994)' in *ANRW* II, 18.5, 1995, pp. 3380-3684.

Brashear, William. 'New Greek Magical and Divinatory Texts in Berlin' in Meyer, Marvin and Mirecki, Paul (eds.). *Ancient Magic and Ritual Power*, Leiden: Brill, 1995.

Bremmer, Jan N. 'The Birth of the Term "Magic"' in *ZFPE,* Bd. 126, 1999, pp. 1-12.

Burkert, Walter. *Ancient Mystery Cults.* London: Harvard, 1987.

Burnett, Charles. 'Arabic, Greek, and Latin Works on Astrological Magic attributed to Aristotle,' in J. Kraye, W. F. Ryan, C B Schmitt (eds.). *Pseudo-Aristotle in the Middle Ages.* London, 1986.

Butler, Edward P. 'Offering to the Gods: a Neoplatonic Perspective' in *Magic, Ritual, and Witchcraft,* Vol. 2, No. 1, Summer 2007, pp. 1-20.

Chambers, John (trans.). *The Divine Pymander and other Writings of Hermes Trismegistus.* New York: Weiser, 1972.

Ciraolo, L. J. and J. Seidel (eds.). *Magic and Divination in the Ancient World.* Leiden and Boston: Brill, 2002.

Ciraolo, L. J. 'Supernatural Assistants in the Greek Magical Papyri' in Meyer, Marvin and Mirecki, Paul (eds.). *Ancient Magic and Ritual Power,* Leiden: Brill, 1995.

Clinton, Kevin. 'A New Lex Sacra from Selinus: Kindly Zeuses, Eumenides, Impure and Pure Tritopatores, and Elasteroi,' in *Classical Philology,* Vol. 91, No. 2, April. Chicago: University of Chicago, 1996, pp. 159-179.

Conybeare, Frederick C. *Christian Demonology.* Piscataway, NJ: Gorgias, 2007, reprinted from *JQR,* Vol. 8, No. 4; Vol. 9, Nos. 1, 3, 4. 1896-97.

Conybeare, Frederick C. 'The Testament of Solomon' in *Jewish Quarterly Review,* Vol. 11, No. 1, Oct. 1898, pp. 1-45.

Cumont, Franz. *Astrology and Religion among the Greeks and Romans.* London: Putnam, rpt. New York: Dover, 1960.

Darby, William and Paul Ghalioungui. *Food: the Gift of Osiris,* Vol. I, New York: Academic Press, 1977.

Davila, James. *Descenders to the Chariot: the People behind the Hekhalot Literature.* Leiden: Brill, 2001.

De la Torre, Emilio Suarez. 'Pseudepigraphy and Magic' in Javier Martinez, *Fakes and Forgers of Classical Literature: Ergo Decipiatur!* Leiden: Brill, 2014. pp. 245-258.

Dickie, Matthew W. 'The Learned Magician and the Collection and Transmission of Magical Lore' in Jordan, David (ed.) *The World of Ancient Magic,* PNIA 4. Bergen, 1999, pp. 163-193.

Dickie, Matthew W. *Magic and Magicians in the Greco-Roman World.* London: Routledge, 2001.

Dieleman, Jacco and Ian Moyer. 'Miniaturization and the Opening of the

Mouth in a Greek Magical Text (*PGM* XII. 270-350),' in *JANER 3*, 2003, pp. 47-72.

Dieleman, Jacco. *Priests, Tongues, and Rites: The London-Leiden Magical Manuscripts and Translation in Egyptian Ritual (100-300 CE)*. Leiden and Boston: Brill, 2005.

Dieterich, Albrecht. *Eine Mithrasliturgie.* Leipzig: Teubner, 1903, rpt. Darmstadt, 1966.

Dodd, David B. and Faraone, Christopher A. (eds.). *Initiation in Ancient Greek Rituals and Narratives*, Routledge, London, 2003.

Dodds, E. R. *The Greeks and the Irrational.* Berkeley: University of California Press, 1951.

Eitrem, Samson. *Les Papyrus Magiques Grecs de Paris.* Kristiania, 1923.

Eitrem, Samson. 'Dreams and Divination in Magical Ritual' in *Magika Hiera: Ancient Greek Magic and Religion* ed. Faraone and Obbink. New York: OUP, 1991, pp. 175-87.

Faraone, Christopher A. 'The Wheel, the Whip and Other Implements of Torture: Erotic Magic in Pindar's Pythian 4.213-19,' in *The Classical Journal*, Volume 89, No. 1, Oct-Nov 1993, Classical Association of the Midwest and South, 1993.

Faraone, Christopher and Dirk Obbink (eds.). *Magika Hiera: Ancient Greek Magic and Religion.* New York: OUP, 1991.

Faraone, Christopher and Roy Kotansky. 'An inscribed Gold Phylactery in Stamford, Conneticut,' in *ZFPE,* Bd. 75, 1988, pp. 257-266.

Faraone, Christopher. 'Binding and Burying the Forces of Evil: The Defensive Use of "Voodoo Dolls" in Ancient Greece,' in *Classical Antiquity,* Vol. 10, No. 2, Oct. 1991, pp. 165-220.

Faraone, Christopher. 'Notes on Three Greek Magical Texts' in *ZFPE* 100, 1994, pp. 81-86.

Faraone, Christopher. 'The Collapse of Celestial and Chthonic Realms in a Late Antique 'Apollonian Invocation' (*PGM* I 262-347),' in Boustan and Reed, eds., *Heavenly Realms and Earthly Realities in Late Antique Religions.* Cambridge: Cambridge University, 2004.

Faraone, Christopher. *Talismans and Trojan Horses: Guardian Statues in Ancient Greek Myth and Ritual.* New York: OUP, 1992.

Flowers, Stephen Eldred. *Hermetic Magic: the Postmodern Magical Papyrus of Abaris.* Boston: Weiser, 1995.

Fowden, Garth. *The Egyptian Hermes, An Historical Approach to the Late Pagan Mind.* Princeton: Princeton University, 1986.

Freke, Timothy and Peter Gandy. *The Jesus Mysteries.* New York: Three Rivers, 1999.

Freke, Timothy and Peter Gandy. *The Hermetica.* New York: Penguin/Tarcher, 1999.

Frankfurter, David. 'The Magic of Writing and the Writing of Magic: the Power of the Word in Egyptian and Greek Traditions' in *Helios* 21, 1994, pp. 189-221.

Frankfurter, David. *Religion in Roman Egypt: Assimilation and Resistance.* Princeton: Princeton University, 1998.

Gager, John G. *Moses in Graeco-Roman Paganism,* Society of Biblical Literature 16. New York: Abingdon, 1972.

Gager, John G. (ed.) *Curse Tablets and Binding Spells from the Ancient World.* New York: OUP, 1992.

Ganszyniec, R. 'Λεκανομαντεία' in *PRE,* 12, 1925, pp. 1879-89.

Gardiner, A. H. 'Professional Magicians in Ancient Egypt' in *Proceedings of the Society for Biblical Archaeology,* 39.

Gee, John. 'The Structure of Lamp Divination' in Ryholt, Kim (ed.). *Acts of the Seventh International Conference of Demotic Studies,* Copenhagen: University of Copenhagen, 1999, 2002.

Godwin, Joscelyn. *The Mystery of the Seven Vowels.* Grand Rapids: Phanes, 1991.

Godwin, Joscelyn. *Light in Extension: Greek Magic from Homer to Modern Times.* St. Paul: Llewellyn, 1992.

Gordon, Richard. 'Reporting the Marvellous: Private Divination in the Greek Magical Papyri' in Peter Schäfer and Hans Kippenberg (eds.) *Envisioning Magic, A Princeton Seminar and Symposium.* Studies in the History of Religions 75. Leiden: Brill, 1997, pp. 65-92.

Graf, Fritz. 'Prayer in Magical and Religious Ritual' in Christopher Faraone and Dirk Obbink (eds.). *Magika Hiera, Ancient Greek Magic and Religion.* New York and Oxford, 1991 rpt. 1997, pp. 188-213.

Graf, Fritz. *Magic in the Ancient World.* London and Cambridge, Mass: Harvard University Press, 1997 rpt. 1999.

Graf, Fritz. 'Magic and Divination: two Apolline Oracles on Magic' in Bohak, Harari and Shaked, *Continuity and Innovation in the Magical Tradition* (Jerusalem Studies in Religion and Culture). Leiden: Brill, 2011, pp. 119-

133.

Griffiths, J. G. *Apuleius of Madauros: The Isis-Book (Metamorphoses, Book XI), EPRO,* 39. Leiden: Brill, 1975.

Harrison, Jane Ellen. *Epilegomena to the Study of Greek Religion and Themis a Study of the Social Origins of Greek Religion.* New York: University, 1962 rpt. 1966.

Heintz, Florent. 'A Greek Silver Phylactery in the MacDaniel Collection,' in *ZFPE,* Bd. 112, 1996, pp. 295-300.

Hort, Arthur (transl. & ed.). *Theophrastus: Inquiry into Plants.* 1, Book I-V. New York: Loeb, 1916.

Hull, John. *Hellenistic Magic and the Synoptic Tradition.* London: SCM, 1974, pp. 5-9, 15-44.

Jackson, Howard. 'The Origin in Ancient Incantatory *Voces Magicae* of some Names in the Sethian Gnostic System,' in *Vigiliae Christianae,* Vol. 43, No. 1, Mar. 1989, pp. 69-79.

Janowitz, Naomi. *Magic in the Roman World: Pagans, Jews and Christians* (*Religion In The First Christian Centuries*) London/New York: Routledge, 2001.

Janowitz, Naomi. *Icons of Power: Ritual Practices in Late Antiquity.* University Park: Pennsylvania State University Press, 2002.

Jeffers, Ann. *Magic and Divination in Ancient Palestine and Syria.* Leiden: Brill, 1996.

Johnson, Janet H. 'The Demotic Magical Spells of Leiden I 384' in *OMRO* 56, 1975, pp. 29-64.

Johnson, Janet H. 'Louvre E3229: A Demotic Magical Text' in *Enchoria 7,* 1977, pp. 55-102.

Johnson, Luke T. *Among the Gentiles: Greco-Roman Religion and Christianity.* New Haven and London: Yale University Press, 2009.

Johnston, Sarah Iles. *Hecate Soteira: a Study of Hekate's Role in the Chaldean Oracles and Related Literature.* Atlanta: Scholars, 1990.

Johnston, Sarah Iles. 'The Song of the Iynx: Magic and Rhetoric in Pythian 4,' in *Transactions of the American Philological Association,* 125, 1995, pp. 177-206.

Johnston, Sarah Iles. 'Rising to the Occasion: Theurgic Ascent in its Cultural Milieu,' in Scafer, Peter, and Kippenberg, Hans G., eds., *Envisioning Magic: A Princeton Seminar and Symposium,* Leiden: Brill, 1997.

Johnston, Sarah Iles. *Restless Dead: Encounters between the Living and the Dead in*

Ancient Greece. Berkeley: University of California, 1999.

Johnston, Sarah Iles. 'The *Testament of Solomon* from Late Antiquity to the Renaissance,' in *The Metamorphosis of Magic* [eds.] Jan Bremmer and Jan Veenstra. Leuven: Peeters, 2002.

Johnston, Sarah Iles. *Ancient Greek Divination*. Oxford: Wiley-Blackwell, 2008.

Johnston, Sarah Iles. 'Ancient Greek Divination' in *Magic, Ritual, and Witchcraft.* Vol. 5, No. 2, Winter 2010.

Johnston, Sarah Iles and Struck, Peter T. (eds.). *Mantikê: Studies in Ancient Divination.* Leiden: Brill, 2005.

Jordan, D. R. 'A Survey of Greek Defixiones not included in the Special Corpora' in *Greek, Roman and Byzantine Studies*, No. 26, 1985, pp. 151-97.

Jordan, D. R. 'A New Reading of a Phylactery from Beirut,' in *ZFPE,* Bd. 88, 1991, pp. 61-69.

Jordan, David, Hugo Montgomery, Einar Thomassen (eds.). *The World of Ancient Magic: Papers From the First International Samson Eitrem Seminar at the Norwegian Institute at Athens 4-8 May 1997.* (Papers From the Norwegian Institute at Athens 4-8), Bergen, 1999.

Kartsonis, Anna. 'Protection against all Evil: Function, Use and Operation of Byzantine Historiated Phylacteries,' in *Byzantinische Forschungen, 20,* 1994, pp. 73-102, plates 1-9.

Kenny, John Peter (ed.). *The School of Moses: Studies in Philo and Hellenistic Religion.* Atlanta: Scholars, 1995.

Kilcher, Andreas. 'The Moses of Sinai and the Moses of Egypt: Moses as Magician in Jewish Literature and Western Esotericism' in *Aries*, Vol. 4, No. 2, p. 150.

Kippenberg, Hans and Guy Stroumsa (ed.). *Secrecy and Concealment: Studies in the History of Mediterranean and Near Eastern Religion.* (Numen Book Series 64) Leiden: Brill, 1995.

Klutz, Todd (ed.). *Magic in the Biblical World: from the Rod of Aaron to the Ring of Solomon.* London: Clark, 2003.

Klutz, Todd (ed.). *Rewriting the Testament of Solomon: Tradition, Conflict and Identity in a Late Antique Pseudepigraphon.* Library of Second Temple Studies No. 53. London: Clarke, 2005.

Kotansky, Roy. *Texts and Studies in the Graeco-Egyptian Magic Lamellae.* Ph.D. Dissertation, University of Chicago, 1988.

Kotansky, Roy. *Greek Magical Amulets.* Opladen: Westdeutscher, 1994.

Kotansky, Roy. 'Greek Exorcistic Amulets' in Meyer, Marvin and Mirecki, Paul (eds.). *Ancient Magic and Ritual Power,* Leiden: Brill, 1995.

Kotansky, Roy and Jeffrey Spier. 'The "Horned Hunter" on a Lost Gnostic Gem' in *HTR* 88:3, 1995, pp.

Lecouteux, Claude. *The High Magic of Talismans & Amulets.* Rochester: Inner Traditions, 2014.

Legge, Francis. 'The Names of Demons in the Magic Papyri' in *Proceedings of the Society of Biblical Archaeology,* Vol. XXIII, 1901, pp. 41-49.

Legge, Francis. *Forerunners and Rivals of Christianity being Studies in Religious History from 330 BC to 330 AD.* 2 Vols., Cambridge: CUP, 1915.

Lesses, Rebecca. 'Speaking Angels: Jewish and Greco-Egyptian Revelatory Adjurations' in *HTR,* Vol. 89, No. 1, Jan, 1996, pp. 41-60.

Lewis, Naphtali. *Greeks in Ptolemaic Egypt.* Oakville: American Society of Papyrologists, 2001.

Lewy, H. *Chaldaean Oracles and Theurgy, Mysticism, Magic and Platonism in the Later Roman Empire.* Paris, 1956, rpt. (ed. Tardieu), Paris, 1978.

LiDonnici, Lynn.'Single-Stemmed Wormword, Pinecones and Myrrh: Expense and Availability of Recipe Ingredients in the *Greek Magical Papyri*' in *Kernos,* 14, 2001.

Lindsay, Jack. *Leisure and Pleasure in Roman Egypt.* London: Muller, 1965.

Luck, Georg. *Arcana Mundi. Magic and the Occult in the Greek and Roman Worlds, A Collection of Texts.* Baltimore: Johns Hopkins University Press, 1985, rpt. London: Crucible, 1987.

Luck, Georg. 'Theurgy and Forms of Worship in Neoplatonism,' in Neusner, Jacob, et al., (ed.), *Religion, Science, and Magic: In Concert and Conflict.* New York: OUP, 1989.

Lycourinos, Damon Z. *Occult Traditions.* Colac: Numen, 2012.

MacMullen, Ramsey. *Christianity and Paganism in the Fourth to Eighth Centuries.* New Haven: Yale University Press, 1997.

Marathakis, Ioannis. *From the Ring of Gyges to the Black Cat Bone: a Historical Survey of the Invisibility Spells,* http://www.hermetics.org/invisibilitas.html, 2007.

Mastrocinque, Attilio. *From Jewish Magic to Gnosticism.* Tübingen: Mohr Siebeck, 2005.

Mead, G. R. S. *Fragments of a Faith Forgotten.* New York: University, 1960.

Meyer, Marvin and Mirecki, Paul (eds.). *Ancient Magic and Ritual Power*

[*Religions in The Græco-Roman World*, Volume 129]. Leiden/New York/London: Brill, 1995.

Mierzwicki, Tony. *Graeco-Egyptian Magick*. Stafford: Immanion, 2006.

Migne, J. P. *Patrologiae Cursus Completus*. Series Greco-Latina. 161 vols. Paris, 1857-1866.

Mirecki, Paul and Marvin Meyer (eds.). *Magic and Ritual in the Ancient World*. (*Religions in the Graeco-Roman World*, Volume 141.) Leiden: Brill, 2002.

Moyer, Ian. 'Thessalos of Tralles and Cultural Exchange' in Scott Noegel (ed.). *Prayer, Magic, and the Stars in the Ancient and Late Antique World*. Pennsylvania: Pennsylvania University, 2003.

Nabarz, Payam. *Mithras Reader: an Academic and Religious Journal of Greek, Roman and Persian Studies*, Vol. 1. Oxford: Twin Serpents, 2006.

Naveh, Joseph, and Shaked, Shaul. *Amulets and Magic Bowls: Aramaic Incantations of Late Antiquity*. Jerusalem: Magnes Press; Leiden: Brill, 1985.

Neugebauer, Otto. *The Exact Sciences in Antiquity*. New York: Dover, 1969.

Nilsson, Martin P. 'The Anguipede of the Magical Amulets' in *HTR* Vol. 44, No. 1, 1951, pp. 61–64.

Nilsson, Martin P. *Greek Folk Religion*. Philadelphia: University of Pennsylvania Press, 1972.

Nock, A. D. 'Greek Magical Papyri' in *The Journal of Egyptian Archaeology* 15, 1929, pp. 219–235.

Noegel, Scott. (ed.). *Prayer, Magic, and the Stars in the Ancient and Late Antique World*. Pennsylvania: Pennsylvania University, 2003.

Ogden, Daniel. *Greek and Roman Necromancy*. Princeton: Princeton University, 2001.

Ogden, Daniel. *Magic, Witchcraft, and Ghosts in the Greek and Roman Worlds: a Sourcebook*. Oxford: OUP, 2002.

Pachoumi, Eleni. 'The Greek Magical Papyri: Diversity and Unity.' Ph.D. thesis Newcastle University, 2007.

Pachoumi, Eleni. 'Divine Epiphanies of Paredroi in the *Greek Magical Papyri*' in *Greek, Roman, and Byzantine Studies*, 51, 2011, pp. 155-165.

Parsons, Peter. *City of the Sharp-Nosed Fish*. London: Phoenix, 2007.

Pax, W. 'Circumambulatio' in *RAC* 3, 1957, pp. 143-52.

Phillips, Richard L. *In Pursuit of Invisibility: Ritual texts from Late Roman Egypt*. Durham: American Society of Papyrologists, 2009.

Pingree, David. 'Petosiris,' in *Dictionary of Scientific Biography*, Charles Coulson Gillespie. New York: Scribners, 1970, pp. 547-49.

Porreca, David. 'Divine Names: A Cross-Cultural Comparison (*Papyri Graecae Magicae, Picatrix, Munich Handbook*)' in *Magic, Ritual, and Witchcraft*, Volume 5, Number 1, Summer 2010. Philadelphia: University of Pennsylvania Press, pp. 17-29

Quibell, J. E. *The Ramesseum*. London: Quaritch, 1898.

Reitzenstein, Richard, (trans.) John E. Steely. *Hellenistic Mystery-Religions; Their Basic Ideas and Significance*. Pittsburgh: Pickwick Press, 1978.

Rice, David and John Stambaugh. *Sources for the Study of Greek Religion*. Corrected edition, Society of Biblical Literature, 1979.

Robinson, James (ed.). *The Nag Hammadi Library in English*. San Francisco: Harper, 1990.

Ronan, Steve (ed.). *The Goddess Hekate*. Hastings: Chthonios, 1992.

Ronan, Stephen, (ed.). 'Hekate's Iynx: An Ancient Theurgical Tool,' in Fideler, David, ed., *Alexandria* 1. Grand Rapids: Phanes, 1991.

Rose, Jenny. *Zoroastrianism: an Introduction*. London: Tauris, 2011.

Sanzi, Ennio. 'Mithras: a *deus invictus* among Persia, stars, Oriental cults and magical gems' in *Charmes et Sortilèges Magie et Magiciens*. Bures-sur-Yvette: Groupe pour l'Étude de la Civilisation du Moyen-Orient, 2002.

Scarborough, John. *Pharmacy's Ancient Heritage: Theophrastus, Nicander, and Dioscorides*. University of Kentucky, 1984.

Scarborough, John. 'The Pharmacology of Sacred Plants, Herbs, and Roots' in *Magika Hiera: Ancient Greek Magic and Religion* ed. Faraone and Obbink. New York: OUP, 1991, pp. 138-174.

Schiffman, L. H., and Michael D. Swartz. *Hebrew and Aramaic Incantation Texts from the Cairo Genizah*. Sheffield: Sheffield Academic, 1992.

Schrire, T. *Hebrew Amulets. Their Decipherment and Interpretation*. London: RKP, 1966.

Schwartz, Martin. 'Sasm, Sesen, St. Sisinnios, Sesengen Barpharangēs, and… "Semanglof",' in *Bulletin of the Asian Institute*, Vol. 10, 1996.

Schwendner, Gregg. 'Under Homer's Spell' in Ciraolo, L. J. and J. Seidel (eds.). *Magic and Divination in the Ancient World*. Leiden: Brill, 2002.

Shaked, Saul (ed.). *Officina Magica: Essays on the Practice of Magic in Antiquity*. Leiden: Brill, 2005.

Sheldon, Suzanne. 'Middle English and Latin Charms, Amulets and Talismans from Vernacular Manuscripts.' Ph.D. dissertation. Tulane University, 1978.

Skemer, Don C. *Binding Words: Textual Amulets in the Middle Ages*. University Park: Pennsylvania State University Press, 2006.

Skinner, Stephen. *Magical Techniques and Implements present in Graeco-Egyptian Magical Papyri, Byzantine Greek Solomonic Manuscripts and European Grimoires.* Ph.D thesis, University of Newcastle, 2014.

Skinner, Stephen. *Complete Magician's Tables.* Singapore: Golden Hoard, 2006; rpt. Woodbury: Llewellyn, 2007, 2011.

Smith, J. Z. 'The Temple and the Magician' in Jonathan Smith, *Map is not Territory: Studies in the History of Religions.* Leiden: Brill, 1978, pp. 172-89.

Smith, Mark. 'A New Version of a Well-known Egyptian Hymn,' in *Enchoria* 7, 1977, pp. 115-49.

Smith, Mark. *The Early History of God: Yahweh and the other deities in Ancient Israel.* Cambridge: Eerdmans, 2002.

Smith, Morton. *Jesus the Magician.* San Francisco: Harper & Row, 1978.

Smith, Morton. 'The History of the Term Gnostikos' in *Studies in the Cult of Yahweh, RGRW* 130, II, Leiden, New York, Cologne: Brill, 1996, pp. 183-193.

Smith, Wesley. 'So-called Possession in Pre-Christian Greece' in *TAPA* 96, 1965. pp. 403-426.

Swartz, Michael D. 'Ritual Procedures in Magical Texts from the Cairo Genizah,' in *Jewish Studies Quarterly* 13:4, 2006, pp. 305-318.

Tanaseanu-Döbler, Ilinca. *Theurgy in Late Antiquity.* Göttingen: Vandenhoeck & Ruprecht, 2013.

Tavenner, Eugene. *Studies in Magic from Latin Literature.* New York: AMS, 1966.

Taylor, Thomas (trans.). *Iamblichus on the Mysteries.* Chiswick: Whittingham, 1821.

Trzcionka, Silke. *Magic and the Supernatural in Fourth-Century Syria.* London: Routledge, 2007.

Uždavinys, Algis. *Philosophy & Theurgy in Late Antiquity.* San Rafael: Sophia Perennis, 2010.

Veldman, Frederick J. *Theurgy and Numbers.* Cold Spring: Waning Moon, 2010.

Vesnel, H. S. 'A twisted Hermes. Another View of an Enigmatic Spell,' in *ZFPE,* Bd. 72, 1988, pp. 287-292.

Wasserstrom, Steven. 'The Magical Texts in the Cairo Geniza,' in Joseph Blau and

Stefan C. Reif (eds.), *Genizah Research after Ninety Years: the Case of Judaeo-Arabic.* Cambridge: Cambridge University Press, 1992, pp. 160-166.

Wilder, Alexander (trans.). *Theurgia, or the Egyptian Mysteries.* London: Rider, 1911.

Wypustek, Andrzej. '*Calumnia Magiae.* Towards a New Study of the Relationship between Greek-Roman Magic and Early Christianity' in *Charmes et Sortilèges Magie et Magiciens.* Bures-sur-Yvette: Groupe pour l'Étude de la Civilisation du Moyen-Orient, 2002.

Selected Later Grimoire Sources

Abraham of Worms, (ed.) Georg Dehn, (trans.) Steven Guth. *The Book of Abramelin.* Lake Worth: Ibis, 2006.

Gollancz, Hermann. *Sepher Maphteah Shelomoh (Book of the Key of Solomon) an exact facsimile of an original Book of Magic in Hebrew.* 1903 and 1914, rpt. (Intro.) Stephen Skinner. York Beach: Teitan, 2008.

Hedegård, Gösta. *Liber Iuratus Honorii.* Stockholm: Almqvist and Wiksell, 2002.

Marathakis, Ioannis. *The Magical Treatise of Solomon or Hygromanteia.* Vol. 8, *SWCM.* Singapore: Golden Hoard, 2011.

Mathers, S. L. MacGregor (trans.). *The Key of Solomon the King (Clavicula Salomonis).* London: Redway, 1889; rpt. London: Kegan Paul, 1909; rpt. Maine: Samuel Weiser, 2000.

Mathers, S. L. MacGregor, (trans.). *The Book of the Sacred Magic of Abramelin the Mage.* London: Watkins, 1900.

Peterson, Joseph. (ed.). *The Lesser Key of Solomon: Lemegeton Clavicula Salomonis: Goetia, Theurgia Goetia, Ars Paulina, Ars Almadel, Ars Notoria.* York Beach: Weiser, 2001.

Skinner, Stephen and David Rankine. *The Goetia of Dr Rudd,* Vol. 3, *SWCM.* London: Golden Hoard, 2007.

Index